Sacred Books of the Buddhists Vol. XXXIV.

PETA-STORIES

TRANSLATION OF THE PALI COMMENTARIES

in

CELEBRATION OF THE CENTENARY

of

THE PALI TEXT SOCIETY

1881-1981

Publication No. 2

ELUCIDATION OF THE INTRINSIC MEANING

SO NAMED

THE COMMENTARY ON THE PETA-STORIES

(Paramatthadīpanī nāma

Petavatthu-aṭṭhakathā)

by

DHAMMAPĀLA

Translated by

U BA KYAW

Edited and Annotated by

PETER MASEFIELD

Published by

THE PALI TEXT SOCIETY, LONDON

Distributed by

ROUTLEDGE & KEGAN PAUL LTD.

London, Henley and Boston

1980

First published 1980

Generous contributions towards the publication of this work have been made by
The Subha Group, Malaysia

UNESCO COLLECTION OF REPRESENTATIVE WORKS

This Buddhist text has been accepted in the series of translations from the literature of Burma, India, Sri Lanka, and Thailand, jointly sponsored by the United National Educational, Scientific, and Cultural Organisation (UNESCO), and the National Commissions for Unesco in these countries

ISBN 0 7100 0604 7

Printed in Great Britain by
Unwin Brothers Limited, The Gresham Press, Old Woking, Surrey

INTRODUCTION

It had been hoped that it would have been possible to include in this work a short introduction discussing such topics as the Buddhist concept of the peta and the (so-called) doctrine of the transfer of merit. Unfortunately this has proved impossible in the time available and will, I hope, be included instead in the translation of the companion volume to the present work – Dhammapāla's commentary on the Vimānavatthu, or Mansion Stories – now in progress. Here it may simply be noted that the reason why individuals arise as petas is by and large because they neglected to show charity to the almsworthy Sāvakasaṅgha, the new seat of the sacrifice and, in a sense, the new Agni. For just as pouring a sacrificial oblation into Agni, the sacrificial fire, resulted in that offering being transferred, through the medium of Agni, to the world of the devas, so similarly does the placing of food in the Sāvakasaṅgha result in the appearance of that food, or its divine counterpart, in the world beyond for one's own use after death. Failure to give such alms – or giving alms to those unworthy of them and thus, unlike the Sāvakasaṅgha and Agni, not in communication with the divine plane – results in one arising on the divine plane after death but with no store laid up for one's sustenance. This plight may however be rectified under certain circumstances by some relative or friend giving alms to the almsworthy and requesting, subsequently, that the divine counterpart produced thereby be assigned for the use of this or that peta. There is in these stories no suggestion of any transfer of merit as such and indeed Dhammapāla on occasion explicitly states that it is not merit that is transferred. On receipt of the assigned divine counterpart of the gift the peta is transformed into a devatā with no suggestion that such a change in status involves rebirth of any kind. Rather we may see the peta and the devatā (who usually possesses a vimāna or mansion) as two aspects of life on the divine plane in the life to come – miserable and happy existences respectively. They both belong to the same world and the assignment of the divine counterpart of a gift simply alleviates the state of suffering to which the peta had hitherto been subject, allowing him henceforth to enjoy the pleasures normally associated with that world.

It may be useful to add a few words introducing the general reader to Dhammapāla's commentarial style. Each story may be said to fall into three distinct parts: (1) an arisen need, or introductory story, explaining the circumstances in which the verses that follow came to be spoken;

(2) those verses themselves; and (3) a commentary on those verses alone. In his introduction (PvA 2) Dhammapāla attributes the first two of these to the Buddha who, when explaining how it was that the verses came to be spoken, himself repeated the verses concerned. Thus only the third part forms the commentary proper. The task of the commentary, apart from clarifying who said which verse, is mainly to explain the meanings of words occurring in the verses rather than to expound upon the doctrine supposedly lying behind those verses. It will thus be found that the commentary abounds in what may appear, especially in translation, as a series of somewhat uninteresting linguistic equivalents whilst remaining relatively silent on issues of doctrinal importance.

Several features of Dhammapāla's commentarial style deserve mention: (1) Pali, unlike English, contains a remarkable variety of grammatically equivalent and alternative verbal forms in a given tense and from the same root and it is frequently Dhammapāla's practice to supply another, and usually more common, equivalent form. In such cases I have followed the method adopted by Ñāṇamoli in his *Minor Readings and Illustrator*, thus: *gave: dajja=datvā* (alternative grammatical form) (PvA 139 on II 9^{68}); similarly *you should say: vajjesi=vadeyyāsi* (alternative grammatical form) (PvA 203 on III 6^{7}). As an example in English of the first pair of alternatives we may compare *he spelt=he spelled* and of the second *he lit=he lighted.*

(2) A similar variety may also be found amongst (a) forms of personal pronouns and (b) case endings of nouns. Thus for example: *I: me=mayā* (PvA 15 on I 3^{2}) which might be compared with the English *thy=your* whilst as an example of alternative case endings we may cite *that lotus pond: pokkharaññā=pokkharaṇiyā* (PvA 157 on II 12^{9}).

(3) Another feature of Pali that is not altogether shared by English is its ability to form compounds and it is frequently the task of Dhammapāla to tell us to which class of compound a given instance belongs. This he does by resolving it into its uncompounded form which results at the same time in a demonstration of the internal relationship holding between its parts. In such cases I have again followed Ñāṇamoli, thus: *and with fraud and deceit: nikativañcanāya ca=nikatiyā vañcanāya ca* (resolution of compound) (PvA 211 on III 9^{5}). It will be clear that in nearly every case a compound required such resolution during its translation into English since 'with fraud-deceit' and the like would make little sense. Sometimes we even find compounds resolved in an alternative grammatical form: *food and drink: annapānamhi=anne ca pāne ca* (resolution of compound in alternative grammatical form) (PvA 25 on I 5^{2}).

(4) It is clear that on occasion Dhammapāla was confronted with variant

readings in his manuscripts and is thus obliged to draw our attention to this by stating the alternative in his commentary accompanied, if necessary, by its effect on the meaning of the verse – see e.g. PvA 103f. on II 7^{17}. At other times certain expressions were clearly ambiguous and at PvA 158 on II 12^{9} Dhammapāla points out that *subhe* might mean 'bright' and thus be descriptive of the grass or alternatively it could be the king's means of addressing the petī when it would mean 'My bright one'.

(5) As with other commentators Dhammapāla sometimes offers edifying etymologies of various words such as that of the term *arahant* at PvA 7 on I 1^{1} but with little or no linguistic justification as though we might say one were in a state of *holiness* since he was *wholly* freed from the *nescience* of an unbeliever. Where the word involved is of a more mundane nature it is possible on occasion to detect a pun and in such cases it is nearly always impossible to maintain the pun in translation. But we may illustrate the style employed in such places by saying that it is as if he were to say that a garment was a *waistcoat* because it was made from the *waste* material left after the *coat* had been made; or that it was a *sarong* because it was a *sari* that had been tied *wrong*; or indeed that the seat was called a *sofa* as one can only lean *so far* before one falls off the edge.

(6) These five features are, however, relatively rare in the commentary as a whole and the normal method followed is for Dhammapāla to quote from each verse lemmas of varying length followed by one or more synonyms, these synonyms themselves often being followed by a further phrase introduced by the word 'meaning', thus: *sorrow (soko)*: mourning, torturing the heart, meaning burning inside (PvA 18 on I 4^{3}). If it be found that one or more verses are not commented upon this is usually because they have appeared in a preceding story and received comment there – this is what Dhammapāla means when he frequently ends his commentary with a note to the effect that the rest is just as already given above. At times the method followed is more complex in that having given the lemma to be commented upon Dhammapāla then repeats that same lemma interspersed with a variety of glosses on individual words to the extent that readability may be thought to suffer: *those who . . . when a great (ceremony of) honouring the stūpa of the Arahant is in progress (ye ca kho thūpapūjāya vattante arahato mahe)*: he clarifies his own great loss allegorically saying, '*You should separate*, you should have separated, you should consider as outsiders, *therefrom*, from that meritorious deed, *those* persons *who*, like me, *make known the disadvantages* of, the faults with, honouring the stūpa *when a great (ceremony of) honour* with respect to *the stupa of the Arahant*, the Perfect Buddha, *is in progress*' (PvA 214 on III 10^{7}), the italicised portions being (approximately) the verse itself. It was thought

advisable to adhere as much as possible to the style of the Pali even though this often results in a sentence that might appear cumbersome to someone unfamiliar with the method employed; if, however, the reader bears in mind Dhammapāla's method he may well, when reading such passages, get more from them than he might had they been recast into more readable English.

(7) Ideally it should be possible to substitute the lemma of the verse with its commentarial gloss and every effort has been made to ensure that this is possible in English if this were so in the case of the original Pali. Thus II 1^{21} reads:

> And I sport and play and enjoy myself, having nothing to fear from any quarter. I, sir, have come to salute the compassionate sage for the world

and the commentary at PvA 77 explains:

I: sāhaṃ=sā ahaṃ (resolution of compound). *Sport (ramāmi)*: find delight. *Play (kīḷāmi)*: gratify my senses. *Enjoy myself (modāmi)*: am delighted at the excellence of my enjoyment. *Having nothing to fear from any quarter (akutobhayā)*: I dwell at ease and as I like lacking fear from any quarter. *I, sir, have come to salute (bhante vanditum āgatā)*: I, sir, have come, that is, I have approached, to salute you who are the means of my acquiring this heavenly excellence.

If one then replaces the lemmas of the verse by their respective glosses one arrives at the following:

> And I find delight and gratify my senses and am delighted at the excellence of my enjoyment – I dwell at ease and as I like lacking fear from any quarter. I, sir, have come, that is, I have approached, to salute the compassionate sage for the world, you who are the means of my acquiring this heavenly excellence.

In preparing this work the following editions of the text have been utilised:

(1) that in the Roman script edited by E. Hardy for the Pali Text Society in 1894/1896 (referred to as 'text' in the notes);

(2) that in Sinhalese script edited by Siri Dhammārāma Tissa Nāyaka Thēra and Māpalagama Chandajōti Thēra and revised by Mahagoda Siri Ñānissara Thēra and published in Colombo in 1917 as part of the Simon Hewavitarne Bequest (referred to as Se);

(3) that in Burmese script being the Chaṭṭhasaṅgāyana edition published in Rangoon in 1958 (referred to as Be).

I have throughout modelled the translation on Hardy's edition since it is this that is most likely to be available to the English reader. Moreover

Hardy's edition remains valuable, in spite of numerous typographical errors generally corrected in Se and Be, due to the wealth of variant readings that it, unlike the latter, preserves. I very much regret that at the time the new edition of the canonical verses of the text, correcting many of these errors, and prepared by Professor Jayawickrama for the PTS was not available to me.

Thanks are due to K. R. Norman and Professor Richard Gombrich for their able resolution of many troublesome passages, to Lance Cousins who first introduced me to the work, to Dr. L. P. N. Perera who helped me from time to time during his stay in Lancaster, and also to my wife for having patiently assisted me in checking the typescript in the closing stages. Last, but certainly not least, I must express my indebtedness to Miss Horner, whose continued interest was a source of constant encouragement.

Peter Masefield
1978

LIST OF ABBREVIATIONS

A :	Aṅguttara-Nikāya
AA :	Commentary on A
Ap :	Apadāna
Asl :	Atthasālinī
AV :	Atharva Veda
B of Disc :	Book of the Discipline
Be :	Burmese edition of PvA
BHSD :	Buddhist Hybrid Sanskrit Dictionary
Buddhist Psych. Ethics :	Buddhist Psychological Ethics
BvA :	Commentary on Buddhavaṃsa
Childers :	A Dictionary of the Pali Language
CPD :	Critical Pali Dictionary
Compendium :	Compendium of Philosophy
Cty :	Commentary
D :	Dīgha-Nikāya
DA :	Commentary on D
Dhp:	Dhammapada
DhpA :	Commentary on Dhp
DhsA :	Commentary on Dhammasaṅgaṇī (Atthasālinī)
Dial :	Dialogues of the Buddha
DPPN :	Dictionary of Pali Proper Names
Dpv :	Dīpavaṃsa
EV :	Elders' Verses
Expos :	The Expositor (DhsA trans)
Gehman :	Stories of the Departed (translator of)
GS :	The Book of the Gradual Sayings
It :	Itivuttaka
J :	Jātaka
Jāt :	Jātaka (No)

Jātaka Stories :	Jātaka (trans)
JPTS :	Journal of the Pali Text Society
KhpA :	Khuddakapātha
KS :	The Book of the Kindred Sayings
M :	Majjhima-Nikāya
M- :	Majjhima-Nikāya (Sutta No)
Manu :	Mānavadharmaśāstra
Mārk. Pur. :	Mārkaṇḍeya Purāṇa
MBh :	Mahābhārata
Mhv :	Mahāvaṃsa
Miln :	Milindapañha
MLS :	Middle Length Sayings
Mvu :	Mahāvastu
Nd[1] :	Mahāniddesa
Nd[2] :	Cullaniddesa
Nett :	Netti-pakaraṇa
PED :	Pali-English Dictionary
pp :	past participle
PTS :	Pali Text Society
Pv :	Petavatthu (with reference)
:	Petavatthu ed. Minayeff (without reference)
PvA :	Commentary on Pv
RV :	Ṛg Veda
S :	Saṃyutta-Nikāya
SA :	Commentary on S
SBE :	Sacred Books of the East
Se :	Sinhalese edition of PvA
SED :	Sanskrit-English Dictionary (Monier-Williams)
Sing. :	Singular
Skt :	Sanskrit
Sn :	Suttanipāta
SnA :	Commentary on Sn
Text :	PTS edition of PvA
Thag or Th1 :	Theragāthā

Thig or Th2 :	Therīgāthā
trans. :	translation
Ud :	Udāna
VA :	Commentary on Vin
Vin :	Vinaya-piṭaka
Vin Texts :	Vinaya Texts
Vism :	Visuddhimagga
vl(l) :	variant reading(s)
Vv :	Vimānavatthu
VvA :	Commentary on Vv

CONTENTS

Introduction vii

Abbreviations xii

I THE SNAKE CHAPTER
(Uragavagga) 1

Inception of the Composition 3

1 Like a Field (Khettūpamā) 6

2 Boar(-faced) (Sūkara) 13

3 Putrid Mouth (Pūtimukha) 16

4 Biscuit Doll (Piṭṭhadhītalika) 20

5 Outside the Walls (Tirokuḍḍa) 23

6 Devourer of Five Sons (Pañcaputtakhādaka) 36

7 Devourer of Seven Sons (Sattaputtakhādaka) 40

8 The Ox (Goṇa) 42

9 Master Weaver (Mahāpesakāra) 46

10 Bald-headed (Khallāṭiya) 50

11 The Elephant (Nāga) 57

12 The Snake (Uraga) 65

II THE UBBARĪ CHAPTER
(Ubbarīvagga) 71

1 Saṃsāramocaka (Saṃsāramocaka) 73

2 The Elder Sāriputta's Mother (Sāriputtattheramātu) 84

3 Mattā Petī (Mattāpetī) 89

4 Nandā (Nandā) 97

5 Maṭṭakuṇḍalin (Maṭṭakuṇḍali) 99

6 Kaṇha (Kaṇha) 100

7 Dhanapāla (Dhanapāla) 107
8 Cūḷaseṭṭhi (Cūḷaseṭṭhi) 113
9 Aṅkura (Aṅkura) 118
10 Uttara's Mother (Uttaramātu) 149
11 The Thread (Sutta) 152
12 Kaṇṇamuṇḍa (Kaṇṇamuṇḍa) 158
13 Ubbarī (Ubbarī) 167

III SMALL CHAPTER
(Cūḷavagga) 177
1 Without Parting (Abhijjamāna) 179
2 Sānuvāsin (Sānuvāsi) 188
3 Rathakāra (Rathakāra) 197
4 Chaff (Bhusa) 202
5 The Boy (Kumāra) 204
6 Serenī (Serinī) 210
7 Deer-hunter (Migaludda) 214
8 Second Hunter (Dutiyaludda) 217
9 False Declaration (Kūṭavinicchayika) 219
10 Contẹmpt for the Relics (Dhātuvivaṇṇa) 221

IV GREAT CHAPTER
(Mahāvagga) 227
1 Ambasakkhara (Ambasakkhara) 229
2 Serissaka (Serissaka) 253
3 Nandaka (Nandaka) 254
4 Revatī (Revatī) 267
5 Sugar-cane (Ucchu) 267
6 The Boys (Kumāra) 270
7 The King's Son (Rājaputta) 273
8 Excrement Eating (Gūthakhādaka) 277

9 Excrement Eating (Gūthakhādaka) 279
10 The Troop (Gaṇa) 280
11 Pāṭaliputta (Pāṭaliputta) 282
12 The Mango (Amba) 284
13 Tree-axle (Akkharukkha) 287
14 Accumulation of Wealth (Bhogasaṃharaṇa) 289
15 The Wealthy Merchant's Sons (Seṭṭhiputta) 290
16 Sixty Thousand Hammers (Saṭṭhikūṭasahassa) 294
Concluding Remarks 298

INDEXES
1 Words and Subjects 300
2 Names 310
3 Some Pali Words discussed in the Notes 315
4 List of Quotations and Allusions 316
5 Words and Senses Not Listed by PED 317
6 Amendments to PED Suggested in the Notes 318

Chapter I

THE SNAKE CHAPTER
[Uragavagga]

ELUCIDATION OF THE INTRINSIC MEANING
THE SO-NAMED COMMENTARY ON THE PETA STORIES

Praise to the Lord, the Arahant, the Perfect Buddha.

[1] AN ACCOUNT OF THE INCEPTION OF THE COMPOSITION:[1]

1 I salute the Saviour of Great Compassion who has gone beyond the ocean of things knowable and who has set forth in various ways things subtle and profound.

2 I salute the utmost Dhamma honoured by the Perfect Buddha by means of which those who are endowed with wisdom and conduct are led from this world.

3 I salute the Ariyasaṅgha, the unsurpassed merit-field of those who, endowed with the qualities of virtue and so on, stand fast in the fruits of the paths.

4 Through this salutation to the Three Jewels merit is thus produced; by means of its effulgence I have removed obstacles everywhere.[2]

5 It is due to a difference in the fruition of this and that deed done by petas in their previous births that this and that existence as a peta has been brought about for them.[3]

6 Clarifying this is that teaching of the Buddhas that demonstrates the fruition of deeds, that particularly gives rise to agitation,

7 And that is well-founded on a thorough understanding (of the subject), namely, the Peta Stories that were rehearsed by the Great Masters in the Khuddaka Nikāya.

8 Relying thoroughly thereon after the manner of their ancient commentary and at various places explaining the particular subject-matter,

9 Resolving, quite clearly and without confusion, the subtle meanings in accordance with the views of the present residents of the Mahāvihāra,[4]

10 I will, as well as I am able, set forth an illuminating exposition of their meaning. Please pay attention to what I, with due reverence, have to say.

[2] Herein the Peta Stories (relate) of this and that being the deed that was the cause of their attaining existence as a peta, beginning with that of the son of a wealthy merchant. Here by the Peta Stories is meant the canonical text that begins with (the verse) 'Like a field are the arahants' (but) which proceeds, however, by way of its clarification. Now these

Peta Stories, by whom were they spoken, where were they spoken, when were they spoken and why were they spoken? These Peta Stories are said to proceed in two parts – by way of an arisen need[5] and by way of questions and answers. Herein that which proceeds by way of an arisen need, this much was spoken by the Lord, whilst the other part was asked by the elder Nārada[6] and so on and answered[7] by this and that peta. Since, however, when this and that[8] (set of) questions and answers was raised[9] by the elder Nārada and so on, the Teacher would take this and that (set) as an arisen need and teach Dhamma to the company assembled there, the entire Peta Stories therefore came to be looked upon as having been spoken by the Teacher himself. When the Teacher had set rolling the Wheel of the Noble Dhamma and was staying here and there, such as at Rājagaha and so on, as a rule this and that teaching involving a Peta Story came about with the purpose of demonstrating the fruition of deeds of beings by way of the questions and answers (that had occasioned) this and that arisen need. This is, thus far, the answer in general to the questions as to by whom they were spoken and so on. It will appear in particular, however, in the exposition of the meaning of this and that story.

As to the three Piṭakas, namely the Vinaya Piṭaka, the Sutta Piṭaka and the Abhidhamma Piṭaka, these Peta Stories are included in the Sutta Piṭaka. As to the five Nikāyas, namely the Dīgha Nikāya, the Majjhima Nikāya, the Saṃyutta Nikāya, the Aṅguttara Nikāya and the Khuddaka Nikāya, they are included in the Khuddaka Nikāya. As to the nine limbs of the Teaching, namely the discourses in prose, in prose and verse, the expositions, the verses, the uplifting verses, the as-it-was-saids, the birth stories, the wonders and miscellanies, they are classified as verses. As to the eighty-four thousand units of the Dhamma[10] acknowledged by the Treasurer of the Dhamma thus:

> 'Eighty-two thousand I received from the Buddha and two thousand from the monk.[11] These eighty-four thousand are the Dhammas (set) rolling'

they are classified as a few of these units of the Dhamma. By recitation sections there are as many as four recitation sections. By chapters they are classified into four chapters: the Snake Chapter, the Ubbarī Chapter, the Small Chapter and the Great Chapter. As to these there are twelve stories in the first chapter, thirteen stories in the second [3] chapter, ten stories in the third chapter and sixteen stories in the fourth chapter: thus it is adorned with fifty-one stories (in all). Herein as to chapters the Snake Chapter is first, as to stories the Like a Field Peta Story is first, and of this, moreover, the first verse (begins:) 'Like a field are the arahants'. Now this is that story.

[1] ganthārambhakathā, Be only.

[2] See vv. 7–8 of the Concluding remarks, PvA 287.

[3] Reading tesaṃ hi with Se Be for text's sattehi.

[4] The Mahāvihāra, situated at Anurādhapura in northern Ceylon, was in Dhammapāla's day the centre of Theravādin orthodoxy; see Walpola Rahula, *History of Buddhism in Ceylon*, Colombo 1966, Appendix I, p. 303f.

[5] atthuppatti; see Minor Readings and Illustrator p. 78, n. 1.

[6] Reading Nārada with Se Be for text's Narada.

[7] bhāsitaṃ, literally spoken.

[8] Reading tasmiṃ tasmiṃ with Se Be for text's tasmiṃ.

[9] Reading ārocite with Se Be for text's āropite.

[10] dhammakkhandha, defined at Asl 27 (Expos i 34); cp DA 24. The Treasurer of the Dhamma was Ananda – see Thag 1048.

[11] Sāriputta, Asl 27; cp Thag 1024 and note thereon at EV i 264 f.

I.1 EXPOSITION OF THE LIKE A FIELD PETA STORY
[Khettūpamāpetavatthuvaṇṇanā]

The Lord, who was staying at the Squirrels' Feeding Ground in the Bamboo Grove at Rājagaha told[1] this concerning a certain peta who had been the son of a wealthy merchant.

It is said that in Rājagaha there was a certain prosperous wealthy merchant owning great wealth, great possessions, abundant material resources and countless koṭis[2] of accumulated wealth. It was through his being endowed with such great wealth that he was known simply as the Mahādhanaseṭṭhi.[3] He had an only son who was much loved and adored. When he reached puberty his parents thought, 'If our son should spend a thousand (pieces) every day for a hundred years even this accumulated wealth would not come to exhaustion. Let him enjoy these possessions as he wishes with a body and mind unwearied by the fatigue of learning a craft.' They did not have him trained in a craft and when he came of age they fetched him a bride of good family who was endowed with youth, beauty and charm, but who was voluptuous and neglected things spiritual. As he enjoyed the pleasures of love with her he did not give even so much as one thought to the Dhamma and became disrespectful to recluses and brahmins and venerable persons and, surrounded by wicked people, he took delight in, and was attached to, the pleasures of the five senses, blindly hankering after them in his delusion. And so he passed his time.

When his parents died, he squandered his wealth, giving to dancers and singers and so on to his heart's content. It was not long before (his wealth) was lost but he managed to live after securing a loan. When he could get no further loan and was being pressed by his creditors, he gave them his arable land and house and so on and dwelt at the hall for the destitute in that same city, eating (what he had got) after wandering about begging with bowl in hand.

Now one day some robbers who had assembled said to him, 'Look here, man, why this hard life of yours? You are young [4] and are endowed with strength, agility and power. Why behave as though deprived of hand and foot? Come! By stealing with us you can get the property of others and live your life in comfort.' 'I do not know how to steal,' he replied. 'We will train you. You just do everything we say,' said the robbers. 'Very well,' he agreed and went with them. The robbers then placed a large club in his hand, broke into the house and, as they entered, they stationed him at the mouth of the breach, saying, 'If anyone else comes here, strike him dead with a single blow from this club.' Blinded by folly and not knowing what was either good or bad for him, he stood there, looking about for the approach of others, whilst the robbers entered the house, took whatever they could lay their hands on, and ran off in all directions as soon as (their presence) became known to the occupants of the house. The occupants of the house arose and, running very quickly and looking about[4] them in all directions, saw the man standing at the door where they had broken in. 'There he is, the wicked robber!' they said and seized him and beat him with the club and so on on his hands and feet. They presented him before the king saying, 'Your majesty, this is the robber who was seized at the mouth of the breach.' 'Have his head cut off!' the king ordered the city-guard. 'Very well, your majesty,' the city-guard said and had him seized and his arms tied tightly behind his back. With a wreath of red kaṇavīra[5] flowers tied around his neck and with his head smeared with brick-powder,[6] he was flogged as he was led towards the place of execution along the path described by the beating of the execution drum,[7] going from road to road and from crossroads to crossroads, as the cry went up, 'This is the plundering robber who was seized in this city!'

Now in that city on that occasion, the city courtesan, named Sulasā, was standing in the palace, looking out through a lattice window, and saw him being led about in that manner. Through having made his acquaintance in the past, compassion for him arose within her as she thought, 'This man who used to enjoy great prosperity in this same city has now come to such misfortune, to such plight and distress.' She sent out four sweetmeats and some water and had it announced to the city-guard, 'May your worthiness pause [5] until this man has eaten these sweetmeats and drunk this water.' Now during this interlude, the venerable Mahāmoggallāna saw his plight as he surveyed (the world) with his heavenly eye;[8] his heart was stirred with compassion and he thought, 'This man has done no meritorious deeds, he has (only) done wicked deeds. For this reason he will arise in hell. But if I go (there) and he gives me the sweetmeats and the water, he will arise amongst the terrestrial devas.[9] It would be a good thing if I were to help him', and he appeared before the man as the sweetmeats and the water were being brought to him. When he saw the elder he thought, with devotion in his heart, 'What is the use of eating these sweetmeats to me who am about to be put to death? But they could be provisions for one going to the other world', and had the sweetmeats and the water given to the elder. With the aim of increasing his devotion, the elder sat down at a spot such that he was just within his vision[10] and ate the sweetmeats and drank the water and then rose from his seat and left. The man was led by his executioners to the place of execution and beheaded. Although he deserved to arise in the superior[11] devaloka on account of the meritorious deed he had performed with respect to the elder Moggallāna, the unsurpassed merit-field, since he thought, 'It is thanks to Sulasā that I obtained this merit-offering', his thoughts at the time of dying were soiled by feelings of affection[12] directed towards Sulasā and he therefore arose at an inferior level, arising as a tree-devatā in a huge banyan tree[13] amidst a densely shaded mountain thicket.

It is said that if, in his youth, he had worked hard and carried on the family line, he would have been foremost amongst wealthy merchants in that same city, whereas if when middle-aged, of middling (status), and if in his old age, of the lowest (status). However if, in his youth, he had gone forth, he would have become an arahant, whereas if when middle-aged he would have become a non-returner or a once-returner, and if in his old age, he would have become a sotāpanna.[14] But they say that through his association with evil friends he became disrespectful and given to bad conduct and to debauchery with women and drink and that in due course he wasted away all his prosperity and arrived at that great plight.

[6] Then later on he saw Sulasā who had gone to the park. Full of lust and desire, he inflicted her with blindness,[15] took her to his own realm and lived intimately with her for seven days and then revealed his identity to her. Her mother, being unable to see her, roamed about in all directions weeping. When the people saw her, they said, 'The worthy Mahāmoggallāna, who is of great psychic power and majesty, should know her whereabouts – you should go and ask him.' 'Very well, good people,' she said and approached the elder and asked him about the matter. The elder said, 'You will see her at the edge of the company when the Lord is teaching Dhamma at the Mahāvihāra[16] in the Bamboo Grove in seven days from now.' Sulasā then said to the devaputta, 'It is not proper for me to dwell in your realm; today is the seventh day and my mother, being unable to see me, will be full of anxiety and grief. Please take me back there, deva.' He took her when the Lord was teaching Dhamma in the Bamboo Grove and set her at the edge of the company and stood invisibly (beside her), whereupon the people, seeing Sulasā, said, 'Sulasā, my dear, where have you been for so many days? Your mother, being unable to see you, has been full of anxiety and grief like one driven to distraction.' She told the people of the incident and when the people asked, 'How did that man, who had pursued wicked deeds in that way and who had done no skilled deed, come to arise as a deva?' Sulasā replied, 'He gave to the worthy elder Mahāmoggallāna the sweetmeats and water that I had had given to him; it was by means of this meritorious deed that he came to arise as a deva.' When the people heard this, their hearts were filled with wonder and surprise and they felt[17] the highest joy and satisfaction at the thought, 'The arahants are indeed the world's unsurpassed merit-field – even the slightest service done for them brings it about that beings arise as devas.'

The monks raised the matter with the Lord whereupon the Lord spoke these verses on account of that arisen need:

1 'Like a field are the arahants, like cultivators those who give; like seed the merit-offering: from these the fruit is produced.

2 [7] This seed, field and cultivation (are desirable) for the petas and for the one who gives; the petas make use of this, whilst the donor through that merit grows.

3 Having done right here what is skilled and honoured the petas, having done that auspicious deed, he goes to the heavenly place.'

1 Herein *like a field (khettūpamā)*: a field is that which nourishes the seed scattered and sown in it and protects it by turning it into great fruit;[18] it is a place for growing paddy seeds and so on – they are[19] like this, like a field, meaning they are similar to a field prepared for ploughing. *The arahants (arahanto)*: those in whom the āsavas are destroyed. They are called 'arahants' because the enemies (*arīnaṃ*) of the defilements[20] and the spokes (*arānaṃ*) of the wheel of saṃsāra[21] have been destroyed (*hatattā*) by them; because of their keeping aloof (*ārakattā*) therefrom;[22] because they are worthy of (*arahattā*) the requisites and so on; and because they do no wicked deed, not even in secret (*arahābhāvā*).[23] For in this connection, just as a field that is well prepared,[24] that is undamaged by weeds and so on, when sown with seed yields great fruit for its cultivator, provided it is watered at the right time and other necessary conditions are fulfilled, even so does he in whose heart the āsavas are destroyed, he who is well prepared[24] and who is without the corruptions of greed and so on, when sown with seed (in the form of) merit-offerings, yield great fruit for the one who gives, provided it is the right time and other necessary conditions are present. For this reason the Lord said, 'Like a field are the arahants.' This is an explanation by way of 'maximum definition',[25] for there is no exclusion[26] of learners and so on also being that field. *Those who give (dāyakā)*: the givers of, those who give away, the requisites such as robes and so on. By their[27] generosity those who give away are those who cut out greed and so on from their own hearts, meaning alternatively that they are those who cleanse and who guard their hearts therefrom. *Like cultivators (kassakūpamā)*:[28] similar to cultivators; just as the cultivator obtains excellent and abundant fruit from his crops if he ploughs his paddy-fields and so on[29] and is zealous as to the cyclical supply and drainage of water and the laying down and protection (of his crops) and so on,[30] even so does the one who gives also obtain excellent and abundant fruit from his gift if he is zealous in his service to, and in his

generosity as regards his merit-offerings for, the arahants.[31] For this reason it was said, 'Like cultivators those who give'.[32] *Like seed the merit-offering (bījūpamaṃ deyyadhammaṃ)*: is given with a distortion of gender, meaning similar to seed the merit-offering, for this is a name for the ten[33] sorts of things that are to be given, such as food and drink and so on. *From these the fruit is produced (etto nibbattate phalaṃ)* means that from these, from (the conjunction of) the one who gives, the recipient and the giving away of the merit-offering [8] the fruit of the gift is produced, arises and continues to exist by way of their being conjoined for quite a long time. In this connection, since the nature of things such as food and drink and so on is none other than to be prepared with the intention of giving them away, therefore 'like seed the merit-offering' is how the merit-offering is taken to be. By means of this designation of the merit-offering, by just this intention of giving away with the thing that is the merit-offering as its object,[34] is its seed-like nature to be seen. It is indeed this (intention), and not the merit-offering as such, that produces the fruit (that consists in) various sorts of rebirth and so on and the various sorts of factors supporting this.

2 *This seed, field and cultivation (etaṃ bījaṃ kasīkhettaṃ)* means the aforesaid seed, the aforesaid field and the cultivation, the so-called means of sowing that seed in that field. For whom are these three desirable? He said, 'For the petas and for the one who gives.' If the one who gives gives a gift on behalf of the petas, this seed, this cultivation and this field are of benefit to both those petas and the one who gives, whilst if he gives a gift that is not on behalf of the petas, then they are of benefit to the one who gives alone – this is the meaning. Then to demonstrate this benefit 'the petas make use of this[35] whilst the donor through that merit grows' was said. Herein *the petas make use of this (taṃ petā paribhuñjanti)*: when a gift is given on behalf of the petas by the one who gives, the petas make use of the fruit of that gift which is of benefit to the petas due to successful attainment of the aforementioned field, cultivation and seed and to the appreciation (shown by the petas). *Whilst the donor through that merit grows (dātā puññena vaḍḍhati)*: whilst the donor, however, on account of his meritorious deed consisting in giving, through the fruit of that meritorious deed increases in his excellence of enjoyment and so on amongst devas and men.[36] For the fruit of a meritorious deed may also be called 'merit' (alone), viz., 'It is by the acquisition of skilled states, monks, that this merit increases'* and so on.

3 *Having done right here what is skilled (idh' eva kusalaṃ katvā)*: having heaped up right here, in this very existence, merit which consists

*D iii 58; also quoted at PvA 120 below.

in giving by way of (giving) on behalf of the petas and which is skilled in the sense that it results in unsullied well-being.[37] *And honoured the petas (pete ca paṭipūjayaṃ)*: venerated[38] by means of a gift on behalf of the petas and released those petas from the misery they were undergoing, for a gift that is being given on behalf of the petas[39] is called 'honouring them'. For this reason, 'For honour has been paid to us' and 'And the highest honour has been paid to the petas' is said.[40] *And (honoured) the petas (pete ca)*: [9] by the word 'and' are included the advantages of giving (experienced) in this very life, such as: one is much loved and adored, one is to be approached and trusted, one is to be honoured and respected, and one is praised and commended by the wise; and so on. *Having done that auspicious deed, he goes to the heavenly place (saggañ ca kamati ṭhānaṃ kammaṁ katvāna bhaddakaṃ)*: having done that auspicious, that lovely, skilled deed, he goes to, he approaches[41] by way of arising in, the devaloka, the place of arising for those who have performed meritorious deeds that has acquired the name 'heavenly' (*saggaṃ*) since it is supreme (*suṭṭhu-aggattā*)[42] in ten attributes such as heavenly life-span and so on.[43] Now here, after having said 'Having done what is skilled' he repeats the words 'Having done that auspicious deed' – this should be regarded as being meant to indicate that as with the (actual) giving away of the merit-offering,[44] so also is the (subsequent) giving away of any thought of (entitlement to) that gift by way of the assignment of the gift itself a skilled deed consisting in giving. Some, however, say that here 'the petas' means 'the arahants' but this is mere fancy on their part because of there being simply no possibility of return for those who have destroyed the āsavas, because of the inappropriateness to them, as to both the state of the seed and so on and the one who gives, of the term 'peta' and because of the appropriateness (of this) to those of the peta-womb (alone).

At the end of this teaching, insight into the Dhamma[45] arose to eighty-four thousand beings, beginning with that devaputta and Sulasā.

By this Elucidation of the Intrinsic Meaning, by this Exposition of this Peta Story, the Exposition of the Like A Field Peta Story is concluded.

[1] Reading kathesi with Se Be for text's kāthesi.
[2] The Indian crore, usually reckoned as 10,000,000.
[3] Literally, the wealthy merchant of great wealth.
[4] Reading olokentā with Se Be for text's olokento.
[5] All texts read rattavaṇṇaviralamālā- here but see PED sv virala where it is suggested that the vl rattakaṇavīramālā be adopted. This latter also garlands the condemned at J iii 59, iv 191, vi 406. Little is known of the flower other than that it was a bush (gaccha) J iii 61, v 420, and that it is contrasted with the tree and creeper Vism 183. Its flowers are cited as characteristic of the colour crimson (mañjettha)

VvA 177, DhsA 317, cp J iii 62, rather than red which is characterised by the bandhujīvaka flower D ii 111 = M ii 14, Vism 174, DhsA 317. A note at Jātaka Stories iv 119 n. 1 suggests the kaṇavīra 'was the vajjhamālā put on the head or neck of a criminal condemned to death'. Compare also SED sv vadhya. A red flower known as the vadamala, or shoe flower, is found in Ceylon and is so called due to its use in garlands for the condemned during the days of the Sinhalese kings. It is considered inauspicious and is never used in offerings to the Buddha, on shrines, or for personal adornment. The Bhikkhu Khantipālo, a botanist before ordination, has written questioning the PED identification of the kaṇavīra with the oleander, Nerium odorum, since most oleanders are either pink or white, rather than red. He feels, moreover, that since the oleander flowers only seasonally, it would prove an unsuitable execution flower which had, like the vadamala, to be available the whole year round. Might perhaps the kaṇavīra have been this vadamala, the single red Hibiscus (Rosa-sinensis)?

[6] Cp D iii 67 = S ii 128; S iv 340ff.; A ii 240ff. for further references to such practices regarding the condemned.

[7] vajjhapahaṭabheridesitamaggaṃ, all texts. PED sv pahaṭa, however, suggests amending to read -paṭaha-.

[8] dibbena cakkhunā.

[9] bhummadevesu.

[10] Reading tassa passantass' eva with Se Be for text's tassa . . . passaṃ tass' eva.

[11] uḷāre devaloke, but with vl uḷārena qualifying the meritorious deed, thus: 'although he deserved to arise in the devaloka on account of the superior meritorious deed he performed with respect to the elder Moggallāna'. Such an interpretation would not be impossible for Moggallāna is a merit-field (cp the hierarchy of the merit-worthy at M iii 255) but it is probable that the superior devaloka here is set in apposition to the inferior level, hīnakāyaṃ, of the sequel. It does not explain, however, Moggallāna's earlier prophesy that he would arise as a terrestrial deva, that is, at this lower level.

[12] sinehena, presumably amounting to more than mere gratitude as the sequel suggests. It is possible that the superior devaloka above refers to the Brahmaloka, or rūpāvacara, and that his failure to attain this is due to his continued attachment to the sense desires of the kāmāvacara. Arising at a low level on account of affection for the opposite sex is a theme that recurs in some later stories.

[13] Ficus indica, or the Indian fig-tree.

[14] This term is usually rendered 'streamwinner' but is more likely to be derived from sota, ear, than sota, stream, and would then mean 'one who had gained the ear', that is, one who had received an oral teaching of the Dhamma and thereby attained insight into the Dhamma as for instance at the end of this story. I therefore leave both this term and the similar expression sotāpatti- untranslated. See my forthcoming doctoral dissertation (University of Lancaster) on this and related issues.

[15] andhakāraṃ māpetvā; compare the similar expression andhaṃ akāsi Māraṃ (M i 159, 174; cp A iv 434) when a darkness is said to be put around Māra, or that Māra is made blind, by one attaining jhāna. The consciousness of one attaining jhāna transcends the kāmāvacara, the limit of Māra's realm with the result that the individual becomes invisible to Māra though Māra no doubt continues to see beings in his own realm. The world of the terrestrial devas is not spatially distinct from the world of men and is merely a different dimension of that world. But since it is a different dimension men generally fail to see devatās. In inflicting Sulasā with blindness the devatā in all probability does nothing more than render her invisible to the world of men, notably her mother, rather than actually deprive her of her sight.

[16] This should not be confused with the Mahāvihāra at Anurādhapura mentioned above.

[17] Reading paṭisaṃvedesi with Be for text's Se pativedesi.

[18] Reading mahapphalabhāvakaraṇena with Se Be for text's mahapphalaṃ bhāvakāraṇena.

[19] Reading etesan ti with Se Be for text's ete santi.

[20] Reading kilesārīnaṃ with Be for text's Se kilesānaṃ.

[21] Reading saṃsāracakkassa with Be for text's Se -vaṭṭassa.

[22] Cp A iv 145 where seven such things are listed.

[23] For a similar etymology of 'arahant' see DA 146; VvA 105f.

[24] Be suggests that it is the seed and the merit-offering that are well prepared.

[25] Reading ukkaṭṭhaniddeso with Se Be for text's ukkaṭṭhanideso; in other words the arahant, the most exalted member of the field, is here pars pro toto.

[26] Text's Se khettassa vā paṭikkhepato should be amended to read khettass' evāpaṭikkhepato; cp Be khettabhāvāpaṭikkhepato. The learners are the sotāpanna, once-returner and non-returner.

[27] Reading tesaṃ with Se Be for text's tena.

[28] Text mis-spells kassūpamā.

[29] Reading -khettādīni kasitvā with Se Be for text's -khettādīnaṃ kassitvā.

[30] vaṭṭūdakadānanīharaṇanidhānarakkhanādīhi.

[31] Reading arahantesu deyya- with Se Be for text's arahante sudeyya-.

[32] Text mis-spells dāyaka; it should read dāyakā as in the verse.

[33] A list of fourteen such items appears at Nd²523, Nd¹373.

[34] Reading deyyadhammavatthuvisayāya pariccāgacetanāya yeva with Se Be for text's deyyadhammavatthuvisayāyapariccāgato nāyayeva; merit-offerings, like seed, have to be given away, planted, if they are to bear fruit at a later date.

[35] taṃ, so Se Be and verse; text omits.

[36] Reading devamanussesu bhoga- with Se Be for text's devamanusse subhoga-.

[37] anavajjasukhavipāka-; cp D i 70 = M i 180 = 269 = 346 = A ii 210 = v 206.

[38] Reading sammānetvā with Se Be for text's sampādetvā; not in PED.

[39] Reading pete with Se Be for text's te.

[40] Pv I 5^{5} and I 5^{12} respectively. The text's punctuation should be corrected to read with Se Be: Tenāha: amhākañ ca katā pūjā ti petānaṃ pūjā ca katā uḷārā ti ca. Pete cā ti ca-saddena. . . .

[41] Reading upagacchati with Be for text's Se uppajjati.

[42] Cp PvA 89 below for a similar explanation.

[43] Enumerated at Pv II 9^{59-60} below.

[44] Reading deyyadhammapariccāgo with Se Be for text's deyyadhammaṃ pariccāgo.

[45] dhammābhisamayo, that is, gaining the Dhammacakkhu S ii 134, the vision of the Dhamma in which the Four Truths are directly perceived, e.g. M i 380; cp Asl. 242f. (Expos. 323ff.) as a result of which one becomes a sotāpanna. It is not therefore 'quasi' conversion as suggested by PED sv abhisamaya.

I.2 EXPOSITION OF THE BOAR(-FACED) PETA STORY
[Sūkarapetavatthuvaṇṇanā]

'Your body is all golden.' This was said when the Teacher was staying at the Squirrels' Feeding Ground in the Bamboo Grove near Rājagaha concerning a certain peta with the face of a boar.

It is said that long ago, during the dispensation of the Lord Kassapa,[1] there was a monk who was **[10]** restrained in body but unrestrained in speech and who would insult and abuse the monks. When he died he arose in hell[2] where he roasted for one Buddha-interval. During this Buddha-period he fell from there and arose, as a residual effect[3] of that same deed, as a peta overcome by hunger and thirst[4] at the foot of the Vulture Peak near Rājagaha. His body was the colour of gold but his face was like that of a boar. Now at that time the venerable Nārada was staying on the Vulture Peak. Having attended at dawn to his bodily ablutions,[5] he took his robe and bowl and as he was going to Rājagaha in search of alms[6] saw on his way that peta and uttered this verse enquiring about the deed he had done:

1 'Your body is all golden, it spreads light in all directions; yet your face is that of a boar – what deed did you do in the past?'

1 Herein *your body is all golden (kāyo te sabbasovaṇṇo)*: your body, your person, is all over the colour of gold, resembling the glow of molten gold. *It spreads light in all directions (sabbā obhāsate disā)*: it shines forth, it radiates, throughout all directions with its radiance; or alternatively the expression 'it spreads light' (*obhāsate*) can imply a causative sense though this is not expressed by its grammatical form,[7] meaning: 'your body is all golden; it lights up (*obhāseti*), it shines forth in, all directions' – this is how it should be regarded. *Yet your face is that of a boar (mukhan te sūkarass' eva)*: but your face is like that of a boar, meaning your face is similar to a boar's face. *What deed did you do in the past? (kiṃ kammam akarī pure)*: he asks what kind of deed he did formerly in a past birth.

That peta, questioned thus by the elder about the deed he had done, answered by uttering this verse:

2 'I was restrained in body; in speech I was unrestrained. For this reason my appearance, Nārada, is such as you see.'

2 Herein *I was restrained in body (kāyena saññato āsiṃ)*: I was restrained with bodily restraint, I was controlled with control in matters concerning the doors of the physical senses.[8] **[11]** *In speech I was unrestrained (vācāyāsim asaññato)*: in matters concerning speech I possessed no control. *For this reason (tena)*: by reason of both this restraint and lack of restraint.[9] *My: me=mayhaṃ* (alternative grammatical form). *Appearance is such as (tādiso vaṇṇo)*: such as you, Nārada, can see for yourself; I am of such a form that my body is human-shaped and the colour of gold but in face I am similar to a boar – this is how it should be construed.

The word 'appearance' (*vaṇṇo*) is to be regarded here as a reference to his skin and his shape.[10]

When the peta had thus answered the point upon which he had been questioned by the elder, making this his reason, he uttered this verse, exhorting the elder:

3 'Therefore I say to you, Nārada, you yourself have seen this; commit no wicked deed by mouth, do not end up with the face of a boar!'[11]

3 Herein *therefore: taṃ=tasmā* (alternative grammatical form). *I (say) to you: tāhaṃ=te ahaṃ* (resolution of compound). *Nārada (Nārada)*: he is addressing the elder. *Say (brūmi)*: tell. *Yourself (sāmaṃ)*: just by yourself. *This (idaṃ)*: he speaks concerning his own body. This is the meaning here: 'Since you, Nārada sir, have seen for yourself how this body of mine is human-shaped from the neck down and boar-shaped (from the neck) up, therefore I speak exhorting you.' What was it the peta[12] said? – 'Commit no wicked deed by mouth, do not end up with the face of a boar!' Herein *no (mā)* is a particle of prohibition. *By mouth: mukhasā=mukhena* (alternative grammatical form). *Kho* (untranslated) is used for emphasis. Do not commit, do not perform, any wicked deed in speech. *Do not end up with the face of a boar (mā kho sūkaramukho ahu)*:[13] simply do not[14] end up with the face of a boar as I have done. But if you are scurrilous and should commit wicked deeds in speech then you would certainly end up with the face of a boar. Therefore he warns him, saying, 'Commit no wicked deed by mouth', in order to prevent the face which is their fruit.

The venerable Nārada then proceeded to Rājagaha in search of alms. After his meal he returned from his almsround and raised the matter with the Teacher who was seated in the midst of the four assemblies. The Teacher said, [12] 'I (also), Nārada, saw that being in the past', and then taught Dhamma explaining in countless different ways[15] the disadvantages connected with bad conduct in speech and the advantages associated with good conduct in speech. That teaching was of benefit to the company assembled there.

[1] The Buddha immediately prior to Gotama.

[2] niraye; some render this 'purgatory' but all births are a purgatory given the law of kamma.

[3] Reading vipākāvasesena with Se Be for text's vipākavasena.

[4] Reading khuppipās' ābhibhuto peto with Se Be for text's khuppipāsāhi guṇūpeto; cp PED sv guṇa.

[5] sarīrapaṭijagganaṃ, not in PED.

[6] Reading piṇḍāya with Se Be for text's piṇḍacāratvāya.

[7] anto-gadha-hetu-atthaṃ, cp CPD sv.

[8] Reading kāyadvārikena with Be; text and Se read kāyañ cārikena.

[9] Reading saṃyamena (ca) asaṃyamena ca with Se Be for text's saññamena ca, (Be omits the first ca).

[10] Reading chaviyaṃ saṇṭhāne ca with Se Be for text's chavisaṇṭhāne 'va.

[11] mā kho sūkaramukho ahu, literally 'do not become boar-faced'.

[12] Reading kim idan ti peto āha for text's kim idan ti petī āha; Se reads kim idam peto āha whilst Be kin ti ceti āha.

[13] Text's punctuation should be amended to read with Se Be: mā karohi. Mā kho sūkaramukho ahū ti ahaṃ viya. . . .

[14] Reading mā ahosi with Se Be for text's ahosi.

[15] Reading anekākāravokāraṃ with Se Be for text's anekā kāravo kāraṃ.

I.3 EXPOSITION OF THE PUTRID MOUTH PETA STORY [Pūtimukhapetavatthuvaṇṇanā]

'You possess a beautiful, heavenly complexion.' This was said when the Teacher was staying at the Squirrels' Feeding Ground in the Bamboo Grove concerning a certain peta with a putrid mouth.

It is said that long ago, at the time of the Lord Kassapa, two young men of good family went forth under his dispensation and were full of virtuous conduct, living a life of austerity and dwelling together in harmony in a certain village settlement. Then a certain monk who was given to wicked deeds and who delighted in slander arrived at their dwelling place. The elders extended him a friendly welcome and provided him with accommodation. On the following day they entered the village with him in search of alms. When they saw this the people showed the three elders the highest reverence in the extreme and served them with a meal of rice-gruel and so on. When he had entered the vihāra he thought, 'This village is an attractive source of food for its people are full of faith and give the choicest almsfood. And this vihāra is shaded and well watered. I could happily live here; but as long as these monks continue to live here this vihāra will afford me no comfort – I will be living like a residential pupil. Well then, I must estrange them from one another and act in such a way that they will not live here again.'

So one day, when the senior elder had instructed the other two,[1] the slanderous monk entered his own dwelling place, spent a little time there and then approached that senior elder, who asked him, 'Why have you come at an improper time, my brother?' 'There is something I ought to mention, sir,' (he replied) and when the elder had given him permission (to speak), he said, 'Sir, this [13] companion elder of yours parades himself like a friend to your face but tells tales about you behind your back as might a rival.' When asked what (it was that) he said, he replied, 'Listen, sir, he speaks to your discredit, saying, "This senior elder is crafty, deceitful and a fraud; he makes his living by wrong means".' 'Do not speak in this way, my brother. This monk would not tell tales about me. He has known my character since the time we were laymen – I have always been of an amiable and lovely nature.' 'If you think in this way due to your purity of heart then that is up to you. But I have no ill-feelings towards him so why should I tell you he had said it if he did not say it? Very well, sir, but you will find out about it yourself after a while,' he said. But that elder, on account of being a puthujjana,[2] wavered, wondering, 'Could it be as he says?', and suspicion arose in his heart, his trust a little shaken. Having estranged the first senior elder, that fool also set that other elder at variance in the aforesaid manner. On the following day, neither elder addressed the other when taking robe and bowl and going to that village in search of alms. When they brought back their almsfood, each ate it in his own dwelling place and, without extending even the slightest courtesy, spent the day right there, whilst at daybreak each went wherever he found convenient without informing the other. When they saw the slanderous monk who had entered that village that could fulfil all his wishes in search of alms, the people asked, 'Where have the elders gone, sir?' 'They quarrelled with one another the whole night. I told them not to quarrel but to live in harmony and that quarrelling leads to misfortune, brings about misery in the future and conduces to unskilled deeds; furthermore much that is of benefit that has already been done is undone[3] by a quarrel – and so on, but they went away without heeding my words.' At this the people begged, 'Let those elders go if they so wish. But you must please dwell here out of pity for us – you will not have any regrets!' 'Very well,' he agreed.[4] When he had stayed there a few days, he thought, 'I have set at variance monks who were virtuous and of lovely character through my greed for a dwelling. I have surely done a very wicked deed!' [14] Overcome by an extremely uneasy conscience he became sick through the weight of his grief and, dying not long afterwards, arose in Avīci.[5]

As the other two companion elders wandered about that country they met in a certain dwelling and exchanged friendly greetings with one another. They informed one another of the words of dissension the monk had spoken and when they realised that there was no truth in it became harmonious (again) and returned in due course to that same dwelling. When the people saw the two elders they were overjoyed and, full of happiness, served them with the four requisites. The elders stayed there being supplied with suitable food and developed insight through the concentration of mind and not long afterwards attained arahantship.

The slanderous monk roasted in hell for one Buddha-interval and arose during this Buddha-period not far from Rājagaha as a peta with a putrid mouth. His body was the colour of gold but worms would come out of his mouth and devour his face here and there. He emitted a foul smell that pervaded far into the atmosphere. Now as the venerable Nārada came down from the Vulture Peak he saw him and asked about the deed he had done with this verse:

1 'You possess a beautiful, heavenly complexion but as you stand in the air, in the sky, worms devour your putrid smelling mouth. What deed did you do in the past?'[6]

1 Herein *heavenly (dibbaṃ)* (usually means): of a divine nature, having attained the state of devahood; here, however, 'heavenly' (means) 'heaven-like'.[7] *Beautiful (subhaṃ)*: shining or in an excellent condition. *Complexion (vaṇṇadhātuṃ)*: colour of the skin. *You possess (dhāresi)*: you bear. *As you stand in the air, in the sky (vehāyasan tiṭṭhasi antalikkhe)*: you stand in the air, in the sky so to speak. Some say, however, that the reading is *vihāyasan tiṭṭhasi antalikkhe* and say this is the meaning as the rest of the words are: 'you stand in the air lighting up[8] the sky'. **[15]** *Putrid smelling (pūtigandhaṃ)*: having the smell of a rotting corpse, meaning foul smelling. *What deed did you do in the past? (kiṃ kammaṃ akāsi pubbe)*: he asks, 'Worms devour your putrid smelling mouth yet your body is the colour of gold. What sort of deed did you do in the past that could be the cause of such an appearance?'

When questioned by the elder about the deed he had done that peta uttered this verse explaining the matter:

2 'I was a wicked and foul mouthed recluse; (though) in the guise of an ascetic, I was unrestrained in mouth. Through my austerity I received this complexion and by my slander this putrid mouth.'

2 Herein *I was a wicked recluse (samaṇo ahaṃ pāpo)*: I was a despicable recluse, a wicked monk. *Foul mouthed (duṭṭhavāco)*: of foul speech; I transgressed against others, I went too far with my mouth, meaning I was one to speak denouncing the virtues of others. An alternative reading is *extremely foul mouthed (atiduṭṭhavāco)*: extremely harsh spoken, fond of bad conduct in speech such as telling lies and slander and so on. *In the guise of an ascetic (tapassīrūpo)*: disguised as a recluse. *In mouth: mukhasā=mukhena* (alternative grammatical form). *Received (laddhā)*: obtained; the word 'and' (*ca*) has the meaning of a conjunction.[9] *I: me=mayā*

(alternative grammatical form). *Through my austerity (tapasā)*: by means of my Brahma-faring. *By my slander (pesuniyena)*: by my malicious speech. *Putrid (pūti)*: putrid smelling.

When that peta had reported the deed that he had done, he then uttered the concluding verse exhorting the elder:

3 'You yourself have seen this, Nārada. Those who possess pity and who are skilled would say, "Neither slander nor tell lies – then you will become a yakkha with all your desires gratified".'

3 [16] Herein *this (tayidaṃ)*: this appearance of mine. *Those who possess pity and who are skilled would say (anukampakā ye kusalā vadeyyuṃ)*: those who are of a pitying nature and who possess compassion, who are skilled and clever in acting for the benefit of others, such as the Buddha and so on, would say just what I am saying – this is the meaning. Showing this exhortation he then said, 'Neither slander nor tell lies – then you will become a yakkha with all your desires gratified.' This is the meaning: neither (utter) slanderous talk nor tell, nor speak, lies: if you renounce telling lies and malicious speech and become restrained in speech, then you will become a yakkha or a deva or one of a deva's retinue.[10] Having obtained the finest heavenly excellence and whatever desire that can be desired,[11] you will be able to go here and there (at pleasure) and be of a nature to amuse yourself by gratifying the senses at will.

When he had heard this, the elder thereupon proceeded to Rājagaha in search of alms. Returning from his almsround after his meal, he raised the issue with the Teacher. The Teacher took it as an arisen need and taught Dhamma. That teaching was of benefit to the company assembled there.

[1] Reading dvinnaṃ with Se Be for text's dinnaṃ.

[2] One who has not attained any of the four supramundane paths of the sotāpanna, once-returner, non-returner and arahant and who therefore, unlike the sāvaka, has not gained insight into the Four Truths afforded by the Dhammacakkhu.

[3] Reading paribhaṭṭhā with Se Be for text's parihaṭṭhā. Gehman has 'gladdened' here but the meaning seems rather that in a fit of rage many of the good states that one had already built up, including calm, are quickly lost.

[4] Reading paṭissuṇitvā with Se Be for text's paṭisuṇitvā.

[5] That is, in the Great Hell of the same name.

[6] Cp III 10[1].

[7] Cp PvA 110.

[8] Reading obhāsento with Se Be for text's abhāsento; vehāyasaṃ is accusative but apparently with locative meaning and this alternative explanation thus suggests that it is the accusative of a variant form of the noun since it is the patient of a missing or understood verb.

[9] Cp Path of Purification p. 165 n. 43.

[10] yakkho vā devo vā devaññataro vā; the precise distinctions between such terms as deva, devatā, devaputta and devaññatara still remain in need of investigation.
[11] Reading kāmitabbaṃ with Be (Se kamitabbaṃ) for text's kāmī kaññaṃ.

I.4 EXPOSITION OF THE BISCUIT DOLL PETA STORY
[Piṭṭhadhītalikapetavatthuvaṇṇanā]

'With reference to whomsoever.' The Teacher, who was staying in the Jeta Grove at Sāvatthī told this concerning an almsgiving of the householder Anāthapiṇḍika.

It is said that the householder Anāthapiṇḍika's grand-daughter, who was still a young girl, was given a biscuit doll by her nurse, who said, 'Take this to play with.' She came to regard it as her own daughter. Then one day whilst playing with it she carelessly let it fall and it broke. At this the girl burst out crying, saying, 'My daughter is dead!', but none of the servants could console her tears.

Now at that same time the Teacher was seated on the appointed seat in the house of the householder Anāthapiṇḍika and that extremely wealthy merchant [17] was seated near the Lord. The nurse went with the girl into the wealthy merchant's presence. When he saw her he said, 'Why is this girl weeping?' The nurse reported the incident to the wealthy merchant and the latter sat the girl on his lap and consoled her, saying, 'I will give alms on behalf of your daughter', and then addressed the Teacher, saying, 'I wish to give alms on behalf of my great grand-daughter, this biscuit doll.[1] Please accept my invitation to you, Lord, and to five hundred monks for the following day's meal.' And the Lord consented with his silence. Then on the next day the Lord went, together with five hundred monks, to the house of that wealthy merchant and, when he had finished his meal, spoke these verses expressing his appreciation:

1 'With reference to whomsoever the unselfish should give alms, whether with respect to former petas or, moreover, to the household devatās,

2 And the Four Great Kings, renowned guardians of the world, namely Kuvera, Dhataraṭṭha, Virūpakkha and Virūlhaka, – when these are honoured the givers are not without fruit.

3 No amount of weeping, sorrow or any other lamentation benefits the peta though their relatives persist in them.

4 But this donation that has been made and firmly planted in the Saṅgha will serve, with immediate effect, their long term benefit.'

1 Herein *with reference to whomsoever (yaṃ kiñcārammaṇaṃ katvā)*: with respect to, on behalf of, whomsoever else one (participates) in auspicious rites and so on. *Should give: dajjā=dadeyya* (alternative grammatical form). *The unselfish (amaccharī)*: the unselfish are so due to an absence of selfishness which is characterised by the inability (to share) their own good fortune[2] in common with others; being of a generous nature, they should give after they have set at a distance stains of the heart such as selfishness and greed and so on – this is the meaning. *Whether with respect to former petas (pubbe pete ca ārabbha)*: whether on behalf of any former ancestors.[3] *Household devatās (vatthudevatā)*: with respect to the devatās that inhabit the house and its grounds and so on – this is how it should be construed. *Or, moreover (atha vā)* indicates that they should give alms in this way with respect also to any other deva or man and so on whomsoever.

2 Herein, after stating 'and the Four Great Kings', indicating to this extent some well-known devas amongst the devas, he again **[18]** says 'Kuvera' and so on referring to them by name. Herein *Kuvera (Kuveraṃ)*: Vessavaṇa. *Dhataraṭṭha (Dhataraṭṭhaṃ)* and so on are the names of the three remaining guardians of the world. *When these are honoured (te c'eva pūjitā honti)*: when these Great Kings, former petas and household devatās are revered by acts on their behalf. *The givers are not without fruit (dāyakā ca anipphalā)*: the givers, those who give alms on behalf of others, are not entirely without fruit; they similarly partake of the fruit of their own alms. Then to show that those who weep, mourn and lament at the death of their relatives do them no good and merely torment themselves, he uttered the verse (beginning:) 'No amount of weeping'.

3 Herein *weeping: ruṇṇaṃ=ruditaṃ* (alternative grammatical form), the shedding of tears. The rest of the words state that this is not to be done. *Sorrow (soko)*: mourning, torturing the heart, meaning burning inside. *Any other lamentation (yā c'aññā paridevanā)* means any lamentation other than weeping and sorrow, such as mumbling 'Where is my only son?' and so on, are not to be done either. The word 'or' (*vā*) under all circumstances denotes an alternative. *No (amount of weeping) benefits the peta (na taṃ petassa atthāya)*: since none of these, neither weeping nor sorrow nor lamentation either helps or benefits the dead peta, they are therefore not to be done, even though their foolish[4] relatives persist in them – this is the meaning. Having thus shown the futility of weeping and so on, he then uttered the verse (beginning:) 'But this donation' showing the usefulness of a donation made to the Saṅgha by a donor with respect to former petas and so on.

4 Herein *this (ayaṃ)*: he speaks pointing to the alms before him that were given by that donor. *But (ca)* is a word (denoting) something additional. He clarifies the distinction by going on to say that just because weeping and so on do not benefit either the peta or anyone else this is not so, however, as regards this donation which will be to their long term benefit. *Kho* (untranslated) is used for emphasis. *Donation (dakkhiṇā)*: almsgiving. *Firmly planted in the Saṅgha (saṅghamhi suppatiṭṭhitā)*:[5] **[19]** firmly planted in the Saṅgha, the unsurpassed merit-field. *Their long term benefit (dīgharattaṃ hitāy' assa)*: the good, the benefit, of that peta for a long time. *Will serve with immediate effect (ṭhānaso[6] upakappati)*: it takes effect straight away, meaning with no time intervening. This is indeed the rule here:[7] if petas express their appreciation when a gift is given on their behalf, they are at once[8] relieved (of their sufferings)[9] by means of its fruit.

When the Lord had thus taught Dhamma and had made those people take delight in giving on behalf of petas, he rose from his seat and departed. On the following day the wife of that wealthy merchant and the rest of his relatives followed his example and inaugurated a great almsgiving lasting as long as a month.[10] Then Pasenadi, king of Kosala, approached the Lord and asked, 'Why is it, Lord, that the monks have not come to my house for as long as a month now?' When the Teacher told him the reason the king too, following that wealthy merchant's example, inaugurated a great almsgiving for the order of monks with the Buddha at its head. And when they saw this his citizens, following the king's example, inaugurated a great almsgiving lasting as long as a month. Thus they inaugurated a great almsgiving that lasted two months, all on account of that biscuit doll.

[1] Reading piṭṭhadhītalikaṃ with Se Be for text's piṇḍa-, though the meaning remains unaltered.

[2] sampattiyā.

[3] pitaro.

[4] Reading aviddasuno with Se Be for text's avindasuno.

[5] Text mis-spells suppatiṭṭhā.

[6] Text erroneously inserts taṃ after ṭhānaso.

[7] Reading ayaṃ hi tattha dhammatā with Se Be for text's ayaṃ hitātthadhammatā.

[8] Reading tāva-d-eva tassa with Se Be for text's tāva devassa.

[9] Text reads bhuñjanti with vl paribhuñjanti suggesting that they enjoy or make use of the food that has just appeared in their vicinity. Se Be, however, both read parimuccanti here, meaning that they are released or set free (from their former sufferings), which I follow. But since, as these stories make abundantly clear, the suffering from which petas are usually freed is that of hunger, the difference between these vll is narrower than might at first sight appear.

[10] So text and Se which both read te māsamattaṃ; Be reads temāsamattaṃ which would mean that it lasted three months.

1.5 EXPOSITION OF THE OUTSIDE THE WALLS PETA STORY[1]
[Tirokuḍḍapetavatthuvaṇṇanā]

'They stand outside the walls.' The Teacher who was staying at Rājagaha told this concerning a large number of petas. Here is that story in detail.

Ninety-two aeons ago there was a city named Kāsipurī where a king named Jayasena reigned. His queen was named Sīrimā and in her womb was conceived the Bodhisatta Phussa who in due course attained (the) perfect enlightenment (of a Buddha). King Jayasena became possessive, thinking, 'My son it is who performed the Great Renunciation and has become a Buddha. Mine alone is the Buddha, mine the Dhamma, mine the Saṅgha', and all the time waited upon them himself, giving no one else an opportunity. The Lord's three brothers, younger brothers by a different mother, thought, **[20]** 'Buddhas indeed arise for the benefit of the whole world, not just for the sake of one person, yet our father does not give anyone else an opportunity. Now how might we get to wait upon the Saṅgha?' And then the thought occurred to them, 'Come on, let's devise some means!' So they made it appear as though there were a disturbance on the border. When the king heard of this 'disturbance on the border' he sent these three sons to pacify the border. They went and pacified things and when they returned the king was pleased and granted them a boon, saying, 'Take whatever you wish.' 'We wish to wait upon the Lord,' they said. 'You may take anything apart from him,'[2] replied the king. 'We do not care for anything else,' they said. 'In that case set a time limit and take him.' They begged for seven years but the king would not give this. They begged successively for six, five, four, three, two years, one year; for seven months, six, five, four months, for three months at which the king said, 'Take him!' They approached the Lord and said, 'Lord, we wish to wait upon the Lord for three months. Lord, may the Lord accept us for this three months' residence of the rainy season.' The Lord consented by his silence. Those three then sent a letter[3] to their agent in that district (where the Lord would be staying), stating, 'The Lord is to be waited upon by us during these three months. First of all build a vihāra and then procure everything that will be needed for waiting upon the Lord.' He sent (word) back when he had procured everything. They dressed in yellow clothes and, together with two thousand five hundred male helpers, conducted the Lord and the order of monks to that district, waiting upon them respectfully, and handed over the vihāra to them and had them pass the rainy season there. Their treasurer, a householder's son and married, had faith and devotion. With due care he gave the items for almsgiving for the order of monks with the Buddha at its head. The agent in that district received these and along with as many as eleven thousand men from that district organised the almsgiving[4] with due care. Now some people there were of corrupt mind. They obstructed the alms, ate the merit-offerings themselves and set fire to the refectory. When they had celebrated the Pavāraṇā ceremony[5] the sons of the king worshipped the Lord [21] and then went back,[6] with the Lord going before them, into their father's presence. After the Lord had gone there he attained Parinibbāna.

In due course the king's sons, their agent in that district and their treasurer died and arose in heaven together with that company (of helpers) whilst those people of corrupt mind arose in the hells. Ninety-two aeons passed thus whilst both (groups of) people arose in heaven after heaven and in hell after hell respectively. Then during this auspicious aeon,[7] at the time of the Lord Kassapa, those people of corrupt mind arose amongst the petas. At that time when people gave alms for the sake of their peta-relatives they dedicated them, saying, 'Let this be for our relatives!' (at which) they attained excellence. Now when those petas saw this they approached Kassapa and asked, 'How, Lord, might we (also) attain such excellence?' The Lord said, 'You will not attain it now. However, in the future there will be a Perfectly Enlightened One named Gotama. At the time of this Lord there will be a king named Bimbisāra who was your relative ninety-two aeons ago. He will give alms to that Buddha and dedicate them to you. Then you will attain (such excellence).' It is said that when he said this it seemed to those petas as though he had said they would attain it on the following day.

Then when one Buddha-interval[8] had passed and our Lord had arisen in the world those three sons of the king, together with a thousand men, also fell from the devaloka and arose in a brahmin clan[9] in the kingdom of Magadha. In due course they went forth into the homeless life of the ascetic and became the three matted-hair[10] ascetics of Gayāsīsa.[11] Their agent in that district became king Bimbisāra and their treasurer, the householder's son, became the wealthy merchant Visākha whose wife, named Dhammadinnā, was the daughter of a wealthy merchant whilst the remainder of that company arose as the king's entourage.

When our Lord had arisen in the world and had spent the seven weeks (following his enlightenment) he came in due course to Benares where he set rolling the Wheel of the Dhamma and instructed[12] first the Group of Five and then the three matted-hair ascetics with their one thousand followers and then went to Rājagaha. [22] He there established in the sotāpatti-fruit king Bimbisāra who had come to visit him that very day, along with eleven myriads[13] of brahmin householders who were inhabitants of Aṅga-Magadha.[14] He accepted the king's invitation to a meal on the following day and the next day entered Rājagaha with Sakka, Lord of Devas, who had assumed the form of a brahmin youth, walking in front of him praising him with the verses that begin:

> 'The tamed with the tamed, the freed with the freed; the Lord, bright as a golden jewel, entered Rājagaha with the former matted-hair ascetics.'[15]

And in the king's residence he accepted a great almsgiving. Now the petas stood surrounding the house, thinking, 'Now the king will dedicate the alms to us', but when he gave the alms the king thought only about a site for the Lord's vihāra, wondering, 'Now where should the Lord stay?', and did not dedicate the alms to anyone. Not getting the alms in this way, those petas lost hope and that night wailed in utter and dreadful distress about the king's residence. The king became agitated and was filled with fear and trembling. At daybreak he told the Lord, 'I heard such a noise (during the night)! Whatever is going to happen to me, Lord?' The Lord said, 'Have no fear, great king, no evil will befall you – you will be all right. The fact is that[16] former relatives of yours who have arisen amongst the petas have been going around for one whole Buddha-interval with the expectation[17] that you would give alms to a Buddha and dedicate them to them. But when you gave alms yesterday[18] you did not dedicate them and they lost hope and wailed in such dreadful distress.' 'Would they receive them, Lord, if (alms) were given now?' (asked the king). 'Yes, great king.' 'Then let the Lord accept my (invitation) for today[19] and I will dedicate the alms to them.' The Lord consented by his silence. The king went to his residence and had a great almsgiving prepared and had the time announced to the Lord. [23] The Lord went to the king's royal court[20] together with the order of monks and sat down on the appointed seat. The petas thought, 'Today we may get something', and went and stood outside the walls and so on. The Lord brought it about that they all became visible to the king. As he gave the water donation the king dedicated it, saying, 'Let this be for my relatives!' At that moment lotus ponds came into being for the petas covered with lotuses[21] and blue water lillies.[22] They bathed and drank in them and with their distress, weariness and thirst allayed[23] they became the colour of gold. The king gave rice-gruel and hard and soft foods and dedicated these and at that very instant heavenly rice-gruel and hard and soft foods[24] came into being. When they ate these their faculties were refreshed.[25] The king gave clothing and lodging and dedicated these and heavenly clothing and palaces variously furnished with couches and covers and so on[26] came into being for them. All this excellence of theirs was made manifest to the king just as the Lord had resolved it should be and when the king saw it he was thoroughly delighted. Then when the Lord had finished his meal and eaten his fill he told king Bimbisāra the Outside the Walls Peta Story in order to show his appreciation:

1 'They stand outside the walls and at junctions and road-forks; they go to their own house and stand at the door-posts.

2 Though abundant food and drink, foods hard and soft, are served, no one remembers those creatures on account of their deeds.

3 So they who possess pity give for their relatives the purest, choicest, timely and fitting food and drink (saying), "Let this be for our relatives! May our relatives be happy!"

4 And those peta-relatives who have gathered and assembled there respectfully show their appreciation for that abundant food and drink (saying),

5 "A long life to our relatives by means of whom we have gained (all this) for honour has been paid to us and those who give are not without fruit!"

6 For there is no cultivation there, nor is there here[27] any cattle-rearing known; nor are there such things as trading and buying and selling with gold – the petas, those who have passed on,[28] are there sustained by what is given from here.[29]

7 As water rained on the uplands flows down to the lowlands [24] even so does what is given from here benefit the petas.

8 Just as swollen streams swell the ocean, even so does what is given from here benefit the petas.

9 "He gave to me, he worked for me, he was a relative, friend and companion to me" – (thus) recalling what they used to do one should give donations for the petas.

10 No amount of weeping, sorrow or any other lamentation benefits the peta though their relatives persist in them.

11 But this donation that has been made and firmly planted in the Saṅgha will serve, with immediate effect, their long term benefit.

12 Now this, the duty to one's relatives, has been pointed out and the highest honour has been paid to the petas; strength has been furnished to the monks and not trifling the meritorious deed pursued by you.'

1 Herein *outside the walls (tiro kuḍḍesu)*: on the further side of the walls. *They stand (tiṭṭhanti)*: this expression asserts their standing in contrast to (other postures) such as sitting and so on,[30] meaning they stand thus outside, beyond, the fences that surround houses. *And at junctions and road-forks: sandhisiṅghāṭakesu ca=sandhīsu ca siṅghāṭakesu ca* (resolution of compound); places where four roads meet, house-junctions, wall-

junctions and light-junctions[31] are called 'junctions' whilst 'road-forks' are places where three roads meet.[32] *Stand at the door-posts (dvārabāhāsu tiṭṭhanti)*: stand leaning against the posts of the city gates and of the doors of houses. *They go to their own house (āgantvāna sakaṃ gharaṃ)*: 'their own house' can be the house of a former relative as well as their own house in which they dwelt as owners. Since they come regarding both these as their own he therefore said, 'They go to their own house.' The Lord said the verse (beginning:) 'They stand outside the walls' showing the king the many petas, who were extremely ugly, deformed and terrible to behold, undergoing[33] the fruit of envy and selfishness and who were stood outside the walls and so on having come to Bimbisāra's residence regarding it as their own house since it was the house of a former relative though they themselves had not formerly dwelt there in the past.[34] He then uttered the second verse (beginning:) 'Though abundant food and drink' showing the dreadful nature of the deed done by them.

2 Herein *abundant (pahūte)*: plentiful, much, meaning as much as is needed. [25] It is permissible to substitute the syllable *pa* for the syllable *ba* [thus transforming *bahu* into text's *pahu*] as in such passages as 'Though possessing plenty he does not support . . .' (*pahu santo na bharati*).* Some however read 'abundant' (*bahuke*) but this is a careless reading.[35] *Food and drink: annapānamhi=anne ca pāne ca* (resolution of compound in alternative grammatical form). *Foods hard and soft: khajjabhojje=khajje ca bhojje ca* (resolution of compound); by means of these (four) he indicated the four sorts of food: that which is eaten, drunk, chewed and savoured. *Are served (upaṭṭhite)*: are begun (*upagamma*) to be set out (*ṭhite*), meaning are given out, are got ready. *No one remembers those creatures (na tesaṃ koci sarati sattānaṃ)*: no one, neither their mother nor father nor son nor grandson remembers those creatures who have arisen on the peta-plane. For what reason? On account of their deeds. By reason of[36] that miserly deed that they themselves did consisting in the failure to give and the prevention of that almsgiving and so on – it is this[37] deed of theirs that does not allow their relatives to remember them. When he had shown how, in spite of the existence of plentiful food[38] and drink and so on, due to that wicked deed there was not even the slightest recollection on the part of those relatives of the petas waiting in expectation of (a gift from) their relatives, the Lord then uttered the third verse (beginning:) '(So they who possess pity) give for their relatives' praising alms given[39] on behalf of relatives who have arisen on the peta-plane.

3 Herein *so (evaṃ)* is a term of comparison. It can be construed in two ways: though they do not remember those creatures on account of

*Sn 98.

their deeds, some give for their relatives *so* they possess pity; and they who possess pity give for their relatives the purest, choicest, timely and fitting food and drink as *so* given in that way by you, great king. Herein *give (dadanti)*: dedicate, consign. *For their relatives (ñātīnaṃ)*: for those connected on the mother's and father's sides. *Who (ye)*: any sons and so on. *Who: honti=bhavanti* (alternative grammatical form). *Possess pity (anukampakā)*: are desirous of their welfare, are seekers of their well-being. *Purest (suciṃ)*: clean, captivating and in accordance with the Dhamma. *Choicest (paṇītaṃ)*: finest. *Timely (kālena)*: at a time when it is proper[40] for those worthy of donations to eat or at the time when their relatives **[26]** have come and are standing outside the walls. *Fitting (kappiyaṃ)*: suitable, seeming, worthy of being eaten by the ariyans. *Food and drink: pānabhojanaṃ=pānañ ca bhojanañ ca* (resolution of compound); by means of this reference[41] he speaks here of all merit-offerings. Then, showing the manner in which these are to be given for the petas, he said, 'Let this be for our relatives! May our relatives be happy!' This is to be construed with the first half of the third verse, thus: 'So they who possess pity give for their relatives saying, "Let this be for our relatives! May our relatives be happy!" ' In this way he gave an indication of the way in which the alms are to be given.[42] Herein *this (idaṃ)* indicates the merit-offering. *Vo* (untranslated) is a mere particle as in (such passages as) 'One of those ariyans who . . .' (*ye hi vo ariyā*).* *Let (this) be for our relatives! (ñātīnaṃ hotu)*: let (this) be for our relations who have arisen on the peta-plane! Some read *our relatives: no ñātīnaṃ=amhākaṃ ñātīnaṃ* (alternative grammatical form).[43] *May our relatives be happy! (sukhitā hontu ñātayo)*: may our relatives who have arisen on the peta-plane be happy, attain happiness in experiencing this (gift's) fruit! Although it was said, 'Let this be for our relatives!', it is not a case of a deed done by one giving fruit for another[44] but simply that things that are being given on their behalf in this way become a condition of those peta-relatives[45] (doing) a skilled deed.[46] Therefore it is this skilled deed that produces its fruit for them at that very instant in accordance with those things. Showing this he uttered the verse beginning: 'And those (peta-relatives who have gathered and assembled) there'.

4 Herein *those (te)*: those peta-relatives. *There (tattha)*: there where the alms are given. *Who have gathered (samāgantvā)*: who have assembled there in order to show their appreciation thinking, 'These relatives of ours will dedicate alms for our sake.' *For that abundant food and drink (pahūte annapānamhi)*: for that abundant food and drink,[47] for the things that are being given on their behalf. *Respectfully show their appreciation (sakkaccaṃ anumodare)*: possessing faith in the fruition of deeds and without

*M i 17.

forsaking their respect[48] and with no derangement of mind [27] they rejoice, they show their appreciation and become full of joy and happiness at the thought, 'May these alms be for our[49] happiness and well-being!'

5 *A long life! (ciraṃ jīvantu)*: may they have a long life, may they be long lived! *To our relatives (no ñātī)*: to our relations. *By means of whom (yesaṃ hetu)*: by reason of whom, dependent upon whom. *We have gained (labhāmase)*: we have gained such excellence. This shows the manner of the praise for their relatives (shown) by the petas who are experiencing the excellence gained by means of their dedication. A donation produces its fruit immediately when three factors are present: the successful attainment of those worthy of donations, the dedication by the one who gives and the appreciation of the petas. Of these the one who gives is the particular means; for this reason they said, 'By means of whom we have gained (all this).' *For honour has been paid to us (amhākañ ca katā pūjā)*: for honour has been paid to us by those who give dedicating (those alms) thus: 'Let this be for our relatives!' *And those who give are not without fruit (dāyakā ca anipphalā)*: since that deed (consisting in giving away)[50] gives its fruit[51] there and then for them in whose hearts it was conceived. Here it may be asked,[52] 'How is it, do only[53] those who have arisen on the peta-plane gain this excellence by means of their relatives or do others also (gain it)?' Nothing need be said here by us since this has been explained as follows* by the Lord himself:

' "Master Gotama, we brahmins give alms and perform the śrāddha[54] rites saying, 'May these alms be of benefit to the petas who were our relatives and blood-relations! May our peta-relatives and blood-relations enjoy these alms!' Master Gotama, are those alms really of benefit to those petas who were our relatives and blood-relations? Do those peta-relatives and blood-relations really enjoy those alms?"

"If they are in the (appropriate) place, brahmin, they are of benefit (to them); if they are in a place that is not (appropriate) they are not."

"But what is the (appropriate) place, master Gotama, and what the place that is not (appropriate)?"

"Here, brahmin, a certain person destroys living beings (takes what has not been given, is of wrong conduct as to sensual desires, speaks falsely,[55] is of slanderous speech, is harsh-spoken, talks frivolously, is covetous, malevolent in mind and)[56] of wrong view. At the breaking up of the body after dying he arises in hell. He sustains himself there, he maintains himself there, on whatever is the food of the creatures of hell. This, brahmin, is a place that is not (appropriate); those alms are of no benefit to one who remains there.

*A v 269–271.

"Here, brahmin, a certain person destroys living beings . . . is of wrong view. At the breaking up of the body after dying [28] he arises in the animal womb. He sustains himself there, he maintains himself there, on whatever is the food of the creatures of the animal womb. This, brahmin, is a place that is not (appropriate); those alms are of no benefit to one who remains there.

"Here, brahmin, a certain person refrains from destroying living beings (refrains from taking what has not been given, refrains from wrong conduct as to sensual desires, refrains from speaking falsely, refrains from slanderous speech, refrains from being harsh-spoken, refrains from talking frivolously, is not covetous, nor malevolent in mind and) is of right view. At the breaking up of the body after dying he arises in the company of human beings. (He sustains himself there, he maintains himself there, on whatever is the food of human beings. This, brahmin, is a place that is not (appropriate); those alms are of no benefit to one who remains there.

"Here, brahmin, a certain person refrains from destroying living beings . . . is of right view. At the breaking up of the body after dying)[57] he arises in the company of the devas. He sustains himself there, he maintains himself there, on whatever is the food of the devas. This,[58] brahmin, is a place that is not (appropriate); those alms are of no benefit to one who remains there.

"Here, brahmin, a certain person destroys living beings . . . is of wrong view. At the breaking up of the body after dying he arises on the peta-plane.[59] He sustains himself there, he maintains himself there, on whatever is the food of the creatures of the peta-plane. Or he sustains himself there, he maintains himself there, on whatever his friends, companions or relatives and blood-relations offer up from here.[60] This, brahmin, is the (appropriate) place; those alms are of benefit to one who remains there."

"But if, master Gotama, that peta who was our relative and blood-relation has not arisen in that place, who is it that enjoys the alms?"

"Other petas, brahmin, who were your relatives and blood-relations who have arisen in that place – these enjoy the alms."

"But if, master Gotama, that peta who was our relative and blood-relation has not arisen in that place and other petas who were our relatives and blood-relations have also not arisen in that place – who is it that enjoys the alms?"

"But this[61] is impossible, brahmin, this cannot be, that that place should be empty for so long a time of those petas who were your relatives and blood-relations. And anyway, brahmin, those who give are not without fruit." '[62]

Then to show that those who have arisen on the peta-plane are sustained by what is given from here in the absence of any other (source) such as cultivation and cattle-rearing and so on that might be a reason of their obtaining excellence (the verse) beginning: 'For (there is) no' was said.

6 Herein *for there is no cultivation there (na hi tattha kasī atthi)*: for there is no cultivation on that peta-plane dependent upon which the petas might live in comfort. *Nor is there here any cattle-rearing known (gorakkh' ettha na vijjati)*: here, on this peta-plane, not only is there no cultivation, there is, moreover, also no cattle-rearing known [29] dependent upon which they might live in comfort. *Nor are there such things as trading (vaṇijjā tādisī n' atthi)*: nor are there even such things as trading which might be a cause of their obtaining excellence. *And buying and selling with gold (hiraññena kayakkayaṃ)*: nor are there even such things as buying and selling with gold which might be a cause of their obtaining excellence. *The petas, those who have passed on, are there sustained by what is given from here (ito dinnena yāpenti petā kālagatā tahiṃ)*: they are sustained, they continue their existence, entirely by what is given from here by their relatives or by their friends and companions. *The petas (petā)*: those creatures who have arisen on the peta-plane. *Those who have passed on (kālagatā)*: those who have passed on on account of its being the time of their death. An alternative reading is *those who have died (kālakatā)*: those who have done their (kammic) time,[63] those who have done their dying, those who have reached their death. *There (tahiṃ)*: on that peta-plane. He then uttered the two verses (beginning:) 'As water rained on the uplands' to illustrate by way of a simile the meaning of what had just been said.

7-8 This is the meaning: just as water poured down by clouds on the uplands, on elevated ground, on high ground, flows down to the lowlands, goes to the hollows, to that portion of the ground that is low-lying, so in that same way do the alms given from here benefit the petas, accrue to them on the appearance of their fruit. The world of the petas where the alms are of benefit is like the low-lying place to which the water flows down. He said accordingly, 'This,[64] brahmin, is the (appropriate) place; those alms are of benefit to one who remains there.' And just as streams, mighty rivers, that become swollen with water falling from mountain clefts and crevices, from gullies and ravines, from pools and great lakes, swell the ocean, even so do alms given from here benefit the petas in the aforesaid manner. Since the petas who go to the house of their relatives desperately hoping that they may get something from there are not able to beg, 'Please give us this!', he therefore uttered the verse (beginning:)

'He gave to me' showing that the son of the family should make a donation recollecting memorable occasions concerning them.

9 This is the meaning: he gave to me those riches or that grain; he worked for me himself completely fulfilling what had to be done; since so and so was connected on my mother's or my father's side he was a relative;[65] **[30]** since he was capable of being my refuge[66] on account of his affection he was a friend; whilst since so and so was my playmate in making mud pies he was a companion. Recalling all this one should give donations for the petas, one should consign the alms (to them). An alternative reading is *a donation is to be given (dakkhiṇā dajjā)*: recalling, by recalling,[67] what they used to do in this manner, with this 'He gave to me' and so on, a donation is to be given for the petas – this is what is said. This is the accusative case (recalling, *anussaraṃ*) with the scope of the instrumental (by recalling, *anussaratā*).[67]

10-11 He uttered the verse (beginning:) 'No amount of weeping' showing that whilst beings persist in continual weeping and sorrow and so on[68] at the death of relatives they give nothing for their benefit and that this weeping and sorrow and so on are merely and entirely to their own self-torture[69] which provides nothing of benefit to the petas. He then uttered a further verse (beginning:) 'But this' to demonstrate the useful nature of the donation given by the king of Magadha. The meaning of these is just the same as that given above.[70]

12 The Lord then uttered the concluding verse (beginning:) 'Now (this), the duty to one's relatives' praising the king on account of these genuine qualities, that is, since by the king giving that donation, by his doing what should be done by one relative for another,[71] the duty to one's relatives has been pointed out, it has been made known[72] to the many people, pointing out and making it known that they too should fulfil their duty to their relatives in this same way; and by causing the petas to come into possession of heavenly excellence the highest honour has been paid to the petas; by his satisfying with food and drink and so on the order of monks with the Buddha at its head strength has been furnished to the monks; and by giving rise to a generous intent accompanied by the quality of pity and so on not trifling the meritorious deed pursued. Herein *the duty to one's relatives (ñātidhammo)*: the performance of what should be done by one relative for another. *Highest (uḷārā)*: beneficial, magnificent. *Strength (balaṃ)*: physical strength. *Pursued (pasutaṃ)*: accumulated. Now here, by means of (the statement) 'Now this, the duty to one's relatives, has been pointed out' the Lord instructed[73] the king with a talk on Dhamma for his indicating[74] the duty to one's relatives is here an instruction.[75] By means of (the statement) 'And the highest honour has been paid to the

petas' he roused him for his praising as 'highest' is here a rousing as to his paying that honour again and again.[76] By means of (the statement) 'Strength has been furnished to the monks' he whetted him for the furnishing of strength to the monks is here a whetting by increasing his effort in furnishing strength in that particular manner.[77] [31] By means of (the statement) 'And not trifling the meritorious deed pursued by you' he made him bristle with joy for the commendation of pursuing meritorious deeds is here making him bristle with joy[78] on account of the nature of his description of his genuine qualities.[79] This is how it should be construed here, this is the way in which it is to be understood.

At the end of this teaching insight into the Dhamma arose to eighty-four thousand beings through properly striving, their hearts having been agitated by this description of the distressing circumstances[80] of arising on the peta-plane. On the day(s) that followed too he taught this same Outside the Walls teaching to devas and men such that for seven days there arose this very same insight into the Dhamma.

[1] The story is also found, with minor differences, at KhpA 201–216, translated at Minor Readings and Illustrator pp. 223–241.

[2] Reading 'etaṃ ṭhapetvā aññaṃ . . .' with Se Be for text's etaṃ ṭhapetvā 'aññaṃ . . .'.

[3] Reading lekhaṃ with Be KhpA for text's likhāpaṇṇaṃ (Se likhitapaṇṇaṃ); cp PED sv likhā.

[4] Reading dānaṃ pavattāpesi with Be KhpA for text's Se dānavatthuṃ pesesi.

[5] Reading pavāritā with Be (KhpA pavārite) for text's Se saparivārā te hi; the Pavāraṇā ceremony marks the end of the residence of the rainy season.

[6] Reading paccāgamiṃsu with Se Be for text's āgamiṃsu.

[7] This present aeon is considered auspicious in that it will see no less than five Buddhas, viz. Kakusandha, Konāgamana, Kassapa, our own Gotama and Metteyya, the Buddha who is yet to come; see for instance Dial ii 6f. for the list of Buddhas in which Kakusandha is said to have been preceded by a further three Buddhas, beginning with Vipassi ninety-one aeons ago. This list is further expanded in texts such as the Buddhavaṃsa and Thūpavaṃsa in which Phussa is said to have appeared in the aeon prior to that in which Vipassi arose, or, as our text states, ninety-two aeons ago, and that Phussa was himself preceded by some seventeen earlier Buddhas.

[8] Buddha-intervals, unlike aeons, are not specific periods since though this auspicious aeon will see five Buddhas, a full sixty aeons elapsed between Vipassi and his successor Sikhi.

[9] Reading brāhmaṇakule with Se Be KhpA for text's -kulesu.

[10] Jaṭilā; see Vin i 24 for a detailed account of these three.

[11] Identified by Malalasekera as the hill somewhat to the southwest of Gayā now known as Brahmayoni and an important place of pilgrimage for Hindus (DPPN i 753). There is a spring (yoni) near the summit which is thought to be connected with the warm water baths of the Brahmakund at Rajgir (Rājagaha) some distance away. It seems likely that the present Brahmakund may be situated upon the same site where the Tapodā Park once stood – cp KS i 14 n. 5 and DPPN i 992.

[12] vinetvā.

[13] nahuta.

[14] Aṅga and Magadha were originally two separate states that seem to have become united by the time of the text.

[15] These verses may be found in full at Vin i 38.

[16] Reading api ca kho with Se Be KhpA for text's atha kho.

[17] Reading paccāsiṃsantā with Se Be for text's paccasiṃsantā.

[18] hīyo, not listed by PED.

[19] Reading ajjatanāya with Se Be KhpA for text's svātanāya, the following day.

[20] See A v 81–82 for the ten risks run by the monk who goes there for alms.

[21] kalama, Nelumbrium.

[22] kuvalaya.

[23] Reading paṭippassaddhadaratha- with Se Be for text's paṭippassaddhā daratha-.

[24] Reading -bhojjāni with Se Be for text's -bhajjāni.

[25] Reading pīṇitindriyā with Se KhpA for text's pi nindiyā (Be pīṇindriyā); cp PED sv nindiya.

[26] Reading dibbavatthapāsādapaccattharaṇaseyyādi-alaṅkāravidhayo with Se Be for text's dibbavatthā dibbapāsādā seyyāpaccattharaṇālaṅkaravidhayo.

[27] Reading ettha with Se Be and cty below for text's etta.

[28] Reading kālagatā with Be KhpA for text's Se kālakatā; cp cty below.

[29] Reading text's 7 a b as 6 e f as required by the cty below.

[30] At A ii 244 the posture of petas is said to be lying flat on their backs.

[31] Reading gharasandhibhittisandhi-ālokasandhiyo with Se Be KhpA for text's gharasandhi bhittisandhi ālokasandhiyo; by 'house-junctions' are meant crevices and joints in houses, by 'wall-junctions' either joints or holes in walls whilst by 'light-junctions' slits for looking through.

[32] Reading siṅghāṭakā ti tikoṇaracchā with Be KhpA (Se siṅghāṭakan ti) for text's siṅghāṭake ti koṇaracchā.

[33] See discussion at Minor Readings and Illustrator p. 228 n. 4.

[34] Reading anajjhāvutthapubbaṃ with Se Be KhpA for text's anajjhāvutthe pubbaṃ.

[35] KhpA 207 claims, on the contrary, that pahūte (the reading of our text) is a careless reading for pahute though our text Se Be are unanimous here.

[36] Reading kāraṇabhāvato with Se Be for text's karaṇabhāvato.

[37] Reading taṃ hi with Se Be KhpA for text's tahiṃ.

[38] Reading anappake pi with Se Be for text's anappakeci.

[39] Se Be add raññā, by the king, here.

[40] Reading paribhogayoggakālena with Se Be for text's -yogya-.

[41] Reading tadupadesena with Be for text's tadupādesena (Se tadapadesen').

[42] Reading dātabbākāranidassanaṃ with Se Be KhpA for text's -kāradassanaṃ.

[43] That is, with no, our, in place of the mere particle vo.

[44] Reading na aññassa phaladaṃ hoti with Se Be for text's aññassa phalaṃ dinnaṃ hoti.

[45] Reading taṃ vatthu ñātipetānaṃ with Se Be for text's vuttapetānaṃ.

[46] It is curious that apart from the hint at PvA 69 below that some petas might be capable of making a tiny amount of merit no mention is made elsewhere throughout the whole of this commentary of what would seem to be a very significant point of doctrine. More often one is led to believe that petas, like all in the lower three gatis, are incapable of either making merit or of the Brahma-faring. It may be that Dhammapāla is here importing an idea from KhpA.

[47] Se Be omit.

[48] Reading avijahantā with Se Be KhpA for text's vijjamānā.

[49] Reading no with Se Be KhpA for text's vo.

[50] Se Be KhpA add pariccāgamayaṃ here.

[51] Reading phaladānato with Se Be KhpA for text's phalādānato.

[52] Reading etth' āha with Be KhpA for text's ettha hi; Se reads tattha hi.

[53] Reading eva with Se Be KhpA for text's evam.

[52] Reading eva with Se Be KhpA for text's evaṃ.

[54] saddhāni – so A v 269, KhpA and our text's vl whereas text, Se Be all substitute puññāni which is less preferable given the context of Brāhmaṇic ritual.

[55] Omitted, apparently in error, at GS v 181.

[56] So A v 269; text Se Be KhpA all abbreviate both here and below.

[57] So A v 270; text abbreviates and should be amended to read with Se Be KhpA manussānaṃ sahavyataṃ uppajjati – pe – devānaṃ sahavyataṃ uppajjati.

[58] Reading idam pi kho with Se Be KhpA for text's idaṃ kho.

[59] pettivisayaṃ; so also A v 270 Se Be. KhpA reads pittivisayaṃ as do the vll of our text and A v 270. See next.

[60] It is clear from the majority of these stories that the food of the creatures of the peta-plane is either repulsive matter such as excrement and urine, pus and blood or, perhaps more frequently, the lack of any food at all. Moreover when alms are assigned to this and that peta we find that it is not so much a case of them being sustained, as petas, by such offerings but rather that, by means of such offerings, they are transformed into yakkhas or vimāna-owning devatās. This would in turn explain the different readings of the previous note since the peta sustained by offerings from relatives and so on approximates more closely to the Brāhmaṇic pitṛ (or intermediary preta) rather than the Buddhist (suffering) peta. In this Aṅguttara passage 'peta' may mean nothing more than 'departed'.

[61] Reading etaṃ with Se Be KhpA for text's taṃ.

[62] Here ends the Aṅguttara quote.

[63] Reading Petā ti pettivisayupapannā sattā. Kālagatā ti attano maraṇakālena gatā. Kālakatā ti vā pāṭho, katakālā . . . with Be KhpA for text's petā pettivisayuppannā kālakatā attano maranakālena gatā. Kālagatā ti vā pāṭho. Katakālā . . . Se resembles our text but with superior punctuation.

[64] Reading idaṃ kho with A v 270 Be KhpA for text's Se idaṃ.

[65] Reading ñāti sinehavasena with Se Be for text's ñātisinehavasena.

[66] Reading tāṇasamatthatāya with Se Be KhpA for text's ṭhāna-.

[67] Reading anussaratā with Se Be KhpA for text's anussaraṇā.

[68] Reading ruṇṇasokādiparā with Se Be KhpA for text's ruṇṇasokādi varā.

[69] Reading attaparitāpanamattaṃ with Se Be for text's attaparitāpanaṃ.

[70] PvA 18–19.

[71] Reading ñātīnaṃ ñātīhi with Se Be KhpA for text's ñātīhi; see also cty below.

[72] Reading pākaṭo kato with Be for text's pākaṭo.

[73] sandassesi; not listed by PED. This and the three following verbs – roused, whetted, made him bristle with joy – are found elsewhere in similar passages describing the process by which a person is led towards insight; see for instance D ii 42 and cp M ii 48, D i 126 etc. At S v 162 the ability is ascribed to Sāriputta.

[74] Reading ñātidhammadassanaṃ with Be for text's Se ñātidhammasandassanaṃ; KhpA reads -nidassanaṃ, pointing out, which agrees with the verse and would therefore be preferable.

[75] Reading h' ettha sandassanaṃ with Be KhpA for text's Se hetusandassanaṃ.

[76] Reading punappuna pūjākaraṇe samādapanaṃ with Se Be KhpA for text's punappunapūjākaraṇasamādapanaṃ.

[77] Reading evaṃ vidhānaṃ balānuppadāne with Se Be for text's eva 'va vidhānatthabalānuppadāne ti.

[78] Reading sampahaṃsanaṃ with Be for text's sampahaṃsaṃ.

[79] Reading -saṃvaṇṇanabhāvena with Se Be KhpA for text's -saṃvaṇṇanatāya.

[80] Reading pettivisayūpapatti-ādīnavasaṃvaṇṇanena with Be KhpA (≏ Se) for text's pettivisayuppattiyā ādīnaṃ 'va saṃvaṇṇanena.

I.6 EXPOSITION OF THE DEVOURER OF FIVE SONS PETA STORY
[Pañcaputtakhādakapetavatthuvaṇṇanā]

'Naked and of hideous appearance are you.' This was said when the Teacher was staying at Sāvatthī concerning a petī who devoured her five sons.

It is said that in a village not far from Sāvatthī the wife of a certain man of property was barren. His relatives said, 'Your chief-wife[1] is barren; we must fetch you another bride', but he was unwilling on account of his affection for his wife. Now when his wife heard the news, she said to her husband, 'I am barren, my lord; another bride must be fetched – do not let the family line be severed', and, being urged by her, he took another bride who in due course became pregnant. The barren woman thought, 'When she has had her son she will become mistress of this house', and, overcome by envy, seeking some means of causing her to miscarry, she satisfied with food and drink and so on a certain female[2] who had gone forth and had her make her miscarry. When she miscarried (the second wife) informed her mother and her mother summoned together her relatives and made them aware[3] of the matter. They accused the barren woman of being responsible for her miscarriage but she denied it, saying, 'I am not responsible.' They replied, 'If you are not responsible for the miscarriage then make an oath!' [32] She made her oath, lying, 'If I am responsible for this miscarriage then may I be destined to a state of misery in which, overcome by hunger and thirst, I might give birth each morning and evening to five sons and then devour them, yet find no satisfaction; moreover, may I always be foul smelling and surrounded[4] by flies!'[5] She died not long afterwards and arose as a petī of hideous appearance not far from that same village. At that time eight elders who had spent the residence of the rainy season in that district and were on their way to Sāvatthī to see the Teacher went for rest to a shaded and well watered spot in the forest not far from that village. The petī then revealed herself to those elders and the senior elder amongst them questioned that petī with this verse:

1 'Naked and of hideous appearance are you; you emit a foul, putrid smell. You are surrounded by flies – now who are you, you who are stood here?'

1 Herein *naked (naggā)*: unclothed. *Of hideous appearance are you (dubbaṇṇarūpāsi)*: extremely deformed are you, endowed with an appearance that is a quite disgusting sight. *A foul smell (duggandhā)*: a disagreeable smell. *You emit a putrid smell (pūti vāyasi)*: you emit the smell of a

rotting corpse from your body. *You are surrounded by flies (makkhikā-parikiṇṇā 'va)*: you are entirely surrounded by bluebottles. *Now who are you, you who are stood here? (kā nu tvaṃ idha tiṭṭhasi)* means who, indeed, are you who are stood here at this spot looking like this and wandering this way and that?

When questioned thus by the elder that petī then spoke these three verses explaining who she was, giving rise to the agitation of beings:

2 'I, sir, am a petī, gone to a miserable existence in the world of Yama; having done a wicked deed, I have gone from here to the world of the petas.

3 At daybreak I give birth to five sons and in the evening again a further five – though I devour them all, even these are not enough for me.

4 [33] My heart smoulders and is scorched with hunger and I can get no water to drink – behold the plight befallen me.'

2 Herein *sir (bhaddante)*: she addresses the elder with respect. *Gone to a miserable existence (duggatā)*: gone to a state of misery. *In the world of Yama (Yamalokikā)*: in the world of the petas which is known by the name of 'the world of Yama' due to its being included therein. *I have gone from here (ito gatā)*: I have gone from here, from the world of men, by arising in the world of the petas, meaning I arose (there after death).

3 *At daybreak (kālena)*: at dawn; this instrumental case has the force of the locative. *Five sons: pañca puttāni=pañca putte*; this was said with a distortion of gender.[6] *And in the evening again a further five (sāyaṃ pañca punāpare)*: and at evening time I again devour a further five sons – this is how it should be construed. *I give birth (vijāyitvāna)*: day in, day out, I give birth to ten sons. *Even these are not enough for me (te pi nā honti me alaṃ)*: even these ten sons are not enough, are insufficient, for warding off my hunger in a single day; *na* here is lengthened to *nā, metri causā.*

4 *My heart smoulders and is scorched with hunger (pariḍayhati dhūmāyati khudāya hadayaṃ mama)*: through being afflicted with hunger and starvation the region of my heart smoulders, burns, is tormented, throughout with the ache of hunger.[7] *And I can get no water to drink (pānīyaṃ na labhe pātuṃ)*: and I can get no water to drink as I wander about here and there overcome with thirst. *Behold the plight befallen me (passa maṃ vyasanaṃ gataṃ)*: she declares to the elder the misery she is suffering, saying, 'Venerable sir, behold what sort of plight has befallen me, both generally and in particular, through having arisen amongst the petas.'

When he heard this the elder uttered this verse questioning her about the deed she had done:

5 'Now what evil deed was done by you by body, speech or mind? As a result of which deed do you devour the flesh of your sons?'

5 Herein *evil deed (dukkataṃ)*: evil conduct. *As a result of which deed? (kissa kammavipākena)*: as a result of what sort of deed, meaning did you destroy a living being or was it some other (deed) such as taking what had not been given and so on? Some read 'as a result of which deed?' (*kena kammavipākena*).

[34] Then that petī, relating to the elder the deed she had done, said:

6 'My co-wife became pregnant and I devised a wicked deed against her: depraved in mind I caused her to miscarry.
7 Her two month old embryo flowed out just like blood; then her mother became angry with me and collected her relatives together; she made me make an oath and (them) abuse me.
8 I told a terrible lie when I made that oath that if this were done by me I might devour the flesh of my sons.
9 It is both as a result of that deed and due to the fact that I lied that I devour the flesh of my sons and am smeared[8] with blood and matter.'

6 Herein *co-wife (sapatī)* is said of a woman with the same husband. *And I devised a wicked deed against her (tassā pāpaṃ acetayiṃ)*: and I planned a wicked and gruesome deed against her, against that co-wife. *Depraved in mind (paduṭṭhamanasā)*: with depraved intent or with a depraved mind.
7 *Two month old (dvemāsiko)*: having been established (in the womb) for two months[9] it was two months old. *Flowed out just like blood (lohitañ ñeva paggharī)*: as it perished it became just like blood and streamed out. *Then her mother became angry with me and collected her relatives together (tad assā mātā kupitā mayhaṃ ñātī samānayi)*: then my co-wife's mother became angry with me and summoned her relatives together. An alternative reading is *tat' assā* which divides into the two words *tato assā* (thereupon her). *Oath (sapathaṃ)*: oath.[10] *And (made them) abuse (paribhāsāpayi ca)*: and (made them) threaten and frighten.
8 *I told a lie when I made that oath (sapathaṃ musāvādaṃ abhāsissaṃ)*: I told a lie when I made that oath, that is, there was no truth in my pointing out that I had not done what I had in fact done, saying, 'If this were done by me might I be such and such.' *If this were done by me I might devour the flesh of my sons (puttamaṃsāni khādāmi sac' etaṃ pakataṃ mayā)*: **[35]** this then shows the nature of oath made, meaning that if this wicked deed, this miscarriage, were done by me, I might devour

nothing but the flesh of my sons in my future renewed becoming and rebirth.

9 *Of that (tassa)*: of that deed of destroying a living being committed by way of that miscarriage. *And due to the fact that I lied (musāvādassa ca)*: and due to that act of lying. *It is both (ubhayaṃ)*: it is on account of the results of both deeds; this accusative case has the force of the instrumental. *I am smeared with blood and matter (pubbalohitamakkhitā)*: I devour the flesh of my sons after I have become smeared with blood and matter through giving birth and tearing (the sons) apart[11] – this is how it should be construed.

When the petī had thus declared the results of her deeds she spoke once more to the elder (saying), 'Venerable sir, I used to be the wife of the man of property so and so in this very village but I was overcome by envy and did a wicked deed and have thus arisen in the peta-womb. Venerable sir, would you please go to the home of that man of property. He will present you with alms – have him dedicate that donation to me for in this way my release from here, from this world of the petas, will come about.' When the elders heard this they (went), pitying her and full of mercy, and entered the home of that man of property in search of alms. When that man of property saw the elders he went out, full of devotion, to meet them, took their bowls, had them be seated and began to feed them with the choicest food. The elders reported the incident to the man of property and had him dedicate the almsgiving to the petī. At that very moment that petī was rid of that misery and, having obtained supreme excellence, she revealed herself that night to the man of property. The elders went in due course to Sāvatthī and raised the issue with the Lord. The Lord took the matter as an arisen need and taught Dhamma to the company assembled there. That teaching was of benefit to those people.

[1] pajāpatī, here clearly not in the sense of 'one who has offspring' or 'having (or rich in) progeny' as suggested by PED sv.

[2] Reading paribbājikaṃ with Se Be for text's paribbājakaṃ.

[3] Reading nivedesi with Be for text's vedesi; Se reads pavedesi.

[4] Reading makkhikāparikiṇṇā with Se Be and v 1 below for text's -parikkhiṇṇā.

[5] At p. 12, line 10, Gehman probably intended us to read 'fate' rather than 'date'.

[6] Masculine accusative plural with neuter inflexion.

[7] udaragginā, literally with the fire of the belly or stomach.

[8] Reading pubbalohitamakkhitā with Se Be for text's -makkhikā both here and in the cty below. In v 1 she was said to be surrounded by flies (makkhikā), no mention being made there of her being smeared (makkhitā) with blood and matter, which she now seems to feel requires explanation rather than the flies. It seems likely that the similarity of the two terms has led to their confusion at some point. Gehman is surely not correct in taking pubba as 'of the past' here.

[9] Reading dvemāsajāto with Se Be for text's dve māsā jāto.

[10] sapanaṃ; not in PED but listed by Childers. Se reads saccāpanaṃ.

[11] Reading paribhijjanavasena with Be for text's Se paribhuñjanavasena; not listed by PED.

I.7 EXPOSITION OF THE DEVOURER OF SEVEN SONS PETA STORY

[Sattaputtakhādakapetavatthuvaṇṇanā]

[36] 'Naked and of hideous appearance are you.' This was said when the Teacher was staying at Sāvatthī concerning a petī who devoured her seven sons.

It is said that in a certain village not far from Sāvatthī there was a lay-follower with two sons who were in the prime of life, handsome and endowed with virtue and good conduct. Their mother despised her husband because of her power of sons, thinking, 'I am possessed of sons',[1] and he, having had enough of her despite, took another bride who not long afterwards became pregnant. The first wife was overcome by envy and persuaded a certain physician, in return for a fee, to cause the miscarriage of her three month old embryo. Now when questioned by her husband and relatives as to whether she was responsible for her miscarriage she lied and denied it saying, 'I am not responsible.' As they did not believe her they said, 'Then make an oath!' She made her oath, saying, 'May I give birth each morning and evening to seven sons and may I devour the flesh of those sons; moreover, may I always be foul smelling and surrounded by flies!' She died in due course and arose in the peta-womb through fruition of her (causing that) miscarriage and of her telling that lie and wandered about not far from that same village eating the flesh of her sons in the aforesaid manner. Now at that time many elders who had spent the residence of the rainy season by staying in that village and were on their way to Sāvatthī to see the Lord were resting for the night at a place not far from that village. The petī then revealed[2] herself to those elders and the senior elder questioned her with this verse:

1 'Naked and of hideous appearance are you; you emit a foul, putrid smell. You are surrounded by flies – now who are you, you who are stood here?'

When questioned by the elder she answered him with three verses:

2 'I, sir, am a petī, gone to a miserable existence in the world of Yama; having done a wicked deed, I have gone from here to the world of the petas.

3 At daybreak I give birth to seven sons and in the evening again a further seven – though I devour them all, even these are not enough for me.

4 [37] My heart smoulders and is scorched with hunger[3] and I can get no refreshment – I am tormented as though burnt by fire.'

4 Herein *refreshment (nibbutiṃ)*: relief from the misery of hunger and thirst. *I can get no (nādhigacchāmi)*: I can obtain no. *I am tormented as though burnt by fire (aggidaḍḍhā va ātape)*: I am tormented with extreme heat as though I were being burnt by fire[4] (since) I can get no refreshment – this is how it should be construed.

When he heard this the elder uttered this verse questioning her about the deed she had done:

5 'Now what evil deed was done by you by body, speech or mind? As a result of which deed do you devour the flesh of your sons?'

That petī then spoke these verses relating how she had arisen in the world of the petas and the reason for her devouring her sons:

6 'I had two sons who had both reached adolescence;[5] endowed with the power of sons[6] I neglected my husband,

7 Whereupon my husband became angry and took another as co-wife; and when she became pregnant I devised a wicked deed against her:

8 Depraved in mind I caused her to miscarry and her three month old embryo fell as putrid blood.

9 Then her mother became angry at this and collected her relatives together; she made me make an oath and (them) abuse me.

10 I told a terrible lie when I made that oath that if this were done by me I might devour the flesh of my sons.

11 It is both as a result of that deed and due to the fact that I lied that I devour the flesh of my sons and am smeared with blood and matter.'

6 Herein *endowed with the power of sons: puttabalūpetā=puttabalena upetā* (resolution of compound); the power derived by way of her sons. *I despised (atimaññissaṃ)*: I spoke against, I disparaged.

8 *Fell as putrid blood (pūtilohitako pati)*: the embryo fell after becoming a bloody corpse.

All the rest is just the same as that immediately preceding with the sole difference that there there were eight elders whilst here there are many and that there there were five sons whilst here there are seven.

[1] Reading puttavatī ahan ti puttabalena with Be (Se reads puttavasena in place of puttabalena) for text's puttavasena alone. See n. 6 below.

[2] Reading dassesi with Se Be for text's dasesi.

[3] Reading dhūmāyati khudāya with Se Be and I 6[4] above for text's dhūmayati kudāya.

[4] Reading ati-uṇha-ātape agginā ḍayhamānā with Be (Se -uṇhe-) for text's ati-uṇha-atāpe aggiḍayhamānā; cp PvA 174.

[5] Reading sampattayobbanā with Se Be for text's -yobhanā.

[6] puttabalūpetā, one of the five powers of women, the others being beauty, wealth, kin and virtue, possessed of which a woman cannot be taken by the neck and thrown out of the family – see S iv 246–248 and KS iv 167 n. 1; it cannot be the strength of the sons as Gehman suggests.

I.8 EXPOSITION OF THE OX PETA STORY
[Goṇapetavatthuvaṇṇanā]

[38] 'Why do you, like a madman.' The Teacher who was staying in the Jeta Grove told this concerning a certain man of property whose father had died.

It is said that in Sāvatthī the father of a certain man of property had died. His heart was stricken with grief at the death of his father and he would wander about like a madman with a lamenting heart asking whomever he saw, 'You've seen my father, haven't you?' But no one could dispel his grief. His potential, however, for realising the sotāpatti-fruit shone in his heart like a lamp in a jar. The Teacher, who was surveying the world towards dawn, saw his potential for realising the sotāpatti-fruit and thought, 'When I have recounted his past actions and relieved his grief it would be proper to give[1] him the sotāpatti-fruit.' On the following day whilst returning from his almsround after his meal he took his attendant[2] and went to the door of his house. When he heard that the Teacher had come he went out to meet him and had him enter his house. When the Teacher was seated on the appointed seat, he himself saluted the Lord and, seated on one side, asked, 'Lord, do you know the place to which my father has gone?' The Teacher then replied, 'Are you asking about your father in this present life, layfollower, or (those) in the long past?' When he heard these words he thought, 'I have had many fathers', at which his grief subsided and he gained a little equanimity. The Teacher then gave him a talk on Dhamma to dispel his grief and, when he knew that his grief had departed and that his heart was ready, then by means of that Teaching on Dhamma which (the Buddhas)[3] have themselves discovered (– ill, uprising, stopping, the way –) he established him in the sotāpatti-fruit and then went to his vihāra. The monks then began to talk amongst themselves in the Dhamma-hall, saying, 'Behold, friends, the great power of the Buddha in that a layfollower who was overcome by the greatest grief[4] has been guided by the Lord into the sotāpatti-fruit in just an instant.' **[39]** The Teacher went there and seated himself[5] on the seat of honour prepared for the Buddha and asked, 'For the purpose of what discussion, monks, are you now seated together here?' The monks reported the topic (of their conversation) to the Lord. When the Teacher said, 'It is not just on this occasion, monks, that I have dispelled his grief; I similarly dispelled it on a former occasion too', they begged him to recount (that incident) of long ago.

Long ago in Benares the father of a certain householder died. He was overcome by grief and lamentation at the death of his father and with a tearful face he wailed[6] and beat his breast as he circumambulated his[7] funeral pile by the right. His son, named Sujāta, was an intelligent and clever young man and full of wisdom and, whilst thinking about some means of removing his father's grief, he saw one day a dead ox outside the city. He brought some grass and water and placed them in front of it and, giving it a mouthful, stood there ordering it as though it were alive, saying, 'Eat, eat; drink, drink!' When the passers-by saw him they said, 'Sujāta, my dear, have you gone quite mad in that you should offer grass and water to a dead ox?', but he said nothing in reply. The people went to his father and said, 'Your son has gone mad and is giving grass and water to a dead ox.' When he heard this that man of property's grief for his father departed. Agitated at the thought, 'They say my son has gone mad', he sped there and reprimanded him, saying, 'Sujāta, are you not wise and clever and full of intelligence? Why are you giving grass and water to a dead ox?', and uttered these two verses:

1 'Why do you, like a madman, cut green grass and mutter, "Eat, eat!", to an old ox whose life is gone?

2 For it is not by food or drink that this dead ox would rise; you are a fool, an oaf, and an idiot just like anyone else.'

1 Herein *why (kin nu)* is a word of interrogation. *Like a madman (ummattarūpo va)*: like one who is by nature mad, like one mentally deranged. **[40]** *Cut: lāyitvā=lāvitvā* (alternative grammatical form). *Green*

grass (haritaṃ tiṇaṃ): fresh grass. *Mutter (lapasi)*: talk idly. *Whose life is gone (gatasattaṃ)*: devoid of life. *Old ox (jaraggavaṃ)*: a frail ox, an ox that has been used for ploughing.

2 *By food or drink (annena pānena)*: by either this green grass or the water you have given. *This dead ox would rise (mato goṇo samuṭṭhahe)*: even if this ox that has died were to regain life it would not rise. *You are a fool, an oaf (tvaṃ 'si bālo ca dummedho)*: you are a fool since you are attached to foolishness, an oaf since you lack that insight known as wisdom. *And an idiot just like anyone else (yathā t' aññ' eva dummati)* means that you thus lament to no purpose just like anyone else lacking insight might. *Yathā taṃ* (untranslated) is a mere particle. *Just like anyone else (aññ' eva)* means that though you possess insight you have become as idiotic as any other idiotic person and talk in a confused manner.[8]

When he heard this Sujāta uttered these two verses to make his intention known to his father:

3 'These legs, this head, this body with its tail and the eyes remain just as they were: this ox might rise,
4 But grandfather's hands, legs, body and head are not to be seen – is it not rather you that is the idiot, weeping at his earthen mound?'[9]

3 This is the meaning: these four legs, this drum-like head together with the tail of this ox still exist, this body with its tail and these eyes remain just as they were before death and lack any sign of having perished.[10] *This ox might rise (ayaṃ goṇo samuṭṭhahe)*: due to this reason the thought might occur to me that this ox might rise, might get up. Some read *I think the ox might rise (maññe goṇo samuṭṭhahe)*: for this reason I might think that this ox might suddenly raise his body; such a notion might present itself to me – this is the meaning.

4 **[41]** Then he taught his father Dhamma saying, 'But grandfather's, but my grandsire's, hands, legs, body and head are not to be seen. It is not rather you alone, father, that is, however, the idiot, the one lacking insight, a hundred, a thousand times over, as you weep at a mound made of earth after enclosing his bones therein? Conditioned things are by nature perishable and perish; you know this[11] so why the lamentation?' When he heard this the father of the Bodhisatta thought, 'My son is wise – he performed this deed to teach me' (and said), 'My dear Sujāta, it is well known that all living beings are subject to death. Henceforth I will mourn no more: so it should be for those such as are able to dispel their grief', and then he spoke four verses in praise of his son:

5 'I was truly ablaze, being like a fire fed with ghee; but now all my sorrow has been extinguished as if I had been sprinkled with water.

6 Truly the dart, the grief, that had pierced my heart has been drawn out. You have dispelled that grief, the grief for my father which had overwhelmed me.
7 With dart withdrawn I am become tranquil and cool; since hearing you, young man, I no longer grieve nor weep.'[12]
8 Just as Sujāta distracted[13] his father from his grief – so act the wise who possess[14] pity.

5 Herein *I was ablaze (ādittaṃ)*: I had been set alight and was burning with the fire of sorrow. *Being: santaṃ=samānaṃ* (alternative grammatical form). *Fire (pāvakaṃ)*: fire. *As if I had been sprinkled with water (vārinā viya osiñcaṃ)*: as if I were being sprinkled[15] with water. *But now all my sorrow has been extinguished (sabbaṃ nibbāpaye daraṃ)*: but now all the distress in my heart has been extinguished.
6 *Truly has been drawn out (abbūḷha vata)*: truly has been driven out. *The dart (sallaṃ)*: the dart of grief. *That had pierced my heart (hadayanissitaṃ)*: the dart that had become lodged in my heart. *That grief which had overwhelmed (sokaparetassa)*: that grief which had overcome. *The grief for my father (pitusokaṃ)*: the grief that had arisen with respect to my father. *You have dispelled (apānudi)*: you have removed.
7 *Since hearing you, young man (tava sutvāna mānava)*: however, since hearing your words, my boy, I now no longer grieve nor weep.
8 *Just as Sujāta (distracted) his father (Sujāto pitaraṃ yathā)*: just as this Sujāta distracted his father from his grief, so also do those other wise people who possess pity, [42] who are by nature helpful, act in the same way, meaning they act to the benefit of their fathers and others.

When he had heard the words of the young man, the father lost his sorrow. He bathed his head, ate (again) and conducted his business and when he died he was one bound for heaven.

When the Teacher had recounted this teaching on Dhamma, he explained the (Four Noble) Truths to those monks, at the end of which many were established in the sotāpatti-fruit.

It was our Saviour of the World[16] who at that time was Sujāta.

[1] dātuṃ; the implication both here and elsewhere in this work is that such potential for realising the sotāpatti-fruit would have remained unrealised had it not been for the gracious intervention of the Buddha.

[2] pacchāsamaṇaṃ, the junior monk that walks behind an elder on his almsround, the Buddha always being so accompanied by Ānanda: see Vin i 46, iii 10; PvA 93. Be reads anādāya, did not take, this attendant.

[3] This should be understood as an extremely condensed version of the stock passage describing the means by which certain individuals were converted by the Buddha;

it can be found in full at, for instance, M i 379f. Cp PvA 195f. Gehman's 'uttering a brief address' misses the point entirely.

[4] Reading sokapareto paramasoko with Se for text's sokaṃ paramosoko; Be reads sokaparidevasamāpanno.

[5] Reading nisinno with Se Be for text's nisimo.

[6] Reading kandanto with Se Be for text's karonto; Be however has rattakkho, with red eyes, in place of 'beat his breast'.

[7] Reading tassa with Se for text's tato; Be omits entirely.

[8] Be omits the entire sentence.

[9] mattikathūpasmiṃ; thūpa (Skt stūpa) in its non-technical Buddhist sense.

[10] Reading abhinnasaṇṭhānāni with Se Be for text's abhinava-.

[11] The text is wrongly punctuated here – the comma following tattha should instead precede it.

[12] vv 5–7 recur at Vv 83$^{8-10}$.

[13] Reading vinivattayi as at II 6^{19} below for text's vinivattanti; cp PED sv vinivaṭṭeti.

[14] Reading honti with Se Be for text's konti.

[15] Reading avasiñcanto with Be for text's Se āsiñcanto.

[16] Lokanātho, an epithet of the Buddha. Gehman wrongly identifies the Sujāta of this story with the (former) Buddha Sujāta. Rather it is a case of our own (Gotama) Buddha recalling an incident in which he, in a former birth as Sujāta and whilst still the Bodhisatta, helped dispel the grief of the very same man to whom he has just given the sotāpatti-fruit; indeed the cty to v 4 calls Sujāta the Bodhisatta. The story appears in a similar form as the Sujāta Jātaka (No. 352) some of whose details Dhammapāla seems here to assume, such as the fact that his father had stopped eating.

I.9 EXPOSITION OF THE MASTER WEAVER PETA STORY [Mahāpesakārapetavatthuvaṇṇanā]

'Excrement and urine, blood and pus.' This was said when the Teacher was staying at Sāvatthī concerning a certain petī who had been a weaver.

It is said that as many as twelve monks had been given a meditation subject[1] in the Teacher's presence and, whilst in search of a dwelling place at the approach of the rainy season, saw a delightful, shaded and well watered spot in the forest with a village for the supply of alms that was neither too far nor too near. They spent the night there and on the following day entered the village in search of alms. Eleven weavers dwelt there. When they saw the monks they became full of joy and led them to their respective[2] homes. When they had waited on them with food and drink they asked, 'Where are you going, sirs?' 'We are going to wherever will prove comfortable for us,' they replied. 'If this be so, sirs, then you should stay right here,' they said, and begged them to enter upon the residence of the rainy season (with them), which the monks accepted. The layfollowers had huts built for them at that place in the forest and presented them to the monks who entered upon the residence of the rainy season there. The chief weaver there waited with due care upon two monks with the four requisites and the others each waited upon one monk. The wife of that chief weaver had neither faith nor devotion but was mean and of wrong view and did not wait with due care upon the monks. When he discovered this (that weaver) fetched her younger sister and put her in charge as mistress of his home. She [43] had faith and devotion and looked after the monks with due care. All of those weavers each gave one cloak to those monks who had spent the rainy season, upon which the mean wife of the senior weaver, being of depraved mind, cursed her husband (saying), 'Whatever food and drink you have given as alms to those recluses who are sons of the Sakya,[3] may it in the next world turn into excrement and urine, blood and pus for you and may those cloaks become red-hot iron plates!' Then in due course that senior weaver died and arose as a tree-devatā[4] in the Viñjha[5] forest endowed with great majesty. But when his miserly wife died she arose as a petī not far from that same dwelling place. She was naked and of hideous appearance and, overcome by hunger and thirst, she approached that terrestrial deva and said, 'My lord, I am unclothed and I wander about overcome by extreme hunger and thirst; please give me some clothes and some food and drink.' He gave her the choicest heavenly food and drink but when she as much as touched them they turned into excrement and urine, blood and pus, and as she put on the cloak it became a red-hot iron plate. Suffering great misery she threw them away and wandered (off) wailing.

Now at that time a certain monk who had spent the rainy season was on his way to salute the Teacher and had entered the Viñjha forest in the company of a large caravan. The caravan proceeded on its journey by night and saw, by day, a densely shaded and well watered spot and unharnessed the oxen and rested for a short while. The monk, however, desired seclusion and went on a little. He laid his upper robe at the foot of a tree, an impenetrable tangle giving dense shade and, exhausted by the night's journey, laid down his tired body and fell asleep. The caravan, having rested, got once more underway but the monk did not awake. He got up in the evening and, unable to see the caravan, [44] set off in the wrong direction and in due course came across the dwelling place of that devatā. When the devaputta saw him he approached in human form and extended a friendly greeting, having him enter his mansion,[6] and gave him some ointment for his feet and so on and sat down in attendance. At this time the petī came, saying, 'My lord, please give me food and drink and a cloak.' He gave these to her but when she as much as touched them they just became excrement and urine, blood and pus, and red-hot[7] iron plates. When he saw this the monk, full of agitation, questioned that devaputta with these two verses:

1 'She eats excrement and urine, blood and pus – of what is this the result? Now what deed did this woman do that she always feeds on blood and pus?

2 New clothes, beautiful and soft, clean and like down, when given to her[8] become like (metal) sheets;[9] now what deed did this woman do?'

1 Herein *of what is this the result? (kissa ayaṃ vipāko)*: of what sort of deed is this the result that she now undergoes? *Now what deed did this woman do? (ayaṃ nu kiṃ kammaṃ akāsi nārī)*: now what deed did this woman do in the past? *That she always feeds on blood and pus (yā ca sabbadā lohitapubbabhakkhā)*: that she all the time feeds on,[10] eats, only blood and pus.

2 *New (navāni)*: recent, having appeared that very minute.[11] *Beautiful (subhāni)*: lovely and fair to behold. *Soft (mudūni)*: pleasant to touch. *Clean (suddhāni)*: of very pure appearance. *Like down (lomasāni)*: with a pile that is pleasant to touch, meaning lovely. *When given to her become like (metal) sheets (dinnān' imissā kiṭakā va bhavanti)*: become similar to (metal) sheets with spikes,[12] similar to copper plates. An alternative reading is 'become worms' (*kīṭakā*[13] *bhavanti*), meaning they come to resemble insects[14] that bite.

[45] When thus questioned by the monk the devaputta spoke two verses explaining the deed she had done in her previous life:

3 'She was my wife, sir, uncharitable, mean and miserly; when I gave to recluses and brahmins, she insulted me and abused me, saying,

4 "Excrement and urine, blood and pus – may you eat what is impure for all time! Let this be your (lot) in the next world and may your clothes be like (metal) sheets!" Having been of such bad conduct she has come here having to eat (impurities) for a long while.'

3 Herein *uncharitable (adāyikā)*: she gave nothing to anyone, she lacked the virtue of generosity. *Mean and miserly (maccharinī kadariyā)*: at first she was mean due to her character (being marred by) the stain of selfishness; through her pursuit[15] time and again (of such conduct) she became extremely mean;[16] (and in the end) she was miserly – this is how it should be construed. He then said 'When I gave (to recluses and brahmins) she (insulted) me' and so on showing (the extent of) her miserliness.

4 Herein *such (etādisaṃ)*: having been of bad conduct in speech and so on of the aforesaid kind. *She has come here (idhāgatā)*: she has come to

this world of the petas, she has come into existence as a petī. *Having to eat (impurities) for a long while (cirarattāya khādati)*: having to eat only excrement and so on for a long time. For whatever the manner[17] of her insult,[18] in that same manner[19] is its resulting fruit also. An insult[20] falls back on oneself, not on him towards whom it was directed, like the fall of a thunderbolt on a peak, the so-called ender of motion on earth.[21]

When he had thus related the deed she had done in the past, the devaputta then spoke[22] once more to the monk (saying), 'Is there, sir, any means by which she might be freed from this world of the petas?' When he said that there was, he said, 'Please tell it, sir.' [**46**] 'If alms be given to a monk or to but one member of the Lord's Ariyasaṅgha and then dedicated to her and she shows her appreciation there will thus be freedom for her from this misery here.' When he heard this the devaputta gave to the monk the finest food and drink and assigned that donation to the petī and the petī immediately refreshed and satiated her faculties and became contented with heavenly food. Then he again gave into the hand of that same monk a pair of heavenly cloaks specifically for the Lord and assigned that donation to the petī, who immediately became dressed in heavenly clothes[23] and decorated with heavenly ornaments and, richly endowed with all she desired, she resembled a deva-nymph.[24] And that monk reached Sāvatthī that very day by the psychic powers of the devaputta. He went into the Jeta Grove, entered the presence of the Lord, saluted him and then gave him the pair of cloaks. He then raised that issue (with the Lord). The Lord took the matter as an arisen need and taught Dhamma to the company assembled there. That teaching on Dhamma was of benefit to those people.

[1] kammaṭṭhānaṃ; generally forty are specified: the 10 kasinas, the 10 loathsome objects, the 10 recollections, the 4 Brahmavihāras, the 4 arūpa-jhānas, the perception of the loathsomeness of food and the analysis of the elements. See Path of Purification, Chs. III–XI.

[2] Reading attano attano with Se Be for text's attano.

[3] Sakyaputtiyānaṃ; see B of Disc ii pp. xliv–xlvi for a discussion of this term. Here it would seem to serve merely to identify the sect without any racial connotation.

[4] rukkhadevatā; at PvA 5 above such arising was considered inferior to that which might have been attained.

[5] See PvA 244 below.

[6] vimānaṃ.

[7] Reading pajjalita- with Se Be and as earlier for text's jalita-.

[8] Reading dinnān' imissā for text's dinnāni missā.

[9] Text reads kiṭakā, Se Be kitakā; the word is uncertain and seems not to appear elsewhere.

[10] Reading bhakkhati with Se Be for text's bhakkā ti.

[11] Reading tāva-d-eva pātubhūtāni with Se Be for text's tāva devapātubhūtāni.

[12] Reading kitakakaṇṭakasadisāni with Se Be for text's kiṭakasadisāni.
[13] So Se Be for text's kiṭakā.
[14] pāṇaka; this sense is not listed by PED but Childers suggests worm, insect, flea etc.
[15] Reading āsevanatāya with Se Be for text's āsevanāya.
[16] Reading thaddhamaccharinī with Se Be for text's thadda-.
[17] Reading yen' ākārena with Se Be for text's yenā pi kārena.
[18] Reading akkuṭṭhaṃ with Be for text's akaṭṭha; Se reads akaṃ.
[19] Reading ten' ev' ākārena with Se Be for text's tena vā kārena.
[20] Reading akkuṭṭhaṃ with Be for text's akaṭṭha; Se reads akantaṃ.
[21] All texts differ widely here and all seem corrupt. Se reads paṭhaviyā matthakasaṅkhāte matthake asanipātaṃ; Be reads pathaviyaṃ kamantakasaṅkhāte matthake asanipāto; whilst text paṭhaviyaṃ matakasaṅkhāte matthake asanipāto though also mentioning two vll of matakasāghātena matake and matakasāghātena matthake. Matthake asanipāto seems all right – cp asanipāto matthake nipati at Ap 123 = 421 – but the rest is quite obscure. The two words preceding matthake were probably intended as a gloss or pun on matthake but it is not at all clear what their original form might have been nor whether matthake here means on a mountain peak or on a human head. I read kamantakasaṅkhāte with Be which I take to be from kram + antaka- but since none of the readings we have at present is likely to be that intended by Dhammapāla, this interpretation is at best uncertain.
[22] Reading bhikkhum āha with Se Be for text's bhikkhuṃ ārabbha . . . āha.
[23] Reading dibbavatthanivatthā with Se Be for text's dibbavatthāni vatthā.
[24] devaccharā, the Vedic apsaras.

I.10 EXPOSITION OF THE BALD-HEADED PETA STORY
[Khallāṭiyapetavatthuvaṇṇanā][1]

'Now who are you (remaining) inside your mansion?' This was said when the Teacher was staying at Sāvatthī concerning a certain bald-headed[1] petī.

It is said that long ago in Benares there was a certain harlot who was extremely beautiful and lovely to behold, charming and endowed with the highest beauty of complexion and who had tresses of extremely captivating hair. Her long black hair was soft, fine and sleek and was curled at the ends; it was set in two bunches and when loosened the tresses would hang down as far as her girdle. When they saw her beautiful hair nearly all the young men there fell in love with her. Unable to bear her beautiful hair, some women, overcome with envy, took counsel together[2] and then bribed her maid-servant to give her a potion that would make her hair fall out. It is said that her servant prepared that potion with her bath-powder and gave it to her at a time when she was bathing in the river Ganges. She moistened her hair well down to the roots and immersed it in the water.

[47] No sooner than she immersed it her hair fell out at the roots and her head resembled a bitter gourd.[3] Then, entirely shorn of hair and looking unsightly like a pigeon with its head plucked,[4] she was, through shame, unable to enter the city. She wrapped a cloth around her head and made her abode at a certain spot outside the city. After a lapse of a few days her shame left her[5] and she pressed some sesamum seed and earned her living by trading in oil and spirituous liquor. One day when two or three drunken men had fallen into a deep sleep she stole their clothes that were hanging loose. Then one day she saw an elder who had destroyed the āsavas going about in search of alms and, with devotion in her heart, led him to her house, had him be seated on the appointed seat and then gave him an oil-cake made from ground sesamum[6] and soaked in oil which he, out of pity for her, accepted and ate whilst she stood with devotion in her heart holding a sunshade above him. The elder showed his appreciation which delighted[7] her heart and then departed. At the very time he showed his appreciation the woman made the wish, 'May my hair be long, soft, sleek and fine and curled at the ends!' She died in due course and as an outcome of her meritorious and demeritorious deeds she arose all alone in a golden mansion in the middle of the ocean. Her hair turned out just as she had wished[8] but she was naked on account of having stolen the men's cloaks. She arose time and again in that golden mansion and, naked, she passed one Buddha-interval there. Then when our Lord had arisen in the world and had set rolling the Wheel of the Noble Dhamma and was in due course staying at Sāvatthī, as many as a hundred[9] traders, residents of Sāvatthī, set out by ship across the mighty ocean[10] heading for Suvaṇṇabhūmi.[11] The ship in which they had embarked was thrown about by the force of rough winds and, drifting here and there, came to that spot whereupon the vimānapetī revealed herself and her mansion to them. When he saw her the senior trader uttered this verse enquiring:

1 [48] 'Now who are you remaining inside your mansion, not coming out? Come out, my dear, let us see you standing outside.'[12]

1 Herein *now who are you remaining inside your mansion? (kā nu anto vimānasmiṃ tiṭṭhantī)*: he asks, 'Now who are you remaining within, inside your mansion? Are you a human or non-human female?' *Not coming out (na upanikkhami)*: not leaving your mansion. *Come out, my dear, let us see you standing outside (upanikkhamassu bhadde tvaṃ passāma taṃ bahiṭṭhitaṃ)*:[12] my dear, let us see you, we wish to see you, standing outside,[12] so please leave your mansion. An alternative reading is 'Blessings to you! Come out!' (*upanikkhamassu bhaddan te*), meaning blessings be to you.

She then uttered this verse explaining her inability to come outside:

2 'Naked, I am (too) distressed and embarrassed[13] to come outside; I am covered (only) by my hair – few are the meritorious deeds that I have done.'

2 Herein *I am (too) distressed (aṭṭiyāmi)*: being naked, I am (too) distressed and miserable to come outside. *Embarrassed (harāyāmi)*: ashamed. *I am covered (only) by my hair (keseh' amhi paṭicchannā)*: I am covered, my body is hidden (only) by my hair. *Few are the meritorious deeds that I have done (puññaṃ me appakaṃ kataṃ)*: few, trifling, are the skilled deeds that I have done, the gift of merely (a cake made from) ground sesamum[14] – this is the meaning.

Then the trader, wishing to give her his cloak, uttered this verse:

3 'Here, I will give[15] you my cloak – put on this garment. When you have put on this garment, then come outside, my pretty one. Come out, my dear, let us see you standing outside.'[16]

3 **[49]** Herein *here (handa)*: take this. *Cloak (uttarīyaṃ)*: an upper garment, worn on top, meaning an outer cloak. *I will give you: dadāmi te= tuyhaṃ dadāmi*[17] (alternative grammatical form). *Put on this garment (imaṃ dussaṃ nivāsaya)*: put on this outer cloak[18] of mine. *My pretty one (sobhane)*: my beautiful one.

So saying he presented her with his outer cloak. She uttered these two verses showing that that which is given in that way does not benefit her and the way in which things given would benefit her:

4 'What is given by your hand into my hand is of no benefit to me. But this layfollower here has faith and is a sāvaka of the Perfect Buddha;

5 Having clothed him, assign that donation to me. Then I will be happy and richly endowed with all I desire.'

4 Herein *what is given by your hand into my hand is of no benefit to me (hatthena hatthe te dinnaṃ na mayhaṃ upakappati)*: what is given by you, good sir, by your hand into my hand is to me of no benefit, does not accrue to me, meaning is not fit for my use.[19] *But this layfollower here has faith (es' etth' upāsako saddho)*: but there is in this collection of people here this layfollower who has gone for refuge to the Three Jewels and who has faith since he possesses faith in the fruition of deeds.

5 *Having clothed him, assign that donation to me (etaṃ acchādayitvāna mama dakkhiṇaṃ ādisa)*: have this layfollower clothed with that cloak that was being given to me and assign that donation to me, give (for

me) a gift that is assigned. *Then I will be happy (tadāhaṃ sukhitā hessaṃ)*: when that is done I will attain happiness and will be dressed in heavenly clothes.

When they heard this the traders bathed and anointed the layfollower and then clothed him with a pair of garments. Those rehearsing the texts then spoke these three verses clarifying this point:

6 'Those traders bathed and anointed him and clothed him with the garments and assigned the donation to her.

7 **[50]** Immediately they dedicated[20] this the result came into being – food, clothing and drink being the fruit of this donation.

8 Thereupon she became pure, clad in fresh, clean clothes, wearing those more fine than those of Kāsi and left her mansion smiling (to indicate), "This is the fruit of your donation".'

6 Herein *him (taṃ)*: that layfollower; the word *ca* (untranslated) is a mere particle. *Those (te)* is to be construed with 'traders'. *Anointed (vilimpitvāna)*: anointed with the finest scent. *Clothed him with the garments (vattheh' acchādayitvāna)*: having fed him curried food of every description endowed with good appearance, fragrance and flavour, they clothed him with two garments – an undergarment and a cloak – meaning they gave him the two (items of) clothing. *Assigned the donation to her (tassā dakkhiṇaṃ ādisuṃ)*: gave that donation for the sake of the petī.

7 *Immediately they dedicated this (samanantarānuddiṭṭhe)*: *anu* (untranslated) is a mere particle; immediately they dedicated the donation to her. *The result came into being (vipāko upapajjatha)*: the result for the petī, that is, this fruit of the donation, came into being. What sort of result? The petī said:[21] *food, clothing and drink (bhojanacchādanapānīyaṃ)*: various foods similar to heavenly foods,[22] variously dyed clothes blazing forth colours similar to heavenly clothes and countless sorts of drink – such was the fruit of that donation that came into being – this is how it should be construed.

8 *Thereupon (tato)*: after receiving the aforesaid[23] food and so on. *She became pure (suddhā)*: her body being pure through bathing. *Clad in fresh, clean clothes (sucivasanā)*: dressed in clean, bright clothes. *Wearing those more fine than those of Kāsi (kāsikuttamadhārinī)*: wearing those more fine than those made from Kāsi cloth. *Smiling (hasantī)*: she left her mansion smiling to indicate, 'Behold, friends, this exquisite fruit of your donation.'

When the traders thus saw for themselves the fruit of their meritorious deed, their hearts were filled with wonder and surprise and they were filled with respect and veneration for the layfollower and honoured him with the añjali salute. He caused them still more devotion with a talk on Dhamma and established them in the Precepts and the Refuges.[24] They questioned the vimānapetī about the deed she had done with this verse:

9 [51] 'Your nicely painted, gleaming mansion is radiant;[25] O devatā, you are asked to inform us of what deed this is the fruit.'

9 Herein *nicely painted (sucittarūpaṃ)*: nicely decorated with paintings of both elephants, horses, men and women and so on,[26] as well as festoons of garlands and creepers. *Gleaming (ruciraṃ)*: delightful and lovely to behold. *Of what deed this is the fruit (kissa kammass' idaṃ phalaṃ)*: of what sort of deed, meaning is it the fruit of one consisting in giving or of one consisting in virtuous conduct?

When thus questioned by them she spoke these verses informing them both that that (mansion) was the extent of the fruit of that trifling skilled deed she had done and that in the future, however, there would be of that unskilled deed (fruit) such as is found in hell:[27]

10 'To a wandering, upright monk I, with a devout heart, gave an oil-cake,[28]

11 As a result of that skilled deed I have for a long while enjoyed myself in this mansion but now there is but a trifle.

12 After four months will come my death and down to the exceedingly severe and terrible hell will I fall:

13 Four-cornered and with four gates, it is divided into equal portions, encircled by an iron wall with a roof of iron above;

14 Its incandescent floor is made of glowing iron – all around a hundred yojanas it spreads, forever standing.[29]

15 There for a long time I will experience painful feelings as the fruit of my wicked deeds – for this reason I am exceedingly sorrowful.'[30]

10 Herein *to a wandering monk (bhikkhuno caramānassa)*: to a certain monk who had broken up the defilements[31] and who was wandering around in search of alms. *An oil-cake (doṇinimmajjanaṃ)*: ground sesamum oozing with oil.[32] *Upright (ujubhūtassa)*: who had attained uprightness through being without the defilements that produce crookedness, deceitfulness and dishonesty of mind. [52] *With a devout heart (vippasannena cetasā)*: with true devotion in heart due to faith[33] in the fruition of deeds.

11 *For a long while (dīghaṃ antaraṃ)*: the words *dīghaṃ* and *antaraṃ* are euphonically connected with the syllable *ma*,[34] meaning for a long time. *But now there is but a trifle (tañ ca dāni parittakaṃ)*: but now there is but a trifle, but little remaining of that deed – the fruit of that meritorious

deed is fully ripe and has reached maturity,[35] meaning I will fall from here before long. For this reason she said:

12 *After four months will come my death (uddhañ catūhi māsehi kālakiriyā bhavissati)*: she points out that after four months, four months further on, in the fifth month (from now), will come her death. *Exceedingly severe (ekantaṃ kaṭukaṃ)*: undesirable in the extreme, meaning it is extremely painful on account of its belonging to the six fields of (sense) impingement.[36] *Terrible (ghoraṃ)*: cruel. *Hell (nirayaṃ)*: hell is called *nir-ayaṃ* as there is nothing here (*nir-*, negative prefix) that makes for ease (*ayaṃ*), for comfort. *Will I fall: papatiss'āhaṃ=papatissāmi ahaṃ* (resolution of compound).[37] And since 'hell' here is to be understood as the Great Hell of Avīci she uttered (the verses) beginning, 'Four-cornered' showing it has the same shape (as Avīci).

13 Herein *four-cornered (catukkaṇṇaṃ)*: with four corners. *With four gates (catudvāraṃ)*: furnished with four gates (with one) at (each of) the four directions. *Divided (vibhattaṃ)*: divided regularly. *Into portions: bhāgaso=bhāgato* (alternative grammatical form). *Equal (mitaṃ)*: matching. *Encirled by an iron wall (ayopākārapariyantaṃ)*: surrounded by a wall made of iron. *With a roof of iron above (ayasā paṭikujjitaṃ)*: covered above by an iron ceiling.

14 *Incandescent (tejasāyutā)*:[38] the flames are continuously joined in a great fire of flame that rises up all around. *All around a hundred yojanas (samantā yojanasataṃ)*: whilst[39] all around outside it is thus in all directions a hundred yojanas, in yojanas one hundred. *Forever (sabbadā)*:[40] all the time. *It spreads (pharitvā)*: it stands pervading.

15 *There (tattha)*: in that Great Hell. *I will experience: vedissaṃ= vedissāmi* (alternative grammatical form); I will undergo. *As the fruit of my wicked deeds (phalañ ca pāpakammassa)* means that this undergoing of painful (feelings) of such a kind will be the fruit of the wicked deeds that were done by me alone.[41]

When she had thus made known the fruit of her deed and her future existence in hell [53] the heart of that layfollower was stirred with compassion and, thinking he might be a (means of) support for her, said, 'By way of but one gift to me, O devatā, did you become richly endowed with all you desire and put in contact with this noble excellence. If you now give a gift to these layfollowers and recall the virtues of the Teacher you will be freed from having to arise in hell. The petī was overjoyed and said, 'Very well', and satisfied them with heavenly food and drink and gave them heavenly clothes and jewels of various kinds. She then gave into their hands a pair of heavenly garments specifically for the Lord and sent this salutation: 'When you reach Sāvatthī, please salute the Teacher with this message from me: "Lord, a certain vimānapetī salutes the Lord with her head at his feet." ' She brought their ship to the port they desired that very same day by means of her psychic power and majesty. Now those traders reached Sāvatthī from that port in due course and entered the Jeta Grove. They gave the Teacher the pair of garments and when they had passed on her salutation they raised that whole issue right from the beginning. The Teacher took the matter as an arisen need and taught Dhamma in detail to the company assembled there. That teaching was of benefit to those people. On the following day those layfollowers gave a great almsgiving to the order of monks with the Buddha at its head and assigned the donation to her. When she fell from the world of the petas she arose in a golden mansion in the realm of the Thirty-three, resplendent with various jewels and with a retinue of a thousand nymphs.

[1] So Se Be for text's Khalātiya-.

[2] Reading sammantetvā with Se for text's samantetvā; Be reads mantetvā.

[3] Reading tittakalābu with Be (Se -lāpu) for text's tintakalābu; cp PED sv tintaka.

[4] Reading luñcitamatthakā with Se Be for text's luñcitapamaṭṭā; cp also PED sv pamaṭṭa where a reading of luñcitapakkhikā is suggested, which Gehman follows.

[5] Be adds tato nivattetvā, she returned from there, here.

[6] Reading doṇinimmajjanaṃ piññākaṃ with Se (Be doṇinimmajjaniṃ p.) for text's doṇinimmijjanaṃ miñjakaṃ; cp cty on v 2 below.

[7] sampahaṃsanto, literally made her bristle with joy; cp PvA 31 where the latter rendering was adopted. Gehman wrongly suggests that it is the elder's heart that is delighted.

[8] Reading patthitākārāyeva with Se Be for text's patthitā kārā yeva.

[9] Be reads sattasatā, seven hundred, here.

[10] See note at PvA 137; the mighty ocean is seventh from Mt. Meru and it is in this ocean that the four continents are located, one of these being India.

[11] Literally the Golden Land and generally identified with lower Burma; see DPPN ii 1262f.

[12] Reading bahiṭṭhitaṃ with Be for text's Se mahiddhikaṃ; the latter would mean they were asking her to display her great psychic power.

[13] Reading harāyāmi with Se Be for text's harāyami.

[14] piññāka-; cp n. 6.

[15] Reading dadāmi with Se Be and as at II 4^{5} for text's dāmi.

[16] See n. 12.

[17] So Se Be; text omits.

[18] Reading uttarisāṭakaṃ with Be (Se uttara-) and in conformity with the preceding sentence but one and also the sentence following for text's uttarīyaṃ sāṭakaṃ.

[19] Reading upabhogayoggaṃ with Se Be for text's upabhogayoyaṃ.

[20] Reading samanantarānuddiṭṭhe with Se Be for text's -udiṭṭhe both here and at II 1^{8}, 2^{9}, 3^{27}, 4^{10}, III 2^{12}, 2^{16}, 2^{21}, 2^{25}, 2^{30} and IV 3^{46}.

[21] The text is poorly punctuated here and should read with Se: Kīdiso ti? Petī āha . . . ; it may however be noted that Dhammapāla earlier attributed these verses to those rehearsing the texts.

[22] Reading dibbabhojanasadisaṃ with Se Be for text's dibbbhojana-.

[23] Reading yathāvuttabhojanādi with Se Be for text's yathāvuttā-.

[24] That is, the fivefold precepts binding upon the laity and the threefold refuges of the Buddha, the Dhamma and the Saṅgha; by taking these they thus became lay-followers themselves, though not, unlike the layfollower here, sāvakas of the Buddha.

[25] Reading pabhāsati with Se Be for text's ca bhāsati.

[26] Reading hatthi-assa-itthipurisādivasena with Se Be for text's atthi assa itthi-.

[27] Earlier we were given to suppose that her theft of the clothes was expiated by her being naked.

[28] Reading doṇinimmajjanaṃ with Se (Be -jjaniṃ) for text's doṇinimmiñjanaṃ; cp n. 6.

[29] Cp M iii 167; A i 141f.; J v 266.

[30] Reading socām' ahaṃ bhusaṃ with Se Be and IV 3[40] for text's socāmīdaṃ bhūtaṃ; II 7[15] reads socām' ahabbhusaṃ in Pv.

[31] bhinnakilesassa.

[32] Reading vissandamānatelaṃ piññākaṃ with Se Be for text's vissandamānatela-miñjakaṃ.

[33] Reading kammaphalasaddhāya with Se Be for text's -sandhāya.

[34] Text should thus be amended to read dīgha-m-antaraṃ.

[35] Reading vipakkavipākattā with Se Be for text's vipākattā.

[36] Cp S iv 126 for an account of this.

[37] The text is poorly punctuated here and should be amended to read with Be: Papatiss' āhan ti papatissāmi ahaṃ. Nirayan ti. . . .

[38] So the verse; text (Se) however (mis)quote as tejasāyuttā (tejasāyutaṃ) here and gloss samāyuttā jālā (samāyuttajālaṃ) whilst Be reads tejasāyutā and samāyutajālā respectively.

[39] Reading evaṃ pana with Se Be for text's evaṃ puna.

[40] Text mis-spells sabbada here.

[41] Reading eva with Be for text's Se evaṃ.

I.11 EXPOSITION OF THE ELEPHANT PETA STORY [Nāgapetavatthuvaṇṇanā]

'One proceeds in front on a white elephant.' This was said when the Teacher was staying in the Jeta Grove concerning two petas who had been brahmins.

It is said that the seven year old venerable Saṃkicca had attained arahantship whilst still in the tonsure-hall and was dwelling as a novice with as many as thirty monks in a forest haunt. [54] After he had defended those monks from impending death at the hands of five hundred robbers and had tamed the robbers and had them go forth, he then went into the Teacher's presence.[1] The Teacher taught Dhamma to the monks and at the end of that teaching they attained arahantship. Then when the venerable Saṃkicca had become old enough and had received ordination he went to Benares with five hundred monks and stayed at Isipatana.[2] The people went into the elder's presence, heard Dhamma and, with devotion in their hearts, formed themselves into groups along the streets, giving alms to new-comers.[3] A certain layfollower there urged the people (to provide) a constant supply of food and they provided this constant supply of food in accordance with their means.

Now there was in Benares at that time a certain brahmin possessed of wrong views who had two sons and a daughter. The elder son of these was a friend of that layfollower. He took him and went into the venerable Saṃkicca's presence and the venerable Saṃkicca taught him Dhamma, at which his heart became tender. Then the layfollower said to him, 'You should give a constant supply of food for one monk.' 'It is not the custom for us brahmins to give a constant supply of food to those recluses who are sons of the Sakya, so I will not give (this).' 'Would you not give[4] food even to me?' he asked. 'How could I not give it?' he replied. 'In that case, then give to one monk what you would give[5] to me.' 'Very well', he agreed and on the following day whilst still very early went to the vihāra, fetched one monk and fed him. As time went on in this way his younger brother and sister saw the conduct of the monks and heard Dhamma and, finding faith in the Teaching, took delight in meritorious deeds. Thus these three people, giving alms according to their means, venerated, respected, esteemed and honoured recluses and brahmins. Their parents, however, had neither faith nor devotion, lacked respect for recluses and brahmins and paid no regard to the performance of meritorious deeds. Relatives asked that their young daughter should be given in marriage to her maternal cousin. [55] But he heard Dhamma in the presence of the venerable Saṃkicca and, filled with agitation, constantly went as one gone forth to his mother's house to eat. His mother tried to entice him with his young maternal female cousin.[6] Because of this he became dissatisfied and approached his preceptor and said, 'I wish to leave the order, sir. Please give me permission.' His preceptor, seeing that he possessed the potential (of becoming a sāvaka), said, 'Wait for just a month, novice.' 'Very well', he agreed and, when one month had elapsed, he addressed (him) in the same manner. His preceptor again said, 'Wait for just a fortnight.' When a fortnight had elapsed and (the preceptor) had been spoken to in the same manner he again said, 'Wait for a week.' 'Very well', he agreed. Inside a week the house of that novice's aunt collapsed when its perished thatch and its old weak walls[7] were struck by the wind and rain and the brahmin and his wife, their two sons and their daughter died when crushed by the house. Of these, the brahmin and his wife arose in the peta-womb whilst their two sons and their daughter amongst the terrestrial devas. Of these, the elder son arose riding on an elephant, the younger in a mule-drawn chariot and the daughter in a golden litter. The brahmin and his wife would each take huge iron hammers and beat one another and swellings, each the size of a huge water-pot, would arise at the places where they were struck, come to a head in an inkling and then burst open. They would split open one another's swellings and, overcome by anger and ruthlessly cursing (each other) with harsh speech, would drink the blood and pus yet not find any satisfaction.

Then the novice (still) overcome with dissatisfaction, approached his preceptor and said, 'I have waited the agreed number of days, sir. I wish to go home, sir. Please give me your permission.' His preceptor then said, 'Come (here) at sunset when it is the fourteenth day of the dark half of the month', and went and stood a little to the rear of the Isipatana vihāra. Now at that time those two devaputtas were going, together with their sister, along that same road to attend an assembly of the yakkhas. Their mother and father followed[8] them with clubs in their hands and with harsh speech. [**56**] They were of dark appearance, burdened with thoroughly tangled, coarse, flying hair,[9] and resembled the burnt trunks of palm trees (struck by) lightning.[10] They were dripping with blood and pus and their bodies were wrinkled – they were an extremely loathsome and disgusting sight. The venerable Saṃkicca then worked his psychic powers in such a way that the novice could see all of them going along and, when he had done so, said, 'Do you see them going along, novice?' 'Yes, sir, I do see (them)' (he replied). 'Well then, question them about the deeds they[11] did.' Those going along he questioned in turn, beginning with the one riding on an elephant. 'You should question the petas following on behind', they said, and the novice addressed the petas with these verses:

1 'One proceeds in front on a white elephant, in the middle in a mule-drawn chariot however, whilst at the rear a maiden is conducted about in a golden litter, entirely lighting up the ten directions.

2 But you, with hammer in hand, with weeping faces and split and broken bodies, what wicked deed did you do whilst in the world of men, on account of which you must drink each other's blood?'

1 Herein *in front (purato)*: foremost of all. *White (setena)*: pale (-coloured). *One proceeds (paleti)*: one goes. *In the middle however (majjhe pana)*: between the one mounted on the elephant and the one mounted in the litter. *In a mule-drawn chariot (assatarīrathena)*: one proceeds by chariot yoked with she-mules – this is how it should be construed. *Is conducted about (nīyati)*: is driven about. *Entirely lighting up the ten directions (obhāsayantī dasa sabbato disā)*: shining forth entirely throughout all the ten directions with the radiance of her

body and with the radiance of her clothes and ornaments[12] and so on.

2 *With hammer in hand (muggarahatthapāṇino)*: those who have hammers in their hands (*pāṇīsu*) (here) reckoned as hands (*hattha-*) are 'with hammer in hand'. 'Hand' (*pāṇi*) by itself[13] is qualified with the word *hattha* due to the fact that it might (otherwise) be taken for the common designation of *pāṇi* as a wooden instrument for smoothing the ground and so on.[14] *With split and broken bodies (bhinnapabhinnagattā)*: with bodies split and broken all over by the blows of the hammers. *You should now drink: pivātha=pivatha (metri causā).*

[57] When thus questioned by the novice, those petas replied with four verses (telling) the entire story:

3 'He who goes in front on an elephant, on a four(-footed) white elephant, he was our elder son. Having given alms, he is now happy and delighted.

4 He who is in the middle in a galloping[15] four-yoked mule-drawn chariot, he was our second son. Unselfish and a master in the practice of giving, he now shines brilliantly.

5 She who at the rear is conducted about in a litter, the wise maiden with the soft eyes of a deer, she was our daughter and youngest born. (Satisfied) with a half portion of her share, she is now happy and delighted.

6 Now in the past they gave alms with devotion in their hearts to recluses and brahmins; we, however, were selfish and abusive to recluses and brahmins. They gave and now gratify themselves whilst we are withered like a cut down reed.'

3 Herein *he who goes in front (purato 'va yo gacchati)*: he goes in front of those who are going along. Another reading is *yo so purato gacchati* (he who goes in front), meaning that one who goes in front thereof. *On an elephant (kuñjarena)*: on an elephant (*hatthinā*) that has acquired the name *kuñjara* since it brings the terrain (*kuṃ*), the earth, to destruction (*jīrayati*); or, alternatively, since it is in glens (*kuñjesu*) that it delights (*ramati*), that it roams about.[16] *On a . . . elephant (nāgena)*: that elephant, the *nāga* to whom nowhere (*na*) is inaccessible (*agamanīyaṃ*) and for whom there is nothing he cannot overcome.[17] *Four(-footed) (catukkamena)*: four-legged. *Elder (jeṭṭhako)*: born earlier.

4 *Four(-yoked) (catubbhī)*: (yoked) with four she-mules. *Galloping (suvaggitena)*:[15] with beautiful movement or with swift movement.

5 *With the soft eyes of a deer (migamandalocanā)*: with eyes casting a soft look like that of a doe. [58] *With a half portion of her share: bhāgaḍḍhabhāgena=bhāgassa aḍḍhabhāgena* (resolution of compound), the

reason being that she gave away a half portion of the share she received for herself. *Happy: sukhī=sukhinī*; this was given here with a distortion of gender.

6 *Abusive (paribhāsakā)*: insulting. *They now gratify themselves (paricārayanti)*: they feast (*cārenti*) their senses at will wherever they like with the heavenly sensual pleasures, or they amuse themselves (*paricariyaṃ*[18] *kārenti*) with their attendants due to the majestic outcome of their meritorious deeds.[19] *Whilst we are withered like a cut down reed (mayañ ca sussāma naḷo va chinno)*: but we are withered like a reed that has been cut down and laid down in the heat of the sun, we are parched and dried up by hunger and thirst and by the deadly blows (we receive) from one another.

When they had thus made known their wicked deeds, they then informed him that they were his aunt and uncle. When he heard this the novice, full of agitation, uttered this verse asking how food could be made available for such wrong-doers:[20]

7 'What is your food? What your bed?[21] How do you sustain yourselves, you who were by nature so very wicked, who though amidst abundant and plentiful wealth, missed[22] (your chance of) happiness and have today attained to misery?'

7 Herein *what is your food? (kiṃ tumhākaṃ bhojanaṃ)*: of what sort is your food? *What your bed? (kiṃ sayānaṃ)*: of what sort your bed? Some read 'what your sleep?' (*kiṃ sayānā*) – of what sort your sleep, meaning in what sort of bed do you sleep?[23] *How do you sustain yourselves? (kathaṃ su yāpetha)*: in what manner do you sustain yourselves? An alternative reading is *kathaṃ vo*[24] *yāpetha=kathaṃ tumhe yāpetha* (alternative grammatical form), meaning how do you sustain yourselves? *You who were by nature so very wicked (supāpadhammino)*: you who were of so very wicked a nature in the extreme. *Though amidst abundant wealth (pahūtabhogesu)*: though being amidst boundless and immense wealth. *Plentiful: anappakesu=na appakesu* (alternative grammatical form); much. *Missed (your chance of) happiness (sukhaṃ virādhāya)*: **[59]** missed, lost (your chance of) happiness through not performing meritorious deeds which are the cause of happiness. Some read 'through missing (your chance of) happiness' (*sukhassa virādhena*).[25] *Have today attained to misery (dukkh' ajja pattā)*: have today, have now, arrived at this misery belonging to the peta-womb.

When thus questioned by the novice, the petas spoke these verses answering the points[26] about which he had enquired:

8 'When we have struck one another, we drink the blood and pus; we drink much but we are not nourished, we are not pleased.

9 So, in fact, do unbestowing mortals lament when after death[27] they become Yama's residents; those who have known[28] and attained wealth but who do not make use of it, nor even perform meritorious deeds,

10 These undergo hunger and thirst hereafter; those petas burn,[29] being for a long time scorched. Having done deeds yielding misery,[30] bitter fruit, they suffer misery.

11 Short-lived[31] indeed are riches and grain and fleeting[31] one's life here; knowing the transient[31] as transient, the wise man should make a refuge.

12 Those who understand this are men skilled in the Dhamma; having heard the speech of the arahants, they do not neglect to give alms.'

8 Herein *we are not nourished (na dhātā homa)*: we are not nourished, not satisfied, not satiated. *Are not pleased: na ruccādimhase=na ruccāma* (alternative grammatical form); we obtain no pleasure, meaning we do not drink it for our pleasure.

9 *So, in fact (icc' eva)*: in just this way. *Do mortals lament (maccā paridevayanti)*: other people also who, like us, have done wrong, do lament and wail. *Unbestowing (adāyakā)*: selfish, lacking the virtue of generosity. *They become Yama's residents (Yamassa ṭhāyino)*: their nature is to reside[32] on the peta-plane, the residence of Yama known as the world of Yama. **[60]** *Those who have known and attained wealth (ye te viditvā adhigamma bhoge)*: those who have known and obtained wealth providing extraordinary happiness, both now and in the future. *But who do not make use of it, nor even perform meritorious deeds (na bhuñjare nā 'pi karonti puññaṃ)*: but who, like us, do not make use of it themselves, nor even perform meritorious deeds consisting in almsgiving by giving to others.

10 *These undergo hunger and thirst hereafter (te khuppipāsūpagatā parattha)*: these beings are overcome by a desire to eat and by thirst hereafter, on the peta-plane in the next world. *(Those petas) burn, being for a long time scorched (ciraṃ jhāyare ḍayhamānā)*: means (those petas) burn,[29] they bemoan, being continually scorched by the fire of an uneasy conscience, thinking, 'We did, alas, no skilled deeds, we did (only) wicked deeds' and so on and by the fire of misery caused by their hunger. *Yielding misery (dukkhudrayāni)*: resulting in misery. *Bitter fruit they suffer misery (anubhonti dukkhaṃ kaṭukapphalāni)*: having done wicked deeds (yielding) undesirable fruit, they suffer misery, they suffer misery characteristic of the woeful state[33] for a long time.

11 *Short-lived (ittaraṃ)*: not long lasting, impermanent, subject to change. *Fleeting one's life here (ittaraṃ idha jīvitaṃ)*: the life of beings here, in this world of men, is fleeting, limited, trifling. For this reason the Lord said, 'He, who lives long, lives but a hundred years or but little longer.'* *Knowing the transient as transient (ittaraṃ ittarato ñatvā)*: ascertaining by means of wisdom that commodities such as riches and grain and so on and human life are fleeting, limited, momentary and not long lasting. *The wise man should make a refuge (dīpaṃ kayirātha paṇḍito)*: the man of wisdom should make a refuge, a support, that will be the basis of his happiness and well being[34] in the next world.

12 *Those who understand this (ye te evaṃ pajānanti)*: those who truly[35] realise the transient nature of human life and wealth, they do not neglect to give alms at all times. *Having heard the speech of the arahants (sutvā arahataṃ vaco)* means having heard the words of the arahants, of ariyans[36] such as Buddhas and so on. The rest is quite clear.

When those petas had explained the points on which they had been questioned by the novice, they said, 'We are your aunt and uncle.' When he heard this, the novice, full of agitation, dispelled his dissatisfaction and fell down with his head at his preceptor's feet, saying, 'Whatever **[61]** pity should be shown out of pity has been shown to me by you, sir. I have certainly been protected from falling into great misfortune.[37] I have now no interest in the household life and will find my delight in the Brahma-faring.' The venerable Saṃkicca then imparted to him a meditation subject suiting his disposition. He devoted himself to that meditation subject and before long attained arahantship. The venerable Saṃkicca raised the issue with the Lord. The Teacher took the matter as an arisen need and taught Dhamma in detail to the company assembled there. That teaching was of benefit to those people.

*S i 108; cp S ii 94.

[1] For details of this frequently quoted incident see DPPN ii 975. Saṃkicca's verses appear at Thag 597–607 and not at 'No. 240' as stated by Gehman.

[2] Site of the famous Deer Park at Sarnath, some six miles from Benares, where the First Sermon was preached. It 'was so called because sages, on their way through the air (from the Himalayas), alight here or start from here on their aerial flight' (DPPN i 324).

[3] Cp A iii 41.

[4] Reading na dassasi with Be for text's Se dassasi na dassasi.

[5] Reading desi taṃ with Se Be for text's desitaṃ.

[6] Be reads bhātudhītāya dārikāya, with the young daughter of her brother, which amounts to the same thing.

[7] Reading dubbalakuḍḍaṃ with Se (Be -kuttaṃ) for text's dubbalaṃ kūṭaṃ.

[8] Reading anubandhanti with Se Be for text's anubajjhanti; cp PED sv anubajjhati.

[9] Reading ākulākulalūkhapatitakesabhārā with Se Be for text's -sukha-.

[10] indaggi-, literally Indra's fire.

[11] Reading imehi with Se Be for text's ime.

[12] Reading vatthābharaṇādippabhāhi with Se Be for text's vattha-.

[13] Reading pāṇi eva with Se Be for text's pāṇi.

[14] Reading bhūmisaṇhakaraṇīyādīsu with Se Be for text's bhūmisaṇhā-; this sense of pāṇi is not listed in PED.

[15] Reading suvaggitena with Se Be and Pv for text's suvagtena and suviggatena in cty below; this sense of vaggati is not listed in PED.

[16] Reading kuñjesu vā ramati caratī ti with Se Be for text's kuñjo suvāram aticarati. Cp VvA 35 for a similar etymology.

[17] Reading nāssa agamanīyaṃ anabhibhavanīyaṃ atthī ti with Be for text's n' assa agati abhibhavanīyam atthī ti (≏ Se). See also Thag 693 and notes at EV i 177; also cty on S i 27. Text's punctuation should read with Se Be, . . . nāgo tena nāgena. Catukkamenā ti. . . .

[18] So Se Be for text's pāricariyaṃ.

[19] Cp ThagA on Thag 96 (quoted at EV i 145).

[20] Text's punctuation should read with Be, 'evarūpānaṃ kibbisakārīnaṃ kathaṃ . . . sijjhantī' ti.

[21] Reading kiṃ sayānaṃ with Se Be for text's kissayanaṃ.

[22] Reading virādhāya with Se Be for text's virāgāya.

[23] All texts vary considerably over minor points here. For consistency's sake I follow Be, kiṃ sayānan ti kīdisaṃ sayanaṃ. 'Kiṃ sayānā ti keci paṭhanti, kīdisā sayanā, kīdise sayane sayathā ti attho.

[24] So Se Be for text's ha; the meaning is unaffected.

[25] So Se Be for text's sukhassa virāgena.

[26] Reading pucchitamatthaṃ with Se Be for text's pucchitamattaṃ.

[27] pecca.

[28] Reading viditvā with Se for text's vivicca; Be reads vidicca.

[29] Reading jhāyare with Se Be for text's ghāyire; similarly jhāyanti in cty below for text's ghāyanti.

[30] Reading dukkhudrayāni for text's dukkhandriyāni, Se dukhudrayāni, Be dukhudrāni; cp PED sv dukkha.

[31] ittaraṃ.

[32] Reading ṭhānasīlā with Se Be for text's ṭhāne sīlā.

[33] apāyikaṃ.

[34] Reading hitasukhādhiṭṭhānaṃ with Se Be for text's hitasukham iṭṭhānaṃ.

[35] Reading yāthāvato with Be (Se yathāvato) for text's yathā vato; cp PED sv yathāva.

[36] That is, a member of the Ariyasaṅgha (cp PvA 1) and thus a sāvaka, or, as here, a Buddha.

[37] Reading mahatā vata 'mhi anatthapātato with Be for text's Se mahato vata 'mhi anatthato pātato.

I.12 EXPOSITION OF THE SNAKE PETA STORY
[Uragapetavatthuvaṇṇanā]

'Just as the snake (having cast aside) its worn out skin.' The Teacher who was staying in the Jeta Grove told this concerning a certain layfollower.

It is said that at Sāvatthī the son of a certain layfollower died. Full of grief and lamentation on account of the death of his son, he would just stay at home, neither going outside nor able to do any work. Then when, towards dawn, the Teacher had emerged from the meditation of the great compassion[1] and was surveying the world with his Buddha Eye,[2] he saw that layfollower. He dressed early that morning and, taking his robe and bowl, went and stood at the door of his house. When the layfollower heard of the Teacher's arrival, he rose quickly and went out to meet him. He took the bowl from his hand, had him enter the house and offered him the appointed seat. The Lord sat on the appointed seat and the layfollower saluted him and then sat at one side. The Lord said, 'Why, layfollower, you appear like one overwhelmed with grief.' 'Yes, Lord, my beloved son has died – for this reason I am overwhelmed with grief' (he replied). The Lord then recited the Snake Jātaka* (with the purpose of) dispelling his grief.

Long ago, there was at Benares in the kingdom of Kāsi a brahmin family named Dhammapāla, all of whom – the brahmin and his wife, his son and daughter, daughter-in-law and servant-girl – were given to cultivating mindfulness of death.[3] [62] Whenever any of them left the house, he would advise the rest of the people and then leave without concern. Then one day the brahmin left the house with his son and went to his field and ploughed whilst his son set fire to some dry grass and sticks. At this a (poisonous) black snake, through fear of being burned, left the hollow of the tree and bit the brahmin's son, who fainted from the effect of the venom, fell down right there and died (thereafter) arising as Sakka, king of devas. When the brahmin saw his dead son, he said to a man he saw passing near where he was working, 'My good man, please go to my house and tell my wife she should bathe and dress in clean clothes and then come here with food for one person and with garlands and scent and so on.' He went there and informed her accordingly and the members of the household did as he said. The brahmin bathed, ate and anointed himself and, surrounded by his attendants, put his son's body on the funeral pile and set fire to it and then stood there as if he were (merely) burning a wooden log, with neither grief nor self-torment but with his mind fixed on the idea of impermanence.

*No. 354.

Now it is our Bodhisatta who was at that time the brahmin's son who had arisen as Sakka.[4] When he contemplated the meritorious deeds he had done in his previous life, he felt pity for his father and his relatives and went there disguised as a brahmin. When he saw that his relatives were not mourning him, he said, 'Hey there – you who are cooking that venison. Please give us some meat; I am hungry!' 'It is not venison, brahmin, it is a human being', he replied. 'Was he your enemy then?' 'He was no enemy but my own flesh and blood, my young son of great virtue.' 'Why do you not mourn when your young son of such virtue is dead?' When he heard this, the brahmin uttered these two verses telling why he was not mourning:

1 'As the snake quits its old skin, its person, and then goes on its way, so at death the peta[5] his useless body.

2 That which is burning is unaware of the lamentation of relatives. Therefore I do not mourn him; he is gone to whatever is his destiny.'

1 [63] Herein *the snake (urago): uraga* is a descriptive term for the serpent: it is on its breast (*urena*) that it moves about (*gacchati*). *Its old skin (tacaṃ jiṇṇaṃ)*: its skin, its slough, which is old, worn out, due to its decrepitude. *Quits its person and then goes on its way (hitvā gacchati santanuṃ)*: just as the snake (passing) between trees, branches, roots or rocks, removes from its body its old skin that is causing it misery, as though removing a close fitting jacket and, having given it up and cast it aside, then goes on its way as it wishes, even so does the being passing through[6] saṃsāra leave his decrepit 'person', his body, due to the exhaustion of his former deeds and then goes on his way, goes on his way in accordance with his deeds, meaning he arises by way of renewed existence. *So (evaṃ)*: he says this pointing to his son's burning body. *His useless body (sarīre nibbhoge)*: his body that has lost its usefulness, that is of no avail; as it was for him, so also is it for others. *The peta (pete)*: when vitality, heat and consciousness have gone, have left the body.[7] *At death (kālakate sati)*: when one is dead.

2 *Therefore (tasmā)*: since, due to the departure of consciousness, the body that is burning is unaware of the pain of being burnt and also the weeping and lamentation of beloved relatives, therefore I do not weep making a pretext of this son of mine. *He is gone to whatever is his destiny (gato so tassa yā gati)*: nonetheless, dead beings are not annihilated; rather, immediately he fell,[8] he was gone to whatever destiny there was said to be in store for him through a deed of that dead person finding its opportunity.[9] He does not wait for the weeping and lamentation of former relatives, nor is anything to any purpose generally accomplished by the weeping of former relatives – this is the meaning.

When the brahmin had thus manifested his skilfulness in thoroughly fixing his mind (on the idea of impermanence), Sakka, disguised as a brahmin, said to the brahmin's wife, 'Good woman, what was the deceased to you?' 'He was my grown up son, sir, whom I carried around in my womb for ten months, suckled and taught to crawl.'[10] 'Even though his father does not weep, it being in a man's nature so to do, surely a mother's heart is tender – why then do you not weep?' When she heard this, she uttered these two verses telling her reason for not weeping:

3 **[64]** 'He came from there without invitation[11] and went from here without permission. As he came, so he went. In such circumstances what is the use of lamentation?

4 That which is burning is unaware of the lamentation of relatives. Therefore I do not mourn him; he is gone to whatever is his destiny.'

3 Herein *without invitation (anabbhito)*: unsummoned; he was not sent for, saying, 'Come, become a son to me!' *From there (tato)*: from where he was before, from the other world.[12] *He came: āgā=āgacchi* (alternative grammatical form). *Without permission (nānuññāto)*: without leave; he was not dismissed by us, saying, 'Go to the other world,[12] my son!' *From here (ito)*: from this world.[13] *Went (gato)*: left. *As he came (yathāgato)*: the way in which he came, meaning he came quite[14] without our invitation. *So he went (tathāgato)*: in that same way he went. As he came on account of his own deeds alone, so he went on account of his own deeds alone; in this way the working of kamma is shown.[15] *In such circumstances what is the use of lamentation? (tattha kā paridevanā)*: as saṃsāra thus rolls on without one's control, what indeed is the use of lamentation on account of death? It shows that it is not fitting and should not be done by one possessing insight.

When he heard what the brahmin's wife had to say, he asked his sister, 'What was he to you, my dear?' 'He was my brother, sir.' 'My dear, surely sisters are fond of their brothers; why then do you not weep?' She uttered these two verses telling her reason for not weeping:

5 'If I were to weep I would become emaciated. What would be the fruit for me in that? It would be yet more distress for our relatives, friends and well-wishers.[16]

6 That which is burning is unaware of the lamentation of relatives. Therefore I do not mourn him; he is gone to whatever is his destiny.'

5 Herein *if I were to weep I would become emaciated (sace rode kisā assaṃ)*: if I should weep I might become emaciated and my body wasted. *What would be the fruit for me in that? (tattha me kiṃ phalaṃ siyā)*: what

indeed might be the fruit, what the advantage, for me in that, in weeping on account of the death of my brother? [65] My brother would not come (back to life) thereby nor even would he go to a happy state thereby – this is the meaning. *It would be yet more distress for our relatives, friends and well-wishers (ñātimittasuhajjānaṃ bhīyo no arati siyā)*: by my mourning him there would just be extreme misery, even more misery, at the death of my brother for our relatives, friends and well-wishers.

When he heard what the sister had to say, he asked his wife, 'What was he to you?' 'He was my husband, sir' (she replied). 'My dear, surely women are fond of their husbands and when they die their widows are destitute. Why then do you not weep?' She too uttered two verses telling her reason for not weeping:

7 'Just as a child cries for the rising moon, so with similar success he who mourns the peta.

8 That which is burning is unaware of the lamentation of relatives. Therefore I do not mourn him; he is gone to whatever is his destiny.'

7 Herein *a child (dārako)*: an ignorant child. *For the moon (candaṃ)*: for the moon's disc. *Rising (gacchantaṃ)*: ascending[17] in the firmament. *Cries (anurodati)*: cries, saying, 'Catch the chariot wheel and give it to me!' *So with similar success (evaṃ sampadam ev' etaṃ)*: the mourning of him who mourns the peta, the dead, is just as successful as, and similar to, the desire to catch the moon as it rises in the sky, since it is wishing for an unobtainable object – this is the meaning.

When he heard what his[18] wife had to say, he asked the servant-girl, 'My dear, what was he to you?'[19] 'He was my master, sir.' 'If so, you will have done your work after being beaten by him. I think, therefore, that you do not weep as you think that by his death you are well rid of him.' 'Do not speak to me thus, sir, it is not [66] befitting. The son of my master acted properly and possessed extreme patience, friendliness and kindness – he was like a son who had grown up at my own breast.' 'Then why do you not weep?' She too uttered two verses telling her reason for not weeping:

9 'Just as, brahmin, a broken water-pot cannot be put together again, so with similar success he who mourns the peta.

10 That which is burning is unaware of the lamentation of relatives. Therefore I do not mourn him; he is gone to whatever is his destiny.'

9 Herein *just as, brahmin, a broken water-pot cannot be put together again (yathā[20] pi brahme udakumbho bhinno appaṭisandhiyo)*: just as indeed, brahmin, a water-jar that has been broken by blows from a hammer

and so on cannot be put together again, cannot be restored to its original condition. The rest is quite self-evident as it has already been stated above.

When Sakka heard this talk on Dhamma from them, he said with devotion in his heart, 'Thoroughly have you cultivated mindfulness of death. From this (day) henceforward, there will be no need for you to labour at ploughing and so on.' He filled their house with the Seven Treasures[21] and exhorted them, saying, 'Do not neglect to give alms; keep the precepts and observe the Uposatha', and, after revealing his (true identity) to them, returned to his own abode. And that brahmin and the others performed meritorious deeds of almsgiving and so on and having lived their full span of years arose in the devaloka.

When the Teacher had recounted this Jātaka and had extracted[22] the dart of sorrow from that layfollower, he afterwards explained the (Four Noble) Truths at the end of which the layfollower was established in the sotāpatti-fruit.

The Exposition of the Snake Peta Story is concluded – thus the exposition of the meaning of the first, Snake, chapter, that is adorned with twelve stories in these Peta Stories of the Khuddaka Nikāya is concluded.[23]

[1] mahākaruṇāsamāpattito.

[2] Cp D ii 38f.

[3] maraṇasatibhāvanā; recollection of death, maraṇānussati, is one of the forty kammaṭṭhānas. See Vism viii 1–41 (Path of Purification pp. 247–259).

[4] In the Jātaka account the Bodhisatta is said to be the father and whilst Sakka appears in the story there is no suggestion that he has any connection with the deceased son.

[5] Perhaps meaning here simply 'departed' or 'dead and gone'.

[6] paribbhamanto, literally roaming or wandering about. No doubt some parallel was also intended between the snake going on its way 'as it wishes' (yathā kāmaṃ) and the being going on its way 'in accordance with his deeds' (yathā kammaṃ).

[7] Reading āyu-usuma-viññāṇe ite kāyato apagate with Se for text's āyusmāviññānato apagate (Be āyu-usmā-); on these three see M i 296, S iii 143, Thig 468 (not Thag as stated at MLS i 356 n. 3) and cp CPD sv āyu.

[8] Reading taṃ cuti-anantaraṃ eva with Se Be for text's ti vuccati tadanantaraṃ eva.

[9] To ripen.

[10] hatthapāde saṇṭhāpetvā, literally established in hand and foot. Gehman offered 'I placed his hands and feet' and Jātaka Stories iii 109 reads 'directed the movements of his hands and feet'; it may mean simply 'brought up'.

[11] Cp Thig 129.

[12] paralokato, usually meaning the 'next world' or the 'world beyond' both with reference to the future and in distinction to the world of men. Here, however, the sense is clearly that of the past and there is nothing to suggest whether it was from the world of men or some other world that he came.

[13] Reading idhalokato for text's dhalokato.

[14] Reading eva with Se Be for text's evaṃ.

[15] See M i 265f. where three things are said to be necessary for conception; cp also M ii 157.

[16] suhajjānaṃ, not listed in PED. Text should read, with Se Be, ñātimitta-, not ñātimittā-.

[17] Reading abbhussukkamānaṃ with Se Be for text's abbhuggamānaṃ, a term commonly used for the movement of heavenly bodies – e.g. M i 317 = S iii 156 = It 20; cp KS iii 133 n. 3.

[18] Reading tassa with Se Be for text's tassā.

[19] Reading tuyhaṃ so with Se Be for text's tvaṃ tassa.

[20] Text misquotes yatthā.

[21] sattaratanabharitaṃ; the expression occurs at S iii 83 where the cty says these are the seven bojjhaṅgas, or factors of enlightenment, but this would seem unlikely here. (The reference in PED sv ratana to S ii 217 is in fact to an instance of ratana[2] and should be amended.) A list of seven moral treasures (dhana) is given at A iv 4ff. (cp Miln 336) but these again seem out of place here. On the other hand it would seem equally unlikely that the seven treasures of the cakkavattin (D ii 16, 172ff., 187ff. etc.) were intended. The Jātaka account states simply that before he left he filled their house with countless wealth (aparimitaṃdhanaṃ katvā).

[22] Reading samuddharitvā with Be for text's, Se, samuṭṭharitvā.

[23] So Be.

Chapter II

THE UBBARĪ CHAPTER

[Ubbarīvagga]

II.1 EXPOSITION OF THE SAṂSĀRAMOCAKA PETA STORY
[Saṃsāramocakapetavatthuvaṇṇanā]

[67] 'Naked and of hideous appearance are you.' This was said when the Teacher was staying in the Bamboo Grove concerning a certain petī in the village named Iṭṭhakāvatī in the kingdom of Magadha.

It is said that in the kingdom of Magadha there were two villages, Iṭṭhakāvatī and Dīgharājī, in which lived many Saṃsāramocaka heretics.[1] A long time ago, some five hundred years past, a certain woman arose in a Saṃsāramocaka family right there in Iṭṭhakāvatī and due to her wrong views she took the life of many insects and grasshoppers and arose amongst the petas where she underwent the misery of hunger and thirst for five hundred years. Then when our Lord had arisen in the world and had set rolling the Wheel of the Noble Dhamma and was in due course staying in the Bamboo Grove, near Rājagaha, she arose yet again in that same Saṃsāramocaka family in that same Iṭṭhakāvatī. Then one day when she was seven or eight years old and was busy playing with other girls on the highway, the venerable elder Sāriputta, who was staying at the Aruṇavatī vihāra near that same village, passed along that road, close by the gate of that village, accompanied by twelve monks. At that moment many girls of that village, who had left the village and were playing close by the gate, after the manner of their parents quickly went with devotion in their hearts and saluted the elder and the other monks with the five-fold prostration.[2] The daughter of that family of non-believers,[3] however, disrespectful and lacking the good manners of virtuous people through her not having collected skilled deeds for a long time, remained standing like one undisciplined.[4] The elder discerned her former conduct, her present arising in a Saṃsāramocaka family and that she was worthy of arising (only) in hell in the future. He realised that if she were to salute him she would not arise in hell and that though she would arise amongst the petas she would attain excellence through him.[5] With his heart stirred with compassion [68] he said to those girls, 'You salute the monks[6] but this girl has remained standing like one undisciplined.'[4] Then those girls grabbed her by the hands, dragged her forward and, with the use of force, made her salute at the elder's feet. In due course she came of age and was given (in marriage) to a certain young man in a Saṃsāramocaka family in Dīgharājī.[7] When she was about to deliver, she died and arose amongst the petas, naked, of hideous appearance, a quite disgusting sight; wandering about she revealed herself during the night to the venerable elder Sāriputta and then stood at one side. When he saw her, the elder questioned her with this verse:

1 'Naked and of hideous appearance are you, emaciated and with prominent veins.[8] You thin one, with your ribs standing out, now who are you, you who are stood here?'

1 Herein *with prominent veins (dhamanisanthatā)*: with a body spread with a network of veins due to an absence of flesh and blood. *With your ribs standing out (upphāsulike)*: with protruding ribs. *You thin one (kisike)*: you with an emaciated body; having formerly said 'emaciated',[9] the words 'you thin one'[10] are repeated with the purpose of showing her extreme emaciation[11] in that her body was mere skin, bone and sinew.

When she heard this, the petī said this verse making herself known:

2 'I, sir, am a petī, gone to a miserable existence in the world of Yama; having done a wicked deed, I have gone from here to the world of the petas.'

Questioned once more by the elder about the deed she had done:

3 'Now what evil deed was done by you by body, speech or mind? As a result of which deed have you gone from here to the world of the petas?',

she spoke three verses showing that after having been selfish and having lacked the virtue of giving she had arisen[12] in the peta-womb and was undergoing great misery thus:

4 **[69]** 'I, sir, had not father, mother nor other relatives even who, possessing pity for me, would urge me saying, "Give a gift with devotion in your heart to recluses and brahmins."

5 From now on for five hundred years I must wander about naked like this, being consumed by hunger and craving – this is the fruit of my wicked deed.

6 I salute you, worthy sir, with devotion in my heart; please have pity on me, O resolute and mighty one. Please give something[13] and assign that to me; release me from this state of misery, sir.'

4 Herein *possessing pity (anukampakā)*: helpful as to her welfare in the next world. *Sir (bhante)*: she is addressing the elder. *Who would urge me (ye maṃ niyojeyyuṃ)*: I had not mother or father or other such relatives of such a kind as who, possessing pity for me, would urge[14] me saying, 'With devotion in your heart give a gift to recluses and brahmins' – this is how it should be construed.

5 *From now on for five hundred years I must wander about naked like this (ito ahaṃ vassasatāni pañcā yaṃ evarūpā vicarāmi naggā)*: having

recollected her existence as a petī in her last birth but two, the petī said this assuming she would now also have to wander about in that way for five hundred years. *Yaṃ* (untranslated)=*yasmā* (alternative grammatical form); since I have not done any meritorious deeds of giving and so on, I have become a petī, naked like this, and I must henceforward wander about for five hundred years – this is how it should be construed. *By craving (taṇhāya)*: by thirst. *Being consumed: khajjamānā*[15]*=khādiyamānā* (alternative grammatical form), meaning being afflicted.

6 *I salute you, worthy sir, with devotion in my heart (vandāmi taṃ ayya pasannacittā)*: with devotion in my heart I salute you, worthy sir. This shows just how little merit it is now possible for me to do.[16] *Please have pity on me (anukampa maṃ)*: [70] please help, please be kind towards me. *Please give something and assign that to me (datvā ca me ādissa yaṃ hi kiñci)*: she said this assuming that when he had given some merit-offering and had assigned that donation to her, there would thereby be release for her from the peta-womb. For this reason she said, 'Release me from this state of misery, sir.'

These three verses were said by those rehearsing the texts to show the manner in which the elder proceeded to act when the petī had thus spoken:

7 ' "Very well", consented Sāriputta, possessing pity, and gave to the monks a morsel, a piece of cloth measuring a hand and a bowl of water and assigned the donation to her.

8 Immediately he dedicated this the result came into being, food, clothing and drink being the fruit of this donation.

9 Thereupon she became pure, clad in fresh, clean clothes, wearing those more fine than those of Kāsi and, bedecked in various clothes and ornaments, she approached Sāriputta.'

7 Herein *to the monks (bhikkhūnaṃ)*: to a monk; this is said with a distortion of number. Some read 'gave to a monk a morsel' (*ālopaṃ bhikkhuno datvā*). *A morsel (ālopaṃ)*: a mouthful,[17] meaning merely one morsel of food. *A piece of cloth measuring a hand (pāṇimattañ ca colakaṃ)*: the size of one hand, meaning a bit of cloth. *And a bowl of water (thālakassa ca pānīyaṃ)*: merely one bowlful of water.

The rest is just as already given in the Bald-headed Peta Story.[18]

Then when the venerable Sāriputta saw that petī who, having come into his presence, was stood with her faculties refreshed, completely pure in complexion and adorned with heavenly clothes and ornaments and lighting up everything around her with her own radiance, he spoke three verses, desiring to have the fruition of deeds explained by her from her own experience:

10 'You who stand with surpassing beauty, devatā, lighting up all directions like the Healing Star,

11 Due to what is such beauty yours? Due to what is this accomplished by you here [71] and that there should arise whatever pleasures your heart holds dear?

12 I ask you, devī of great majesty, what meritorious deed did you do when you were human? Due to what is your shining majesty thus and your beauty radiates in all directions?'[19]

10 Herein *surpassing (abhikkantena)*: extremely lovely, meaning very beautiful. *With beauty (vaṇṇena)*: with complexion. *Lighting up all directions (obhāsentī disā sabbā)*: shining in all the ten directions with a single light. In what manner? He said, 'Like the Healing Star'. This star has acquired the name *Osadhī* since excessive (*ussanna-*) radiance is contained (*dhīyati*) by it or since it contributes to giving strength[20] to medicines (*osadhīnaṃ*): just as it stands shedding light all about it, even so do you (stand) lighting up all directions – this is the meaning.

11 *Due to what? (kena)*: the word 'what' (*kiṃ*) in its interrogative form; this is the instrumental case in the sense of (asking for the) cause, meaning due to what cause? *Yours: te=tāva* (alternative grammatical form). *Such (etādiso)*:[21] this is said with reference to how it appears at the moment. *Due to what is this accomplished by you here? (kena te idha-m-ijjhati)*: due to what especially meritorious deed is this fruit of good conduct that is now being received by you accomplished, produced, here, at this place? *There should arise (uppajjanti)*: there should come into existence. *Pleasures (bhogā)*: outstanding possessions and means such as clothes and ornaments and so on that have acquired the name 'pleasures' (*bhogā*) through being fit to be enjoyed (*paribhuñjitabbattena*). *Whatever (ye keci)* means (all) pleasures are embraced and included, without remainder, for this is an expression embracing (everything) without remainder, as in that of 'whatever is compounded' (*ye keci saṅkhārā*). *Your heart holds dear (manaso piyā)*: that are endeared to your heart, meaning that are dear to your heart.

12 *I ask (pucchāmi)*: I put the question, meaning I wish to know. *You: taṃ=tvaṃ* (alternative grammatical form). *Devī (devi)*: she is a devī due to her being endowed with heavenly majesty. For this reason he said, 'Of great majesty'. *When you were human (manussabhūtā)*: when you were born amongst men and had attained the human state. This is said in accordance with the general rule that beings perform meritorious deeds whilst they remain in a human existence. This is the meaning of these verses in brief only. It should, however, be understood just as has already been

given in detail in the Commentary on the Mansion Stories (section) of this Elucidation of the Intrinsic Meaning.

[72] The petī, questioned thus by the elder, spoke the remaining verses, clarifying the reason as to how this excellence of hers had been received:

13 'The compassionate sage for the world saw[22] me gone to a miserable existence – yellowish,[23] emaciated, famished, naked and with a wrinkled skin.[24]

14 He gave to the monks a morsel, a piece of cloth measuring a hand and a bowl of water and assigned the donation to me.

15 Behold the fruit of that morsel: for one thousand years I shall eat food curried with many flavours, enjoying the gratification of all my desires.

16 Behold what kind of result there is of a piece of cloth measuring a hand: as many clothes as were in the whole of king Nanda's realm,

17 Still more than that, sir, are my clothes and coverings of silk and wool, linen and cotton.

18 Many and costly are they – they even hang down from the sky and I just put on whichever takes my fancy.[25]

19 Behold what kind of result there is from a bowl of water: deep, four-cornered and well laid out lotus ponds,[26]

20 With clear water and beautiful banks, cool and fragrant, covered with lotuses and water lilies, the water full of lotus filaments,

21 And I sport and play and enjoy myself, having nothing to fear from any quarter. I, sir, have come to salute the compassionate sage for the world.

13 Herein *yellowish (uppaṇḍukiṃ)*: having become yellowish.[27] *Famished (chātaṃ)*: wishing to eat, overcome with hunger. *With a wrinkled skin (sampatitacchaviṃ)*: with the skin of my body chapped and broken. *For the world (loke)*: this shows the range of the compassion of the one here said to be 'compassionate'. *Me (taṃ maṃ)*: me in that condition, me in a state that certainly (calls for) compassion as already mentioned. *Gone to a miserable existence (duggataṃ)*: gone to a state of misery.

14 *He gave to the monks a morsel (bhikkhūnaṃ ālopaṃ datvā)*: and so on indicates the way in which the elder acted out of compassion.

15 [73] Herein *food (bhattaṃ)*: boiled rice, meaning heavenly food. *For one thousand years (vassasataṃ dasa)*: for ten times a hundred years is said to be a thousand years;[28] this is the accusative case in the sense of a continuous period of time. *Curried with many flavours, enjoying the gratification of all my desires (kāmakāminī anekarasasavyañjanaṃ)*: I shall eat

food curried with many flavours, endowed with yet other desirable sense pleasures – this is how it should be construed.

16 *A piece of cloth (coḷassa)*: this indicates the meritorious deed consisting in giving[29] with this as its object under the general heading of merit-offerings. *Behold what kind of result (vipākaṃ passa yādisaṃ)*: behold the fruit, the result so-called, of that gift of a piece of cloth, sir, of what kind, of what form, it is. In case (one should ask) 'What?', the petī said,[30] 'As many (clothes as were in the whole) of king Nanda's (realm)' and so on.

Now in this connection who was this king Nanda?

It is said that long ago, when the human life-span was ten thousand years, a man of property who was a resident of Benares saw a certain Paccekabuddha in his forest haunt when taking a walk in the forest. The Paccekabuddha had been making a robe there but had folded it up and begun to put it aside, the binding being insufficient.[31] When the man of property saw this, he said, 'What are you doing, sir?' Though nothing was said by him due to his few wants,[32] he realised that the robe material was not sufficient,[33] laid his outer cloak at the Paccekabuddha's feet and went away.[34] The Paccekabuddha took it and, adding it to the binding, made the robe and put it on. At the end of his (natural) life the man of property died and arose[35] in the realm of the Thirty-three. He enjoyed heavenly excellence there for his entire life-span and after falling from there arose in a family of special advisers (to the king) in a certain village at a place a yojana distant from Benares. At the time he came of age, the new-month festivity was announced in that village. He said to his mother, 'Mother, please give me a cloak so that I can take part in the new-month festivity.' She got out a clean garment and gave it to him. 'Mother, this is rough' (he said). She got out another and gave it to him but he refused this too. Then his mother said to him, 'Son, ever since we were born in this house we have not had any merit for acquiring clothes finer than these.' 'I will go to a place for obtaining it, mother.' 'Go then, son, I wish that you might this very day acquire sovereignty of the city of Benares.' [74] 'Very well, mother', he replied. He saluted his mother, circumambulated her by the right[36] and said, 'Goodbye, mother.' 'Goodbye, son.' It is said that the thought[37] occurred to her thus, 'Where can he go? He will just sit here or there about the house.' But urged on by way of his meritorious deeds[38] he left the village and went to Benares where he lay down to sleep on an auspicious slab of stone after covering himself from the head down. Now that was the seventh day following the death of the king of Benares. When the king's special advisers and chief-priest had performed the funeral rites, they sat in the royal courtyard and took counsel, saying, 'There is one daughter of the king but no son – a kingdom with no king does not endure.

We must despatch the carriage of state.'[39] They harnessed four Sindh horses the colour of the white lotus and installed in the carriage the five-fold royal regalia[40] headed by the white umbrella. They then despatched the carriage and had the music struck up at the rear. The carriage left by the eastern gate headed towards the park. Some said, 'The carriage is going along headed towards the park through habit. Turn it back!' But the chief-priest said, 'Do not turn it back!' The carriage circumambulated the boy by the right and then stood ready to be mounted. The chief-priest lifted a corner of the covering, inspecting the soles of his feet,[41] and said, 'Let this (boy) be our refuge – he is capable of creating a single realm of the four great continents and the two thousand surrounding islands', and then had the music struck up three times, saying, 'Strike up the music! Strike it up again!'[42] The boy then uncovered his face, looked around him, and said, 'On what business have you come here, my friend?' 'Your majesty, the kingdom has come to you.' 'Where is your king?' 'He has gone to heaven, my lord.' 'How many days past?' 'Today is the seventh day.' 'Is there no son or daughter?' 'There is a daughter, your majesty, but no son.'[43] 'Well then, in that case I will rule.' They straightaway erected a pavillion for anointing him, adorned the king's daughter with all her ornaments, took her to the park and anointed the boy. When he had been anointed, they presented him with clothes worth a hundred thousand (pieces). 'What is this, my friend',[44] he asked. 'Your underclothes,[45] your majesty.' 'They are not rough are they, my friend?' [75] 'There are none finer[46] than these amongst any of the clothes used by men, your majesty.' 'Did your king dress like this?' 'Yes, your majesty.' 'I do not think your king possessed merit. Bring me the golden water jug and I will get some clothes.' They brought the golden water jug. He stood up, washed his hands, rinsed his mouth and, taking[47] some water in his hands, sprinkled it in an easterly direction, whereupon eight wish-granting trees broke through the solid ground and rose up. He again took some water and sprinkled it to the south, to the west and to the north, thus (sprinkling it) in each of the four directions. In each of all of the directions he produced eight (trees) so that there rose up thirty-two wish-granting trees (in all). Some say that in each direction he produced sixteen (trees) so that there were sixty-four wish-granting trees (in all). He dressed in one heavenly garment, wrapped one about him, and said, 'Have it proclaimed by beat of drum that in the realm of king Nanda no thread spinning women need spin thread (any longer).' He had them raise the umbrella and, dressed and adorned and mounted on the back of the most stately elephant, entered the city, went up into the palace and enjoyed great excellence.

So time went on until one day the queen, seeing the excellence of the king, showed her compassion by saying, 'You certainly ought to show more restraint.'[48] When asked, 'What do you mean, devī?', she said, 'You have excellence to excess, your majesty. At some time in the long past you must have done skilled deeds but now you do no skilled deeds for your future well being.' 'To whom can we give? There are no virtuous ones.' 'This Jambudīpa,[49] your majesty, is not devoid of arahants. You just prepare the alms and I will get the arahants',[50] she said. On the following day the king had a great almsgiving prepared. The queen wished, 'If there are arahants in this direction may they come here and accept alms from us', and prostrated herself facing the northern direction. No sooner than the queen was lying down than the Paccekabuddha Paduma, eldest of the five hundred Paccekabuddhas who were sons of queen Padumavatī and who were dwelling in the Himālaya, addressed his brothers, saying, 'King Nanda is inviting you, good sirs[51] – you should accept his (invitation).' They consented and straightaway went through the air and descended at the northern gate. [76] The people informed the king, saying, 'Five hundred Paccekabuddhas have come, your majesty.' The king went together with the queen and saluted them, took their bowls and had the Paccekabuddhas go up into the palace. There he gave them the alms. When the meal was over they lay themselves down,[52] the king at the feet of the senior member of that company and the queen at the feet of the younger ones,[53] saying, 'You worthy ones will not go short of the requisites; our meritorious deeds will not diminish. Please give us your consent as to staying here.' Having made them consent, he had dwelling places built in the park and supported the Paccekabuddhas for the rest of their lives. When they attained Parinibbāna, he had the sacred festivities[54] performed and had the funeral rites performed with sandalwood and so on and then took their relics and installed them in a stūpa. Filled with agitation at the thought, 'If death must come even to these great rishis of such great majesty, what can be said of those like me?', he installed his eldest son as ruler and himself went forth into the homeless life of the recluse. The queen, wondering what she might do now that the king had gone forth, went forth herself. Dwelling in the park the two of them caused the jhānas to arise and passed their time in the ease of jhāna[55] and at the end of their lifespan they arose in the Brahmaloka. It is said that the elder Mahākassapa,[56] a mahāsāvaka of our Teacher, was that king Nanda and Bhaddā Kāpilānī[57] his queen consort. For the ten thousand years that this king Nanda himself wore heavenly clothes he made his whole realm just like Uttarakuru[58] and would give heavenly garments to all-comers. Now it was with reference to this magnificence of heavenly clothes that the petī said, 'As many clothes as were in the whole of king Nanda's realm.' Herein *in the realm (vijitasmiṃ)*: in the kingdom. *Clothes (paṭicchadā)*: clothes (*vatthāni*); they are called 'clothes' (*paṭicchadā*)[59] since (people) clothe themselves (*paṭicchādenti*) with them.

Now showing that her magnificence was now even greater than the magnificence of king Nanda[60] the petī said, 'Still more than that, sir, are my clothes and coverings' and so on.

17 Herein *than that (tato)*: still more than the clothes that belonged to king Naṇda are my clothes, that is, my garments. *Clothes and coverings (vatthāni 'cchādanāni)*: underclothes and outer clothes. [77] *Of silk and wool: koseyyakambalīyāni=koseyyāni c'eva kambalāni ca* (resolution of compound). *Linen and cotton (khomakappāsikāni ca)*: clothes of linen and clothes made of cotton.

18 *Many (vipulā)*: many and great in length and breadth. *Costly (mahagghā)*: of very great value through being costly. *Hang down from the sky (ākāse 'valambare)*: remain hanging down in the sky. *Whichever takes my fancy (yaṃ yaṃ hi manaso piyaṃ)*: and I just take whichever takes my fancy and put it on and wrap it round me – this is how it should be construed.

19 *Behold what kind of result there is from a bowl of water (thālakassa ca pānīyaṃ vipākaṃ passa yādisaṃ)*: behold what kind and just how great is the result of this, a mere bowlful of water given and appreciated. Indicating this she said, 'Deep, four-cornered' and so on. Herein *deep (gambhīrā)*: unfathomable. *Four-cornered (caturassā)*: rectangular in shape. *Lotus ponds: pokkharañño=pokkharaṇiyo* (alternative grammatical form). *Well laid out (sunimmitā)*: well laid out in accordance with her deed.

20 *With clear water: setodakā=seta-udakā,*[61] (resolution of compound); (and)[62] strewn with white sand. *With beautiful banks (supatitthā)*: with beautiful bathing places. *Cool (sītā)*: with cool water. *Fragrant (appaṭigandhiyā)*: with an entrancing[63] aroma, lacking any disagreeable odour. *The water full of lotus filaments (vārikiñjakkhapūritā)*: filled with water that is covered with the hairy filaments of lotuses and blue water lilies and so on.

21 *I: sāhaṃ=sā ahaṃ* (resolution of compound). *Sport (ramāmi)*: find delight. *Play (kīḷāmi)*: gratify[64] my senses. *Enjoy myself (modāmi)*: am delighted at the excellence of my enjoyment. *Having nothing to fear from any quarter (akutobhayā)*: I dwell at ease and as I like[65] lacking fear from any quarter. *I, sir, have come to salute (bhante vanditum āgatā)*: I, sir, have come, that is, I have approached, to salute you who are the means of my acquiring this heavenly excellence.

That which is not analysed here as to its meaning is given elsewhere.

When this had thus been said by the petī, the venerable Sāriputta, relating the story in detail to the people – residents of the two villages of Iṭṭhakāvatī and Dīgharājī, who had come into his presence – agitated them and released them from their wicked Saṃsāramocaka heresy[66] and then established them as layfollowers. [78] This issue became well known to the monks and the monks raised it with the Lord. The Lord took the matter as an arisen need and taught Dhamma to the company assembled there. That teaching was of benefit to those people.

[1] It is not clear who these were nor in what their heresy consisted. At Jātaka Stories vi 117 king Aṅgati may be found saying, 'There is no door to heaven: only wait on destiny. Whether thy lot be happiness or misery, it is only gained through destiny: all will at last reach deliverance from transmigration (saṃsārasuddhi); be not eager for the future.' It could be that they are Ājīvikas since the doctrine attributed at D i 54 to Makkhali-Gosāla is there similarly called saṃsārasuddhi – 'purification through transmigration' (Dial i 73).

[2] A kneeling añjali salute in which the forehead, edges of the hands and the knees touch the ground.

[3] Reading assaddhakulassa with Se Be for text's assadhā kulassa.

[4] Reading asikkhitā with Se for text's āsikkhitā (Be alakkhikā).

[5] Reading mamaṃ with Se Be for text's namaṃ.

[6] Reading bhikkhū with Se Be for text's bhikkhuṃ.

[7] PED sv rāji suggests dīgharājiyaṃ here means 'of long lineage' but it is almost certainly a reference to the above-mentioned village and should have been given in the text with a capital letter.

[8] Reading dhamanisanthatā with Se Be for text's dhamanisaṇṭhitā both here and throughout.

[9] Reading kisā with Se Be and verse for text's kise.

[10] Reading kisike with Se Be and verse for text's kisikā.

[11] Reading kisabhāvadassanatthaṃ with Se Be for text's kisabhāva dassanatthaṃ.

[12] Reading nibbattitvā with Se Be for text's nibbattetvā.

[13] Reading yaṃ hi with Se Be for text's yāhi.

[14] Reading niyojeyyuṃ with Se Be and verse for text's yojeyyuṃ.

[15] So Se Be and verse for text's khajjamāno.

[16] Traditionally petas were thought incapable of any meritorious deeds – hence the need of relatives to do this on their behalf. See however the remarks at PvA 26 above.

[17] As much as is made into a small ball when eating with the fingers.

[18] I.10 above.

[19] These verses recur at Vv 9[1,2,4].

[20] Reading anubalappadāyikā ti katvā with Se Be and VvA 53 for text's anubalappadānā hutvā; anubalappadāyika is not listed in PED but cp CPD sv. According to PED sv osadhī, 'Childers calls it Venus but gives no evidence; other translators render it "morning star". According to Hindu mythology the lord of medicine is the moon (oṣadhīśa), not any particular star.' No doubt it is the moon that was expected to be understood here. We need not be misled by the word 'star' (tārakā) for this may be used just as easily of the moon – see Sn 687 where the moon is said to be the 'bull of stars' (tārāsabha). Moreover the morning star, however bright, could hardly be said to light up all about it as required here. Cp also S i 65; A v 62; It 20.

[21] Reading Etādiso ti with Se Be; text omits ti. Verse 10 should thus be amended to read Kena te 'tādiso. . . .

[22] Reading addakkhi with Se Be for text's dakkhasi.

[23] Reading uppaṇḍukiṃ with Se Be for text's upakaṇḍakiṃ both here and in cty below where it is defined as uppaṇḍukajātaṃ.

[24] Reading sampatitacchaviṃ with Be for text's appaṭicchaviṃ; see also PED sv appaṭicchaviṃ which also recommends this reading but which gives no entry at the appropriate place; Se reads āpatitacchaviṃ.

[25] Literally whichever my heart holds dear, as above.

[26] Reading pokkharañño with Se Be and III 2[25] below for text's pokkhāraññā.

[27] Reading uppaṇḍukajātaṃ with Se Be for text's upakaṇḍakajātaṃ.

[28] Reading vassasahassan ti vuttaṃ with Se Be for text's vassasahassan nivuttaṃ; PED entry for nivutta[1] should probably be deleted.

[29] Reading dānamayaṃ puññaṃ with Se Be for text's dānapuññaṃ.

[30] Text reads yathārūpan ti petī āha as does Se though it seems this is Hardy's emendation since he states that all MSS. read ce ti or ve ti for petī. Be has yathārūpaṃ. Kin ti ce ti āha. I emend to read yathārūpaṃ. Kin ti ce petī āha.

[31] Reading appahonte with Se Be for text's appabhonte.

[32] Reading appicchatāya with Se Be for text's apicchatāya.

[33] Reading nappahoti with Se Be for text's tassa hoti.

[34] Reading agamāsi with Se Be for text's āgamāsi.

[35] Reading nibbattitvā with Se Be for text's nibbattetvā.

[36] padakkhiṇaṃ katvā, that is, circumambulating a person whilst keeping one's right side turned towards that person, or in other words clockwise and the way of the sun. It was normally performed three times (e.g. VvA 173, 219) as a means of saying farewell, as here, or as a means of greeting one newly arrived. The practice was also common in Scotland where it was known as 'walking the deasil' around someone – for a detailed investigation see W. Simpson, *The Buddhist Praying Wheel*, London 1896.

[37] Reading cittaṃ with Se Be for text's pi taṃ.

[38] Reading puññaniyāmena with Se Be for text's puññāniyāmena.

[39] phussarathaṃ, a wonderful state carriage that ran of its own accord to find a new ruler when there was no heir to the throne; cp J ii 39, iii 238, v 248, vi 39ff.

[40] rājakakudhabhaṇḍaṃ – the yaktail fan (vālavījanī), turban (uṇhīsa), sword (khagga), umbrella (chatta) and slippers (pādukā); see e.g. J v 264. At D i 7 they appear amongst the items for self-adornment from which Gotama holds himself aloof.

[41] He would have been looking for the auspicious marks, normally totalling thirty-two, possessed by all Buddhas and Cakkavatti monarchs – cp J iii 239. Details of these marks can be found in the Lakkhaṇa Suttanta (D iii 142ff.) and of the career of the Cakkavatti, or wheel-turning king, in the Cakkavatti-Sīhanāda Suttanta (D iii 58ff.). It seems Asoka was considered such a monarch, by the Buddhists at least. Whereas Buddhas turn the wheel of the Dhamma spiritually, the Cakkavatti monarch turns it in a temporal sense, conquering neighbouring kingdoms (without force) so that their rulers may be made to administer the territory in accordance with the Dhamma – see verse 10 of the Concluding Remarks below. Here it may be noticed that the Cakkavatti conquers not only the whole of Jambudīpa but the other three continents as well together with the five hundred smaller islands that surround each continent. See notes at PvA 137.

[42] Reading paggaṇhatha puna pi paggaṇhathā ti with Se Be for text's paggaṇhathā ti puna pi paggoṇhathā ti.

[43] Reading deva putto with Se Be for text's devaputto.

[44] Reading tātā ti with Se Be for text's tātā li.

[45] Reading nivāsanavatthaṃ with Se Be for text's nivāsanatthaṃ.

[46] Reading sukhumataraṃ with Se Be for text's sukkhumataraṃ.

[47] Reading ādāya with Se Be for text's ādaya.

[48] Reading aho tapassī, literally you should be an ascetic, with Se Be for text's aho vata sirī.

[49] 'Land of the Rose-apple', that is, India – see notes at PvA 137.

[50] Reading arahante with Se Be for text's aharante.

[51] Reading mārisā with Se Be for text's marisā.

[52] Reading nipajjitvā with Se Be for text's nippajjitvā.

[53] saṅghatthera and saṅghanavaka – elder and novice – terms usually applicable to grades of monk but perhaps not in this sense in the case of Paccekabuddhas.

[54] sādhukīḷitaṃ – cp SA i 284.

[55] jhānasukhena; as one of the five jhāna factors sukha, or ease, is present in the first three jhānas only.

[56] See GS i 16 and DPPN ii 476–483 for his details.

[57] So Se Be for text's Bhaddakapilā; see GS i 22 and DPPN ii 354f. for her details.

[58] The northern of the four continents where there are no wants and where no labour is necessary since everything needed is granted; see notes at PvA 137 and also D iii 199ff.

[59] So Se Be and verse for text's paṭicchādā; cp PvA 185 below.

[60] Reading Nandarājasamiddhito with Se Be for text's Nandarājā samiddhito.

[61] So Se Be; text repeats setodakā.

[62] Se alone adds ca here. Setodakā literally means 'with white water', presumably appearing white due to the presence of the white sands beneath.

[63] surabhi; not listed in PED.

[64] Reading paricāremi with Se Be for text's paricarāmi.

[65] Reading serī sukhavihārinī with Se Be for text's serimukhavihārinī.

[66] saṁsāramocanapāpakammato mocetvā, released them from the wicked deed of saṃsāramocana, their heresy no doubt being regarded as a wicked deed of mind.

II.2 EXPOSITION OF THE ELDER SĀRIPUTTA'S MOTHER PETĪ STORY

[Sāriputtattheramātupetivatthuvaṇṇanā][1]

'Naked and of hideous appearance are you.' This was said when the Teacher was staying in the Bamboo Grove concerning a petī who had been the mother of the venerable elder Sāriputta in her last birth but four.

One day the venerables Sāriputta, Mahāmoggallāna, Anuruddha and Kappina were staying in a certain forest haunt not far from Rājagaha. Now there was in Benares at that time a brahmin owning great riches, great wealth, immense hoards of gold and silver, who would give food, drink, clothing and bed and so on to recluses and brahmins, indigents, tramps,[2] wayfarers and beggars, as a well might give water. He gave to all-comers according to occasion and desert,[3] stocking a range of gifts consisting of everything that should be bestowed such as water for (washing) the feet, (ointments) for soothing the feet and so on,[4] as well as serving the monks with due care with food and drink and so on for their morning meal. When going to other areas, he would say to his wife, 'My dear, please continue with due care this form of almsgiving just as I have arranged it, without allowing it to decline.' 'Very well', she agreed[5] but when he had left she put an end to the form of almsgiving he had arranged for the monks. She would show to travellers who approached in search of a dwelling an old abandoned[6] shed at the back of the house, saying, 'You can stay here', whilst when travellers came there in search of food and drink and so on, she would say, 'Eat excrement; drink urine, drink blood; eat your mother's brains!' and curse them with the name of whatever is impure and loathsome.

She died in due course and swept up by the power of her deeds arose in the peta-womb, undergoing misery commensurate with her misconduct in speech. [79] Recollecting their connection in an earlier birth and desiring to enter the presence of the venerable Sāriputta, she reached his vihāra[7] but the (guardian) devatās of that vihāra refused her admission to the vihāra. It is said that she had been the elder's mother in her last birth but four. She therefore said, 'In my last birth but four I was the mother of the worthy elder Sāriputta; please give me admission through the gate to see the elder.' When they heard this, the devatās granted her admission. When she had entered, she stood at the end of the walk-way[8] and revealed herself to the elder. When the elder saw her, his heart was stirred with compassion and he questioned her with this verse:

1 'Naked and of hideous appearance are you, emaciated and with prominent veins. You thin one, with your ribs standing out, now who are you, you who are stood here?'

On being questioned by the elder, she spoke these five verses in reply:

2 'I was your own mother in other former births but now I have arisen on the peta-plane, endowed with hunger and thirst.

3 The thrown out, the expectorated, sputum, nose-mucus, phlegm, the fat of those being burnt and the blood of delivered women,

4 And the blood from wounds and that from severed noses and heads – overwhelmed by hunger I eat what is attached to men and women.

5 I feed on pus and blood of cattle[9] and of men and am without shelter and without home,[10] resting on the black bed.

6 Give, dear son, a gift for me and when you have given make it over to me – surely then I will be freed from eating pus and blood.'

2 Herein *I was your own mother (ahan te sakiyā mātā)*: I was your own mother who brought you into the world. *In other former births (pubbe aññāsu jātisu)*: though being your mother, it was not in this birth but in other former births, in my last birth but four – this is how it should

be regarded. *But now I have arisen on the peta-plane (uppannā pettivisayaṃ)*: but now I have come to the world of the petas by way of rebirth. **[80]** *Endowed with hunger and thirst (khuppipāsāsamappitā)*: provided with hunger and thirst, meaning being overcome with an incessant desire to eat and to drink.

3 *The thrown out (chaḍḍitaṃ)*: the thrown up, meaning the vomited.[11] *The expectorated (khipitaṃ)*: the impurities that leave the mouth upon expectoration. *Sputum (khelaṃ)*: spittle. *Nose-mucus (siṅghāṇikaṃ)*: the impurities that leave the nose after streaming down from the brains. *Phlegm: silesumaṃ=semhaṃ* (alternative grammatical form).[12] *The fat of those being burnt (vasañ ca ḍayhamānānaṃ)*: the fat and oil of corpses that are being burnt on the funeral pile. *And the blood of delivered women (vijātānañ ca lohitaṃ)*: and the blood of women who have delivered; the impurities of the womb are included by the word 'and'.

4 *From wounds (vaṇitānaṃ)*: from wounds that have arisen. *That (yaṃ)*: the blood – this is (the word) with which it connects. *From severed noses and heads (ghānasīsacchinnaṃ)*: I eat the blood from severed noses and also from severed heads – this is how it should be construed. This 'from severed noses and heads' is a heading for (further) teaching. Since I also eat the blood from severed hands and feet and so on, the[13] blood from these may also be regarded as included by (the expression) 'from wounds'. *Overwhelmed by hunger (khudāparetā)*: overcome by a desire to eat. *What is attached to men and women (itthipurisanissitaṃ)*: this indicates that she eats what is attached to the bodies of men and women as aforesaid and other[14] things such as the skin, flesh, sinew and pus and so on.

5 *Of cattle (pasūnaṃ)*: of goats, cows and buffaloes and so on.[15] *Without shelter (alenā)*: without refuge. *Without home (anagārā)*: without a dwelling. *Resting on the black bed (nīlamañcaparāyanā)*: lying on a bed of impurities that have been abandoned[16] in a cemetery. Or, alternatively, 'black' (*nīla*) refers to the cemetery ground with its many ashes and embers, meaning lying on just this as though it were a bed.

6 *Make it over to me (anvādisāhi me)*: please give an assigned gift dedicating it in such a way that the donation that has been given will be of benefit to me.[17] *Surely then I will be freed from eating pus and blood (app' eva nāma muñceyyaṃ pubbalohitabhojanā)*: surely I will be freed from this life as a petī eating pus and blood by means of your dedication.

When he heard this the venerable elder Sāriputta consulted, on the following day, the three elders, that is, the elder Mahāmoggallāna and so on, and, going together with them **[81]** to Rājagaha in search of alms, came to the dwelling of king Bimbisāra. When the king saw the elder, he saluted him and asked him of the reason for his visit, saying, 'For what purpose have you come here, venerable sir?' The venerable Mahāmoggallāna informed the king of the incident. The king said, 'You have my permission, reverend sir', and then dismissed the elders. He summoned his minister who looked after everything and commanded, 'Have four huts built near the city in a grove that is shaded and well watered.' He divided his inner city[18] into three in accordance with their particular expertise, had the four huts roofed,[19] and then went there himself and did what had to be done. When the huts were completed, he had all the food offerings[20] prepared and all the proper requisites[21] such as food, drinks and clothes and so on got ready for the order of monks with the Buddha at its head and then handed all this over to the venerable elder Sāriputta. The elder then gave all this on behalf of that petī to the order of monks of the four quarters[22] with the Buddha at its head. The petī showed her appreciation to him and arose in the devaloka, richly endowed with all she desired. On a later day she approached the venerable elder Mahāmoggallāna, saluted him and then remained while the elder questioned her. She told him in detail about how she had arisen as a petī and as a devī. For this reason it was said:

7 'When he had heard what his mother had to say, Upatissa,[23] possessing pity, consulted Moggallāna, Anuruddha and Kappina.
8 He built four huts[24] and he gave those huts together with food and drink to the Saṅgha of the four quarters and then dedicated that donation to his mother.
9 Immediately he dedicated this the result came into being, food, drink and clothing being the fruit of this donation.
10 Thereupon she became pure, clad in fresh, clean clothes, wearing those more fine than those of Kāsi and, bedecked in various clothes and ornaments, she approached Kolita.'[25]

8 Herein *he gave to the Saṅgha of the four quarters: saṅghe cātuddise adā=cātuddisassa saṅghassa adāsi* (alternative grammatical form), meaning he handed over (to them).

[82] The rest has just the meaning stated.

The venerable Mahāmoggallāna then questioned that petī:

11 'You who stand with surpassing beauty, devatā, lighting up all directions like the Healing Star,
12 Due to what is such beauty yours? Due to what is this accomplished by you here and that there should arise whatever pleasures your heart holds dear?
13 I ask you, devī of great majesty, what meritorious deed did you do

when you were human? Due to what is your shining majesty thus and your beauty radiates in all directions?'

She then answered, saying, 'I was the mother of Sāriputta'[26] and so on. The rest has just the meaning stated.

Then the venerable Mahāmoggallāna raised the issue with the Lord. The Lord took the matter as an arisen need and taught Dhamma to the company assembled there. That teaching was of benefit to those people.

[1] So Be for text's Se Sāriputtattherassa Mātu-.

[2] Reading -kapaṇaddhika- with Se Be for text's -kapaniddhika-.

[3] Reading yathārahaṃ with Se Be for text's yathā rahaṃ.

[4] Reading pādodakapādabbhañjanādidānānupubbakaṃ sabbābhideyyaṃ with Be (≏ Se) for text's pādodakapādabbhañjanādidānaṃ anupubbakaṃ sabbapātheyyaṃ.

[5] Reading paṭissuṇitvā with Se Be for text's paṭisuṇitvā.

[6] Reading chaḍḍitaṃ with Se Be for text's chaḍḍhitaṃ.

[7] This vihāra was presumably in the forest haunt in which he was earlier said to be staying.

[8] caṅkamanakoṭiyam, a long strip of ground on which one walks up and down when developing mindfulness; cp also GS iii 21 n. 2.

[9] Reading pasūnaṃ with Se Be for text's pasunaṃ.

[10] Reading anagārā with Se Be for text's anagarā.

[11] Reading vantan ti with Se Be for text's vantan ii.

[12] silesuma is the diaeretic form of the contraction semha; cp PED sv silesuma.

[13] Text wrongly begins a new sentence here.

[14] Reading aññañ ca with Se Be for text's aññañ.

[15] Cp II 13[12], PvA 166 and AV XI 2 9.

[16] Reading chaḍḍitamalamañcasayanā with Se Be for text's chaḍḍitamalā mañcasayanā.

[17] Reading mayhaṃ upakappati tathā uddisa pattidānaṃ dehi with Se Be for text's mayhaṃ uddissa paṭidānaṃ dehi.

[18] antepure, sometimes harem but here apparently the various craftsmen in his palace or city.

[19] Adopting the text's vl paṭicchādesi for all texts' paṭicchāpesi.

[20] balikaraṇaṃ; a fivefold offering on behalf of relatives, guests, petas, the king and the devatās can be found at A ii 68 (cp A iii 45).

[21] parikkhāre; various lists are to be found, the earliest of which being probably that of four, viz. robe, almsfood, bed and seat, and medicines, commonly encountered throughout this text. Cp PED sv.

[22] Things may be donated to monks in either of two ways, either to an individual monk for his own use or to a monk (or monks) on behalf of the whole Saṅgha. In the latter case what is given then becomes saṅghika or the property of the Saṅgha and cannot be disposed of by individual monks. When a monk wishes to make a presentation of some item to a visiting layman he normally does so stating at the same time that it is not saṅghika, implying thereby that it is his own property to be disposed of as he wishes. See Vin i 250 where these two methods are clearly distinguished and cp also II 3[25], III 2[10, 14]. See also S. Dutt, *Early Buddhist Monachism*, 1960, pp. 67ff. The merit earned by a gift to the order of monks of the four quarters might be expected to surpass that earned by a gift to an individual monk, even were the latter an arahant. However on the basis of the principle laid down at M i 236f. it would seem that the merit earned by Bimbisāra would have been that of a gift to the individual

Sāriputta alone, whilst that earned by Sāriputta (and assigned to the petī) was that earned by this subsequent gift to the order of the four quarters and thus considerably greater.

[23] The personal name of Sāriputta (M i 150) and, according to some accounts, the name of his village.

[24] catasso kuṭiyo katvā, presumably by persuading the king to do this on his behalf as the story above suggests; the cty below is silent.

[25] The personal name of Mahāmoggallāna after his village of the same name. This verse is to be found in Se and Be as well as our text and Gehman's note that it 'is only in the Burmese MS., Phayre Collection' should perhaps be deleted.

[26] The wording here strongly suggests that there were originally further verses in answer to the questions posed in vv 12–13. Whilst neither our text, Se nor Be contains these, two MSS. later consulted by Hardy add a further verse:

Through that gift of Sāriputta I enjoy myself, having nothing to fear from any quarter. I, sir, have come to salute the compassionate sage for the world.
(Sāriputtassa dānena modāmi akutobhayā muniṃ kāruṇikaṃ loke taṃ bhaddante vanditum āgatā ti)

and one of these MSS. apparently inserted after v 13 and before this additional verse a repetition of vv 2–5 above but with the exception that the 'I was your own mother' (ahan te sakiyā mātā) of v 2 is now replaced by 'She was the mother of Sāriputta' (Sāriputtassa sā mātā) which closely resembles the 'I was the mother of Sāriputta' (Sāriputtass' āhaṃ mātā) seemingly quoted here by Dhammapāla (see JPTS 1904–5 p. 149 and Pv).

II.3 EXPOSITION OF THE MATTĀ PETĪ STORY
[Mattāpetivatthuvaṇṇanā]

'Naked and of hideous appearance are you.' This was said when the Teacher was staying in the Jeta Grove concerning a petī named Mattā.

It is said that in Sāvatthī there was a certain man of property who had faith and devotion. His wife, who was known by the name of Mattā, had neither faith nor devotion and was of an angry disposition and barren. Now that man of property, out of fear that the family line would be cut off, took a bride named Tissā from a similar clan. She had faith and devotion and was dear and charming to her husband. She became pregnant before long and after ten months gave birth to a son. His name was Bhūta. She became mistress of the house and supported four monks with due care. The barren (wife) became jealous[1] of her. One day they both bathed their heads and were standing with wet hair. The man of property was in love with Tissā on account of her qualities and would often stand talking with her with a solemn heart. Being unable to bear this and overcome with envy Mattā swept the house and poured the rubbish she had collected over Tissā's head. She died in due course and arose in the peta-womb undergoing, through the power of her deeds, a misery that was fivefold. This [83] misery is made known by the text. Then one day as evening[2] wore on she revealed herself to Tissā who was bathing at the back of the house. When she saw her Tissā questioned her with this verse:

1 'Naked and of hideous appearance are you, emaciated and with prominent veins. You thin one, with your ribs standing out, now who are you, you who are stood here?'

The other spoke in reply with this verse:

2 'I am Mattā, you are Tissā. I was your co-wife in the past. Having done a wicked deed I have gone from here to the world of the petas.'

2 Herein *I am Mattā, you are Tissā (ahaṃ Mattā tuvaṃ Tissā)*: you are named Tissā whilst I am named[3] Mattā. *In the past (pure)*:[4] in my previous existence. *I was: ahuṃ=ahosiṃ your: te*[5]*=tuyhaṃ* (alternative grammatical forms) co-wife.

Tissā questioned her once more about the deed she had done with this verse:

3 'Now what evil deed was done by you by body, speech or mind? As a result of which deed have you gone from here to the world of the petas?'

The other then explained the deed she had done with this verse:

4 'I was quick-tempered and harsh, I was envious, mean and crafty. Having said ill words of you I have gone from here to the world of the petas.'

4 Herein *quick-tempered (caṇḍī)*: of an angry disposition. *Harsh (pharusā)*: harsh spoken. *I was: āsiṃ=ahosiṃ* (alternative grammatical form). *Of you I: tāhaṃ=taṃ ahaṃ* (resolution of compound). *Ill words (duruttaṃ)*: ill speech, useless talk.

From here onwards they continued to exchange conversation with these verses:

5 'I, too, know all this, how quick-tempered you were; but there is something else that I would ask you: why are you covered with dust?'

6 'You had bathed your head and were clean clothed and adorned; yet I was still more so, even more adorned than you.

7 Whilst I looked on you conversed[6] with our husband whereupon you caused intense envy and anger to be born in me.

8 [84] At this I took some dust and poured that dust over you. It is as a result of that deed that I am covered with dust.'

9 'I, too, know all this, (how) you poured dust over me; but there is something else that I would ask you: why are you eaten up with the itch?'

10 'We both went to the edge of the forest to fetch medicinal herbs. You brought back medicinal herbs whilst I the kapikacchu.[7]

11 Then without your knowing it I scattered them over your bed. It is as a result of that deed that I am eaten up with the itch.'

12 'I, too, know all this, (how) you scattered them over my bed; but there is something else that I would ask you: why are you in the nude?'

13 'There was an assembly of companions, a coming together[8] of relatives took place; and you were asked along with our husband but I not.

14 Then without your knowing it I removed your clothes. It is as a result of that deed that I am in the nude.'

15 'I, too, know all this, (how) you removed my clothes; but there is something else that I would ask you: why do you smell of excrement?'

16 'I threw your scents and garlands and costly ointments into the latrine – that wicked deed was done by me. It is as a result of that deed that I smell of excrement.'

17 'I, too, know all this, (how) that wicked deed was done by you; but there is something else that I would ask you: why do you have a miserable existence?'

18 'Whatever wealth was to be found in our house belonged to both of us equally – yet though merit-offerings were at hand I made no refuge for myself. It is as a result of that deed that I have a miserable existence.

19 Even then you spoke to me, saying, "You are pursuing wicked deeds; surely it is not by wicked deeds that a happy state is easily attained".'

20 'You approached me from the wrong side[9] and what is more you were jealous of me too. Behold what sort of result there is from wicked deeds.

21 [85] You had house, servants and these ornaments. These are now enjoyed[10] by others – possessions are not everlasting.

22 Bhūta's father is now coming home from the market. Maybe he will give you something. Do not go from here till then.'

23 'Naked and of hideous appearance am I, emaciated and with prominent

veins. This is shameful for women. Do not let Bhūta's father see me.'

24 'Well what can I give you or what can I do for you by which you might be happy and richly endowed with all you desire?'

25 'Four monks as of the order and four as individuals[11] – please feed these eight monks and assign that donation to me; then I will be happy and richly endowed with all I desire.'

26 'Very well', she consented. She fed eight monks, clad them in clothes and assigned that donation to her.

27 Immediately she dedicated this the result came into being, food, clothing and drink being the fruit of this donation.

28 Thereupon she became pure, clad in fresh, clean clothes, wearing those more fine than those of Kāsi and, bedecked in various clothes and ornaments, she approached her co-wife.

29 'You who stand with surpassing beauty, devatā, lighting up all directions like the Healing Star,

30 Due to what is such beauty yours? Due to what is this accomplished by you here and that there should arise whatever pleasures your heart holds dear?

31 I ask you, devī of great majesty, what meritorious deed did you do when you were human? Due to what is your shining majesty thus and your beauty radiates in all directions?'

32 'I am Mattā, you are Tissā. I was your co-wife in the past. Having done a wicked deed I have gone from here to the world of the petas; but now, through the gift given by you, I enjoy myself, having nothing to fear from any quarter.

33 May you live long, my sister, with all your relatives (and may you attain) the abode of the Vasavattis, the place that is free of sorrow and pollution.

34 Behave here in accordance with the Dhamma and give gifts, my pretty one; remove the stain of selfishness together with its root and go blameless to the heavenly place.'

5 [86] Herein *I, too, know all this, how quick-tempered you were (sabbaṃ aham pi jānāmi yathā tvaṃ caṇḍikā ahu)*: this 'I was quick-tempered and harsh' that you said, I, too, know all this – how you were quick-tempered, of an angry disposition, harsh spoken, envious, mean and crafty. *But there is something else that I would ask you (aññañ ca kho taṃ pucchāmi)*: but now there is something else that I would ask you. *Why are you covered with dust? (kenāsi paṃsuguṇṭhitā)*: due to what deed are you covered with dust and rubbish, meaning (due to what deed) have (dust and rubbish) been poured all over your body?

6 *You had bathed your head (sīsaṃ nahātā)*: you had bathed from the head down. *Still more so (adhimattaṃ)*: more excessively. *Even more adorned (samalaṅkatarā)*: thoroughly and most exquisitely adorned. An alternative reading is *exceedingly (adhimattā)*: extremely drunk, drunk with conceit and pride, meaning riddled with conceit. *Than you (tayā)*: than you, my dear.

7 *You conversed with our husband (sāmikena samantayi)*: you spoke with our husband, talking to one another.

9 *Eaten up with the itch (khajjāsi kacchuyā)*: devoured by scabies,[12] meaning afflicted (therewith).

10 *To fetch medicinal herbs: bhesajjahārī=bhesajjahāriniyo* (alternative grammatical form); fetching medicines.[13] *We both (ubhayo)*: we two, meaning you and I. *To the edge of the forest (vanantaṃ)*: to the forest. *You brought back medicinal herbs (tvañ ca bhesajjaṃ āhari)*: you brought back medicinal herbs that would be good for you, as prescribed by the physicians. *Whilst I the kapikacchu (ahañ ca kapikacchuno)*: whereas I brought back kapikacchu fruits, fruits that are unpleasant to touch. The kapikacchu is alternatively called 'sayaṃ guttā',[14] in which case it means I brought back sayaṃ guttā leaves and fruits.

11 *I scattered them over your bed (seyyaṃ ty āhaṃ samokiriṃ)*: I scattered your bed all over with kapikacchu fruits and leaves.

13 *Of companions (sahāyānaṃ)*: of friends. *An assembly (samayo)*: a meeting. *Of relatives (ñātīnaṃ)*: of kinsmen. *A coming together (samitī)*: a gathering. *Asked (āmantitā)*: invited to a festivity. *Along with our husband (sasāminī)*: along with our lord, meaning along with the one who supports us. *But I not (no ca kho 'haṃ)*: but I was not asked – this is how it should be construed.

14 *I . . . your clothes: dussaṃ ty āhaṃ=dussaṃ te ahaṃ* (resolution of compound). *Removed (apānudiṃ)*: seized, took away by stealing.

16 [87] *Costly (paccagghaṃ)*: fresh, or very costly. *I threw (athāresiṃ)*: I cast. *Smell of excrement (gūthagandhinī)*: smell with the odour of excrement, emit the smell of faeces.

18 *Whatever wealth was to be found in our house (yaṃ gehe vijjite dhanaṃ)*: whatever wealth was received in our house belonged to us both as relatives, to you and to me, equally and evenly. *Were at hand (santesu)*: were known. *Refuge (dīpaṃ)*: support; she speaks with reference to meritorious deeds.

19 When that petī had explained the points on which she had been questioned by Tissā, she spoke once more, saying, 'Even then you (spoke) to me' and so on, confessing the guilt she felt at not having formerly heeded her words. Herein *even then (tad eva)*: even[15] then, at that same

time that I remained in my existence as a human. An alternative reading is 'in the very manner' (*tath' eva*), meaning that which has now come about has done so in the very manner (in which you spoke to me). *To me (maṃ)*: she refers to herself. *You (tvaṃ)*: Tissā. *Spoke (avaca)*: told. '(You are pursuing) wicked deeds' and so on was said to show the manner in which she spoke. The text has 'wicked deeds'. You are performing only wicked deeds but a happy state is not easily attained by wicked deeds – rather it is a state of misery that is easily attained (thereby). She says that it (has now come about) in the very manner in which she had formerly spoken exhorting her.

When she heard this, Tissā uttered the three verses beginning, 'You approached me from the wrong side':

20 Herein *you approached me from the wrong side (vāmato maṃ tvaṃ paccesi)*: you had a wrong opinion of me – though I desired your welfare you took me to be acting hostilely. *You were jealous of me: maṃ usuyyasi= mayhaṃ usuyyasi* (alternative grammatical form); you envied me. *Behold what sort of result there is from wicked deeds (passa pāpānaṃ kammānaṃ vipāko hoti yādiso)*: she says, 'Behold for yourself what sort of result there is from wicked deeds and how very terrible it is.'

21 *These are now enjoyed by others (te aññe paricārenti)*: these houses, servants and these ornaments that were formerly possessed by you are now enjoyed, made use of, by others. *These (ime)* is given with a distortion of gender.[16] *Possessions are not everlasting (na bhogā honti sassatā)*: these possessions are indeed not everlasting, are not stable, (enduring only) as long as one's time (in a given existence) and have to be left behind when going (on to a new existence).[17] Therefore on this account envy and selfishness should not be entertained – this is the meaning.

22 [88] *Bhūta's father is now (idāni Bhūtassa pitā)*: Bhūta's, my son's, father, the man of property, is now. *From the market: āpaṇā=āpaṇato* (alternative grammatical form); coming, returning, to this home. *Maybe he will give you something (app' eva te dade kiñci)*: when the man of property has come home he may well give you something fit to be given as a merit-offering. *Do not go from here till then (mā su tāva ito agā)*: she says out of compassion, 'Do not go from here, from this yard at the back of the house, until then.'

23 When she heard this, the petī uttered the verse (beginning:) 'Naked and of hideous appearance am I', making known how she felt disposed. Herein *this is shameful for women (kopīnam etam itthīnaṃ)*: this nakedness and hideousness and so on that is shameful[18] for women must be kept apart[19] due to its need to be covered. *Do not let Bhūta's father see me (mā maṃ Bhūtapitāddasa)*: 'Therefore do not let Bhūta's father, that man of property, see me', she says shamefully.

24 When she heard this Tissā was filled with (a desire to) help and uttered the verse (beginning:) 'Well what can I give you.' Herein *well (handa)* is a particle put in metri causā. What can I give you?: *kin t'āhaṃ dammi=kin te ahaṃ dammi* (resolution of compound); shall I give you clothes or food? *Or what can I do for you? (kiṃ vā ca te karom' ahaṃ)*: or what other service can I do for you here at this time?

25 When she heard this, the petī uttered the verse (beginning:) 'Four monks as of the order.' Herein *four monks as of the order and four as individuals (cattāro bhikkhū saṅghato cattāro pana puggale)*: four monks from the order of monks[20] representing the Saṅgha and four monks as individuals – please feed eight such monks to their satisfaction and assign that donation to me, please give for me a gift that is assigned. *Then I will be happy (tadāhaṃ sukhitā hessaṃ)* means that when you have dedicated[21] that donation to me I will then be happy, will attain happiness, and be richly endowed with all I desire.

When she heard this, Tissā informed her husband of the matter and on the following day he fed eight monks and assigned the donation to her. She straightaway attained heavenly excellence and once more approached Tissā. To illustrate this point those rehearsing the texts inserted the three verses beginning: ' "Very well", she consented.' As she stood there after approaching, Tissā questioned her[22] with the three verses that begin: '(You who stand) with surpassing beauty.' **[89]** The other disclosed her identity with the verse (beginning:) 'I am Mattā' and showed her appreciation with the verse (beginning:) 'May you live long', thereafter exhorting her with the verse (beginning:) 'Behave here in accordance with the Dhamma.'

32 Herein *given by you: tava dinnena=tayā dinnena* (alternative grammatical form).

33 *The place that is free of sorrow and pollution (asokaṃ virajaṃ ṭhānaṃ)*: the heavenly place that is free of sorrow due to the absence of sorrow and that is free of pollution due to the absence of sweat and dirt – she says all this with reference to the devaloka. *The abode (āvāsaṃ)*: the place.[23] *Of the Vasavattis (Vasavattinaṃ)*: of those exercising (*vattentānaṃ*) their power (*vasaṃ*) with heavenly supremacy.[24]

34 *Together with its root (samūlaṃ)*: together with the blemish of greed, for the blemish of greed is indeed the root of selfishness. *Blameless (aninditā)*: without reproach, praiseworthy. *Go to the heavenly place (saggam upehi ṭhānaṃ)*: may you go to the heavenly place, meaning may you be one destined to a happy state that is called 'heavenly' (*saggaṃ*)[25] as it is supreme (*suṭṭhu-aggattā*) in its range of sense objects such as those that are visible and so on. The rest is quite self-evident.[26]

Tissā then raised the issue with that man of property. The man of property raised it with the monks and the monks raised it with the Lord. The Lord took the matter as an arisen need and taught Dhamma to the company assembled there. When they heard this those people, having received this agitation, removed the stain of selfishness and so on and became given to the virtue of giving and so forth and were those destined to a happy state.

[1] Reading usūyati with Se Be for text's dussayati.

[2] Reading sañjhāya with Be (Se saṃjjhāya) for text's saññāya.

[3] Reading Mattā nāma with Se Be for text's Mattā.

[4] Reading pure ti with Se Be for text's pure.

[5] Reading te ti with Se Be for text's te.

[6] Reading samantayi with Se Be for text's āmantayi.

[7] Mucuna pruritus.

[8] Reading samitī with Se Be for text's samitiṃ.

[9] vāmato, literally from the left. Compare the auspicious practice of circumambulation by the right e.g. PvA 74 above.

[10] Reading paricārenti with Se Be for text's parivārenti.

[11] Cp PvA 81.

[12] kacchurogena, literally by the kacchu- or itching-disease.

[13] osadhī – cp PvA 71 above.

[14] Literally self-protected – in virtue of its unpleasant nature. Be reads sayaṃ bhūtā throughout which would mean self-grown or self-dependent.

[15] Reading eva with Se Be for text's evaṃ.

[16] It should be neuter nominative plural, imāni, agreeing with tān'evābharaṇāni, and not ime, masculine, as in the verse.

[17] Cp PvA 175 below. This is perhaps a somewhat unusual statement of impermanence in that it is here the impermanence of the possessor that renders the objects possessed impermanent rather than any inherent quality in those objects themselves.

[18] kopīnaṃ, literally the pudenda and by extension both what is shameful (cp Latin pudere, be ashamed) and also loincloth. See also PvA 172 below. Gehman's 'Here is my loincloth' is hardly correct. This sense of kopīnaṃ is given by Childers but is not listed in PED.

[19] Reading rundhanīyaṃ with Se Be for text's rundhamānaṃ.

[20] Reading bhikkhusaṅghato with Se Be for text's bhikkhū saṅghato.

[21] Reading mama uddisissasi with Se Be for text's mamādisissasi.

[22] Reading pana naṃ with Se Be for text's pattaṃ.

[23] ṭhānaṃ – so Be for text's adiṭṭhānaṃ; Se reads adhiṭṭhānaṭṭhānaṃ, fixed place, here. Cp PED sv adhiṭṭhāna.

[24] Reading ādhipateyyena with Se Be for text's adhi-.

[25] Reading saggaṃ with Se Be for text's sagaṃ; cp the similar etymology at PvA 9 above.

[26] Reading uttānaṃ with Se Be for text's vuttānaṃ.

II.4 EXPOSITION OF THE NANDĀ PETA STORY
[Nandāpetavatthuvaṇṇanā]

'Dark and of hideous appearance are you.' This was said when the Teacher was staying in the Jeta Grove concerning a petī named Nandā.

It is said that in a certain village not far from Sāvatthī there was a lay-follower named Nandasena who had faith and devotion. However his wife, who was named Nandā, had neither faith nor devotion and was mean, quick-tempered and harsh spoken; she lacked reverence for, and was disobedient to, her husband and insulted and abused her mother-in-law with a voice (as loud as) a kettle-drum. She died in due course and arose in the peta-womb staying not far from that same village **[90]** and one day revealed herself not far from the layfollower Nandasena as he was leaving that village. When he saw her he addressed her with this verse:

1 'Dark and of hideous appearance are you, harsh and horrible to behold. You are red(-eyed) and have long, protruding (teeth). I do not think you can be human.'

1 Herein *dark (kāḷī)*: of dark complexion; she was similar to burnt cinders in complexion. *Harsh (pharusā)*: rough. *Horrible to behold (bhīrudassanā)*: terrible to behold, frightening. An alternative reading is *bhārudassanā,*[1] grave-looking,[2] meaning unsightly[3] due to her hideousness and so on. *Red (piṅgalā)*: red-eyed. *Long, protruding (kaḷārā)*: long, protruding teeth. *I do not think you can be human (na taṃ maññāmi mānusiṃ)*: I do not think you are human, I think you are just a petī[4] – this is the meaning.

When she heard this, the petī uttered this verse explaining who she was:

2 'I am Nandā, Nandasena, I was your wife in the past. Having done a wicked deed I have gone from here to the world of the petas.'

2 Herein *I am Nandā, Nandasena (ahaṃ Nandā Nandasena)*: my lord[5] Nandasena, I am named Nandā. *I was your wife in the past (bhariyā te pure ahuṃ)*: I was[6] your wife in my previous birth.

After this is the layfollower's question:

3 'Now what evil deed was done by you by body, speech or mind? As a result of which deed have you gone from here to the world of the petas?'

She then answered him, saying:

4 'I was[7] quick-tempered and harsh and I also lacked reverence for

you. Having said ill words of you I have gone from here to the world of the petas.'

He spoke once more:

5 'Here, I will give you my cloak: put on this garment. When you have put on this garment then come and I will take you to the house.

6 [91] Clothes, food and drink shall you obtain when you have gone to the house. And you will behold your sons and see your daughters-in-law.'[8]

She then spoke these two verses to him:

7-8 'What is given by your hand into my hand is of no benefit to me. But please satisfy with food and drink monks who are endowed with virtue, free of lust and who have heard much[9] and assign that donation to me – then I will be happy and richly endowed with all I desire.'

These three verses were said by those rehearsing the texts:

9 ' "Very well", he consented and dispensed abundant alms – food, drink, hard food, clothing[10] and lodging, sunshades and scents and garlands and various sorts of sandals – to monks who were endowed with virtue, free of lust and who had heard much. Having satisfied them with food and drink he assigned the donation to her.

10 Immediately he dedicated this the result came into being, food, clothing and drink being the fruit of this donation.

11 Thereupon she became pure, clad in fresh, clean clothes, wearing those more fine than those of Kāsi and, bedecked in various clothes and ornaments, she approached her husband.'

From here onwards are the verses of the exchange of conversation between the layfollower and the petī:

12 'You who stand with surpassing beauty, devatā, lighting up all directions like the Healing Star,

13 Due to what is such beauty yours? Due to what is this accomplished by you here and that there should arise whatever pleasures your heart holds dear?

14 I ask you, devī of great majesty, what meritorious deed did you do when you were human? Due to what is your shining majesty thus[11] and your beauty radiates in all directions?'

15 'I am Nandā, Nandasena, I was your wife in the past. Having done a wicked deed I have gone from here to the world of the petas; but

now, through the gift given by you, I enjoy myself, having nothing to fear from any quarter.

16 May you live long, householder, with all your relatives, [92] (and may you attain) the abode of the Vasavattis, the place that is free of sorrow and pollution.

17 Behave here in accordance with the Dhamma and give gifts, householder; remove the stain of selfishness, together with its root, and go blameless to the heavenly place.'

9 Herein *dispensed abundant alms (dānaṃ vipulam ākiri)*: inaugurated a great almsgiving as though strewing merit-offering seeds on the field of those worthy of donations.

The rest is just the same as in the immediately preceding story.

When she had thus explained to Nandasena her heavenly excellence and the reason for it she went to her own dwelling. The layfollower raised the issue with the monks and the monks raised it with the Lord. The Lord took the matter as an arisen need and taught Dhamma to the company assembled there. That teaching was of benefit to those people.

[1] So Be; text merely repeats bhīrudassanā; Se reads bhīrudassakā. Cp PvA 142 below.
[2] Reading bhāriyadassanā with Se Be for text's bhariya-.
[3] Reading duddasikā with Se Be for text's duddassikā.
[4] Reading petiṃ eva ca taṃ with Se Be for text's petivacanaṃ.
[5] Reading sāmi with Se Be for text's sami.
[6] Reading ahosiṃ with Se Be for text's ahosi.
[7] Reading c'āsiṃ with Se Be for text's c'āsi.
[8] Reading suṇisāyo with Se Be for text's sūtisāye.
[9] bahussute, the equivalent of being 'well read' in a community in which teachings were passed on orally.
[10] Reading vatthasenāsanāni with Se Be for text's vutthaṃ senā-.
[11] Reading evañjalitānubhāvā with Se Be for text's -bhavā.

II.5 EXPOSITION OF THE MAṬṬAKUṆḌALIN PETA STORY
[Maṭṭakuṇḍalipetavatthuvaṇṇanā]

'Adorned, wearing polished earrings.' This was said when the Teacher was staying in the Jeta Grove concerning the devaputta Maṭṭakuṇḍalin.[1] Herein whatever was to be said is exactly as given in the Exposition of the Maṭṭakuṇḍalin Mansion Story in the Exposition of the Mansion

Stories[2] (section) of this Elucidation of the Intrinsic Meaning and should therefore be understood just as already given there.

In this case it is the story of the devaputta Maṭṭakuṇḍalin from when he became a vimāna-devatā onwards.[3] (His father) the brahmin Adinnapubbaka had gone to the cemetery through grief for (the loss of) his son and was wandering around his funeral-pyre weeping when (his son) the devaputta, with the purpose of dispelling[4] his grief, abandoned his deva-form and revealed himself as a peta that was overcome with misery and, with arms clasped (in sorrow) was wailing, 'Ah, moon! Ah, sun!'[5] Even though it was included in the text of the Mansion Stories his story is to be regarded as also included in the text of the Peta Stories for the reason that anyone who has left the human state may be referred to by the designation 'peta'.[6]

[1] The name means 'polished earrings'.
[2] VvA 322–330.
[3] See Stories of the Mansions pp. 144–147.
[4] Reading sokaharaṇatthaṃ with Be for text's sokāvahar- (Se sokāpahar-).
[5] Se Be read haricandanussado, with an application of yellow sandalwood (on the skin), here. Though he is so described at Vv 83[1] he is also said in the introductory story immediately preceding this verse to be crying out 'Ah, moon! Ah, sun!' The reading of our text seems preferable given the way in which the story develops, since Maṭṭakuṇḍalin pretends to be seeking the moon and the sun as wheels for his chariot. In lamenting not being able to obtain them he is at least seeking what can be seen and Adinnapubbaka thereupon realises his own foolishness in seeking what can no longer be seen, that is, his dead son. See also the following Peta Story.
[6] manussattabhāvato apetattā petapariyāyo pi labbhati eva. It would seem that 'peta' here can mean nothing more than 'departed' yet such an explanation would surely allow the inclusion of any story concerning a deceased person which can hardly be Dhammapāla's intention. Rather it might be supposed that this story had been included since Maṭṭakuṇḍalin is said to have assumed the form of a peta. Curiously this is not mentioned in the VvA version where Maṭṭakuṇḍalin appears instead as a brahmin youth, adorned, wearing polished earrings and so on and owning a golden chariot.

II.6 EXPOSITION OF THE KAṆHA PETA STORY
[Kaṇhapetavatthuvaṇṇanā]

[93] 'Arise, Kaṇha, why are you lying down?' The Teacher who was staying in the Jeta Grove told this concerning a certain layfollower whose son had died.

It is said that in Sāvatthī the son of a certain layfollower had died. Pierced by the dart of grief he would not bathe, eat, go about his business nor go and wait upon the Buddha. He would only talk in a confused manner, saying, 'Where are you, my dear young son? Where have you gone so soon, forsaking me?' and so on. The Teacher, who was surveying the world towards dawn, saw his potential for realising the sotāpatti-fruit and on the following day went to Sāvatthī in search of alms, surrounded by the order of monks. When he had finished his meal, he dismissed the monks and went with his attendant, the elder Ānanda, to the door of his house. The servants informed the layfollower of the Teacher's arrival and then had the Teacher be seated on the seat they had prepared. Then they looked for the layfollower and led him into the Teacher's presence. When he saw him seated at one side, he asked, 'What, are you in mourning, layfollower?' When he said, 'Yes, Lord', he said, 'Layfollower, the wise men of old heard a tale from the wise men and did not bewail a son who had died',* and, when begged by him, recounted (that tale) of long ago.

It is said that long ago in the city of Dvāravatī there were ten royal brothers – Vāsudeva, Baladeva, Candadeva, Suriyadeva, Aggideva, Varuṇadeva, Ajjuna, Pajjuna, Ghaṭapaṇḍita and Aṅkura. Of these, the son dear to the great king Vāsudeva died. The King was overwhelmed by grief at this; he neglected all his obligations, made the añjali salutation to his bed[1] and then lay down talking in a confused manner. At that time Ghaṭapaṇḍita thought, 'Except for me, there is no one who can dispel my brother's grief. I shall dispel his grief by means of a trick.'[2] So he assumed the appearance of a madman and, gazing up at the sky, roamed through the entire city, saying, 'Give me the hare![3] Give me the hare!', and the entire city was shaken with the news that Ghaṭapaṇḍita had gone mad. At that time the (king's) special adviser, named Rohiṇeyya, went to king Vāsudeva [94] and uttered this verse, beginning conversation with the king:

1 'Arise, Kaṇha, why are you lying down? What good does dreaming do you?[4] He who is your own brother, your heart and your right eye, has been overpowered by the winds[5] – he is yearning for the hare,[6] Kesava!'

1 Herein *Kaṇha (Kaṇha)*: he addresses Vāsudeva with his family name. *What good does dreaming do you? (ko attho supinena te)*: what profit indeed is there for you in dreaming? *Own brother (sako bhātā)*: brother by the same mother. *Your heart and your right eye (hadayaṃ cakkhuñ ca dakkhiṇaṃ)* means who is just like your heart and your right eye. *Has been overpowered by the winds (tassa vātā balīyanti)*: the winds of insanity

*J iii 155.

continuously arising in him have strengthened, increased and overpowered him. *He is yearning (jappati)*: he is talking in a confused manner, saying, 'Give me the hare!' *Kesava (Kesava)*: it is said he was called 'Kesava' on account of his beautiful hair; he is addressing him with this name.

The Teacher, the one who had become a Perfect Buddha, then uttered this verse elucidating how he arose from his bed when he heard these words:

2 'When he heard Rohiṇeyya's words, Kesava hastily arose, stricken with grief for his brother.'

The king arose and quickly descended from the palace and then went into Ghaṭapaṇḍita's presence, seized him firmly with both hands and, talking with him, spoke these three verses:

3 'Why do you, like a madman, mutter, "Hare, hare!" about this whole Dvāraka? What kind of hare do you want?

4 One made of gold? One made of jewels? One made of copper? One made of silver even? Or one made from precious stones? (No matter,) I will have that hare made for you.

5 There are also other little hares that roam the woods and forest – I will bring you these too. What kind of hare do you want?'

3 [95] Herein *like a madman (ummattarūpo)*: as one who is mad. *Whole (kevalaṃ)*: entire. *Dvāraka (Dvārakaṃ)*: roaming about this city of Dvāravatī. *Mutter, 'Hare, hare!' (saso saso ti lapasi)*: mumble, 'Hare, hare!'
4 *One made of gold: sovaṇṇamayaṃ=suvaṇṇamayaṃ* (alternative grammatical form). *One made of copper (lohamayaṃ)*: one made of bronze. *One made of silver (rūpiyamayaṃ)*: one made of silver coin.
5 He coaxed Ghaṭapaṇḍita with a hare with the intention (of discovering) his need for a hare, saying, 'Say what it is that you want. Why grieve? There are also other little hares that roam the woods in the forest – I will bring you these, if you will just say, my honourable friend,[7] what kind of hare you want.'

When he heard this Ghaṭapaṇḍita uttered this verse:

6 'I do not want those hares, hares that inhabit the earth. I want the hare from the moon. Bring that one down for me, Kesava!'

6 Herein *bring down: ohara=ohārehi* (alternative grammatical form).

When the king heard this he became dejected, thinking, 'Without doubt my brother has become as one who is mad', and uttered this verse:

7 'Now,[8] my relative, you will surely throw away your sweet life. You

long for what should not be longed for[9] when you want the hare from the moon.'

7 Herein *my relative (ñāti)*: he addresses his younger brother. Now this is the meaning here: 'My dear relative, I think that you will throw away your extremely sweet life if you long for what should not be longed for.'

When Ghaṭapaṇḍita heard what the king had to say, he stood there motionless, saying, 'Brother, knowing as you do that there will be a loss of life for one who, longing for the hare from the moon, does not obtain it, why do you bewail a son who has died[10] whom you cannot obtain?', and uttered this verse elucidating this point:

8 **[96]** 'If you, Kaṇha, thus know the manner in which you advise others, then why do you, even today,[11] bewail a son who died in the past?'

8 Herein *if you, Kaṇha, thus know (evañ ce Kaṇha jānāsi)*: if you thus know, my brother, great king Kaṇha, that a thing that is unobtainable is indeed not to be longed for. *The manner in which (you advise) others (yath' aññaṃ)*: and (though) knowing this, yet you do not act in the manner in which you advise others. *Why (do you bewail) a son who died in the past? (kasma pure mataṃ puttaṃ)* means then why do you, even today, bewail a son who died more than four months since? Thus, whilst standing in the middle of the road, he said, 'At least I only long for what can be seen, whereas you grieve for the sake of one who can be seen no longer', and then uttered two verses teaching him Dhamma:

9 'But this cannot be obtained, either by human or non-human, that "A son born to me should not die." Whence can that which is not to be obtained be obtained?

10 Neither by a mantra, by the root of a medicinal herb, by medicines, nor by wealth is it possible to bring back the peta that you bewail, Kaṇha.'

9 Herein *that (yaṃ)* means but this that you long for; that 'A son born to me should not die', cannot be obtained, it is not possible to obtain this, either by human or deva, my brother. So whence might this be obtained, by what means would it be possible to obtain this, since this thing that is unobtainable is not to be obtained.

10 *By a mantra (mantā)*: by means of a mantra. *By the root of a medicinal herb: mūlabhesajjā=mūlabhesajjena* (alternative grammatical form). *By medicines (osadhehi)*: by various kinds of medicines. *Nor by wealth (dhanena vā)*: nor even by wealth amounting to a hundred koṭis. This is

what is said: 'It is not possible to bring back, by means of these mantras and so on, the peta that you bewail.'

Then showing his brother that it is not possible to prevent this (thing) called death, either by wealth or birth or knowledge, morality or meditation,[12] Ghaṭapaṇḍita [97] taught the king Dhamma with these five verses:

11 'Those of great wealth, great possessions, even kṣatriyas possessing kingdoms – even these, abounding in riches and grain, are not free of old age and death.

12 Kṣatriyas, brahmins, vaiśyas, śūdras, caṇḍālas and pukkusas – even these and others are not, through their birth, free of old age and death.

13 Those who recite the mantras of the sixfold lore devised by Brahmā – even these and others are not, through that knowledge, free of old age and death.

14 And rishis even, those ascetics who are tranquil and who have the self controlled – even these ascetics must take leave of this body when the time comes.

15 The arahants,[13] those with self developed, who have done what had to be done and are āsava-free – (even) they have to lay down this body upon exhaustion of their meritorious and wicked deeds.'

11 Herein *those of great wealth (mahaddhanā)*: extremely wealthy on account of the great wealth they have hoarded. *Those of great possessions (mahābhogā)*: endowed with great excellence of possessions similar to the possessions of the devas. *Possessing kingdoms (raṭṭhavanto)*: possessing entire kingdoms. *Abounding in riches and grain (pahūtadhanadhaññāse)*: they have boundless riches and grain on account of the riches and grain they have left over for their daily use after laying down (sufficient) to cover their needs for three or four years. *Even these are not free of old age and death (te pi no ajarāmarā)*: even those kṣatriyas of great prosperity such as Mahāmandhātu[14] and Mahāsudassana[15] and so on were not free of old age and death, meaning they have surely entered into the mouth of death.

12 *These (ete)*: the aforementioned kṣatriyas and so on. *Others (aññe)*: those who belong to the immediately following class such as Ambaṭṭha and so on.[16] *Through their birth (jātiyā)* means they are not free of old age and death on account of their birth.

13 *The mantras (mantaṃ)*: the Vedas. *Recite (parivattenti)*: repeat and intone; or, alternatively, *recite (parivattenti)*: mumble whilst performing the oblations and worshipping (*anuparivattentā*). *Of the sixfold lore (chaḷaṅgaṃ)*: connected with the six branches reckoned as phonetics,

rules prescribing ceremonial and sacrificial ritual, etymology, grammar, astronomy and prosody and so on. *Devised by Brahmā (brahmacintitaṃ)*: devised, spoken, by Brahmā for the sake of the brahmins. [98] *Through that knowledge (vijjāya)* means that they are not free of old age and death even though they are endowed with knowledge similar to that of Brahmā.

14 *Rishis (isayo)*: they are rishis (*isayo*) by reason of their striving after (*esanā*) restraint and self control and so on.[17] *Tranquil (santā)*: of a tranquil nature in body and speech. *Who have the self controlled (saññatattā)*: who have the mind controlled by the restraint of lust and so on.[18] *Ascetics (tapassino)*: they practice austerity (*tapo*) consisting in mortification (*tapana*) of the body. Again *ascetics (tapassino)*: those who are restrained.[19] This shows that though they have become those who rely on austerity in this way and desire to attain release by means of the body (none the less even) those who are restrained[19] and so on must simply take leave of this body. Or, alternatively, *rishis (isayo)*: they are rishis (*isayo*) by reason of their striving after (*esanā*) the higher moral virtues and precepts and so on.[17] In this sense they are tranquil through the cessation of those wicked states that are opposed to it. They have the self controlled by restricting the mind to one object[20] alone. They are ascetics on account of the burning energy they apply to the (four) right efforts.[21] They are ascetics on account of their burning up of lust and so on through right application[22] – this is how it should be construed.

15 *Those with self developed (bhāvitattā)*: those with the mind developed by meditation[23] with the Four (Noble) Truths as a meditation subject.[24]

When he heard this talk on Dhamma by Ghaṭapaṇḍita, the king, relieved of the dart of grief and with devotion in his heart, then spoke the remaining verses in praise of Ghaṭapaṇḍita:

16 'I was truly ablaze, being like a fire fed with ghee; but now all my sorrow has been extinguished as if I had been sprinkled with water.

17 Truly the dart, the grief, that had pierced my heart has been drawn out. You have dispelled that grief, the grief for my son which had overwhelmed me.

18 With dart withdrawn I am become tranquil and cool; since hearing your words I no longer grieve nor weep.

19 Just as Ghaṭa distracted his elder brother from his grief – so act the wise who possess pity.

20 [99] As Ghaṭa followed his elder brother with good advice (so also is) he who has such advisers and attendants (so followed).

19 Herein *just as Ghaṭa (distracted) his elder brother (Ghaṭo jeṭṭhaṃ va*

bhātaraṃ) means just as Ghaṭapaṇḍita by skilful means[25] and with a Dhamma talk distracted his elder brother, who was overcome with grief for his son who had died, from that grief for his son, so also do those other wise people who possess pity act in the service of their relatives.

20 *He who has such (yassa etādisā honti)*: this is a verse from the Perfect Buddha. This is its meaning: just as, in the manner in which, Ghaṭapaṇḍita followed (*anvesi=anudesi*, alternative grammatical form) king Vāsudeva, who was overwhelmed with grief for his son, with good advice with the purpose of dispelling that grief, (so) also is anyone else who has acquired such wise advisers[26] (so followed); how could there be grief for him?

The rest of the verses are of the same meaning[27] as given above.[28]

When the Teacher had recounted this teaching on Dhamma, he said, 'So it was, layfollower, that the wise men of old dispelled their grief for a son when they heard a tale from the wise men. He then explained the (Four Noble) Truths and applied a Jātaka (thereto), at the end of which that layfollower was established in the sotāpatti-fruit.

[1] Be reads aṭaniṃ pariggahetvā, grasped the leg (of the bed).

[2] upāya; cp PvA 20.

[3] sasaṃ, rabbit or hare, which is to be seen – more clearly in the east – on the surface of the moon. See especially the Sasapaṇḍita Jātaka (No. 316) where it is said that Sakka painted the image on the moon as an aeon-long tribute to the virtue of the Bodhisatta when once a hare. It is thus equivalent to our saying, 'Give me the man in the moon!'

[4] Cp S i 198 = Sn 331.

[5] tassa vātā balīyanti, literally, the winds have become strong for him, that is, the winds of the body that can cause discomfort, whether physical or emotional. Compare our own past use of the 'vapours'. Here it seems to mean that he has lost his senses. The verse and episode recur at J iv 84ff.

[6] Reading sasaṃ with Se Be for text's Ghaṭo.

[7] bhaddamukha, literally auspicious-faced; see M ii 53 and KS i 100 n. 3.

[8] Reading nūna with Se Be for text's nanda; see Gehman (39 n. 3) and PED sv nanda.

[9] Reading apatthiyaṃ with Be for text's Se apatthayaṃ; cp PED sv pattheti.

[10] Reading alabhitvā jīvitakkhayo bhavissatī ti jānanto kasmā mataṃ puttaṃ with Se Be for text's alabhitvājīvitakkhayaṃ patto ti jānanto kasmā tava puttaṃ mataṃ.

[11] Reading ajjā 'pi with Se Be for text's ajāpi.

[12] bhāvanāya.

[13] Reading arahanto with Be for text's Se viharantā; vv 11–15 recur at Vv 63[13,15–18].

[14] Probably a reference to king Mandhātā; see Jāt 258 and DPPN ii 444f.

[15] A cakkavattin known for his abundant possessions – see D ii 169ff., Jāt 95 and DPPN ii 575f.

[16] That is, the brahmin class (vaṇṇa), though there is clearly some irony in Dhammapāla's choice of Ambaṭṭha as an example since in the Ambaṭṭha Sutta (D i 87ff.) the Buddha traces Ambaṭṭha's ancestry to union with a slave-girl. See also DPPN i 151f. and 153 where the following appears: 'Nor were the Ambaṭṭhas

brahmins by birth; some of them were farmers and traders and some even sold their daughters for gold' and where a note is added stating that 'they were called "brahmins" by courtesy, vohāravasena. According to the Mānavadhammaśāstra (sic) they were not sprung from kṣatriya father and a slave (presumably śūdra) mother, as given in the Ambaṭṭha Sutta, but from a brahmin father and a Vaiśya mother.' As examples of mixed vaṇṇa they would have been considered inferior, especially to the kṣatriyas whom the Buddha praises for having committed incest in order to maintain purity of the line (D i 92).

[17] Cp PvA 163, 265 for similar.

[18] It is said that Sāriputta makes his 'mind turn according to his wish and turns not by the mind's wish' (A iv 34; cp M i 214f., S v 70ff.).

[19] Reading saṃvarakā with Se Be for text's saṃvarākā.

[20] Reading ekārammaṇe with Se Be for text's ekārammaṇā.

[21] Reading sammappadhāna with Se Be for text's sama-; the sixth rung of the eightfold path – see M iii 251 and A ii 15–17.

[22] sammayogā rāgādīnaṃ santapanena tapassino ti – so Se Be; text omits entirely.

[23] bhāvanā; cp PvA 139.

[24] This does not appear amongst the forty mentioned at PvA 42 above.

[25] upāyakosallena; cp the Mahāyāna notion of upāya-kauśalya.

[26] Reading aññassāpi etādisā paṇḍitā amaccā paṭiladdhā assu tassa with Se Be for text's aññassa etādisā paṇḍitā amaccā santi saṃvijjamānassa tassa.

[27] Reading vuttatthā with Be for text's vuttattā.

[28] PvA 41f.

II.7 EXPOSITION OF THE DHANAPĀLA PETA STORY
[Dhanapālapetavatthuvaṇṇanā]

'Naked and of hideous appearance are you.' This was said when the Teacher was staying in the Jeta Grove concerning the peta Dhanapāla.

It is said that before the Buddha had arisen there was in the city of Erakaccha in the kingdom of the Dasaṇṇas[1] a wealthy merchant named Dhanapālaka who had neither faith nor devotion and who was miserly and held the natthika[2] heresy. His activities are made known by the text.[3] When he died he arose as a peta in a desert wilderness. His body was the size of a palmyra[4] trunk. His skin was bloated and rough and he was terrible, hideous and extremely deformed – a quite disgusting sight. Overcome by hunger and thirst and with his tongue sticking out of his parched throat[5] he roamed about this way and that for fifty-five years without getting (so much as) a ball of cooked rice as food or a drop of water (to drink). [**100**] Then when our Lord had arisen in the world and had set rolling the Wheel of the Noble Dhamma and was, in due course, staying in Sāvatthī, some traders, who were residents of Sāvatthī, filled as many as five hundred carts with goods, went to Uttarāpatha,[6] sold their goods (there) and loaded their carts with goods received in return. As they were returning they came at evening time upon a certain dried-up stream.[7] They unharnessed their oxen there and made their camp for the night. Then that peta, overcome by thirst, came in search of something to drink. When he did not get even so much as a drop of water there, he fell prostrate, bereft of hope, like a palmyra cut down at its roots.[8] When they saw him the traders questioned him with this verse:

1 'Naked and of hideous appearance are you, emaciated and with prominent veins. You thin one, with your ribs standing out, now who are you, good sir?'

whereupon the peta disclosed his identity:

2 'I, sir, am a peta, gone to a miserable existence in the world of Yama; having done a wicked deed, I have gone from here to the world of the petas.'

Questioned once more by them about the deed he had done:

3 'Now what evil deed was done by you by body, speech or mind? As a result of which deed have you gone from here to the world of the petas?',

he spoke these verses depicting his past, present and future circumstances, from his former place of arising onwards, and giving them an exhortation:

4 'There is a city of the Dasaṇṇas, the famous Erakaccha. I was in the past a wealthy merchant there – as Dhanapāla I was known.
5 Eighty cartloads of gold were mine; mine abundant gold and many pearls and precious stones.
6 Though of such great wealth[9] I was not fond of giving. I shut the door before I ate lest beggars should see me.
7 I was without faith and mean, miserly and abusive. I had the habit of obstructing many people whilst they were giving and performing.
8 **[101]** Saying, "There is no result from giving. From where would come the fruit of self-restraint?",[10] I destroyed lotus ponds and other drinking places, planted pleasure gardens, wayside watering places and bridges at places where it is difficult to cross.
9 I did no lovely deed. I did (only) wicked deeds. When I fell from there, I arose on the peta-plane, tormented by hunger and thirst. For fifty-five years since I died,
10 I am not conscious of having eaten or of having drunk water. He

who was restrained comes to ruin. He who comes to ruin was restrained. It is said that the petas indeed know that he who was restrained comes to ruin.

11 I in the past was so restrained. I did not give though abundant wealth (existed); though merit-offerings were at hand, I made no refuge for myself.

12 I later felt remorse as my own deeds (began to) reach fruition.[11] After four months will come my death,

13 And down to the exceedingly severe and terrible hell will I fall: four-cornered and with four gates, it is divided into equal portions, encircled by an iron wall, with a roof of iron above;

14 Its incandescent floor is made of glowing iron; all around a hundred yojanas it spreads, forever standing.

15 There for a long time I will experience painful feelings as the fruit of my wicked deeds – for this reason I am exceedingly sorrowful.

16 Therefore I say to you, "My blessings to you, each one of you assembled here. Do not commit a wicked deed either openly or in secret.

17 For if you do or will do a wicked deed there will be no escape from misery for you, even if you fly up[12] and run away.

18 Be respectful to mother, respectful to father; honour the elders in the family; (show reverence for) recluses and brahmins – in this way you will go to heaven".'

4 Herein *of the Dasaṇṇas (Dasaṇṇānaṃ)*: of the kingdom of the Dasaṇṇas or of the kings of that name.[13] *Erakaccha (Erakacchaṃ)*: is the name of that city. *There (tattha)*: in that city. *In the past (pure)*: **[102]** formerly, in a past existence. *As Dhanapāla I was known (Dhanapālo ti maṃ vidu)*: as the wealthy merchant Dhanapāla did they know me. He uttered the verse beginning 'Eighty' showing why this particular name was given to him at that time.[14]

5 Herein *eighty cartloads (asīti sakaṭavāhānaṃ)*:[15] twenty khārī[16] loads are said to equal one cart(load). Eighty of these cartloads of gold and likewise kahāpaṇas[17] in fact were mine – this is how it should be construed. *Mine abundant gold (pahūtaṃ me jātarūpaṃ)*: abundant gold measuring countless bhāras;[18] it is (to be) connected with (the verb) 'were'.

6 *I was not fond of giving (na me dātuṃ piyaṃ ahu)*: I was not fond of giving gifts. *Lest beggars should see me (mā maṃ yācanakāddasuṃ)*: I shut the door of the house before I ate thinking, 'The beggars must not see me.'

7 *Miserly (kadariyo)*: extremely mean. *Abusive (paribhāsako)*: when

he saw (people) giving alms he would threaten[19] them with fear. *Whilst they were giving and performing (dadantānaṃ karontānaṃ)*: this is the genitive case with the sense of the accusative – when they were giving alms and performing meritorious deeds. *Many people (bahujanaṃ)*: many beings. Whilst they were giving and performing, I had the habit of obstructing, I hindered, many people, a multitude of beings, from (doing) that meritorious deed.

8 'There is no result from giving' and so on – this is a statement of his reasons for his hindering the alms and so on. Herein *there is no result from giving (vipāko n'atthi dānassa)*: there is indeed no fruit from acts of giving. He elucidates that merit alone is merit and that (giving) is just a loss of wealth. *Of self-restraint (saṃyamassa)*: the self-restraint of the precepts. *From where would come the fruit? (kuto phalaṃ)*: from where indeed would the fruit be obtained? Keeping the precepts is quite useless – this is the meaning. *Pleasure gardens (ārāmāni)*: pleasure gardens and groves. *Wayside watering places (papāyo)*: sheds with drinking water. *At places where it is difficult to cross (dugge)*: at places where it is difficult to proceed due to water and swamps. *Bridges (saṅkamanāni)*: causeways.

9 *When I fell from there (tato cuto)*: when I fell from the world of men. *Fifty-five: pañcapaṇṇāsa=pañcapaññāsa* (alternative grammatical form). *Since I died (yato kālaṅkato ahaṃ)*: from the time that I died onwards.

10 *I am not conscious (nābhijānāmi)*: for all that time I am not aware of having eaten or of having drunk anything. *He who was restrained comes to ruin (yo saṃyamo so vināso)*: that restraint by way of greed and so on of not giving to anyone – **[103]** that is indeed ruin for such beings in that it is the cause of the great plight of arising as petas in the peta-womb. *He who comes to ruin was restrained (yo vināso so saṃyamo)*: with this he speaks of the certainty of the aforementioned fact. *It is said the petas indeed know (petā hi kira jānanti)*: the word 'indeed' (*hi*) is here used for emphasis and the word(s) 'it is said' (*kira*) indicate that it is from hearsay; restraint, the lack of generosity with merit-offerings, is the cause of ruin. It is said that only petas know of this fact due to their being personally overcome by it. Not so humans. It is not possible[20] for even though humans, like petas, are to be seen being overcome by hunger and thirst and so on, petas however are much better aware of this fact since they are familiar with the deeds they did in their previous existence. For this reason he uttered (the verse) beginning, 'I in the past was so restrained'.

11 Herein *I was so restrained (saṃyamissaṃ)*: I myself also exercised restraint in, shrank from, the performance of meritorious deeds such as giving and so on. *Though abundant wealth (bahuke dhane)*: though great wealth was known.

16 *Therefore: taṃ=tasmā* (alternative grammatical form). *To you: vo=tumhe* (alternative grammatical form). *My blessings to you (bhaddaṃ vo)*: my blessings, best wishes and good luck to you – this is the rest of the words. *Each one of you assembled here (yāvant' ettha samāgatā)*: each one of you, as many as have come together here, should all listen to what I have to say – this is the meaning. *Openly (āvi)*: publicly, being visible to others. *In secret (raho)*: covertly, being not (so) visible. Do not commit, do not perform, any wicked, despicable, unskilled deed either openly by means of body and speech, such as destroying living beings and telling lies and so on, or in secret by way of covetousness and so forth.[21]

17 *For if . . . a wicked deed (sace taṃ pāpakaṃ kammaṃ)*: for if you should do a wicked deed now, or if you should do one in the future, then there is indeed no escape, no release, from the misery that is its fruit, such as (arising) in the four states of loss[22] such as the hells and so on, or, if amongst men, of being short-lived. *Even if you fly up and run away (upaccā 'pi palāyitaṃ)* means that there is simply no escape even for those rising up and travelling through the sky. (Some) text(s) also (read) *deliberately (upecca)*: because of the conclusion that it would pursue you whether you run this way or that; there is no escape from that for you even if you run away deliberately, intentionally, [**104**] meaning that it will simply ripen when there is a conjunction of other necessary conditions of place of destination[23] and time and so on. This fact is also to be elucidated by this verse:

> 'Neither in the sky nor in the midst of the sea nor by entering into the clefts of mountains is there known a place on earth where, stationing oneself, one might escape (the fruit of) one's wicked deeds.'*[24]

18 *Respectful to mother (matteyyā)*:[25] to one's mother's benefit. *Be (hotha)*: perform services and so on for them. *Respectful to father (petteyyā)*: this is to be understood in the same way. *Honour the elders in the family: kule jeṭṭhāpacāyikā=kule jeṭṭhakānaṃ apacāyanakarā* (resolution of compound). *Recluses (sāmaññā)*: honour the recluses. In the same way *brahmins (brahmaññā)* means honour those who have cast out wickedness.[26] *In this way you will go to heaven (evaṃ saggaṃ gamissatha)* means that after performing those meritorious deeds in the manner already stated by me you will arise in the devaloka.

Whatever has not had its meaning explained here is to be understood exactly as already given in the above Bald-headed Peta Story[27] and so on.

When they had heard what he had to say, those traders, filled with agitation and pitying him, took a bowl of water, had him lie down and

*Dhp 127 = Miln 150.

then sprinkled it into his mouth. Thereafter the people did this many times but the water that he longed for would not go down his throat[28] due to the fruit of that peta's wicked deeds. How then might his thirst be quenched? They asked him whether he had not[29] got a little relief. 'Even were so much as one drop of the water so many people are sprinkling into me so many times to enter my throat, yet there would still be no escape from this peta-womb', he said. When the traders heard this they were filled with extreme agitation and said, 'But are there any means by which your thirst can be quenced?' **[105]** He said, 'When this wicked deed is exhausted and alms have been given to the Tathāgata or the Tathāgata's sāvakas[30] and one dedicates that almsgiving to me, I will be freed from this peta-state.'[31] When they heard this those traders went to Sāvatthī, approached the Lord and raised the issue with him. They took the Refuges and the Precepts and for seven days gave a great almsgiving to the order of monks with the Buddha at its head and assigned this to the peta. The Lord took that matter as an arisen need and taught Dhamma to the four assemblies and the people abandoned the stain of selfishness and greed and so on and took delight in meritorious deeds of giving and so forth.

[1] Cp DPPN i 1064.

[2] Literally the 'there-is-not-ist' heresy. Such a doctrine is attributed at D i 55 to Ajita Kesakambalin and amounts to a denial of many tenets central to Buddhism, for example a denial that there is any benefit to be got from almsgiving (the theme of this text), that good and bad deeds bear any fruit, that there is a world beyond and that there are those who have gained liberation. See A. K. Coomaraswamy, 'Some Pali Words', *Harvard Journal of Asiatic Studies* IV, 2, 1939 pp. 149ff.; cp PvA 215, 244ff. and verses IV 3^{26-27}.

[3] pālito, the canonical verses below. See note at PvA 112 below.

[4] Borassus flabelliformis.

[5] PED sv kaṇṭha cites this as appearing at PvA 260 and that which appears at PvA 260 as appearing here.

[6] See note at PvA 111 below.

[7] Reading sukkhanadiṃ with Se Be for text's rukkhamūlaṃ.

[8] Reading bindumattam pi pānīyaṃ alabhitvā vigatāso chinnamūlo viya tālo chinnapādo pati with Se Be for text's bindumattaṃ pi alabhitvā ravi. Tato so chinnamūlo viya tālo chinno pati. I have rendered chinnapādo pati as 'fell prostrate' though this means more literally 'fell, cut down at his feet', in parallel with the palmyra being cut down at its roots.

[9] Reading dhanassā 'pi with Se Be for text's dhanassāmi.

[10] Part of the natthika heresy – see IV 3^{23} below.

[11] Reading attakammaphalūpago with Se Be for text's -phalupeto.

[12] Reading upaccā 'pi with Se Be for text's upacchāpi; cp S i 209; Thig 248 and note at EV ii 109.

[13] Reading vā rājūnaṃ with Se for text's vararājūnaṃ; Be reads simply rājūnaṃ and gives their name, both here and in the verse, as the Paṇṇas.

[14] Dhanapāla means 'guardian of wealth'.

[15] So Se Be; text reads simply sakaṭavāhānaṃ.

[16] A measure, usually of grain, of unknown quantity. At A v 173 = Sn p 126 mention is made of a Kosalan khārī load and it may have varied according to region.

[17] Reading asīti hiraññassa tathā kahāpaṇassa ca with Se Be for text's asītīhi raññassa kahāpaṇassa. The kahāpaṇa was a coin, usually of gold, but also of silver or copper.

[18] A measure of gold: 1 bhāra = 20 tulās = 2000 palas (SED 753). This sense is not listed in PED.

[19] Reading santajjako with Se Be for text's santajjito.

[20] Text mispunctuates and should read with Se Be: na manussā ti. Na-y-idaṃ yuttaṃ manussānaṃ pi.

[21] Cp the verses of Piyaṅkara's mother at S i 209.

[22] apāya – birth in hell, as a peta, an asura or an animal.

[23] gati.

[24] Cp note at PvA 148 below.

[25] Text mis-spells metteyyā.

[26] That is, the arahant; see especially Dhp 383–423.

[27] I.10 above.

[28] Reading adhogalaṃ with Se Be for text's udhogalaṃ.

[29] Reading kāci with Be for text's Se kā pi.

[30] That is, the sotāpanna, sakadāgāmin, anāgāmin and arahant and those on the respective paths, categories which extend to include laymen and devas as well as monks. They are sāvakas, or hearers, in the sense that they have acquired right view by means of the Dhammacakkhu through having heard a teaching on the Four Truths. See M i 380 and KhpA 183 and my doctoral thesis (University of Lancaster). As such they comprise the Ariyasaṅgha of PvA 1, 110 and are to be distinguished from the order of monks even though some monks may be included.

[31] Reading petattato with Se Be for text's petato.

II.8 EXPOSITION OF THE CŪḶASEṬṬHI PETA STORY [Cūḷaseṭṭhipetavatthuvaṇṇanā]

'You who have gone forth are naked and emaciated, sir.' This was said when the Teacher was staying in the Bamboo Grove concerning the peta Cūḷaseṭṭhi.

It is said that in Benares there was a householder named Cūḷaseṭṭhi who had neither faith nor devotion and who was mean and miserly and who had no respect for the performance of meritorious deeds. When he died he arose amongst the petas, his head shaven, without clothes and with a body devoid of flesh and blood that was mere bone, sinew and skin. His daughter Anulā, however, who was dwelling in her husband's home at Andhakavinda[1] prepared[2] some alms materials such as rice and so on with the desire of feeding some brahmins on behalf of her father. When he learned of this, the peta, travelling there full of hope through the sky, reached Rājagaha at the time at which king Ajātasattu was walking up and down on the upper storey of the royal palace, being unable to sleep because of an uneasy conscience and unpleasant dreams after having taken, incited by Devadatta, the life of his father. When he saw that peta travelling through the sky [**106**] he questioned him with this verse:

1 'You who have gone forth are naked and emaciated, sir. Where are you going by night and for what reason? Tell me this – we should be able, I might present to you possessions with all.'

1 Herein *who have gone forth (pabbajito)*: who are a recluse. It is said that the king said, 'You who have gone forth are naked and emaciated' and so on thinking him to be a naked recluse on account of his nakedness and shaven head. Herein *for what reason? (kissa hetu)*: on what account? *I might present to you possessions with all (sabbena vittaṃ paṭipādaye tuvaṃ)*: I might present to you, I might procure[3] for you, in accordance with your wish, possessions that are means of support for your comfort, along with all usable items or, alternatively, with all (possible) endeavour; surely[4] we should be able to act in this way. Therefore *tell me this (ācikkha me taṃ)* means explain to me the reason why you have come.

Questioned thus by the king, the peta spoke three verses explaining his situation:

2 'The city of Benares is renowned from afar; I was a householder there, prosperous but mean. I did not give and had a mind that craved enjoyment. Through bad conduct I have reached Yama's realm.

3 I am exhausted by the needle because of these; for this very reason I go amongst my relatives for the sake of something to eat but they lack the virtue of generosity and do not believe that there is any fruit of giving in the next world.

4 Yet my daughter mutters constantly, "I will give alms for my fathers and grandfathers". [**107**] The brahmins are being served what she has got ready and I am going to Andhakavinda to eat.'[5]

2 Herein *renowned from afar (dūraghuṭṭhaṃ)*: acclaimed from afar by way of praise for its qualities, meaning well-known and famous everywhere. *Prosperous: aḍḍhako=aḍḍho* (alternative grammatical form), meaning of great prosperity. *Mean (dīno)*: small-minded, of a disposition not to give. For this reason he said, 'I did not give.' *I had a mind that craved enjoyment (gedhitamano āmisasmiṃ)*: I was bent on craving with my thought set on sensual enjoyment.[6] *Through bad conduct I have reached Yama's*

realm (dussīlena Yamavisayamhi patto): through deeds of bad conduct done by me I have reached Yama's realm, the world of the petas.

3 *I am exhausted by the needle (so sūcikāya kilamito)*: I am exhausted, I am being pierced continually, by hunger which has acquired the name 'the needle' due to its similarity to a needle in the matter of piercing. Alternatively the reading is in fact 'exhaustion' (*kilamatho*). *Because of these (tehi)*: by reason of these aforesaid wicked deeds of having been mean and so on. As the peta recalled those wicked deeds he became extremely dejected and therefore spoke in this manner: *for this very reason (ten' eva)*: because of this same misery of hunger. *I go amongst my relatives (ñātīsu yāmi)*: I go, I make my way, to the presence of my relatives. *For the sake of something to eat (āmisakiñcihetu)*: on account of some small amount of food, meaning longing for some food. *But they lack the virtue of generosity and do not believe that there is any fruit of giving in the next world (adānasīlā na ca saddahanti, 'dānaphalaṃ hoti paramhi loke')*: as with me, so also in that same way do other people lack the virtue of generosity and do not believe that there is for sure any fruit of giving in the next world. Because of this, like me, they too will become petas and experience great misery – this is the meaning.

4 *Mutters (lapate)*: talks. *Constantly: abhikkhaṇaṃ=abhiṇhaṃ* (alternative grammatical form), repeatedly. What did she mutter? She said, 'I will give alms for my fathers and grandfathers.' Herein *for my fathers (pitunnaṃ)*: for my parents, or for my father's younger and elder brothers.[7] *For my grandfathers (pitāmahānaṃ)*: for my grandfathers and great grandfathers.[8] *What she has got ready (upakkhaṭaṃ)*: what she has prepared. *Are being served (parivisayanti)*: are being fed. *To Andhakavinda (Andhakavindaṃ)*: to the city of that name. *To eat: bhottuṃ=bhuñjituṃ* (alternative grammatical form).

[**108**] From here onwards was said by those rehearsing the texts:

5 'The king said to him, "After you have partaken of that you should return quickly; I too will pay honour. Tell me if there is any condition for we will listen to any statement of conditions[9] that is credible."

6 "So be it", he said and departed. But those who ate the food there were not worthy of the donation. So he went back[10] once more to Rājagaha and appeared before the lord of men.

7 Seeing that the peta had come back again, the king said, "What should I give? Tell me if there is any condition through which you could be happy for a long while to come."

8 "When you have served the Buddha and the Saṅgha with food, drink

and robes, your majesty, then assign that donation for my benefit. In this way I could be happy for a long while to come."

9 Therefore the king descended and straightway gave with his own hand alms beyond compare to the Saṅgha; he reported the affair to the Tathāgata and assigned the donation to that peta.

10 Thus honoured and extremely radiant, he appeared before the lord of men and said, "I am now a yakkha possessed of the highest psychic power. No humans are similar or equal to me in psychic power.

11 Behold this unlimited splendour of mine dedicated by you[11] after you had given beyond compare to the Saṅgha. [**109**] I will be satisfied, continually and always, with plenty and I will go about happy, O deva amongst men".'

5 Herein *the king said to him (tam avoca rājā)*: king Ajātasattu said to the peta who remained standing after speaking in that way. *After you have partaken of that (anubhaviyāna tam pi)*: after you have partaken of the alms that have been got ready by your daughter. *You should return (eyyāsi)*: you should come back. *Will pay: karissaṃ=karissāmi* (alternative grammatical form). *Tell me if there is any condition (ācikkha me taṃ yadi atthi hetu)*: tell me, explain to me, if there are any means. *That is credible (saddhāyitaṃ)*: that is to be believed. *Any statement of conditions (hetuvaco)*: any statement concerned with conditions, meaning make a statement together with the means (thereto), such as, 'It will be of benefit to me when a gift is made at such and such a place and in such and such a manner.'

6 *'So be it', he said (tathā ti vatvā)*: 'Very well', he said. *There (tattha)*:[12] at Andhakavinda, the place where (the food) was being served. *But those who ate the food were not worthy of the donation (bhuñjiṃsu[13] bhattaṃ na ca pana dakkhiṇārahā)*: those who ate the food were brahmins of bad conduct, meaning those who ate it were not virtuous and worthy of the donation. *Once more: punāparaṃ=puna aparaṃ* (resolution of compound), he went back in turn to Rājagaha.

7 *What should I give? (kiṃ dadāmi)*: the king asked the peta, 'What sort of gift should I give you?' *Through which you (yena tuvaṃ)*: by means of which you. *For a long while to come (ciratarаṃ)*: for a long time. *Happy (pīṇito)*: (how) you could be contented, meaning please explain this.

8 *When you have served (parivisayāna)*: when you have fed. *Your majesty (rāja)*: he is addressing Ajātasattu. *For my benefit (me hitāya)*: for the sake of my benefit, for (the sake of) release from this state of being a peta.

9 *Therefore (tato)*: for this reason, because of that statement; or, alternatively, *therefrom (tato)*: from the palace. *Descended (nipatitvā)*: came out. *Straightway (tāva-d-eva)*: just then, at the time that the sun was rising. (The king) gave alms on the very same[14] morning on which the peta went back and revealed himself to the king. [**110**] *With his own hand: sahatthā= sahatthena* (alternative grammatical form). *Beyond compare (atulaṃ)*: immeasurable, finest,[15] choicest. *Gave to the Saṅgha: daditvā saṅghe= saṅghassa datvā* (alternative grammatical form). *He reported the affair to the Tathāgata (ārocayi pakaṭiṃ Tathāgatassa)*: he reported news of the affair to the Lord saying, 'This gift, Lord, has been made with reference to a certain peta'. And when he had reported this, he assigned (*ādisittha= ādisi*, alternative grammatical form) the donation to that peta in the very same way in which that gift was of benefit to him.[16]

10 *He (so)*: the peta. *Honoured (pūjito)*: honoured with the donation that was being given. *Extremely radiant (ativiya sobhamāno)*: extremely brilliant with heavenly splendour.[17] *He appeared: pāturahosi=pātubhavi* (alternative grammatical form); he revealed himself before the king. *I am now a yakkha (yakkho 'haṃ asmi)*: released[18] from the state of being a peta, I have become a yakkha, I have attained the state of a devatā. *No humans are similar or equal to me in psychic power (na mayham iddhisamasadisā manussā)*: there are no humans who are similar to me in this excellence of possessions or who are equal to me in this excellence of splendour.[19]

11 *Behold this unlimited splendour of mine (passānubhāvaṃ aparimitaṃ mamayidaṃ)*: showing his excellence personally to the king he says, 'Behold this unlimited heavenly splendour of mine.' *Dedicated by you after you had given beyond compare to the Saṅgha (tayānudiṭṭham atulaṃ daditvā saṅghe)*: after you had given the finest alms beyond compare to the Ariyasaṅgha[20] they were dedicated by you out of pity for me. *I will be satisfied, continually and always, with plenty (santappito satataṃ sadā bahūhi)*: I will be satisfied, I will be happy, continually, without interruption, and always, at all times, for so long as life lasts there even, on account of your satisfying the Ariyasaṅgha with plenty of merit-offerings such as food, drink and clothes and so on. *I will go about happy, O deva amongst men (yāmi ahaṃ sukhito manussadeva)*: he begged leave of the king saying, 'Therefore I am happy now, O deva amongst men, O great king, and I will go to whatever place I please.'

[**111**] When the peta had gone after begging leave in that way, king Ajātasattu raised the matter with the monks. The monks approached the Lord and raised it (with him). The Lord took the matter as an arisen need and taught Dhamma to the company assembled there. When they

heard this, the people abandoned the stain of selfishness and took delight in meritorious deeds of giving and so forth.

[1] A village just outside Rājagaha.

[2] Reading dānūpakaraṇāni sajjesi with Se Be for text's dānūpakaraṇā nisajjesi; cp PvA 278.

[3] Reading sampādeyyaṃ with Se Be for text's sammā deyyaṃ; Se Be read paṭipādaye in verse but paṭipādeyyaṃ in cty.

[4] Reading app' eva nāma with Se Be for text's app' eva.

[5] Reading bhottun ti with Se (Be bhuttun ti) for text's bhottun' tī ti.

[6] Reading kāmāmise laggacitto with Se Be for text's kāmāmiseḷaggacitto.

[7] Reading cūḷapitumahāpitūnaṃ with Be (Se culla-) for text's cūḷapitu mahāpitūnaṃ.

[8] ayyakapayyakānaṃ; cp SED sv āryaka which is said to have been a ceremony for the manes, that is, the petas.

[9] Reading hetuvaco with Se Be and IV 1[31] below for text's hetuvahe.

[10] Reading paccāgami with Se Be and cty below for text's pacchā gamī.

[11] Reading tayānudiṭṭhaṃ here and in cty with Be Se (Se cty -udd-) for text's tayānusiṭṭhaṃ.

[12] Reading tatthā ti with Se Be for text's Tattha bhuñjiṃsū ti.

[13] Text mispunctuates and should read with Se Be . . . parivesanaṭṭhāne. Bhuñjiṃsu. . . .

[14] Reading eva with Se Be for text's evañ ca.

[15] Reading uḷāraṃ with Se Be for text's oḷāraṃ.

[16] Reading ārocetvā ca yathā taṃ dānaṃ tassa upakappati evaṃ tassa ca petassa dakkhiṇaṃ ādisittha ādisi with Se Be for text's āropetvā ca yathā uḷāraṃ paṇītaṃ dānaṃ datvā taṃ dānaṃ petassa upakappati, evaṃ tassa dakkhiṇaṃ ādisittha ādisi.

[17] Reading dibbānubhāvena with Se Be for text's dibbabhāvena.

[18] Reading mutto with Se Be for text's mato.

[19] Reading ānubhāva- with Se Be for text's anubhāva-.

[20] See note at PvA 105 above.

II.9 EXPOSITION OF THE AṄKURA PETA STORY
[Aṅkurapetavatthuvaṇṇanā]

'That purpose for which we were going.' The Teacher who was staying at Sāvatthī told this concerning a peta named Aṅkura. In this case Aṅkura is happily no peta but on account of his activities being connected with a peta this is therefore called the Aṅkura Peta Story. Here is the story in brief.

In the city[1] of Asitañjana in the Kaṃsabhoga region of Uttarāpatha[2] there were born to Upasāgara, son[3] of king Mahāsāgara, ruler of Uttaramadhurā,[4] and to Devagabbhā, daughter of Mahākaṃsaka (the following children: a daughter) Añjanadevī and her ten brothers Vāsudeva, Baladeva, Candadeva, Suriyadeva, Aggideva, Varuṇadeva, Ajjuna, Pajjuna, Ghaṭapaṇḍita and Aṅkura – in all eleven kṣatriyas. Beginning with the city of Asitañjana, Vāsudeva and his brothers, by the discus, brought to their death all the kings in the sixty-three thousand cities of this entire Jambudīpa, ending at Dvāravatī. Whilst dwelling at Dvāravatī they divided the kingdom into ten parts. However they had forgotten their sister Añjanadevī and, when they remembered her again, they said, 'We should divide it into eleven parts', but Aṅkura, the youngest of them all, said, 'You can give her my share. I will make a living by trade and you can send me taxes from your respective provinces.' 'Very well', they agreed and having given his share to their sister the nine kings lived on in Dvāravatī.[5] Aṅkura, however, engaged in trade and constantly gave great almsgivings. Now he had a **[112]** slave who was keeper of his stores[6] and who had his interests at heart. With devotion in his heart Aṅkura procured a daughter of good family and gave her (in marriage) to him. He died just as his son was being born and Aṅkura, at the birth, gave him the food and remuneration he was to have given to his father. Then when the youth came of age the question arose amongst the royal family as to whether he was a slave or not. When Añjanadevī heard about this she cited the example of the cow and freed him from his slavery saying, 'The son of a freewoman is himself a freeman.' But the youth, through shame, could not bear to live there and went to the city of Bheruva where he took (as his wife) the daughter of a tailor and earned his living by the art of tailoring. There was at that time in the city of Bheruva a wealthy merchant named Asayhamahāseṭṭhi[7] who gave great almsgivings for recluses and brahmins, indigents, tramps,[8] wayfarers[9] and beggars. The tailor, full of joy and happiness, would raise his right arm and point out the Asayhaseṭṭhi residence to those not knowing the wealthy merchant's house saying, 'Go there and get whatever is available.' His deeds are recorded in the text.[10] In due course he died and arose in the desert as a terrestrial devatā in a banyan tree with a right hand that granted desires. Now in that same Bheruva there was a man who superintended[11] Asayhaseṭṭhi's alms but who himself had neither faith nor devotion and who was of wrong view and disrespectful about the performance of meritorious deeds. When he died he arose as a peta not far from the dwelling place of that devaputta. The deeds that he did are recorded in the text. When Asayhamahāseṭṭhi died, however, he went into companionship with Sakka, king of the devas, in the realm of the Thirty-three.

Now after some time Aṅkura took his goods on five hundred carts, as did a certain brahmin also on five hundred carts. With these one thousand carts the two men entered upon a road in the desert wilderness and lost their way. After wandering around there for many days they exhausted their grass, water and food. Aṅkura had messengers on horseback[12] search for water in the four directions. Then that yakkha with the hand that granted desires saw the plight they had got into and [113] recalling some service Aṅkura had rendered him in former days thought, 'Well now, I must help him', and showed him the banyan tree in which he lived. It is said that that banyan tree was full of twigs and branches, with thick foliage giving dense shade and with countless thousands of new shoots (so that it stood) one yojana in length, breadth and height. Aṅkura was overjoyed on seeing it and pitched camp[13] underneath it. The yakkha raised his right hand and at first satisfied all the people with water, thereafter giving to anyone whatever it was that he wanted. When those people had been satisfied with as many different kinds of food and drink and so on as they desired and were recovering from the fatigue of the journey, that brahmin trader, reasoning improperly,[14] thought thus, 'When we have gone from here to Kamboja in search of wealth, then what shall we do? But if we were to seize this yakkha now by means of some trick and put him on a cart we could then just go back to our own city.' With this in mind he uttered two verses informing Aṅkura of his plan:

1 'That purpose for which we seekers of wealth were going to Kamboja can be satisfied by this yakkha that grants desires. Let us take this yakkha!

2 When we have taken this yakkha, either with his consent or by force, and put him on a cart we can go quickly to Dvāraka.'

1 Herein *that purpose for which (yassa atthāya)*: that reason for which. *To Kamboja (Kambojaṃ)*: to the kingdom of Kamboja. *Seekers of wealth (dhanahārakā)*: seeking to gain wealth by the sale of goods. *That grants desires (kāmadado)*: that gives whatever is desired. *Yakkha (yakkho)*: devaputta. *Let us take: nīyāmase=nayissāma* (alternative grammatical form).

2 *With his consent (sādhukena)*: by begging him. *By force (pasayha)*: having overpowered him with the use of force. *On a cart (yānaṃ)*: on a comfortable cart. *To Dvāraka (Dvārakaṃ)*: to the city of Dvāravatī. This is the meaning here: we want to go from here to Kamboja for a purpose. That purpose, to be realised by that journey,[15] can be accomplished right here. This is a yakkha that grants desires. [114] Therefore we will beg this yakkha and (proceed) with his consent or, if he is not won over, then we will put him on a cart with the use of force, tie him to the hind part in the cart and then quickly go with him from here to the city of Dvāravatī.

However when the brahmin had spoken in this way Aṅkura, steadfast in the Dhamma of the worthy man,[16] uttered this verse opposing what had been said:

3 'One should not break the branches of the tree in whose shade one would sit or lie, for injuring a friend would be wicked indeed.'

3 Herein *one should not break (na bhañjeyya)*: one should not cut off. *Injuring a friend: mittadubbho=mittesu dubbhanaṃ* (resolution of compound); causing them harm. *Would be wicked (pāpako)*: injuring a friend would be inauspicious. The tree whose cool shade dispels the fatigue of the man overpowered by the heat – one should not even think of wickedness towards it, so how much less living beings? Now this devaputta is a worthy man who has been of great service and who obliged us by relieving our misery.[17] One should not think of doing anything harmful towards him. Surely he is rather to be honoured – this is what he is pointing out.

When he heard this the brahmin, relying on the well established principle that doing away with hypocrisy is the basis of success, uttered this verse setting himself in opposition to Aṅkura:

4 'One would cut down the trunk even of the tree in whose shade one would sit or lie if such were one's need.'

4 Herein *if such were one's need (attho ce tādiso siyā)*: if one's need should be for such a collection of timber, then one would cut down the trunk of that tree even, so how much more its branches and so on – this is the meaning.

When the brahmin had spoken in this way Aṅkura uttered this verse upholding the Dhamma of the worthy man alone:

5 'One should not harm the leaves of the tree in whose shade one would sit or lie, for injuring a friend would be wicked indeed.'

5 **[115]** Herein *one should not harm the leaves (na tassa pattaṃ hiṃseyya)*: one should not cause even so much as one leaf of that tree to fall, so how much less the branches and so on – this is the meaning.

Once more the brahmin uttered a verse upholding his own viewpoint:

6 'One would pull it up together with its roots even, (pull up) that tree in whose shade one would sit or lie if such were one's need.'

6 Herein *one would pull it up together with its roots even (samūlaṃ pi taṃ abbuyha)*: one would pull it up there, that is, lift it up, together with its roots even, accompanied by its roots even.[18]

When the brahmin had spoken in this way Aṅkura spoke these three verses wishing to render it meaningless:

7 'A man should not plan a wicked deed even in his mind against him in whose house he has stayed for one night even and where he has obtained food and drink – gratitude is extolled by worthy men.

8 He should not plan a wicked deed even in his mind against him in whose house he has stayed and (by whom) he has been served with food and drink – the hand not given to injury burns the one who injures a friend.[19]

9 He to whom formerly a lovely deed was done and who later harms (his benefactor) with a wicked deed is a clean-hand-destroyed man – he will not behold good fortune.'

7 Herein *whose (yassa)*: the person whose. *For one night even (ekarattim pi)*: in (whose) home he has stayed for so little as but one night even.[20] *Where he has obtained food and drink (yatth' annapānaṃ puriso labhetha)*: in whose presence anyone has obtained food and drink or any nourishment. **[116]** *(A man) should not plan a wicked deed even in his mind against him (na tassa pāpaṃ manasā 'pi cetaye)*: (a man) should not think of, should not long for, bad luck or misfortune for that person even in his mind, so how much less in body and speech. Why so? *Gratitude is extolled by worthy men (kataññutā sappurisehi vaṇṇitā)*: gratitude is indeed praised by Buddhas and so on, the foremost amongst worthy men.
8 *Has been served (upaṭṭhito)*: has been served with food and drink, has been waited upon with the words, 'Please take this, please eat this.' *The hand not given to injury (adubbhapāṇī)*: the hand not given to harming, the hand that is restrained. *Burns the one who injures a friend (dahate mittadubbhiṃ)*: it burns, it destroys, the person who injures a friend. An offence committed against persons who are endowed with good intentions and without fault by another brings ruin for this same other without exception. As regards its practical import[21] the person who is without fault indeed burns him. For this reason the Lord said, 'He who wrongs a man who is without fault, a man who is cleansed and without blemish, upon that same fool does that wicked deed recoil, like fine dust thrown against the wind.'*
9 *He to whom formerly a lovely deed was done (yo pubbe katakalyāṇo)*: the person to whom some good was done, some service was rendered, by anyone virtuous. *And who later harms (his benefactor) with a wicked deed (pacchā pāpena hiṃsati)*: and who at some future occasion afflicts with a wicked deed, with bad luck and misfortune, that one who obliged him. *Is a clean-hand-destroyed man (allapāṇihato poso)*: he is destroyed, he is afflicted, in the aforesaid manner by the performance of

*Dhp 125.

that service with a clean hand, by the one who obliged him, (doing so) with a clean hand, with a washed hand. Or, alternatively (his own) clean hand is destroyed, it is destroyed[22] by his afflicting the one who obliged him; he is an ungrateful man. *He will not behold good fortune (na so bhadrāni passati)*: the person stated will not behold, that is, will not find, will not obtain, happiness either in this world or the next.

[117] The brahmin, defeated thus by Aṅkura upholding the Dhamma of the worthy man, said nothing further and became silent. The yakkha, however, having heard this exchange of conversation between the two of them and though angry with the brahmin thought, 'Let it be for now – I will decide later what is to be done with this wicked brahmin', and then uttered this verse showing the extent of his inability to be overcome by anyone:

10 'Not by deva nor man nor dominion am I easily subdued[23] – a yakkha am I, attained to the highest of psychic powers, far-ranging and endowed with beauty and strength.'

10 Herein *by deva (devena)*: by any deva. *By man (manussena vā)*: just the same is to be applied here also. *Nor by dominion (issariyena vā)*: neither by dominion over devas nor by dominion over men – in this connection 'dominion over devas' means the divine potency[24] of the Four Great Kings, Sakka, Suyāma[25] and so on whilst 'dominion over men' means the potency stemming from meritorious deeds of a wheel-turning (monarch)[26] and so on. Therefore by 'dominion' are included those of great majesty amongst devas and men. Even devas of great majesty are not able to overcome men who are sustained by the fruit of their meritorious deeds and when there is no failure of those means,[27] so how much less others. *Haṃ* (untranslated) is a particle denoting inability. *Not easily subdued (na suppasayho)*: indestructible. *A yakkha am I attained to the highest of psychic powers (yakkho 'ham asmi paramiddhipatto)*: by way of my own meritorious deeds I have entered the state of a yakkha. There is none who is equal to the yakkha.[28] Moreover I have attained to the highest of psychic powers, I am possessed of the highest, the utmost, psychic power of the yakkha. *Far-ranging (dūraṅgamo)*: able to go to far off places in an inkling. *Endowed with beauty and strength (vaṇṇabalupapanno)*: endowed with,[29] possessed of, beauty and physical strength. By means[30] of this three-worded mantra he shows his own invincibility. Perfect in appearance, he is revered by others; because of his possession of that beauty [118] he is not to be confounded even by the unusual. His possession of that (good) appearance is said[31] to be the reason for his invincibility.

From here onwards there is an exchange of conversation in fifteen verses between Aṅkura and the devaputta:

11 'Your hand is all golden, a five-bearer, and flows with honey; juices of various flavours trickle (from it) – I think you must be Purindada.'

12 'I am no deva nor gandhabba[32] nor even Sakka Purindada; as a peta you should know me, Aṅkura, who am come here from Bheruva.'

13 'What was your conduct, what your behaviour, previously when you were in Bheruva? By what (aspect of the) Brahmafaring (came) the meritorious deed that resulted in this hand?'

14 'I was previously a tailor in Bheruva; at that time I suffered great hardship and led a very hard life. I had nothing to give,

15 But my workshop was quite close to Asayha, a man of faith and a master in the practice of giving, a man of conscience who performed meritorious deeds.

16 Beggars would come there and wayfarers of a variety of clans and they would ask me for the Asayha residence saying, "Blessings to you! Where should we go – where are the alms given out?"

17 So questioned I would raise my right arm and point out the Asayha residence to them saying, "Blessings to you! You should go there – the alms are given out there at the Asayha residence."

18 For this reason my hand grants desires, for this reason my hand flows with honey, by this (aspect of the) Brahmafaring (came) the meritorious deed that resulted in this hand.'

19 'It is said that you did not give alms to anyone with your own hand but that rejoicing at the alms of another you raised your hand and showed (the way).

20 For this reason your hand grants desires, for this reason your hand flows with honey, by this (aspect of the) Brahmafaring (came) the meritorious deed that resulted in this hand.

21 The pious man, sir, who gave those alms with his own hand – when he left the human body to which quarter did he go?'

22 'I do not know the going and coming of Aṅgīrasa, the one who endures what is beyond endurance,[33] **[119]** but I have heard in the presence of Vessavaṇa[34] that Asayha has gone into companionship with Sakka.'

23 'It is sufficient to do lovely deeds and to give alms as is fitting. After seeing this hand that grants desires, who would not perform meritorious deeds?

24 When I have gone, then, from here and have got back to Dvāraka I will provide alms which will bring me happiness.

25 I will give food and drink, clothing and lodging, wayside watering places, wells and bridges at places where it is difficult to cross.'

11 Herein *your hand (pāṇi te)*: your right hand. *Is all golden (sabbasovaṇṇo)*: is all over the colour of gold. *A five-bearer (pañcadhāro)*: (it is said to be) a 'five-bearer' since with its five fingers it has bearers of things that are desired by others. *Flows with honey (madhussavo)*: is flowing[35] with sweet juices. For this reason he said, *juices of various flavours trickle (from it) (nānārasā paggharanti)*, meaning many different sorts of juices – sweet, bitter, astringent and so on[36] – flow[37] (from it). When a yakkha's hand that grants desires is dispensing various hard and soft foods that are full of such flavours as sweetness and so on it is said that it 'flows with honey'. *I think you must be Purindada (maññe 'han taṃ Purindadaṃ)*: I think you must be Sakka Purindada, meaning I think you must be Sakka, king of the devas, who is of such great majesty.
12 *I am no deva (n' amhi devo)*: I am no well known deva such as Vessavaṇa and so on. *Nor gandhabba (na gandhabbo)*: I am not even a deva belonging to the company of gandhabbas. *Nor even Sakka Purindada (na pi Sakko Purindado)*: I am not even Sakka, king of the devas, who has acquired the name Purindada through having previously (*pure*) provided alms (*dānassa*) in a former existence.[38] What was he[39] then? He said, *as a peta you should know me, Aṅkura (petam Aṅkura jānāhi)*: you should know me as one who has arisen as a peta, Aṅkura my good sir, you should take me to be a peta of great psychic power. *Who am come here from Bheruva (Bheruvamhā idhāgataṃ)*: who, after falling from the city of Bheruva, am come here by way of my appearing in this banyan tree here in the midst of this desert wilderness, meaning who am arisen here.
13 *What was your conduct, what your behaviour, previously when you were in Bheruva? (kiṃsīlo kiṃsamācāro Bheruvasmiṃ pure tuvaṃ)*: earlier, in a former existence, when you were dwelling in the city of Bheruva, **[120]** what was your conduct, what your behaviour? After adopting[40] what kind of conduct that was characteristic of your turning back[41] from wicked deeds, because of behaviour that was characteristic of your having turned towards[42] the performance of meritorious deeds, of what kind of behaviour, meaning of what kind of behaviour were you with respect to skilled behaviour such as giving and so on? *By what (aspect of the) Brahmafaring (came) the meritorious deed that resulted in this hand? (kena te brahmacariyena puññaṃ pāṇimhi ijjhati)*: by means of what aspect of the excellent Brahmafaring is there such fruit of a meritorious deed as this that now ripens and takes effect in your hands, meaning please tell me this. By 'meritorious deed' was meant the fruit of a meritorious deed,

through an elision of the second word (of the compound). For it was certainly this that was called 'merit' in, 'It is by the acquisition of skilled states in this way, monks, that this merit increases',* and so on.

14 *A tailor (tunnavāyo)*: a needle worker. *I led a very hard life: sukicchavutti=suṭṭhu kicchavuttiko* (resolution of compound); I had a life of extreme misery. *I suffered great hardship (kapaṇo)*: I was poor, meaning I was in a wretched state. *I had nothing to give (na me vijjati dātave)*: I had nothing that was worthy of being given, nothing to give to tramps, recluses and brahmins, though I did have thoughts of giving alms – this is the meaning.

15 *Workshop (āvesanaṃ)*: house, or a room for doing work. *Quite close to Asayha (Asayhassa upantike)*: near the house of the great wealthy merchant Asayha. *A man of faith (saddhassa)*: possessed of faith in the fruition of deeds. *A master in the practice of giving (dānapatino)*: as regards the practice of giving he was a master through overcoming greed and through an excellence of generosity that continued without interruption.[43] *Who performed meritorious deeds (katapuññassa)*: who performed deeds of good conduct in the past. *A man of conscience (lajjino)*: one who was by nature disgusted by wicked deeds.

16 *There (tattha)*: to that workshop of mine. *Beggars would come (yācanakā yanti)*: beggar-folk would come desiring to beg something from Asayhaseṭṭhi. *Of a variety of clans (nānāgottā)*: of many different clans and regions. *Wayfarers (vanibbakā)*: those who sing one's praises (*vaṇṇadīpakā)*[44] who wander around declaring[45] their state of need with a mouthful of praise and so on for the virtues of, and for the fruits of, the meritorious deeds and so forth of him who gives. *And they would ask me (te ca maṃ tattha pucchanti)*: *tattha* (untranslated) is a mere particle; those beggars and so on would ask me for the residence of Asayha, the wealthy merchant. The versifiers require two patients in such places.[46] **[121]** *Blessings to you! Where should we go – where are the alms given out? (Kattha gacchāma bhaddaṃ vo kattha dānaṃ padīyati)*: this shows the way in which they asked. This is the meaning here: Blessings be to you! We have come after hearing that alms are given out here by Asayhaseṭṭhi. Where are the alms given out? Or where should we go – by going where will we be able to get them?

17 *So questioned I would point out (tesāhaṃ puṭṭho akkhāmi)*: when questioned in this way by those travelling-folk about the place where they could receive (the alms) I would respectfully[47] raise my right arm and tell them of the Asayhaseṭṭhi residence thinking, 'Through not having performed meritorious deeds in the past I am now unable to give anything

*D iii 58; also quoted at PvA 8.

to such as these. However I may produce much merit even by so little as joyfully[48] telling them of the means of obtaining these by showing them the house where the alms are given out. For this reason he said, 'I would raise my right arm' and so on.

18 *For this reason my hand grants desires (tena pāṇi kāmadado)*: on account of making known the alms of another, because of mere rejoicing with due respect at gifts made by another, my hand now grants desires like the wish-granting tree, like the santāna-creeper,[49] it grants desires bestowing whatever is wanted. *For this reason my hand flows with honey (tena pāṇi madhussavo)*: it has come to dispense pleasant things.

19 *It is said that you did not give alms (na kira tvaṃ adā dānaṃ)*: 'it is said' (*kira*) is a particle denoting hearsay. It is said that you did not give away your own property, that you did not give any alms whatsoever to anyone, whether recluse or brahmin, with your own hand, by your own hand. *But that rejoicing at the alms of another (parassa dānaṃ anumodamāno)*: but that you stayed merely rejoicing at gifts made by others for the sake of others thinking, 'Oh, what a great almsgiving you are bestowing!'

20 *For this reason your hand grants desires (tena pāṇi kāmadado)*: for this reason this hand of yours grants desires in this way. Oh, how wonderful indeed is the destiny of meritorious deeds! – this is the meaning.

21 *The pious man, sir, who gave those alms with his own hand (yo so dānaṃ adā bhante pasanno sakapāṇīhi)*: through respect he addresses the devaputta as 'sir'. [122] For merely[50] rejoicing at gifts made by another, sir, such is the fruit, such the majesty, that (has come) to you. But it was Asayha, the great wealthy merchant,[51] who gave that great almsgiving and who became devoted in heart at the time that he bestowed that great almsgiving with his own hand. *When he left the human body (so hitvā mānusaṃ dehaṃ)*: when he forsook this human state here. *To which (kiṃ)*: to which one of the. *Nu so* (untranslated): *nu* is a mere particle. *Quarter did he go? (disataṃ gato)*: (in which) direction, (to which) place, did he go; he asked about the fate of Asayhaseṭṭhi in the world to come saying, 'What sort of destiny did he end up with?'

22 *The one who endures what is beyond endurance (asayhasāhino)*: he is one who endures what is beyond endurance on account of his enduring the responsibility[52] of the worthy man in matters of generosity[53] and so on which would not be able to be endured, to be borne, by others who are mean and overcome by greed. *Of Aṅgīrasa (Aṅgīrasassa)*: of (him) from whose limbs (*aṅga*) brightness emanates, *rasa*[54] being a metaphorical expression for 'brightness'. It is said that when he saw beggars coming the highest joy and happiness would arise in him and his complexion would become bright. He spoke in this manner having seen this for himself.[55]

The going and coming (gatiṃ āgatiṃ vā): I do not know the going,[56] that is, that he has gone from here to such and such a destiny, nor the coming, that is, that he has come here from that place at such and such a time – this is not within my power. *But I have heard in the presence of Vessavaṇa (sutañ ca me Vessavaṇassa santike)*: nevertheless I have heard this in the presence of the Great King Vessavaṇa whilst in attendance upon him. *That Asayha has gone into companionship with Sakka (Sakkassa sahavyataṃ gato Asayho)*: that Asayhaseṭṭhi has entered into companionship with Sakka, lord[57] of the devas, meaning he has arisen in the realm of the Thirty-three.

23 *It is sufficient to do lovely deeds (alam eva kātuṃ kalyāṇaṃ)*: it is proper and seeming to do whatever is a lovely, skilled and meritorious deed. However to show that there is in this connection that which is easy and open to all, 'And to give alms as is fitting' was said. It is sufficient to give alms in accordance with one's power and means. Then he mentioned the reason: *after seeing this hand that grants desires (pāṇikāmadadaṃ disvā)*: inasmuch as by the mere telling of the way to the dwelling of a master in the practice of giving after previously rejoicing at the meritorious deeds done by another this hand that grants wishes is seen. After seeing this [123] *who would not perform meritorious deeds? (ko puññaṃ na karissati)*: who like me would not perform meritorious deeds that would be one's support (in the life to come)? Having shown his esteem for the performance of meritorious deeds in this vague fashion he now utters the two verses beginning: 'When I (have gone from here)' showing his self-commitment.

24 Herein *I: so=so ahaṃ* (alternative grammatical form). *Hi* (untranslated) is an emphatic particle. *Then (nuna)*[58] is a particle of reflection. *When (I) have gone from here (ito gantvā)*: when I have left this desert region. *And have got back to Dvāraka (anuppatvāna Dvārakaṃ)*: and have got back to the city of Dvāravatī. *I will provide (paṭṭhapayissāmi)*: I will bestow.

The yakkha was overjoyed when Aṅkura thus vowed that he would give alms and encouraged him in acts of charity saying, 'You should give alms freely, my good sir. I will assist[59] you by arranging things in such a way that your merit-offerings will not become exhausted.' (Turning to the brahmin he continued) 'Whilst you, brahmin trader, do not know your own measure when you say that you wish to carry off one such as me with the use of force', and, after causing his goods to disappear, terrified him, threatening to harm him with the attack of a yakkha.[60] Aṅkura then pleaded with him in many ways and pacified him by making the brahmin apologise and (thereby) brought about the restoration of all his goods. As night approached he dismissed the yakkha and, whilst continuing on his way, saw not far from him a certain peta that was an extremely disgusting sight. He uttered this verse enquiring about the deed he had done:

26 'For what reason are your limbs[61] distorted and your face contorted; and (why) do your eyes trickle? What wicked deed was done by you?'

26 Herein *distorted (kuṇā)*: bent, crooked, not straight. *Contorted (kuṇalīkataṃ)*: distorted, deformed,[62] with a grimace. *Trickle (paggharanti)*: flow with impurities.[63]

The peta then spoke three verses:

27 **[124]** 'I was in charge of the gifts in the almshouse of Aṅgīrasa, that home-loving householder and a man of faith.

28 When I saw beggars there who were come in need of food I stepped to one side and contorted my face.

29 For that reason my limbs are distorted and my face contorted; (this is why) my eyes trickle – this was the wicked deed done by me.'

27 Herein *of Aṅgīrasa (Aṅgīrasassa)* and so on: he praises Asayhaseṭṭhi with these (attributes). *Home-loving (gharam esino)*: one who stays at home, residing in a house. *In the almshouse (dānavissagge)*: in the house where the alms are given out, at the place of distribution. *I was in charge of the gifts (dāne adhikato ahuṃ)*: I was placed in charge of administering the almsgiving, of the distribution of the merit-offerings.

28 *I stepped to one side (ekamantaṃ apakkamma)*: when he sees beggars who are come in need of food the man who superintends the gifts should not leave the house where those gifts are given out. He should stay at that very place and, full of joy and happiness and with a clear complexion, should give the gifts with his own hand or have them given out properly by others. I, however, did not act in this way – when from afar I saw beggars coming I stepped to one side and kept out of sight. Having stepped (aside) I contorted my face, I distorted and screwed up my face.

29 *For that reason (tena)*: since, in the period during which I had been appointed by the master to administer the almsgiving, I became afflicted with meanness when the time came to serve the gifts and left the house where the gifts were given out, I have attained[64] this crookedness of foot; (since) I failed to give what I should have given with my own hands, I have attained[64] this crookedness of hand; (since I failed to have) the clear features that I should have had,[65] I have attained[64] this crookedness of face; (whilst since by my failure to look on) with the loving eyes with which I should have looked on, I gave rise to[66] this dimness of vision.

Therefore my fingers [125] and toes have become bent and distorted, my face contorted, of unsightly appearance[67] and screwed up, and my eyes trickle with impure, foul smelling, loathsome[68] tears – this is the meaning.

For this reason he said:

30 'For that reason my limbs are distorted and my face contorted; (this is why) my eyes trickle – this was the wicked deed done by me.'

When he heard this Aṅkura uttered this verse reproaching the peta:

31 'It serves you right, you wretched man, that your face is contorted and that your eyes trickle, since you contorted your face at the gift of another.'

31 Herein *it serves (you) right (dhammena)*: it is with quite fitting cause.[69] *You: te=tava* (alternative grammatical form). *You wretched man (kāpurisa)*: you despicable man. *Since: yaṃ=yasmā* (alternative grammatical form). *At the gift of another: parassa dānassa=parassa dānasmiṃ* (alternative grammatical form), or, alternatively this alone is the reading.

Aṅkura once more uttered a verse reproaching that wealthy merchant, that master in the practice of giving:

32 'How could one rely on another when giving a gift of food and drink, hard food, clothing and lodging?'

32 This is the meaning: when giving a gift how indeed could a man rely on another, have it carried out and effected by another? He himself should attend to it in person and should give it with his own hand alone. He should himself be superintendent in this. Otherwise his merit-offering might come to ruin in an inappropriate place,[70] whilst those worthy of donations would waste away with hunger.[71]

[126] When he had thus reproached him he uttered two verses showing[72] the line of action he was about to take:

33 'When I have gone, then, from here and have got back to Dvāraka I will provide alms which will bring me happiness.

34 I will give food and drink, clothing and lodging, wayside watering places, wells and bridges at places where it is difficult to cross.'

The meaning is just as already given.

These four verses were then inserted by those rehearsing the texts to show how Aṅkura acted:

35 'When he had turned back from there and had got back to Dvāraka Aṅkura provided alms which would bring him happiness.

36 He gave food and drink, clothing and lodging, wayside watering places, wells and bridges at places where it was difficult to cross.

37 "Who is hungry? And who is parched? Who will put on[73] these clothes? Whose oxen are exhausted? – They may harness a draught bullock from these. Who wants a sunshade? And perfume? Who flowers? Who some sandals?" –

38 So did barbers, cooks and scent-sellers[74] always cry out, both morning and evening, there at Aṅkura's dwelling.'

35 Herein *from there (tato)*: from that desert wilderness. *When he had turned back (nivattitvā)*: when he had turned back again. *And had got back to Dvāraka (anuppatvāna Dvārakaṃ)*: and had got back to the city of Dvāravatī. *Aṅkura provided alms (dānaṃ paṭṭhayi Aṅkuro)*: Aṅkura established a great almsgiving of everything necessary for the road from a store-house that was kept completely full by the yakkha. *Which would bring him happiness (yaṃ taṃ assa sukhāvahaṃ)*: which would produce happiness for him in both the present[75] and the future.

37 *Who is hungry? (ko chāto)*: let whoever wants to eat come and eat what he likes – this is the meaning and is to be applied to the rest too. *Parched (tasito)*: [127] thirsty. *Will put on (paridahissati)* means will dress in and wear.[76] *Are exhausted (santāni)*: are in a state of fatigue. *Oxen (yoggāni)*: draught bullocks yoked to chariots.[77] *They may harness a draught bullock from these (ito yojentu vāhanaṃ)*: they may take whichever draught bullock they like from this collection of oxen here and harness it. *Who wants a sunshade? (ko chatt' icchati)*: let whoever wants a sunshade of the sort made from rushes and so on take this – this is the meaning and is to be applied to the rest too. *Perfume (gandhaṃ)*: perfumes made from the four perfume ingredients and so on.[78] *Flowers (mālaṃ)*: flowers of the sort that are knotted together and those that are not so knotted.[79] *Some sandals (upāhanaṃ)*: sandals of the sort that have heel coverings and so on.[80]

38 *So (iti su)*: *su* (untranslated) is a mere particle. (They cried out) just so, meaning: 'Who is hungry? And who is parched?' and so on. *Barbers (kappakā)*: bath attendants.[81] *Cooks (sūdā)*: those who prepare meals. *Scent-sellers (Māgadhā)*: those who deal in scents. *Always (sadā)*: all the time, day in, day out, both morning and evening, did they cry out, call out, there at Aṅkura's dwelling – this is how it should be construed.

As time went on with this great almsgiving thus being bestowed that house where the gifts were given out became (only) sparsely[82] and occasionally (visited) by travelling-folk on account of their satiation. When Aṅkura saw this he became dissatisfied due to his lofty intent to give alms and summoned the young man named Sindhaka, whom he had appointed[83] in connection with his almsgiving, and uttered two verses:

39 ' "Aṅkura sleeps easily" – so the people believe of me; I sleep with difficulty, Sindhaka, since I see no beggars.

40 "Aṅkura sleeps easily" – so the people believe of me; (but), Sindhaka, I sleep with difficulty, the wayfarers being so few.'

39 Herein *'Aṅkura sleeps easily' – so the people believe of me (sukhaṃ supati Aṅkuro iti jānāti maṃ jano)*: 'The noble[84] Aṅkura who is endowed with fame and wealth, a master in the practice of giving, due to his attainment of wealth and successful almsgiving sleeps easily, **[128]** he falls asleep with ease and wakes up easily' – in this way the people esteem me. *I sleep with difficulty, Sindhaka (dukkhaṃ supāmi Sindhaka)*: but I sleep only with difficulty, Sindhaka. Why? *Since I see no beggars (yaṃ na passāmi yācake)*: since I do not see as many beggars receiving my merit-offerings as I had wished, meaning it is because of this.

40 *The wayfarers being so few (appake su vanibbake)*: the wayfaring-folk being so few and far between, I sleep with difficulty – this is how it should be construed. *Su* (untranslated) is a mere particle, the meaning being when there are so few wayfaring-folk.

When he heard this Sindhaka, desiring that he make more clear his lofty inclination towards giving, uttered this verse:

41 'If Sakka, lord of the Thirty-three and of all the world, were to grant you a boon, when choosing, what boon would you choose?'

41 This is the meaning: if Sakka, lord of the devas[85] of the Thirty-three and also of all the world, were to grant you, should grant you, a boon saying, 'Choose whatever boon your heart longs for, Aṅkura', when choosing, when wishing,[86] what boon, what kind of boon, might you choose?

Aṅkura then spoke two verses truly declaring his intent:

42–43 'If Sakka, lord of the Thirty-three, were to grant me a boon I would choose that boon from Sakka thus: that when I get up at sunrise there should appear heavenly foods and virtuous beggars, that whilst I am giving they should not be exhausted, that after I have given I should feel no regret and that my heart should be devoted as I give.'

42–43 Herein *when I get up (kāluṭṭhitassa me sato)*: when I arise in the early morning full of energy and vigour for honouring and waiting upon those who are worthy of a donation and in need. **[129]** *At sunrise (suriyuggamanaṃ pati)*: at the moment the sun comes up. *There should appear* *heavenly foods (dibbā bhakkhā pātubhaveyyuṃ)*: there should arise food that belongs to the devaloka. *And virtuous beggars (sīlavanto ca yācakā)*: and that there should be virtuous beggars who are of a lovely nature. *Whilst I am giving they should not be exhausted (dadato me na khīyetha)*: whilst I give to all-comers my merit-offerings should not be exhausted, should not come to an end. *After I have given I should feel no regret (datvā nānutappeyyāhaṃ)*: after I have given alms that should be given I should feel no regret when I find that someone was unworthy (of those alms). *My heart should be devoted as I give (dadaṃ cittaṃ pasādeyyaṃ)*: my heart should be devoted whilst I am giving, I should give only when there is devotion in my heart. *I would choose that boon from Sakka thus (evaṃ Sakkavaraṃ vare)*: I would choose a fivefold boon from Sakka, lord of the devas, thus: the blessings of good health, of merit-offerings, of those worthy of donations, of unlimited merit-offerings and of being their donor. In this connection by 'when I get up' (is meant) the blessing of good health; by 'there should appear heavenly foods' the blessing of merit-offerings; by 'and virtuous beggars' the blessing of those worthy of donations; by 'whilst I am giving they should not be exhausted' the blessing of unlimited merit-offerings; and by 'after I have given I should feel no regret and that my heart should be devoted as I give' the blessing of being their donor. These five things are wished for on account of their being boons;[87] they are to be understood,[88] in short, as being for the purpose of those meritorious deeds consisting in giving being lofty.

When Aṅkura thus declared his intent a man named Sonaka, who was seated there and who was well versed in prudent behaviour, spoke two verses wishing to prevent him from giving to excess:

44 'One should not bestow all one's possessions on another; one should both give alms and protect one's wealth. **[130]** Therefore wealth is better than giving – families cease to exist through giving to excess.

45 Neither the failure to give nor giving to excess are praised by the wise. Therefore wealth is better than giving; one should proceed with moderation – this is the way of the resolute.'

Wishing to put him to the test[89] Sindhaka afterwards uttered once more[90] (the verses) beginning: '(One should) not (bestow) all one's possessions'.

44 Herein *all one's possessions (sabbavittāni)*:[91] all one's possessions and means of both an animate and an inanimate variety, meaning one's articles of wealth. *On another: pare=paramhi* (alternative grammatical form), meaning on behalf of another (*parassa*). *One should not bestow (na pavecche)*: one should not give thinking, 'Those worthy of donations are

available', and not retain anything, meaning one should not make a sacrifice of all one's property. *One should both give alms (dadeyya dānañ ca)*: one should not make everything an item for almsgiving; moreover one should give alms in accordance with one's means after assessing one's income and expenditure. *And protect one's wealth (dhanañ ca rakkhe)*: one should look after one's wealth by obtaining what has not been obtained, by guarding what has been obtained and by securing what is protected; or alternatively one should protect one's wealth in the following way, this being the basis of almsgiving:

> 'One (quarter) of one's possessions should one enjoy; two (quarters) should one put to work; whilst the fourth part should one put aside or else one will be in trouble.'*[92]

Indeed these three paths are to be pursued with mutual modification say the lawgivers. *Therefore (tasmā)*: since when protecting one's wealth and when making gifts one is acting for one's benefit in both worlds[93] and since giving is based on wealth, therefore wealth is better than, is superior to, giving, and giving to excess is not to be practised – this is the meaning. For this reason he said, *families cease to exist through giving to excess (atippadānena kulā na honti)*: families cease to exist, no longer continue (to exist), meaning they are annihilated, through an attachment to giving to excess when one does not know the extent of one's wealth upon which such giving is dependent. Now establishing the fact that this is praised by the wise[94] [131] he uttered the verse (beginning:) 'Neither the failure to give nor giving to excess.'

45 Herein *neither the failure to give nor giving to excess (adānaṃ atidānañ ca)*: neither the total failure to give even a handful of rice or a ladleful of food nor giving to excess, the so-called generosity in which the limits are exceeded, are praised, are applauded, by the wise who possess insight and in whom wisdom has arisen. By the total failure to give one is indeed excluded from well being in the next world whilst by giving to excess one's family line cannot continue in this very life. *One should proceed with moderation (samena vatteyya)*: wise in the ways of the world one should follow, unreproached,[95] a middle path avoiding both extremes.[96] *This is the way of the resolute (sa dhīradhammo)*: in the aforesaid[97] matter of giving (to excess) and the failure to give this is the way of the resolute, of those who are endowed with steadfastness and who are skilled in right conduct and good behaviour – he elucidates that this is the way trodden by them.

When he heard this Aṅkura declared the line of action that he would

*D iii 188.

take with these four verses (attempting) to make him change his mind:

46 'Truly, sir, I would rather that I should just continue to give and that true and worthy men should associate with me – as a cloud filling up the lowland would I satisfy all wayfarers.

47 When one sees beggars one's complexion becomes clear and when one has given one is delighted – this is happiness for the one who dwells at home.

48 When one sees beggars one's complexion becomes clear and when one has given one is delighted – this is the successful performance of the sacrifice.[98]

49 Just before the gift one should be happy, when giving one's heart should be devoted, whilst when one has given one is delighted – this is the successful performance of the sacrifice.'

46 Herein *truly I would rather (aho vata)*: truly it were well. *Sir (re)* is a form of address. *That I should just continue to give: aham eva dajjaṃ= ahaṃ dajjam eva* (alternative grammatical form). This is the meaning in brief here: **[132]** even if, as they say, this is the view[99] of those skilled in proprieties, that wealth is better than giving, I would still prefer that I should just continue to give. *And that true and worthy men should associate with me (santo ca maṃ sappurisā bhajeyyuṃ)*: and that on the occasion that I give true, tranquil and virtuous worthy men of (good) conduct in body, speech and mind should associate with me, should approach me. *As a cloud filling up the lowland (megho[100] 'va ninnaṃ paripūrayanto)*: and truly I would rather that I should satisfy them, fulfilling[101] the wishes of all wayfarers like a great cloud pouring down on the lowlands, on the low-lying places.

47 *When one sees beggars (yassa yācanake disvā)*: when he sees beggars the complexion of the home-loving person becomes clear and faith arises as he thinks, 'Waiting upon them at the earliest possible moment will truly be a merit-field for me', whilst when he has given alms to them in accordance with his means he is delighted, his heart is seized with joy and happiness. *This (taṃ)*:[102] this sighting here of the beggars, this devotion of heart at seeing them and this being delighted after having given alms as is fitting.

48 *This is the successful performance of the sacrifice (esā yaññassa sampadā)*: this is the accomplishment, the fulfilment, of the sacrifice, meaning its completion.[103]

49 *Just before the gift one should be happy (pubbe 'va dānā sumano)*: just before (the gift), from the preparation of the alms materials onwards, one should be happy, one should become full of happiness at the intention of delivering[104] (the gift) thinking, 'I will lay down a hoard that will

follow me as the foundation of my excellence in the next world.'[105] *When giving one's heart should be devoted (dadaṃ cittaṃ pasādaye)*: when giving, when placing the merit-offering in the hand of one worthy of donations,[106] one's heart should be devoted thinking, 'From wealth that is worthless I am making a gift of value.' *Whilst when one has given one is delighted (datvā attamano hoti)*: whilst when one has given out the merit-offerings to those worthy of donations, one is delighted, very pleased, full of joy and happiness at the thought, 'I have carried out what was ordained by the wise. Oh, this is good, this is excellent!' *This is the successful performance of the sacrifice (esā yaññassa sampadā)*: [**133**] the fulfilment of the three intentions which are happily held and accompanied by a belief[107] in the fruition of deeds – the intentions before, during and after delivering (the gift) – this is the successful performance of, the accomplishment of, the sacrifice; it is not otherwise – this is the meaning.

When Aṅkura had thus declared the line of action he was to take he day in, day out, maintained a great almsgiving, his intent on giving being all the more increased. Because of this the whole kingdom at that time put its work aside for the festivities.[108] When that great almsgiving was in progress the people who had received all the necessary means of existence abandoned their respective labours and roamed about at pleasure. Due to this the royal treasuries became empty and the kings thereupon sent a messenger to Aṅkura to say, 'On account of your alms, sir, our economy has been ruined and our treasuries have become empty. You should learn the proper (extent to which alms should be given).'

When he heard this Aṅkura went to Dakkhiṇāpatha[109] and in the Tamil region had a large number of alms-halls built at a place not far from the sea and, maintaining great almsgivings, remained there for the rest of his life, arising at the breaking up of the body after dying in the realm of the Thirty-three. Those rehearsing the texts spoke these verses showing the glory of his gifts and his heavenly arising:

50 'Sixty thousand cartloads of food were given constantly to the people at the residence of Aṅkura who had an eye towards meritorious deeds.

51 Three thousand cooks,[110] adorned with jewelled earrings, who superintended the gifts for the sacrifice owed their livelihood to Aṅkura.

52 Sixty thousand men, young men adorned with jewelled earrings, chopped firewood at Aṅkura's great almsgiving.

53 [**134**] Sixteen thousand women, all adorned and bejewelled, prepared[111] the various (ingredients) at Aṅkura's great almsgiving.

54 Sixteen thousand (women), all adorned and bejewelled, stood ready with ladle in hand at Aṅkura's great almsgiving.

55 This kṣatriya gave much to many, he gave for a long while, thoughtfully, with due care and with his own hand, again and again.

56 Aṅkura maintained his great almsgiving for a long period, for many fortnights and months, (for many) seasons and years.

57 After Aṅkura had thus given and performed sacrifices for that long period he quit the human body and reached the Thirty-three.'

50 Herein *sixty thousand cartloads: saṭṭhivāhasahassāni=vāhānaṃ saṭṭhisahassāni* (resolution of compound); food, sixty thousand cartloadsful of fragrant husked rice and so on, was given constantly, day in, day out, to the people, to groups of beings, at the residence of Aṅkura who had an eye towards meritorious deeds, who was intent on giving, who was inclined towards giving – this is how it should be construed.

51 *Three thousand cooks (tisahassāni sūdā hi)*: as many as three thousand cooks to prepare the meal. And these referred to (here) are only the head cooks – it should be understood that each one of these had countless others to do his bidding. Some read *tisahassāni sūdānaṃ* here (alternative grammatical form). *Adorned with jewelled earrings (āmuttamaṇikuṇḍalā)*: wearing variously jewelled and ornamented earrings. But this is merely an example for they were also adorned, wearing bracelets and girdles and so on. *Owed their livelihood to Aṅkura (Aṅkuraṃ upajīvanti)*: they lived dependent upon him, meaning they were dependent upon him for their living. *Who superintended the gifts for the sacrifice (dāne yaññassa vyāvaṭā)*: [**135**] who entered eagerly upon superintending the gifts, upon the sacrificial act, for the sacrifice, for that Great Sacrifice[112] so-called.

52 *Young men chopped firewood (kaṭṭhaṃ phālenti māṇavā)*: young people who were dressed and adorned chopped, split, firewood for cooking the various exquisite foods both hard and soft and so on.

53 *The various (ingredients) (vidhā)*: those spices that are recommended as suitable additions to food. *Prepared (piṇḍenti)*: mixed by grinding together.

54 *With ladle in hand (dabbigāhā)*: with spoon in hand. *Stood ready (upaṭṭhitā)*: they went and stood at the place where the meals were served.

55 *Much (bahuṃ)*: a great deal, an abundance. *To many (bahūnaṃ)*: to a countless number. *Gave (pādāsi)*: gave in various ways. *For a long while (ciraṃ)*: for a long time; he had arisen when the human life-span was twenty thousand years,[113] giving much to many for all that long time. To show the manner in which he gave 'with due care' and so on was said. Herein *with due care (sakkaccaṃ)*: with respect,[114] with that which is

wanted[115] and without contempt. *With his own hand: sahatthā=sahatthena* (alternative grammatical form); not merely by means of a command. *Thoughtfully (cittiṃ katvā)*:[116] he honoured (them) with his thoughts given over to respect and esteem. *Again and again (punappunaṃ)*: many times; he did not do it once or on a few occasions, he gave on countless occasions – this is how it should be construed. Now it was to clarify just what he did again and again that they spoke the verse (beginning:) '(Aṅkura maintained his great almsgiving for a long period,) for many (fortnights and) months.'

56 Herein *for many months (bahumāse)*: for many and countless months, beginning with the month of Citta.[117] *Fortnights (pakkhe)*:[118] for many fortnights, the dark and bright halves (of the month). *(For many) seasons and years (utusaṃvaccharāni ca)*: for many seasons such as spring and summer and so on and for many years, each beginning with the month of Citta; this is throughout the accusative case in the sense of a continuous period of time. *For a long period (dīghaṃ antaraṃ)*: for a long period of time. After having already explained that 'he gave for a long while' referred to his maintaining that almsgiving for a long time, (this verse) beginning: '(Aṅkura maintained his great almsgiving for a long period,) for many (fortnights and) months' was repeated to emphasise that he maintained this without interruption – **[136]** this is how it should be regarded.

57 *Thus (evaṃ)*: in the manner stated. *Had given and performed sacrifices (datvā yajitvā ca)*: these are one and the same in meaning;[119] had given by way of giving out merit-offerings to those who were worthy of donations (and), again, performed sacrifices by way of the Great Sacrifice, giving to all in need as much as they desired in the manner stated, that is, that '(this kṣatriya) gave much to many'. *He quit the human body and reached the Thirty-three (so hitvā mānusaṃ dehaṃ Tāvatiṃsūpago ahu)*: at the end of his life Aṅkura gave up the human state and reached a group of devas of the Thirty-three by way of rebirth. Whilst he was enjoying heavenly excellence after thus arising amongst the Thirty-three there was, in the time of our Lord, a young man named Indaka who, with devotion in heart, had spoon-alms[120] dealt to the venerable elder Anuruddha as he wandered about in search of alms. He died in due course and arose, by means of the majesty of that meritorious deed that had gone to the field, amongst the Thirty-three as a devaputta of great majesty and great psychic power, shining brilliantly and surpassing the devaputta Aṅkura in the ten attributes of heavenly appearance and so on. For this reason it was said:

58 'After giving a spoonful of food to Anuruddha Indaka quit the human body and reached the Thirty-three.

59 In ten ways Indaka outshone Aṅkura: in appearance, voice, taste, fragrance and touch (all) pleasing to the mind,
60 In length of life and fame, in complexion, happiness and sovereignty – (thus) Indaka outshone Aṅkura.'

59 Herein *in appearance (rūpe)*: in the matter of appearance, meaning with respect to his excellence of appearance. *Voice (sadde)* and so on: the same is to be applied to these too.
60 *In length of life (āyunā)*: in life-span. But is not the life-span of the devas[121] said to be of a definite length? That is true but only as a general rule for, indeed, death comes to some devas prematurely[122] due to the failure of the means[123] and so on. Indaka, however, will complete a full three koṭis and sixty thousand years besides. For this reason it was said that he outshone in length of life.[124] *In fame (yasasā)*: [137] in his excellence of a large[125] retinue. *In complexion (vaṇṇena)*: in his excellence of physical form. This blessing of the condition of his appearance could be indicated just by the phrase 'in appearance' (in the preceding verse). *In sovereignty (ādhipaccena)*: in supremacy.

Whilst Aṅkura and Indaka were enjoying heavenly excellence after arising thus amongst the Thirty-three our Lord, in the seventh year following his supreme enlightenment, performed the Twin Miracle[126] on the night of the full moon in the month of Āsāḷhī[127] at the foot of the Gaṇḍamba tree near the gate to the city of Sāvatthī. He went in due course, taking three steps,[128] to the realm of the Thirty-three and seated himself on the Paṇḍukambala Rock[129] at the foot of the Coral Tree[130] in order to teach the Abhidhamma.[131] Shining brilliantly like the sun that is newly arisen on the Yugandhara mountains[132] he outshone with the radiance from his own body the brightness of those companies of devas and Brahmās who had assembled there from the ten (thousand)[133] world systems. He saw Indaka seated close by and Aṅkura seated twelve yojanas distant and uttered this verse with the aim of explaining (the importance of) the successful attainment of those worthy of donations:

> 'A great almsgiving was given by you, Aṅkura, for a long period. You are seated too far away[134] – come into my presence.'

When he heard this Aṅkura said, 'Lord, I gave out many merit-offerings for a long time and though I maintained a great almsgiving, because of the absence of any successful attainment of those worthy of donations, there was, like seed sown in a field of barren soil, no rich fruit (therefrom). But for Indaka, though he (gave but) a gift of spoon-alms, because of his successful attainment of one worthy of donations, there is produced, like seed sown in a field of fertile soil, this extremely rich fruit.' Those rehearsing the texts spoke these verses illustrating this point:

61 'When the Buddha, the noblest of men, was staying on the Paṇḍukambala Rock at the foot of the Coral Tree in the Thirty-three,

62 The devatās assembled in the ten (thousand) world systems and paid homage to the Buddha as he sojourned on top of the Mount.

63 No deva outshone the Buddha in appearance – excelling all those devas the Buddha alone shone brilliantly.

64 **[138]** At that time Aṅkura was twelve yojanas away whilst Indaka, outshining him, was close to the Buddha.

65 The Buddha, looking at both Aṅkura and Indaka, spoke these words paying honour[135] to those worthy of donations,

66 "A great almsgiving was given by you, Aṅkura, for a long period. You are seated too far away – come into my presence."

67 Prompted by the one with self developed Aṅkura replied saying, "Of what use are those gifts to me? They were devoid of any worthy of donations,

68 Whereas this yakkha Indaka gave some trifling gift and outshines us as does the moon the host of stars.

69 Just as, when even much seed is planted in a field of barren soil[136] it yields no abundant fruit nor pleases its cultivator,

70 Even so do many gifts, when established amongst those of poor conduct, yield no abundant fruit nor please their donor.

71 And just as, when little seed, even, is planted[137] in a field of fertile soil and suitable[138] showers are bestowed, the fruit pleases its cultivator,

72 Even so is there great fruit when even the slightest meritorious action is done with respect to those of such a nature as to possess virtue and good qualities." '

61 Herein *in the Thirty-three (Tāvatiṃse)*: in the realm of the Thirty-three. *On the Paṇḍukambala Rock (silāyaṃ paṇḍukambale)*: when the Buddha, the noblest of men, was staying on the rock throne named the Paṇḍukambala – this is how it should be construed.

62 *The devatās assembled in the ten (thousand) world systems (dasasu lokadhātūsu sannipatitvāna devatā)*: the devatās of the sphere of sense-desire and the devatās of the Brahmā(-worlds) assembled together in the ten thousand cakkavaḷas, the so-called field of rebirth, to pay homage to the Buddha, the Lord, and with the aim of hearing the Dhamma. For this reason it was said: 'And paid homage to the Buddha as he sojourned on top of the Mount', meaning on top of Sineru.

64 [**139**] *At that time Aṅkura was twelve yojanas away (yojanāni dasa dve ca Aṅkuro 'yaṃ tadā ahu)*: at that time, at the time that he faced the Teacher, Aṅkura of the aforementioned conduct was twelve yojanas distant, meaning that he was seated at a place twelve yojanas distant from the place where the Teacher was seated.

67 *Prompted by the one with self developed (codito bhāvitattena)*: prompted by the Perfect Buddha, by the one with the mind developed through cultivation of the ariyan paths and training in the (ten) perfections.[139] The verses beginning: 'Of what use are those (gifts) to me?' were spoken by Aṅkura in reply to the Teacher. Herein *they were devoid of any worthy of donations (dakkhiṇeyyena suññataṃ)*: 'Since my gifts at that time were devoid, empty, lacking, of any worthy of donations, of what use therefore are those gifts to me?' he says, scorning his meritorious deeds of giving.

68 *Yakkha (yakkho)*: devaputta. *Gave: dajjā=datvā* (alternative grammatical form). *Outshines us (atirocati amhe hi)*: he shines brilliantly exceeding that of those like me; *hi* (untranslated) is a mere particle. It means he shines brilliantly, outshining and surpassing us. As does what did he say? As does the moon the host of stars.

69 *Of barren soil (ujjaṅgale)*: that is an extremely hard piece of ground; some say it means 'saline'. *Is planted (ropitaṃ)*: is sown; or is sown, dug up and replanted. *Nor pleases (na pi toseti)*: nor delights; or there is no joy produced through its scanty fruition.

70 *Even so (tath' eva)* means just as, when even much seed is planted in a field of barren soil it yields no abundant fruit, no rich fruit, nor pleases its cultivator thereby, even so do even many gifts, when established[140] amongst those of poor conduct, amongst those lacking morality, yield no abundant fruit, no great fruit, nor please their donor thereby.

71 *And just as, (when little seed), even, (is planted in a field) of fertile soil (yathā pi bhaddake)*: the meaning should be construed as the reverse of what has been said of the two (preceding) verses – this is how it should be understood. Herein *and suitable showers are bestowed (sammādhāraṃ pavecchante)*: and rain showers are properly sent forth, meaning when the (sky-)deva pours down every five, ten or fifteen days.

72 *As to possess good qualities (guṇavantesu)*: as to apply themselves to good qualities such as the jhānas and so on. *To those of such a nature (tādisu)*: [**140**] to those who have attained such characteristics as are agreeable and so on. *Action (kāraṃ)* is given with a distortion of gender,[141] meaning a service. What kind of service did he say? A meritorious one.

These verses were inserted by those rehearsing the texts:

73 'Gifts are to be given with discrimination – then what is given is of

great fruit. When gifts have been given with discrimination their donors go to heaven.

74 Giving with discrimination is praised by the Sugata.[142] That which is given to those who are worthy of donations here in this world of the living is of great fruit as is seed sown in a field of fertile soil.'

73 Herein *with discrimination: viceyya=vicinitvā* (alternative grammatical form); when one has ascertained by means of wisdom that (the proposed recipient of the gift) is a merit-field. The rest is quite self-evident throughout.

Beginning with (the verse:) 'A great almsgiving was given by you', this Aṅkura Peta Story was raised by the Teacher[143] in the realm of the Thirty-three before the devatās of the ten thousand cakkavāḷas with the aim of explaining (the importance of) the successful attainment of those worthy of donations. When he had taught the Abhidhamma there for three months for the sake of the Mahāpavāraṇā ceremony[144] that Deva of Devas[145] descended from that devaloka, surrounded by troops of devas[146] to the city of Saṅkassa.[147] In due course he reached Sāvatthī and, whilst staying in the Jeta Grove, taught in detail in the midst of the four assemblies with the aim of explaining (the importance of) the successful attainment of those worthy of donations, beginning with 'That purpose for which we were going'[148] and brought the teaching to a climax with a discourse on the Four (Noble) Truths. At the conclusion of the teaching insight into the Dhamma[149] arose to countless thousands of koṭis of beings.

[1] Reading Asitañjananagare with Se Be and below for text's -nigame.

[2] Literally, the North Road, 'the great northern route now known as the Grand Trunk Road or as Rāh-i-Azam connected the principal capitals and trading centres like Tāmralipti, Campā, Pāṭaliputra, Vārāṇasī, Kauśāmbī, Kānyakubja, Mathurā, Hastināpura, Śrughna, Śākala, Takṣaśilā, Puṣkalāvatī, Kāpiśī, Bamyan, Bāhlīka and Kamboja. Probably it was the greatest overland route in Asia along which numerous caravans plied throughout the year', V. S. Agrawala in *The Bhakti Cult and Ancient Indian Geography* (ed. D. C. Sircar), Calcutta 1970, p. 144. In time, however, the term came to denote 'the whole of Northern India, from Aṅga in the east to Gandhāra in the north-west, and from the Himālaya in the north to the Vindhyā in the south. The chief divisions included in this territory are . . . Kasmīra-Gandhāra and Kamboja' (DPPN i 363). Gandhāra and Kamboja approximate to modern Kashmir and the North-West Frontier; cp B. N. Chaudhury, *Buddhist Centres in Ancient India*, Calcutta 1969, Chapter 2.

[3] Reading puttaṃ with Se Be for text's puttā.

[4] Madhurā, or Mathura, is frequently called Uttaramadhurā, northern Madhurā, to distinguish it from Madurai in Tamil Nadu. Mathura is an important centre for the followers of Kṛṣṇa. This story should be read in conjunction with the Ghaṭa Jātaka

which is an interesting variant of some of the material later welded into the Kṛṣṇa legend – the Vāsudeva of our story being Kṛṣṇa – mixed up with some of the details of II 6.

[5] Text mis-spells Dvārāvatiyaṃ here.

[6] Reading bhaṇḍāgāriko with Se Be for text's bhāṇḍagāriko.

[7] Literally, Asayha the wealthy merchant; cp PvA 3.

[8] Reading -kapaṇaddhika- with Se Be for text's -kapaṇiddhika-; cp PvA 78.

[9] Reading -vaṇibbaka- with Se PvA 78 for text's Be -vanibbaka-.

[10] pāliyaṃ, the canonical section and here presumably the verses below although at PvA 2 Dhammapāla more than suggested that the introductory story should also be seen as having originated with the Buddha himself; cp PvA 99.

[11] Reading vyāvaṭo with Se Be and text prior to Hardy's emendation to 'vyāvaṭo at PvA 303.

[12] Reading assadūtehi with Se Be for text's assa dūtehi.

[13] khandhāvāra, usually the halting place of a caravan; PED sv speculates on whether this might be the origin of the English term.

[14] Reading ayoniso manasi karonto with Se Be for text's ayoniso ummujjanto.

[15] Reading tena gamanena sādhetabbo attho with Se Be for text's tena dhanena sādhetabbā ti attho.

[16] sappurisa, usually a technical term and synonymous with ariya and sāvaka; cp M i 8 and cty on v 7 below.

[17] Reading dukkhapanūdako bahūpakāro with Se Be for text's dukkhapanudano bahupakāro.

[18] Reading samūlam pi sahamūlena pi with Se Be for text's saha mūlena samūlaṃ pi.

[19] This verse, together with v 3 above, recur at J vi 310.

[20] Reading ekarattimattam pi kevalaṃ with Be for text's ekarattimattaṃ na kevalaṃ (Se ekarattimattam pi, na kevalaṃ).

[21] atthato; cp A. K. Coomaraswamy, 'Some Pali Words', *Harvard Journal of Asiatic Studies* IV, 2, 1939 sv vyañjana (pp. 171–181).

[22] Reading hato allapāṇihato nāma with Se Be for text's hato allapāṇinā.

[23] suppasayho; pasayha was rendered 'by force' in v 2.

[24] iddhi, usually rendered 'psychic power'.

[25] These are the rulers of the various devalokas of the kāmāvacara and are said to surpass the devas of their realms in the ten ways mentioned at vv 59–60 below; cp A iv 242.

[26] The wheel-turning monarch, or cakkavattin, forms the subject of the Cakkavatti-Sīhanāda Suttanta (D iii 58–79); see also D ii 172–177. His treasures are discussed in detail at M iii 172–177 where his happiness, the ultimate in human happiness, is said not to count when set beside that of the devas.

[27] Reading payogavipattiyaṃ with Be (Se -ttiyā) for text's -vippattiyaṃ.

[28] Reading yakkho 'va samāno na yo vā so vā with Se Be for text's yakkho vasamāno nayo vāso vā.

[29] Reading upapanno with Se Be and verse for text's uppanno.

[30] Reading mantappayogādīhi with Se Be for text's mantayogādīhi; cp PvA 96.

[31] Reading vuttā. Ito paraṃ with Se Be for text's Vutta ito paraṃ.

[32] A heavenly musician, usually belonging to the realm of the Four Great Kings. They are under the sway of Dhataraṭṭha, Great King of the eastern quarter (D ii 257, iii 197) but dwell 'in the fragrance of root-wood, in the fragrance of heart-wood, in the fragrance of pith . . . bark . . . sap . . . in that of leaves . . . flowers . . . savours . . . scents' (KS iii 197).

[33] asayhasāhino, of the one who endures (sāhino) what is beyond endurance (asayha), a play on the proper name Asayha; the whole expression – asayhasahīno Aṅgīrasassa – is usually an epithet of the Buddha, e.g. It 32; Thag 536 etc.

[34] Vessavaṇa, another name for Kubera, encountered at I 4[2]. He is one of the Four Great Kings, who rules over the northern quarter with the aid of his troops of yakkhas to which this yakkha no doubt belongs.

[35] Reading madhurarasavissandako with Se Be for text's -visandako.

[36] Reading madhurakaṭukakasāvādibhedā with Se Be for text's -katukasavādibhedā.

[37] Reading vissandanti with Se Be for text's visandanti.

[38] Cp the alternative accounts given at MLS ii 52 n. 5.

[39] Reading ahosī ti with Se Be for text's ahosin ti.

[40] Reading samādāya with Se Be for text's samādāyo.

[41] nivattana-.

[42] Reading saṃvattitapuññakiriyālakkhaṇena with Be for text's paṭipuñña-, Se pattipuñña-.

[43] Readings vary somewhat here. I follow Be (≙ Se) dāne nirantarappavattāya pariccāgasampattiyā lobhassa ca abhibhavena patibhūtassa for text's dānena nirantarappavattāya pariccāgasampattiyā lobhassa cāga-abhibhavena patibhūtassa.

[44] So Se Be for text's vaṇidīpakā.

[45] Reading pavedentā with Se Be for text's pavedento.

[46] That is, the verb here takes two patients, both in the accusative: (they) would ask me (maṃ) for the residence (nivesanaṃ).

[47] ādarabhāvaṃ uppādetvā, literally having given rise to thoughts of esteem, esteem, that is, for the principle itself that gifts to the spiritually worthy result in merit.

[48] Reading pītiṃ uppādento with Se Be for text's pi uppādento.

[49] Perhaps a celestial tree in Sakka's heaven – cp SED sv santāna. PvA 176 states that Sakka's Nandana Grove contains the wish-granting tree *and so on* and B. Walker's *Hindu World*, London 1968, ii 218 names five trees to be found there: (1) mandāra; (2) pārijāta; (3) saṃtānaka; (4) chandana; and (5) kalpa-vṛkṣa, or the wish-granting tree. The third of these, the santāna, is said to ensure progeny and the continuation of one's line forever if its leaves are chewed.

[50] Reading tāva with Se Be for text's tava.

[51] Reading Asayhamahāseṭṭhi with Be (Se Asayhamahāseṭṭhi nāma) for text's Asayhamahāseṭṭhinā.

[52] Reading sappurisadhurassa with Se Be for text's sappurisassa madhurassa.

[53] Reading pariccāgādi with Se Be for text's paricāgādi.

[54] So Se Be for text's rassa. Cp cty on Thag 536 at Ev i 207f. Rasa usually has the meaning of taste, flavour and so on.

[55] Following Se Be, text should have a full stop, not a colon, after evam āha.

[56] Reading gato ti gatiṃ vā with Se Be for text's gato ti vā.

[57] inda, Skt. Indra.

[58] Cp PvA 282.

[59] sahāyakiccaṃ karissāmi, literally I will do what a friend should do.

[60] Reading yakkhavihiṃsakāya with Se Be for text's yakkhaṃ vihiṃsakāya.

[61] aṅgulī; it might also be taken as fingers and toes but the cty on v 29 suggests otherwise.

[62] All texts disagree here. Text reads sakuṇitaṃ (vl saṃkuṇḍitaṃ); Be reads saṃkuṇitaṃ and Se saṅkucitaṃ; PED sv kuṇalin recommends reading saṅkucitaṃ. The meaning is little affected.

[63] Reading asuciṃ (Se asucī) vissandanti with Se Be for text's asuci vissandenti.

[64] Reading āpajjiṃ with Se Be for text's āpajji.

[65] Reading bhavitabbe with Se Be for text's bhavitabbaṃ.

[66] Reading uppādesiṃ with Se Be for text's uppādesi.

[67] Reading virūparūpaṃ with Se Be for text's virūparūpena.

[68] Reading asuciduggandha- with Se Be for text's asuci duggandha-.

[69] Cp PvA 286.

[70] aṭṭhāne; cp PvA 27f. above for a definition.
[71] Reading chātena with Se for text's sātena, Be dānena; cp chāto also in v 37.
[72] Reading dassento with Se Be for text's dento.
[73] Reading paridahissati with Be for text's Se parivassati; cp PED sv paridahati.
[74] Māgadhā, literally people from Magadha.
[75] Reading sampati with Se Be for text's sampatti.
[76] Reading nivāsessati pārupissati ca with Be for text's paridahissati nivāsessati pārupissati va (Se paridahessati nivāsessati pārupissati ca).
[77] Reading ratha- with Se Be for text's rattha-.
[78] PED sv catur gives these as saffron, jasmine, Turkish (tarukkha) and Greek (yavana) incense but cites no authority; cp Milinda's Questions ii 213 n. 3.
[79] Reading ganthitāganthitabhedaṃ with Se Be for text's gaṇṭhikādibhedaṃ, (flowers) of the gaṇṭhikā variety and so on. The gaṇṭhikā appears as the gaṇḍikā at Vv 35⁴, VvA 161 identifying it as the red bandhujīvakā flower – cp M ii 14; D ii 111; Vism 174. Stories of the Mansions p. 74 n. 4 states this is the hibiscus whereas PED, SED sv both take it as the Pentapetes phoenicea, SED adding that 'it is a plant with a red flower which opens at midday and withers away the next morning'. Mālā, here rendered flowers in accordance with the adopted reading, often means a garland and the cty thus explains mālā as either flowers knotted into a garland or flowers in general.
[80] khallabaddhādibhedaṃ; see B of Disc iv 246 n. 6 and Vin Texts ii 15.
[81] nahāpakā; barbers seem to have had the dual role of hairdressing and preparing baths.
[82] Se viralaṃ, Be viraḷaṃ; text omits.
[83] niyuttaṃ, similarly used in the cty to v 29 of the man appointed by Asayhaseṭṭhi and a practice criticised by Aṅkura in v 32.
[84] rājā; he was of course a prince but does not seem to have fulfilled any royal duties.
[85] Se Be add devānaṃ here.
[86] Reading patthayamāno with Se Be for text's paṭṭhayamāno.
[87] Reading atthā varabhāvena with Be for text's attāvarabhāvena; Se reads atthāvahanabhāvena.
[88] Reading veditabbā with Se Be for text's veditabbaṃ.
[89] Reading vīmaṃsitukāmo with Se Be for text's vimaṃsi ukāmo.
[90] Reading puna with Se Be for text's pana.
[91] So Se Be; text wrongly has na sabbavittāni.
[92] Cp Dial iii 180 n. 3 where it is stated that according to Buddhaghosa almsgiving and other personal expenditure are to come from the first quarter, those to be enjoyed.
[93] Reading ubhayalokahitāya with Se Be for text's ubhayattha lokahitāya; this world and the world to come are meant.
[94] Reading pasaṃsitamevatthaṃ with Se Be for text's pasaṃsitāya pi taṃ evatthaṃ.
[95] agarahitena; Be alone reads samāhitena, composed or collected in mind and thus perhaps 'balanced', here.
[96] avisamena, literally not unevenly, and a gloss on samena, with moderation, and therefore 'not lacking moderation'; the extremes are the failure to give and giving to excess.
[97] Reading yathāvuttā with Se Be for text's yathāvuttaṃ.
[98] Reading yaññassa sampadā here and in the following verse with Be for text's Se puññassa sampadā. Yañña-sampadaṃ appears at D i 128 in a similar context, the reinterpretation and redirection of the brāhmaṇic sacrificial ritual.
[99] Reading vādo ti ye vadanti pi with Se for vādo vadanti te; Be reads vādo tava hotu.
[100] Text mis-spells mego here.
[101] paripūrento; this same verb was rendered 'filling up' when applied to the cloud

in the verse and the translation obscures the intended parallel somewhat.

[102] Reading tan ti with Be for text's taṃhi (Se taṃ hi).

[103] Reading nipphatti with Se Be for text's nibbatti.

[104] Reading muñcanacetanāya with Se Be for text's muñcanaṃ cetanāya.

[105] Cp PvA 253.

[106] Reading dakkhiṇeyyahatthe with Se Be for text's dakkhiṇe hatthe.

[107] Reading kammaphalasaddhānugatānaṃ with Se Be for text's kammaphala-laddha-.

[108] Reading unnaṅgalāni with Se Be for text's dunnaṅgalāni.

[109] Like the Uttarāpatha discussed above, this seems originally to have denoted the road leading to the south but in later time the area lying between the south bank of the Ganges and the Godāvarī. By the time of this text its denotation has been extended so as to include the whole of peninsular India in that the Tamil region is said to be part of it. It is also from this term that the more familiar Deccan is derived. See DPPN i 1050 and B. N. Chaudhury, op. cit., pp. 225ff.

[110] Reading tisahassāni sūdā hi with Se Be for text's janā tisahassā sūdā.

[111] piṇḍenti, literally made into a piṇḍa, the lump of food in the shape of a small ball that was given as food for the pitṛs in brāhmaṇic ritual as well as in almsgiving generally. They usually consisted of meat or flour.

[112] Mahāyāga, the four brāhmaṇic sacrifices of the assamedha, horse sacrifice, purisamedha, human sacrifice, sammāpāsa, throwing of pegs, and vājapeyya, soma-offering – see e.g. S i 76; A ii 42; Sn 303; and discussion at KS i 102 n. 1 and GS ii 50 n. 1 etc. PED sv yajati states that 'in the Pali literature it refers (with yañña, sacrifice) either (when critical) to the Brāhmaṇic rites of sacrificing to the gods according to the rules initiated in the Vedas and Vedic literature; or (when dogmatical) to the giving of alms to the bhikkhu. In the latter sense it implies liberal donation of all the necessities of a bhikkhu.' However it should not be forgotten that charity and hospitality towards the brahmin was also understood as a sacrifice, as Aṅkura's pre-Buddhist charity here confirms, and such charity was often given on behalf of the deceased (cp PvA 27f.). It is moreover precisely this pre-Buddhist, brāhmaṇic concept of sacrifice to the almsworthy that the Petavatthu is seeking to redirect, away from the barren soil of the brahmin and towards the merit-field of the Sāvakasaṅgha, the members of which are said to be 'worthy of alms, worthy of hospitality, worthy of offerings, worthy of reverence' (all qualities hitherto assumed by the brahmin) and thus 'the world's unsurpassed merit-field' (e.g. D iii 227; M i 37; S ii 69f.; A i 222 etc.). See R. Amore, *The Concept and Practice of Doing Merit in Early Theravāda Buddhism*, University Microfilms, Ann Arbor, Michigan 1971, and J. Gonda, *Loka: World and Heaven in the Veda*, Amsterdam 1966.

[113] For the variation in the human life-span cp especially D iii 58–79.

[114] Reading sādaraṃ with Se Be for text's ādaraṃ.

[115] Reading anapaviddhaṃ with Se Be for text's anāviddhaṃ; cp M iii 22; MLS iii 72 n. 3; GS iv 262 n. 6.

[116] On this expression see also M iii 22, 24; A iii 171f., iv 392; MLS iii 72 n. 2, where these four, sakkaccaṃ, cittiṃ katvā, sahatthā and anapaviddhaṃ are combined with āgamanadiṭṭhiko, (giving) with regard to the future, that is, believing in the fruition of deeds.

[117] Reading bahumāse ti cittamāsādike with Se Be for text's bahumāse ti cittamāse ti cittamāsādike. Citta, Skt Caitra, is March–April and first month of the year.

[118] Reading Pakkhe ti with Se Be for text's tatthāpi.

[119] Reading atthato ekam eva with Se Be for text's atthato.

[120] Cp Vin i 55, Thag 934 and note at B of Disc iv 72 n. 2.

[121] Reading nanu ca devānaṃ with Se Be; text has nanūpadevānaṃ, but it is not (the life-span) of the minor devas. This would seem to be the only occurrence of the term upadeva and perhaps suspect given the lack of support from Se Be.

See A i 213f. for details of the life-spans of the devas of the kāmaloka heavens.

[122] antarā, literally in between, midway, during etc.; cp the similar (Theravādin) interpretation of the antarā-parinibbāyin as one who attains parinibbāna before half the life-span usual to the heaven into which he has appeared has passed.

[123] Cp PvA 117.

[124] In all 30,060,000 human years. According to A i 213f. the life-span of those in the Thirty-three is 36,000,000 human years.

[125] Reading mahatiyā with Se Be for text's mahati.

[126] This is said to be performed at Sāvatthī by all Buddhas. In response to a challenge by some heretics the Buddha announced his intention of performing this miracle at the Gaṇḍamba tree. The heretics uprooted all the surrounding mango (amba) trees but Gaṇḍa, the royal gardener, gave the Buddha a ripe mango as alms-food. This the Buddha ate and then handed the seed to Ānanda for the gardener to plant, whereupon a tree instantaneously appeared. The Buddha created a jewelled walk in the air by the side of the tree and standing thereon performed the Twin Miracle, 'so called because it consisted in the appearance of phenomena of opposite character in pairs – e.g. producing flames from the upper part of the body and a stream of water from the lower, and then alternatively. Flames of fire and streams of water also proceeded alternatively from the right side of his body and from the left. From every pore of his body rays of six colours darted forth, upwards to the realm of Brahmā and downwards to the edge of the Cakkavāḷa.' (DPPN ii 682f., which see for further details.) The episode is said to have lasted sixteen days during which he preached to those present.

[127] Skt Āṣāḍha, June–July.

[128] Reading anukkamena tipadavikkamena with Se Be for text's vītikkamena. According to Vism xii 72, 'he stood with one foot on the surface of the Earth, and placed the second on Mount Yugandhara. Then again he lifted his first foot and set it on the summit of Mount Sineru.' The Thirty-three is located on this summit. Legend has it that on a visit to Ceylon the Buddha similarly departed by stepping on Siripāda, or Adam's Peak, to which an annual pilgrimage winds its way to visit the impression left by his foot. Compare the three strides of Viṣṇu at e.g. RV vii 99[1], 100[3], viii 13[27] etc.

[129] This is the throne of Sakka, lord of the Thirty-three. It is said to be made of stone the colour of the jayasumana flower (DA 482) and from time to time it glows with heat as an indication to Sakka that a righteous person needs his protection (J v 92), that a deed of the Buddha requires his assistance (J i 330, iv 315ff.) or that virtuous deeds have been performed (J iv 401ff., v 278ff.).

[130] Each world has its own special tree (S v 237ff.), that of the Thirty-three being the Pāricchattaka, Erythrina indica, the Coral or Umbrella tree (see n. 49). It is said to have shed its flowers onto the deathbed of the Buddha (D ii 137). Cp Vv 22[2]; A iv 117ff. and GS iv 78 n. 1–4.

[131] He went to teach this to his mother who had been reborn there.

[132] Buddhist cosmography conceived a world that had at its centre an incredibly high mountain, known as Meru or Sineru, that was completely surrounded by an ocean. This ocean was in turn surrounded by a circular mountain chain known as the Yugandhara mountains, half the height of Meru, and themselves surrounded by an ocean. This pattern repeated itself, Meru being encircled alternately by seven concentric oceans and mountain chains, each of the latter being half the height of its predecessor. Beyond the seventh chain lay the Mighty Ocean in which were situated the four continents, one at each of the cardinal points, that in the south being Jambudīpa, or India. Finally a further wall of mountains encircled this Mighty Ocean marking the horizontal limits of this world. The heaven of the Four Great Kings extended from the earth's surface (hence the inclusion of terrestrial devas such as those in banyan trees) to the summit of Meru, above which was situated the realm

of the Thirty-three. The sun travelled clockwise around Meru near the summit of the Yugandhara mountains, that is, at half the height of Meru and it was thus as a result of the sun disappearing behind Meru that night (Meru's shadow) was cast over a portion of the earth's surface. The newly 'arisen' sun was really the reappearance of the sun from behind Meru at its constant height of the Yugandhara mountains. Beyond the realm of the Thirty-three lay a further four heavens of the kāmāvacara, or sphere of sense desire. Above this lay the sixteen Brahmalokas of the rūpāvacara, or sphere of form, surmounted in turn by the four worlds of the arūpāvacara, or sphere of formlessness. The horizontal system of concentric mountain chains and oceans is usually referred to by the term cakkavāḷa. Cp A i 227f.

[133] The cakkavāḷa together with its heavens and subterranean hells was considered the basic cosmological unit though varying numbers of cakkavāḷas were believed to exist adjacent to one another. Originally only ten seem to have been conceived, perhaps one in each of the ten directions (cp D ii 139). More common, however, is reference to the thousandfold world system (D i 46 = A i 276; A i 227, 281f., v 59f.; M i 213, 328; S v 175f.) whilst on occasion mention is made of Brahmās who are in charge of world systems that are one, two, three, four, five and even ten thousandfold (M iii 101; cp D ii 261), the ten thousandfold world system also appearing at D ii 12 etc. It may be that on occasion by 'world system' was meant but a single cakkavāḷa; whilst on others a group of one thousand such cakkavāḷas, in which case 'ten world systems' would mean ten systems each of one thousand cakkavāḷas, one in each of the ten directions. This seems to be the way in which Dhammapāla has understood it in the cty below. A somewhat different arrangement of multiple world systems can be found at A i 227f.

[134] Reading atidūre with Se Be and v 66 for text's avidūre.

[135] Reading sambhāvento with Be for text's Se pabhāvento.

[136] Reading ujjaṅgale with Se Be for text's ujjhaṅgale.

[137] Reading piropitaṃ with Se Be for text's viropitaṃ.

[138] Cp KS v 328 n. 5.

[139] The ariyan paths are the supermundane paths of the sotāpanna, once-returner, non-returner and arahant. See the Cariyāpiṭaka (passim); Vism ix 124; and I. B. Horner, *Ten Jākata Stories*, London 1957, each illustrating one of the ten perfections.

[140] Reading patiṭṭhāpitaṃ with Se Be for text's patiṭṭhapitaṃ.

[141] As though neuter (after puññaṃ) instead of masculine.

[142] Reading sugatappasaṭṭhaṃ with Se Be for text's -ppaseṭṭhaṃ; Sugata is an epithet of the Buddha.

[143] Reading Tayidaṃ Aṅkurapetavatthu. Satthārā with Se Be for text's Tayidaṃ Aṅkurapetavatthuṃ. Satthā.

[144] The ceremony marking the end of the three months' retreat of the rainy season.

[145] An epithet of the Buddha.

[146] This episode is a favourite subject in Buddhist art. Cp Vism xii 79: 'The Blessed One descended by the middle flight of stairs made of crystal; the deities of the six sense-sphere heavens by that on the left side made of gold; and the deities of the Pure Abodes, and the Great Brahmā, by that on the right made of silver. The Ruler of Gods held the bowl and robe. The Great Brahmā held a three-league-wide white parasol. Suyāma held a yak-tail fan. Five-crest the son of the gandhabba descended doing honour to the Blessed One with his bilva-wood lute measuring three quarters of a league. On that day there was no living being present who saw the Blessed One but yearned for enlightenment' (Path of Purification, p. 429f.); cp DPPN ii 974.

[147] So Se Be for text's Saṅkasa.

[148] The opening words of v 1 but also quoted at the very beginning of the story; it is therefore impossible to know which Dhammapāla had in mind here, though given his remarks at PvA 2 it may well have been the latter.

[149] Cp PvA 9.

II.10 EXPOSITION OF THE UTTARA'S MOTHER PETA STORY
[Uttaramātupetavatthuvaṇṇanā]

'A monk who had gone for his midday rest.' This is the Uttara's Mother Peta Story. Here is the explanation[1] of its meaning.

When the First Council had been inaugurated at the Teacher's Parinibbāna, the venerable Mahā-Kaccāyana **[141]** was staying together with twelve monks in a certain forest-haunt not far from Kosambi. Now at that time a certain special adviser of king Udena, who had formerly managed his affairs in that city, died. So the king sent for his son, a young man named Uttara, and appointed him to that position of management saying, 'Now you must administer those affairs that were managed by your father.' 'Very well', he agreed[2] and went one day to the forest taking some carpenters along in order to get some timber for repairs in the city. Whilst there[3] he approached the dwelling place of the venerable elder Mahā-Kaccāyana and saw the elder seated there alone and wearing robes made of rags from the dust heap. Becoming devout at (the sight of) his posture alone, he saluted him, extending a friendly greeting, and then sat down at one side. The elder then expounded Dhamma to him. When he heard Dhamma he became full of devotion to the Three Jewels[4] and, having been established in the Refuges,[5] invited the elder, saying, 'Please accept out of pity my (invitation), sir, to you and the monks for the following day's meal.' The elder consented by his silence. He then left that place, went to the city and informed other layfollowers, saying, 'I have invited the elder for the following day. You, too, should come to my house where the gifts are to be given out.' Early the next day he had the choicest hard and soft foods prepared, had it announced that it was time and then went out to meet the elder who was approaching with the twelve monks. He saluted them and had them enter the house in front of him. When the elder and the monks were seated on seats spread with suitable and costly coverings, he honoured them with scent, flowers, incense and lamps and satisfied them with the choicest food and drink. Full of devotion and with his hands clasped in the añjali[6] salute he listened to their appreciation. When the elder was going, after appreciation for the meal had been shown,[7] he took his bowl and following him left the city. Having him turn back he begged him, 'You should visit my house permanently, sir', and returned after learning of the elder's acceptance. Waiting thus upon the elder, he became established in his exhortation **[142]** and reached the sotāpatti-fruit. He had a vihāra built and made all his relatives find faith in the Teaching. His mother, however, had a heart possessed by the stain of selfishness and she abused him thus, 'May this food and drink that you thus give to recluses against my wishes turn out to be blood for you in the next world!' She did, however, allow one spray of peacock tail feathers to be given on the Great Day of that vihāra. When she died she arose in the peta-womb and due to her approval of that gift of the spray of peacock tail feathers her hair was black, sleek, curled at the ends, fine and long. When she went down to the water of the river Ganges thinking, 'I will drink', that river became full of blood. For fifty-five years she roamed about, overcome by hunger and thirst. Then one day she saw the elder Kaṅkhārevata[8] seated on the bank of the Ganges taking his midday rest. She approached him after covering herself with her hair and begged[9] him for some water. With reference to this (the following) was said, these two initial verses having been inserted here by those rehearsing the texts:

1 'That petī who was hideous and horrible to behold approached a monk who had gone for his midday rest and who was seated on the bank of the Ganges.

2 Her hair was extremely long and hung down as far as the ground. Covered by her hair she addressed the recluse thus.'

1 Herein *horrible to behold (bhīrudassanā)*: terrible to behold, looking very angry. An alternative reading is 'looking like Rudra' (*ruddadassanā*),[10] meaning looking disgusting and grave.[11]

2 *Hung down as far as the ground: yāva bhummāvalambare=yāva bhūmi tāva olambanti* (resolution of compound in alternative grammatical form). Firstly 'monk' and afterwards 'recluse' are both said with reference to the elder Kaṅkhārevata.

The petī approached the elder and, begging him for water, uttered this verse:

3 'For fifty-five years since I died [143] I am not conscious of having eaten or of having drunk water. Please give me some water, sir – I am parched for want of water.'

3 Herein *I am not conscious of having eaten (nābhijānāmi bhuttaṃ vā)*: throughout that long interval of time I am not conscious of having eaten food or of having drunk water, meaning I have not eaten or drunk. *Parched (tasitā)*: thirsty. *For want of water (pāniyāya)*: 'Please give me some water, sir, since I have been wandering about in search of water' – this is how it should be construed.

From here onwards are the verses of the exchange of conversation between the elder and the petī:

4 'This cool water of the Ganges flows down from the Himālaya – you can take some from here and drink. Why beg me for water?'

5 'Sir, if I myself take water from the Ganges it turns into blood for me. That is why I beg for water.'

6 'Now what evil deed[12] was done by you by body, speech or mind? As a result of which deed does the Ganges become blood for you?'

7 'My son, Uttara, sir, had faith and was a layfollower; against my will he bestowed on recluses robes and almsfood, requisites and lodging,

8 But I, vexed by selfishness, abused him saying, "May the robes and almsfood, the requisites and lodging, that you bestow on recluses against my will,

9 May this become blood for you in the next world, Uttara!" It is as a result of that deed that the Ganges becomes blood for me.'

4 Herein *from the Himālaya (Himavantato)*: from the king of mountains that has acquired the name 'the Himālaya'[13] on account of its vast amounts of snow (*himassa*). *Flows down (sandati)*: proceeds from. *From here (etto)*: from this, from the mighty Ganges. *Why? (kiṃ)*: he points out, 'For what reason do you beg me for water?[14] Go down to the river Ganges and drink as much as you like.'

5 **[144]** *It turns into blood for me (lohitaṃ me parivattati)*: because[15] of a wicked deed the water, as it flows, becomes blood for me, turns into, changes into, blood. The water becomes blood as soon as she has taken hold of it.

7 *Against my will (mayhaṃ akāmāya)*: against my wishes. *Bestowed (pavecchati)*: gave. *Requisites (paccayaṃ)*: requisites for the sick.

9 *This (etaṃ)*: 'May the requisites, such as robes and so on, that you bestowed on, that you gave to, recluses – may this become blood for you in the next world, Uttara!' It is as a result of this, the wicked deed done by way of this curse[16] – this is how it should be construed.

Then the venerable Revata gave some water to the order of monks on behalf of that petī, went in search of alms and gave the food he had gathered to the monks. He gathered rags from rubbish heaps and so on, washed them and made them into cushions and carpets[17] and gave them to the monks. And in this way that petī gained heavenly excellence. She went into the presence of the elder and showed the elder the heavenly excellence she had acquired. The elder explained the issue to the four assemblies that had come into his presence and then gave a talk on Dhamma. The people, full of agitation, thereby became free of the stain of selfishness and took delight in skilled states such as the virtue of giving and so on.

This Peta Story is to be regarded as having been included in this collection at the Second Council.

[1] Reading -vibhāvanā with Se Be for text's -vibhavanā; cp PED sv.
[2] Reading so ca sādhū ti sampaṭicchitvā with Se Be; text omits.
[3] Reading tattha with Se Be for text's tattho.
[4] The Buddha, the Dhamma and the Saṅgha.
[5] Reading saraṇesu patiṭṭhāya with Se Be for text's saraṇe supatiṭṭhāya.
[6] Reading katañjalī with Se Be for text's katañjali.
[7] Reading katabhattānumodane with Se Be for text's -ānumodanena.
[8] Cp A i 24; Thag 3.
[9] Reading yāci. Taṃ with Se Be for text's yācitaṃ.
[10] Readings vary considerably here. I follow Se: bhayānakadassanā ruṭṭhadassanā. Ruddadassanā ti vā pāṭho for text's bhayānakadassanā rudassanā, bhīru-dassanā ti vā pāṭho. Be reads bhayānakadassanā. Ruddadassanā ti vā pāṭho. This is the Vedic deity Rudra, subsequently associated with one of the terrific aspects of Śiva.
[11] Reading bībhacchabhāriyadassanā with Se Be for text's bībhacchā bhīrudassanā; cp PvA 90.
[12] Reading dukkatam with Se Be and elsewhere for text's dukkhaṭaṃ.
[13] Himavant – literally possessing snow.
[14] Reading pāniyaṃ with Se Be for text's pāniyan ti.
[15] Reading pāpakammavasena with Se for text's Be pāpakammaphalena.
[16] Reading abhisapanavasena with Se Be for text's abhisampannavasena; cp PED sv. Text wrongly inserts a full stop before Uttara.
[17] Reading dhovitvā bhisiñ ca cimilikañ ca katvā with Se Be for text's dhovitvābhisiñci cimillikañ ca katvā and as amended in PED sv abhisiñcati. It is probably better to read bhisiñ ca, cushions or mattress covers (cp Vin Texts ii 210 n. 2; B of Disc ii 47 n. 1) rather than 'bhisiñci, aorist of abhisiñcati, to sprinkle (and by extension to dye – cp B of Disc v 211 n. 6 concerning phosituṃ). Cimilikā, of uncertain meaning according to PED, seems to mean a kind of carpet. See B of Disc ii 241 n. 8, v 210 n. 4 and Vin Texts iii 167 n. 2. Buddhadatta's *English-Pali Dictionary* gives it as a rendering of 'pillow-case'.

II.11 EXPOSITION OF THE THREAD PETA STORY [Suttapetavatthuvaṇṇanā]

'In the past I (gave) to a monk, to one gone forth.' This is the Thread Peta Story. How did it originate?

It is said that more than seven hundred years before our Teacher had arisen there was in a certain village not far from Sāvatthī a young man who supported a Paccekabuddha. When he came of age his mother fetched on his behalf a certain daughter of good family from a clan of equal standing but on the very day that he was to be married the young man, who had gone with some friends to bathe, was bitten by a snake and died. They even say that it was because he was possessed by a yakkha.[1] **[145]** Although he was in the position of having done many skilled deeds on account of his support[2] for that Paccekabuddha yet because of his attachment to that girl he arose as a vimānapeta but of great psychic power and majesty. Desiring to fetch the girl to his mansion he wondered, 'Now by what means might she perform a deed to be experienced in this very life[3] and enjoy the pleasures of love with me here?' Whilst he was considering how she could experience the excellence of heavenly enjoyment he saw a Paccekabuddha making robes. He went in human form and saluted him and asked, 'Do you have any need of thread, sir?' 'We are making robes, layfollower' (he replied). He pointed out the home of the girl, saying, 'Well then, you should go and beg some thread at a place such as that.' The Paccekabuddha went there and stood at the door of the house. When she saw the Paccekabuddha standing there, she realised that the worthy one was in need of some thread from her and, with devotion in her heart, gave him a ball of thread. Then that non-human in human form went to the house of the girl, begged her mother and dwelt with her for a few days. To help her mother he filled all the vessels in their home with money and gold and wrote above his name on them all, saying, 'This wealth that has been given by the devas is not to be taken by anyone', and then took the girl and went to his mansion. Her mother, having acquired this abundant wealth, gave to her own relatives and to indigents and tramps and so on[4] and also made use of it herself. As she was dying she told her relatives, 'If my daughter comes show her this wealth', and then died.

Then seven hundred years later when our Lord had arisen in the world and had set rolling the Wheel of the Noble Dhamma and was in due course staying at Sāvatthī, dissatisfaction arose to that woman who was dwelling with the non-human. She spoke to him saying, 'My lord, please take me back to my own home', and then spoke these verses:

1 'In the past I gave[5] to a monk, to one gone forth, the thread for which he came and begged me. [**146**] As a result of that[6] abundant fruit is received and many koṭis of clothes have appeared for me.

2 Your mansion is strewn with flowers and delightful; it has countless paintings and is attended by men and women. I make use of it and clothe myself yet the abundant possessions are still not exhausted.

3 Accordingly, as the result of that same deed, happiness and pleasure are received here. When I have gone once more to (the world of) men I am determined to do meritorious deeds. Please take me, my lord.'

1 Herein *to a monk, to one gone forth (pabbajitassa bhikkhuno)*: this is said with reference to the Paccekabuddha. He is one gone forth[7] in the highest sense on account of his having renounced the stains of sense desire and so on in his own heart, leaving no remainder. He is worthy of being

called 'monk' (*bhikkhu*) on account of his having destroyed the defilements (*bhinnakilesattā*). *The thread (suttaṃ)*: the cotton thread. *He came (upagamma)*: he approached my home. *Begged me (yācitā)*: he begged me by going about for alms employing the recognised bodily posture that intimated[8] that 'The ariyans stand (merely) indicating – this is the ariyans' begging.'[9] *Of that (tassa)*: of that gift of thread. *As a result abundant fruit is received (vipāko vipulaphal' ūpalabbhati)*: as a result abundant fruit of the highest yield, the greatest yield, is now received, is now experienced. *Many (bahū)*: countless. *Koṭis of clothes: vatthakoṭiyo=vatthānaṃ kotiyo* (resolution of compound), meaning countless hundreds of thousands of different sorts of clothes.

2 **[147]** *It has countless paintings (anekacittaṃ)*: it has various kinds of painted works or[10] it is decorated with countless jewels such as pearls and gems and so on. *Is attended by men and women (naranārīsevitaṃ)*: is served by men and women as attendants.[11] *I make use of it (sāhaṃ bhuñjāmi)*: I enjoy the use of this mansion. *Clothe myself (pārupāmi)*: dress myself, put on, whatever I desire amidst the countless koṭis of clothes. *The abundant possessions (pahūtavittā)*: the abundant possession of the necessities of life, of great wealth and great prosperity. *Are still not exhausted (na ca tāva khīyati)*: yet those possessions are not exhausted, do not diminish, do not come to an end.

3 *Accordingly, as the result of that same deed (tass' eva kammassa vipākam anvayā)*: accordingly, by means of, by reason alone of that same meritorious deed of a gift of thread, the resulting happiness and pleasure consisting in what is agreeable and honey-like are received here, in this mansion. *Have gone once more to men (gantvā puna-m-eva mānusaṃ)*: have reached once more the world of men. *I am determined to do meritorious deeds (kāhāmi puññāni)*: I will do meritorious deeds that will yield exceptional happiness for me, or those from which this excellence has been obtained by me – this is the meaning. *Please take me, my lord (nay' ayyaputta maṃ)* means please take me (*naya=nehi*, alternative grammatical form) to the world of men, my lord.

When he heard this, that non-human, unwilling to go both out of pity and also because of his attachment to her, uttered this verse:

4 'It is seven hundred years since you came here. You will be old and advanced there and all your relatives will have died. What will you do when you have gone to that place from here?'

4 Herein *seven (satta)*: this is an attribute with an omission of inflexion, or a peculiar expression[12] in the ablative case. *Hundred years: vassasatā=vassasatato* (alternative grammatical form); it is upwards of seven

hundred years since you came here, since you came to this mansion, meaning it is seven hundred years since you came here. [**148**] *You will be old and advanced there (jiṇṇā ca vuḍḍhā ca tahiṃ bhavissasi)*: you have kept your youthful appearance for all this time by means of the majesty of that deed by which you are sustained here with heavenly food and temperature.[13] But when you have gone from here, due to the exhaustion of that deed and on account of the food and temperature of men, you will be old aged and advanced in years there in that world of men. *And all your relatives will have died (sabbe ca te kālakatā 'va ñātakā)*: in that such a long time has gone by all your relatives will have died. Therefore what will you do when you have gone to that place, to that world of men, from here, from this devaloka? Stay here, spend the rest of your life right here – this is the meaning.

When he had thus spoken, she again spoke, disbelieving what he had said, and uttered this verse:

5 'It is just seven years since I came here endowed with heavenly happiness. When I have gone once more to (the world of) men, I am determined to do meritorious deeds. Please take me, my lord.'

5 Herein *it is just seven years since I came here (satt' eva vassāni idhāgatāya me)*: my lord, it seems to me that only seven years have passed since I came here. She spoke in this way not realising that much time had gone by due to having been endowed with heavenly happiness for seven hundred years. When she had thus spoken that vimānapeta gave her advice in a number of ways, 'You will not live there upwards of seven days from now. There is some wealth given by me and set aside by your mother. Give this to recluses and brahmins with the wish that you might arise right here.'[14] When he had said this he took her by the arm and set her in the middle of her village,[15] telling her that she should exhort the other people who also came there to perform meritorious deeds as their means allowed, and then departed. For this reason it is said:

6 [**149**] He took her firmly by the arm and led her back, elderly and feeble, saying, 'You should tell other people who have also come here, "Perform meritorious deeds then happiness will be received." '

6 Herein *he (so)*: the vimānapeta. *Her (taṃ)*: the woman. *Took firmly by the arm (gahetvāna pasayha bāhāyaṃ)*: took her by the arm as if by force. *Led her back (paccānayitvāna)*: took her once more to the village in which she had been born and had grown up. *Elderly (theriṃ)*: as an elderly woman,[16] meaning old and advanced (in years). *Feeble (sudubbalaṃ)*: feeble on account of her age and decrepitude. It is said that immediately she left that mansion she became old, advanced (in years), stricken in years, had lived her span and was at the close of her life.[17] *You*

should tell: vajjesi=vādeyyāsi (alternative grammatical form). To show her the sort of thing she was to say, 'Other people (who have) also' and so on was said. This is the meaning: 'You, my dear, should perform meritorious deeds and you should tell, you should exhort, other people who have also come here to see you, saying, "My honourable friends,[18] even if your head or clothes[19] be ablaze[20] you should ignore this and perform meritorious deeds such as the virtue of giving and so on, for when meritorious deeds are performed the happiness that is their fruit will certainly be received[21] – there is to be no doubt as regards this!" '

When he had said this and had gone from there, the woman went to the dwelling place of her relatives and made herself known to them. She took the wealth that they presented and, giving alms to recluses and brahmins, exhorted all those coming into her presence with this verse:

7 'Petas, and human beings likewise, were seen by me as they came to grief through not having done what is good, **[150]** as well as devas and men, the race set firm in happiness, after doing deeds that were to be experienced as happiness.'

7 Herein *through not having done (akatena)*: through not having brought about, through not having themselves accumulated. *What is good (sādhunā)*: skilled deeds. This is the instrumental case with the sign of modality.[22] *As they came to grief (vihaññanti)*: as they met with distress. *That were to be experienced as happiness (sukhavedanīyaṃ)*: meritorious deeds resulting in happiness. *Set firm in happiness (sukhe ṭhitā)*: established in happiness; an alternative reading is 'borne along in happiness' (*sukhedhitā*),[23] meaning they grow and prosper[24] accompanied by happiness. This is the meaning here: just as petas, and human beings likewise, were seen by me coming to grief, meeting with the distress of hunger and thirst and so on and undergoing great misery through not having done what is skilled and through having done what is not skilled, (so also) the race belonging to devas[25] and men was seen by me set firm in happiness after doing deeds that were to be experienced as happiness – through having done skilled deeds and through not having done deeds that are not skilled. This (was seen by me) with my own eyes. Therefore be intent on the performance of meritorious deeds, keeping far away from wickedness.

Having thus exhorted them, she inaugurated a great almsgiving for recluses and brahmins that lasted seven days. On the seventh day she died and arose in the Thirty-three. The monks raised the issue with the Lord. The Lord took the matter as an arisen need and taught[26] Dhamma to the company assembled there. He explained in particular the great advantage and the great fruitfulness of alms inaugurated with respect to

Paccekabuddhas. When they heard this the people became free of the stain of selfishness and took delight in meritorious deeds such as giving and so on.

[1] Reading yakkhagāhenā ti pi with Se Be for text's yakkhagāhenāpī ti.

[2] Reading upaṭṭhānena bahuṃ with Se Be for text's upaṭṭhāne na bahuṃ. The meaning here is the very opposite of that suggested by Gehman which missed the point that attachment for a member of the opposite sex at the time of dying tended to lessen any kammic reward to which one would have otherwise been entitled – such a theme recurs from time to time, beginning with the first story; see PvA 5 above.

[3] Cp PvA 242.

[4] Reading kapaṇaddhikādīnañ ca with Se Be for text's kapaṇi-; cp PvA 78.

[5] Reading adāsiṃ with Se Be for text's adāsi.

[6] Reading tassa, with Se Be, as the first word of the third line of the verse rather than, with text, as the last word of the second line.

[7] That is, renounced the world.

[8] Reading vuttāya kāyaviññatti- with Se Be for text's vuttakāya viññatti-.

[9] uddissa ariyā tiṭṭhanti esā ariyānaṃ yācanā ti. This recurs at J iii 354 and Miln 230; it is quoted at SnA 318 and a similar passage can be found at Mvu iii 419, 420. According to the Jātaka cty the ariyans are said to stand motionless and speechless. They do not gesture by altering the posture of their bodies nor do they break their silence in order to attract attention. Rather they remain motionless and speechless, merely indicating their need of alms. Cp the discussions at Miln 229f.

[10] Se Be both add vā here.

[11] Reading paricārakabhūtehi with Se Be for text's parivāraka-; cp PvA 205.

[12] paccattavacanaṃ, more usually the accusative case.

[13] utu, temperature, one of the four causes (paccaya) of the elements (bhūta), the cause of material form (rūpa), the others being kamma, citta and āhāra (food, as here). See CPD sv utu for further details.

[14] For the role that wishing or choice can play in determining one's next birth see M i 289f., iii 99ff.

[15] Reading gāmamajjhe ṭhapetvā with Se Be for text's gāmam ajjhoṭhapetvā.

[16] Reading thāvariṃ jiṇṇaṃ with Se Be for text's thāvarijiṇṇaṃ.

[17] This is stock – see M i 82; Vin ii 88, iii 2 etc.

[18] Reading bhadramukhā with Se Be for text's -mukkha; cp n. 7 at PvA 95 above.

[19] Reading celaṃ with Se Be for text's colaṃ.

[20] This imagery recurs fairly frequently – cp S i 108, iii 143, v 440; A ii 93, iii 308, iv 320, v 93ff. etc.

[21] Reading upalabbhati with Se Be for text's upalabhati.

[22] That is, with an ablative inflexion.

[23] So Se Be for text's sukhe diṭṭhā.

[24] Reading phītā with Se Be for text's ṭhitā.

[25] Reading devamanussapariyāpannā with Se Be for text's manussāpariyāpannā.

[26] Reading desesi with Se Be for text's dassesi.

II.12 EXPOSITION OF THE KAṆṆAMUṆḌA PETA STORY
[Kaṇṇamuṇḍapetavatthuvaṇṇanā]

'The steps of your stairway are golden.'[1] This was said when the Teacher was staying at Sāvatthī concerning the Kaṇṇamuṇḍa petī.

It is said that long ago, **[151]** at the time of the Buddha Kassapa, there was in the city of Kimbilā a certain layfollower who was a sotāpanna and who was of one faith with five hundred other layfollowers. He pursued meritorious deeds such as planting pleasure-groves, compacting causeways and building bridges and so on and whilst staying there he had a vihāra built for the Saṅgha and would go with them from time to time to that vihāra. Their wives were also layfollowers and whilst going to the vihāra from time to time in harmony with one another and with perfumes, garlands and ointments and so on in their hands they would rest on the way in pleasure-groves and rest-houses and so forth before continuing. Then one day some rogues, who were seated together in one of those rest-houses, noticed their beauty as they left after having rested there and became attracted to them. When they realised that they were endowed with the quality of virtuous conduct they began to talk amongst themselves (wondering), 'Who could breach the virtue of anyone of these?' 'I could', said one of them. They made a bet saying, 'We bet a thousand. If you do it we must give you a thousand but if you do not do it you must give us a thousand.' Trying[2] in countless ways, out of greed (for the money) and fear (of losing the bet), he played a seven-stringed vīṇa,[3] producing sweet notes, as they came to the rest-house. Singing songs of an erotic nature[4] with a sweet voice he caused, by means of the sound of that song,[5] a certain woman amongst them to breach her virtue, committed adultery with her and won the thousand from those rogues. Those who lost the thousand to him reported (the matter) to her husband. Not believing them he asked her, 'Are you such as these men say?' 'I know of nothing like that', she objected. When he did not believe her she pointed to a dog standing nearby and made an oath saying, 'If I did such a wicked deed as this, may that shorn-eared black dog devour me wherever I am born!' **[152]** Though the other five hundred women knew the woman to be an adultress, when asked, 'Did she or did she not commit a wicked deed like that?', they lied saying, 'We know of no such thing', and made an oath saying, 'If we do know of this then may we be her slaves in all our (future) existences!'

Now that adulterous woman wasted away due to her heart being tormented by an uneasy conscience and, not long afterwards, died. She arose as a vimānapetī on the shore of Lake Kaṇṇamuṇḍa, one of the seven Great

Lakes[6] on the Himālaya, the king of mountains, and on all sides of her mansion there arose a lotus pond suitable for her to experience the results of her deeds.[7] When the remaining five hundred women died they arose as her slaves on account of making that oath. Through the fruit of the meritorious deeds done previously she enjoyed heavenly excellence there during the day but at midnight, urged on by the force of her wicked deeds, she rose from her bed and went to the edge of the lotus pond. When she got there a black dog the size of a young elephant, terrific[8] in appearance, with shorn ears, with long and protruding, sharp, cruel fangs, his eyes wide open and resembling the burnt embers of acacia[9] wood, his tongue striking out like an uninterrupted succession of flashing lightning,[10] with sharp and cruel claws and hideously long, shaggy hair, thereupon came and threw her to the ground, violently devouring her like one overcome by extreme hunger. When he had made a mere skeleton of her, he took her by his fangs, cast her into the lotus pond and then disappeared. When thrown therein she immediately reverted to her normal form and, after climbing out to her mansion, lay down on her bed. The others however just underwent the misery of slavery to her. They continued to live there in this way until five hundred and fifty years had elapsed whereupon they became dissatisfied as they continued to enjoy heavenly excellence in the absence of any men. Now there was there a river that issued from lake Kaṇṇamuṇḍa and that flowed into the river Ganges after passing through a mountain cleft. **[153]** Near their dwelling place was a wooded region that was like a pleasure-grove and embellished with heavenly fruits, mango trees, jack and breadfruit trees[11] and so on. They thought thus, 'Now if we were to throw these mango fruits into that river surely some man would see that fruit and come here out of greed for (such) fruit and then we could amuse ourselves with him.'[12] And they did just this. Some of the mango fruits they threw in were seized by ascetics, some by foresters and some of them adhered to the bank. One however reached the current of the Ganges and in due course reached Benares. Now at that time the king of Benares was bathing in the waters of the Ganges in an enclosure of copper-netting and that fruit, carried along by the current of the river, went in due course and adhered to that copper-netting. When the king's men saw that huge heavenly mango fruit that was full of colour, fragrance and flavour they presented it to the king. The king took a portion and, in order to test it, gave it to a robber, who was being kept in the prison awaiting execution,[13] to eat. When he had eaten it he said, 'Your majesty, never before have I eaten such a mango; this must, I think, be a heavenly mango fruit.' The king gave him a further slice and when he had eaten it his grey hair and wrinkles disappeared and he became extremely captivating in appearance, like one still in his youth. When the king saw this he was filled with wonder and amazement, ate the mango fruit and obtained elegance in body. He asked his men, 'Where are such mango fruits to be found?' 'It is said on the Himālaya, the king of mountains, your majesty', the men said and, when asked, 'Is it possible to fetch them?', they said, 'The foresters will know, your majesty.' The king sent for the foresters, told them of the matter and then consulted them. He gave a thousand kahāpaṇas to a forester in a wretched state and sent him forth [154] saying, 'Go quickly and fetch this mango fruit for me.'

He gave the thousand kahāpaṇas to his wife and children, took his provisions for the journey and followed the Ganges upstream in the direction of lake Kaṇṇamuṇḍa. When he had passed beyond the ways of men he saw an ascetic at a spot sixty yojanas below lake Kaṇṇamuṇḍa. Going along the route described by him he again saw an ascetic at a spot thirty yojanas (further on). Going along the route described by him he again saw another ascetic at a place fifteen yojanas (further on) and told him of the reason for his journey. The ascetic advised him saying, 'From here onwards you should leave this mighty Ganges and follow this small river upstream until you see a mountain cleft when you should take a firebrand and enter at night. As the river does not flow at night this is therefore a fit (time) for you to proceed. When you have gone on a few yojanas you will see the mangoes.' He did just this and at sunrise he reached that extremely captivating mango grove that resounded with the song[14] of flocks of birds of many varieties and that was embellished with clusters[15] of trees whose spread out branches were bent low under the weight of the fruit they bore,[16] the area being resplendent with a network of rays from a variety of jewels. When those non-human women saw him coming in the distance they ran up to him saying, 'This man belongs to me! This man belongs to me!' As soon as he saw them,[17] however, he was frightened as he was not one who had done meritorious deeds that would entitle him to enjoy heavenly excellence there with them and, crying aloud, ran off and reported the incident to the king when he reached Benares. When the king heard this he was filled with a desire to see those women and to eat those mango fruits, so he entrusted his kingdom to his special advisers and, on the pretext of going on a hunting trip, armed himself with bow and quiver, put on his sword and then went along the road indicated by the forester accompanied by a small retinue of men. He stationed his men at a place a few yojanas distant and continued taking just the forester and in due course he sent him back from there too [155] and entered the mango grove as the sun was rising. When the women saw him like a newly arisen devaputta they went out to meet him. When they realised he was the king they were filled with affection and esteem. They bathed him with due care and beautifully adorned him with heavenly clothes, ornaments, garlands, scents and ointments and led him up to their mansion where they fed him heavenly foods of the choicest flavours and waited on him according to his wishes.

Then after one hundred and fifty years had gone by the king arose at midnight and, whilst seated, saw that adulterous petī going to the edge of the lotus pond. He followed her, desiring to discover where she could be going at that time (of night), and saw her being devoured by the dog when she got there. He pondered (the matter) for three days without understanding what it was all about, then decided it must be her enemy and took (the dog's) life, shooting it with a sharp arrow. He then plunged[18] the woman into the pond and, when he saw that she had regained her former appearance, he questioned her about the incident with these verses:

1 'The steps of your stairway are golden and strewn with sands of gold;[19] the white water lilies[20] there are lovely, sweetly fragrant and pleasing to the mind;[21]

2 Covered with various trees and pervaded with all kinds of scents; covered with various lotuses,[22] overspread[23] with white lotuses;[24]

3 Entrancing, they waft a lovely fragrance around when fanned by the breeze;[25] resounding with the cries of swans[26] and herons, ringing with the sound of the ruddy goose;[27]

4 Crowded with flocks of various birds and full of the various songs of those flocks; the trees bearing[28] a variety of fruits and woods bearing[28] a variety of flowers;[29]

5 **[156]** – The like of such a city as this is not (found) amongst men. And you have many palaces made of silver[30] and gold; (6) dazzling, they shine forth throughout the four directions.

6 These who are your maid-servants, (these) five hundred slaves of yours, (7) they wear bracelets and bangles and their heads are adorned with chaplets of gold.[31]

7 Many couches are yours, made of silver and gold (8) and covered with (hides of the) kadalī antelope, well prepared and strewn with long-haired woollen fleeces.[32]

8 When you have gone to rest thereon you are richly endowed with all you desire, (9) yet when midnight arrives you rise from there and go out;

9 You go to the pleasure-ground and (10) you stand on the bright green grassy edge that completely surrounds that lotus pond,

10 Whereupon a crop-eared[33] dog devours you limb by limb (11) and

when he has devoured you and made a skeleton of you, you then plunge into the lotus pond and your body becomes just as it was before.

11 (12) Then with limbs restored, beautiful and lovely to behold, you put on clothes and come into my presence.

12 (13) Now what evil deed was done by you by body, speech or mind? As a result of which deed does that crop-eared dog devour you limb by limb?'

1 Herein *the steps of your stairway are golden (sovaṇṇasopānaphalakā)*: the steps of your stairway are made of gold. *And strewn with sands of gold (sovaṇṇavālukasanthatā)*: and strewn[34] all around with sands made of gold. *There (tattha)*: on the lotus pond. *White water lilies: sogandhiyā= sogandhikā* (alternative grammatical form). *Lovely (vaggū)*: beautiful, gleaming. *Sweetly fragrant (sucigandhā)*: with a lovely fragrance.

2 *Pervaded with all kinds of scents*[35] *(nānāgandhasamīritā)*: pervaded throughout with scented winds because of the many kinds of entrancing scents. **[157]** *Covered with various lotuses (nānāpadumasañchannā)*: with the surface of the water covered with many and various red lotuses.[36] *Overspread with white lotuses (puṇḍarīkasamotatā)*: besprinkled with white lotuses.[37]

3 *Entrancing, they waft a fragrance around (surabhi sampavāyanti)*: the lotus pond as a whole emits[38] a lovely scent – this is the meaning. *Resounding with the cries of swans and herons (haṃsakoñcābhirudā)*: filled with the cries of swans and herons.

4 *Crowded with flocks of various birds (nānādijagaṇākiṇṇā)*: full of flocks of various birds. *And full of the various songs of those flocks (nānāsaragaṇāyutā)*: and filled with the combined resonance of many varieties of birds. *The trees bearing a variety of fruits (nānāphaladharā)*: bearing[39] many kinds of fruits, having branches[40] that are continually bent by the weight of the various fruit. *And woods bearing a variety of flowers (nānāpupphadharā vanā)* means and woods that bestow many kinds of entrancing blooms; 'woods' (*vanā*) is given with a distortion of gender.[41]

5 *The like of a city is not amongst men (na manussesu īdisaṃ nagaraṃ)*: the like of such a city as this (one) of yours is not found amongst men, meaning it is not known in the world of men. *Made of silver (rūpiyāmayā)*: made of silver coin. *Dazzling (daddalhamānā)*: extremely brilliant. *They shine forth (ābhenti)*: they blaze forth. *Throughout the four directions: samantā caturo disā=samantato catasso pi disā* (alternative grammatical form).

6 *These who are your: yā temā=yā te imā* (resolution of compound). *Maid-servants (paricārikā)*: those who perform services. *They (tā)*: those maid-servants. *Wear bracelets and bangles (kambukāyuradharā)*: are decorated with armlets and bangles of conch-shell. *Their heads are adorned with chaplets of gold (kañcanāveḷabhūsitā)*: tufts of their hair are decorated with golden hangings.[42]

7 *Covered with kadalī antelope (kadalimigasañchannā)*: spread over with coverings of kadalī antelope hides. *Well prepared: sajjā=sajjitā* (alternative grammatical form); fit for sleeping on. *Strewn with long-haired woollen fleeces (goṇakasanthatā)*: strewn[43] with a long-haired fleecy rug.

8 *Thereon (yattha)*: on that couch. *When you have gone to rest: vāsūpagatā=vāsaṃ upagatā* (resolution of compound), meaning when you have lain down to sleep. *When midnight arrives (sampattāya aḍḍharattāya)*: when midnight has come. *From there (tato)*: from that couch.

9 *That lotus pond: pokkharaññā=pokkharaṇiyā* (alternative grammatical form). [**158**] *Green (harite)*: blue-green.[44] *Grassy (saddale)*: covered with young grass. *Bright (subhe)*: clean; or, alternatively, it is a form of addressing her – 'My bright one'. You go and stand, and remain, my dear, on the green grassy edge that completely surrounds that lotus pond – this is how it should be construed.

10 *Crop-eared (kaṇṇamuṇḍo)*: with torn ears, with shorn ears. *He has devoured you: khāyitā āsi=khāditā ahosi* (alternative grammatical form). *Made a skeleton of you (aṭṭhisaṅkhalikā katā)*: made a mere skeleton of you. *Just as it was before (yathā pure)*: like it was before being devoured by the dog.

11 *Then (tato)*: after plunging into the lotus pond. *With limbs restored (aṅgapaccaṅgā)*: fully restored in all limbs.[45] *Beautiful (sucārū)*: very pleasing to the mind. *Lovely to behold (piyadassanā)*: looking lovely. *Come (āyāsi)*: come.

When questioned thus by the king, the petī uttered five verses relating her story to him from the very beginning:

13 (14) 'In Kimbilā there was a householder, a layfollower with faith;
I was his wife but of bad conduct and adulterous.

14 (15) My husband said this (to me) whilst being thus adulterous,
"This is not fitting nor seeming – that you should be adulterous
against me in this way."

15 (16) I told a terrible lie when I made that oath saying, "I have not
been adulterous against you either in body or in thought.

16 (17) If I have been adulterous against you either in body or in
thought, then may that crop-eared dog devour me limb by limb."

17 (18) It is both as a result of that deed and due to the fact that I lied that for seven hundred years since I have undergone being devoured limb by limb by that crop-eared dog.'

13 **[159]** Herein *in Kimbilā (Kimbilāyaṃ)*: in the city of that name. *Adulterous (aticārinī)*: when a wife[46] has transgressed[47] against her husband she is called adulterous because of her conduct.
14 My husband said this to me whilst I was being adulterous – this is how it should be construed.[48] 'This is not fitting' and so on shows the manner in which he spoke. Herein *this is not fitting (n'etaṃ channaṃ)*: this is not proper. *This is not seeming (n'etaṃ paṭirūpaṃ)* is just a synonym[49] for this. *In this way (yaṃ)*: in that act of succumbing. *Should be adulterous: aticarāsi=aticarasi* (alternative grammatical form); or, alternatively, this (latter) is alone the reading, meaning that you should be adulterous against me in this way, your adultery on that occasion – this is not fitting nor is this seeming.
15 *Terrible (ghoraṃ)*: heinous. *Oath (sapathaṃ)*: oath.[50] *Made: abhāsissaṃ=abhāsiṃ* (alternative grammatical form).
16 *If I: sacāhaṃ=sace ahaṃ* (resolution of compound). *Against you: taṃ=tvaṃ* (alternative grammatical form).
17 *Of that deed (tassa kammassa)*: of that wicked deed, of that deed of bad conduct. *And due to the fact that I lied (musāvādassa ca)*: and due to the fact that I lied with the aforesaid 'I have not been adulterous.' *Both (ubhayaṃ)*: as a result of both. *I have undergone (anubhūtaṃ)* means I have been undergoing. *Since (yato)*: since (I did) that wicked deed.

When she had thus spoken she uttered two verses praising the service he had rendered her:

18 (19) 'And you, your majesty, came here for my sake and have been of great service; I am well rid of the crop-eared one and am without sorrow, having nothing to fear from any quarter.

19 (20) I bow before you, your majesty, and beg you with the añjali salute: enjoy these non-human sensual pleasures, your majesty, amuse yourself with me.'

19 Herein *your majesty (deva)*: she is addressing the king. *Of the crop-eared one: kaṇṇamuṇḍassa=kaṇṇamuṇḍato* (alternative grammatical form); this is the genitive case in (the sense of) the ablative.

Then the king tired of living there and made known his intention to leave. When she heard this that petī, because of her attachment to the king, **[160]** uttered the verse (beginning:) 'I bow before you, your majesty', begging him to stay right there. But the king, resolute in his desire to leave, uttered the concluding verse, announcing his intention:

20 (21) 'I have enjoyed these non-human sensual pleasures[51] and amused myself with you. My fortunate one, I beg you, please take me back quickly.'

20 Herein *I (beg) you: tāhaṃ=taṃ ahaṃ* (resolution of compound). *My fortunate one (subhage)*: you who are connected with fortune. *Please take me back (paṭinayāhi maṃ)*: please take me back to my city. The rest is clear throughout.

When the vimānapetī heard what the king had to say she was unable to endure their separation. With a heart perplexed and sick with grief, her body trembling, even though she pleaded in various kinds of ways, she could not persuade him to stay there. She took the king to the city with many jewels of great value and led him up to the palace and, after she had wept and wailed, she returned to her own dwelling place. Now when the king saw this, full of agitation, he performed meritorious deeds such as giving and so on and became bound for heaven. Then when our Lord had arisen in the world and had set rolling the Wheel of the Noble Dhamma and was in due course staying at Sāvatthī, the venerable Mahāmoggallāna when wandering one day in the mountains saw that woman with her retinue and asked her about the deed she had done. She related everything to the elder from the very beginning. The elder raised the issue with the Lord who took the matter as an arisen need and taught Dhamma to the company assembled there. The people, having received this agitation, gave up[52] wicked deeds, performed meritorious deeds such as giving and so on, took delight in Dhamma[53] and became bound for heaven.

[1] Text's sovaṇṇasapānaphalakā should be amended to read sovaṇṇasopāna- with verse.

[2] Reading vāyamamāno with Be for text's Se gāyamāno.

[3] One of India's classical instruments, somewhat similar to the lute. See A. K. Coomaraswamy, 'Some Pali Words', *Harvard Journal of Asiatic Studies* IV, 2, 1939, p. 167.

[4] Reading kāmapaṭisaṃyuttagītāni with Be for text's Se kāmamati-.

[5] madhura, rendered throughout as sweet, has underlying connotations of intoxication and flattering and so on. It was therefore no doubt the lure of the music rather than the melody alone that enticed her to act in the way she did.

[6] The others are Anotatta, Sīhapapāta, Rathakāra, Kuṇāla, Chaddanta and Mandākini; see D i 54; A iv 101; J ii 92; cp DA 164 for a different set.

[7] Cp PvA 228.

[8] bheravarūpo, like Bhairava in appearance. Bhairava, like Rudra (PvA 142), was associated with a terrific aspect of Śiva and is particularly ferocious. Bhairava is the national deity of Nepal.

[9] Reading suvipphālita- for text's suvipphalita-; cp PED sv. Se reads suvipphūlita-khadiraṅgārapuñjasadisanayano (Be suvipphulita-).

[10] Reading nirantarappavattavijjullatāsaṅghātasadisajivho with Se (Be -vijjulatā-) for text's nirantarapavattivipulasaṅghātasadisajivho.

[11] Reading panasalabujādīhi with Be for text's pana salabujādīhi, that is, panasa, the jackfruit tree, Artocarpus integrifolia, and labuja, the breadfruit tree, Artocarpus lacucha or incisa; the suggestion that we should read salaḷa- at PED sv labuja should probably be deleted.

[12] Reading tena with Se Be for text's tehi.

[13] Reading vajjhacorassa with Se Be for text's vajjacorassa; PED sv vajjha does not notice.

[14] Reading -ūpakūjitaṃ with Se Be for text's -ūpakujitaṃ.

[15] Reading taruganopasobhitaṃ with Se Be for text's tarugaṇe palobhitaṃ.

[16] Reading phalabhārāvanata- with Se Be for text's phalabhāravinata-.

[17] Se Be add tā here.

[18] Se Be read otāretvā, made her go down, for text's ogāhetvā. I follow our text since this reading accords better with ogāhasi of v 11 upon which all texts agree. Be adds here that he made her go down after he had beaten her.

[19] Reading -santhatā with Be for text's Se -saṇṭhitā.

[20] sogandhiyā, literally pleasant smelling; the Nymphaea lotus. Not listed by PED which gives only sogandhika.

[21] Cp Dhp 58.

[22] paduma, Nelumbium speciosum; they can be either red, white, blue, yellow or pink.

[23] Reading samotatā with Be for text's samāgatā; Se reads samogatā. Cp Vv 44[12], 81[6].

[24] puṇḍarīka; according to Childers it may also denote a fragrant kind of mango.

[25] 2 c d and 3 a b = Vv 44[12], 81[6].

[26] haṃsa, swan or goose, the king of birds and thus by extension applicable to the arahant, the 'king' of men – Sn 220f., 1134; Dhp 91, 175. It is also the vāhana, or steed, of Brahmā and is usually interpreted as a symbol of purity when it appears in Buddhist architecture.

[27] cakkavāka, Anas Casarca.

[28] Reading -dharā with Se Be for text's -dadā.

[29] The first four verses are to be understood as all describing the vimānapetī's residence, the like of which is not to be found in the world of men. The ordering of the various epithets contained in these verses, as they have come down to us, is rather muddled. As already noted (n. 25) 2 c d and 3 a b appear twice in Vv as a single verse and it is a prominent feature of these verses that they begin a topic half way through a verse and conclude it in the first half of the following verse. This strongly suggests that they have either become muddled or that one or more half verses have at some time got lost. Be attempts to rectify this by taking 6 a b as 5 e f and then continuing half a verse behind, so to speak. This is adopted here and numbers in brackets are inserted to indicate the numbering of our text. One may feel that it would have been better had Be instead read 5 a b as 4 e f. On the basis of context it would seem plausible to reconstruct these verses as follows: 2 a b 4 c d > 1 a b c d for these trees are those of her mango grove and the pond is surely not to be understood as being covered by trees, as Gehman suggested; then 1 a b c d > 2 a b c d; 2 c d 3 a b > 3 a b c d; and 3 c d 4 a b > 4 a b c d with perhaps the addition of 5 a b as 4 e f, since it is possible that the missing half verse belonged to v 5.

[30] Reading sovaṇṇarūpiyāmayā with Be for text's -rūpiyamayā (Se -rupiyāmayā); similarly in v 7 where text reads -ruciyāmayā and Se correctly -rūpiyāmayā.

[31] Reading kañcanāveḷabhūsitā with Se Be for text's -celabhūsitā; cp III 9[3] and Vv 36[2].

[32] Reading sajjā goṇakasanthatā with Se Be for text's -saṇṭhitā.

[33] kaṇṇamuṇḍo; cp lake Kaṇṇamuṇḍa above which may be understood as meaning 'with blunt corners'.

[34] Reading santhatā with Be and verse for text's Se saṇṭhitā.

[35] Cp PvA 164.
[36] rattapaduma-, with red padumas.
[37] setapadumehi, with white padumas.
[38] Reading vāyati pokkharaṇī ti with Se Be for text's vāyanti, pokkaranī ti.
[39] Reading -dhārino with Be for text's Se -dāyino.
[40] Reading -sākhattā with Se Be for text's -sākhaggā.
[41] Masculine nominative plural, vanā, for neuter, vanāni.
[42] Reading suvaṇṇavaṭaṃsakasamalaṅkata- with Se Be for text's suvaṇṇavatthaṃ katasamalaṅkata-.
[43] Reading -santhatā with Se Be for text's -saṇṭhitā.
[44] nīla; this term can denote blue-green, blue-black or dark-blue and 'serves as a general term to designate the "coloured-black" as opposed to the "coloured-white" (pīta yellow), which pairs (nīla-pīta) are both set off against the "pure" colour-sensations of red (lohitaka) & white (odāta), besides the distinct black or dark (kaṇha). Therefore n. has a fluctuating connotation' (PED sv nīla).
[45] Reading paripuṇṇasabbaṅgapaccaṅgavatī with Se Be for text's paripuṇṇasabh-.
[46] Reading jāyā hi patiṃ with Se for text's jāyāpatī; Be reads bhariyā hi patiṃ.
[47] Reading atikkamma caraṇato with Se Be for text's atikkamacaraṇato; cp CPD sv atikkama.
[48] Omitting, with Se Be, the initial aticaramānāyā ti of our text.
[49] Reading vevacanaṃ with Se Be for text's vacanaṃ.
[50] sapanaṃ; cp PvA 34.
[51] Reading bhuttā amānusā kāmā with Be for text's bhutvā amānusā kāmā; Se reads bhutvā amānuse kāme.
[52] Reading oramitvā with Se.Be for text's otaritvā.
[53] dhammābhirato; Se Be omit.

II.13 EXPOSITION OF THE UBBARĪ PETA STORY
[Ubbaripetavatthuvaṇṇanā]

'There was a king, Brahmadatta.' The Teacher, who was staying in the Jeta Grove told this Ubbarī Peta Story concerning a certain layfollower.

[161] It is said that at Sāvatthī the husband of a certain female lay-follower had died and that she, sick with misery at their being separated, would go mourning for him to his funeral pyre and weep. When the Lord saw that she possessed the potential for realising the sotāpatti-fruit his heart was stirred with compassion and he went to her home and sat down on the appointed seat. The layfollower approached the Lord, saluted him and then sat down at one side. The Teacher then asked her, 'Are you in mourning, layfollower?' When she said, 'Yes, Lord, I mourn being separated from a loved one', he recounted (an incident) of long ago, desiring to dispel her grief:

Long ago, in the city of Kapila in the kingdom of Pañcāla,[1] there was a king named Cūḷani-Brahmadatta.[2] He abandoned the ways of going astray[3] and was given to working for the welfare of the people in his realm, governing his kingdom without violating the tenfold code of a king.[4] Desiring on one occasion to hear what was being said in his kingdom, he took the guise of a tailor, left the city unaccompanied and wandered from village to village, from district to district. When he saw that the whole kingdom was free of thieves and unoppressed[5] and that men were living on friendly terms – indeed, that they even left the doors of their houses open – he turned back joyfully. As he was coming towards the city, he entered the house of a widow who led a miserable existence in a certain village. When she saw him she said, 'Now who are you, sir, and from which place have you come?' 'I am a tailor, madam, and I wander about doing tailoring jobs for a fee. If you have any tailoring jobs then give me some food and some remuneration[6] and I will do them for you too.' 'We do not have any jobs that need doing,[7] nor food and remuneration.[8] You will have to work for another, sir', she said. Whilst dwelling there for a few days he saw her daughter who was endowed with a sign of future good fortune and merit and asked the mother, 'Is this daughter already married to anyone or is she still unmarried: If she is not married to anyone then give her to me for I am capable of providing you with the means[9] for a life of comfort.' 'Very well, sir', she replied and gave her to him. He dwelt with her for a few days and then gave her a thousand kahāpaṇas, saying, 'I will return in just a few days, **[162]** my love; do not despair',[10] and went to his city. He had the road between the city and that village levelled and decorated and then went there in great royal splendour. He stood the girl on a pile of kahāpaṇas, bathed her with gold and silver water pots, conferred on her the name of Ubbarī and appointed her to the position of queen-consort. He gave the village to her relatives and led her to the city in great royal splendour. Enjoying the pleasures of love with her he experienced a reign of comfort as long as he lived and died at the end of his natural span. When he died and his funeral rites had been performed, Ubbarī, her heart pierced by the dart of grief at their being separated, went to his funeral pyre where she paid honour for many days with scents and flowers and so on, praised the king's virtues and thereafter circumambulated his funeral pyre by the right,[11] weeping and wailing like one driven to distraction.

Now at that time our Lord was the Bodhisatta and he had gone forth in the life of a rishi and had attained both the jhānas and the abhiññās. Whilst staying in a certain forest haunt in the neighbourhood of the Himālaya he saw by means of his deva-like vision Ubbarī pierced by the dart of grief. He travelled through the air and then, making himself visible, remained in the air and asked people who were stood here and there, 'Whose funeral pyre is this? And for the sake of whom[12] does this woman weep,[13] wailing, "O Brahmadatta, O Brahmadatta"?' When they heard this those people said, 'This, sir, is Ubbarī, wife of Brahmadatta, who ever since he died has gone to his funeral pyre and wept, wailing and calling out his name "Brahmadatta".'

Those rehearsing the texts inserted these six verses elucidating the matter:

1 'There was a king, Brahmadatta, a bull amongst the Pañcālas' charioteers; then after many days and nights that king died.

2 His wife Ubbarī went to his funeral pyre and wept; seeing Brahmadatta no (more) she wept, "O Brahmadatta!"

3 [**163**] Now a rishi came there, a sage[14] of perfect moral conduct and he there questioned those who were met there, saying,

4 "Whose is this funeral pyre that is pervaded with all kinds of scents? Whose this wife that weeps for a husband gone far from here, who seeing Brahmadatta no (more) weeps, 'O Brahmadatta!'?"

5 And those there explained, those who were met there, saying, "Brahmadatta's, O blessed one;[15] Brahmadatta's, good sir.

6 His is this funeral pyre that is pervaded with all kinds of scents and his this wife that weeps for a husband gone far from here, who seeing Brahmadatta no (more) weeps 'O Brahmadatta!'." '

1 Herein *there was: ahu=ahosi* (alternative grammatical form). *The Pañcālas' (Pañcālānaṃ)*: of the inhabitants of the Pañcāla kingdom; or merely of the Pañcāla kingdom, for though[16] it is only one country it is denoted by the plural expression 'the Pañcālas' which has come about on account (of its being the name) of the royal princes that belong to that country.[17] *A bull amongst charioteers (rathesabho)*: like a bull amongst charioteers, meaning a mighty charioteer.

2 *To his funeral pyre (tassa āḷāhanaṃ)*: to the place where the body of the king had been cremated.

3 *Rishi (isi)*: he is a rishi (*isi*) by reason of his striving after (*esanā*) accomplishments such as the jhānas and so on.[18] *There (tattha)*: to the place where Ubbarī was standing,[19] meaning to the cemetery. *Came: āgacchi=agamāsi* (alternative grammatical form). *Of perfect moral conduct (sampannacaraṇo)* means that in moral conduct he is perfect, he is possessed of, and perfect in, these fifteen accomplishments classed under moral conduct:[20] he is accomplished in virtue, has control over the doors of his senses, knows moderation in eating, is intent on vigilance, (is possessed of) the seven excellent things[21] and (can attain) the four jhānas of

the sphere of form. *A sage (muni)*: a sage is one who is sagacious (*munāti*), who knows what is to his own benefit and what is to the benefit of others. *And he there questioned those (te ca tattha apucchittha)*: he asked those people who were in that place. *Who were met there (ye tattha su samāgatā)*: those people who were met here and there in that cemetery. *Su* (untranslated) is a mere particle. An alternative reading is 'who were met there' (*ye tatthāsuṃ samāgatā*), where *were: āsuṃ=ahesuṃ* (alternative grammatical form).

4 [164] *That is pervaded with all kinds of scents*[22] *(nānāgandhasameritaṃ)*: that is pervaded throughout and perfumed by many kinds of scents. *From here (ito)*: from the world of men. *Gone far (dūragataṃ)*: he refers to the fact that he is gone to the world beyond.[23] *Weeps, 'O Brahmadatta' (Brahmadattā ti kandati)*: she invokes him by wailing and proclaiming his name thus: 'O Brahmadatta'.

5 *Brahmadatta's, O blessed one, Brahmadatta's, good sir (Brahmadattassa bhaddante Brahmadattassa mārisa)*: O great sage of sound mind and body, this is the funeral pyre of king Brahmadatta and this is the wife of that same king Brahmadatta. May Brahmadatta receive your blessing, O blessed one,[24] for it is through a regard for their welfare of great rishis[25] like you that there is welfare and happiness for those stationed in the world beyond – this is the meaning.

When the ascetic heard their words he went out of pity into Ubbarī's presence and uttered this verse with the purpose of dispelling her grief:

7 'Eighty-six thousand with the name of Brahmadatta have been cremated on this funeral pyre. For which of these do you mourn?'

7 Herein *eighty-six thousand (chaḷāsītisahassāni)*: in number eighty thousand plus six hundred more besides. *With the name of Brahmadatta (Brahmadattassa nāmakā)*: of that name 'Brahmadatta'. *For which of these do you mourn? (tesaṃ kaṃ anusocasi)*: he asks, 'For which Brahmadatta of these eighty-six thousand Brahmadattas do you mourn? On account of which has your grief arisen?'

When she had been thus questioned by the rishi, Ubbarī uttered this verse showing the Brahmadatta she meant:

8 'The king who was the son of Cūḷani, a bull amongst the Pañcālas' charioteers; it is for him that I mourn, sir, my husband who granted all my desires.'

8 Herein *the son of Cūḷani (Cūḷaniputto)*: the son of the king of that name.[26] [165] *Who granted all my desires (sabbakāmadaṃ)*: who was one

to give me everything whatsoever it was I wanted; or, alternatively, who would give all beings what they wanted.

When Ubbarī had thus spoken the ascetic once more uttered two verses:

9 'All were kings with the name of Brahmadatta; all were sons of a Cūḷani and bulls amongst the Pañcālas' charioteers.
10 To all in turn did you act as queen-consort; why do you forsake those previous ones and mourn (only) this last one?'

9 Herein *all were (sabbe 'va 'hesuṃ)*: all of those that number eighty-six thousand were kings with the name of Brahmadatta, were sons of a Cūḷani and bulls amongst the Pañcālas' charioteers; these conditions of being a king and so on had amongst them no peculiar distinction, even on a single point.
10 *Did you act as queen-consort (mahesittam akārayi)*: and to all of them in turn did you act[27] in the office of chief queen and consort, meaning you attained (that office). *Why? (kasmā)*: he asks, 'Amongst all those people, none of whom were distinguished[28] either in their role as husband or in their personal qualities, why, for what reason, do you abandon those previous kings and mourn only this last one?

When she heard this Ubbarī, filled with agitation, once more uttered a verse to that ascetic:

11 'Was I myself a woman for that long time, good sir, I of whom you speak as having been a woman often in saṃsāra?'

11 Herein *myself: ātume=attani* (alternative grammatical form). *Was I a woman? (itthibhūtāya)*: did I go into existence as a woman? *For that long time: dīgharattāya=dīgharattaṃ* (alternative grammatical form). This is the meaning here: was I myself a woman, was I only a woman for all that time or did I also go into existence as a man? *I of whom (you speak) as having been a woman: yassā me itthibhūtāya=yassā mayhaṃ itthibhūtāya* (alternative grammatical form); I of whom you speak, that is, you relate, great sage, as having been a woman thus, of having been queen-consort so often in saṃsāra. An alternative reading is 'Oh, I myself remember that I was a woman' (*ātumo*[29] *itthibhūtāya*).[30] Herein *Oh, I remember (ā)* is a particle denoting recollection.[31] *Myself (tumo)*: by myself (*sayaṃ*); this is recollected, known, by me. *That I was a woman (itthibhūtāya)*: that I went into existence as a woman **[166]** – there was continual arising[32] thus for me for so long a time. Why? Since[33] (it is) I of whom you speak, great sage, as having been a woman often in saṃsāra (saying), 'To all in turn did you act as queen-consort'[34] – this is how it should be construed.[35]

When he heard these words the ascetic then uttered this verse showing that there is in saṃsāra no such law that a woman is only a woman and a man only a man:[36]

12 'You were a woman, you were a man, you also went to womb of cattle. The limit of this long past is thus not to be seen.'

12 Herein *you were a woman, you were a man (ahu itthi ahu puriso)*: at times you were a woman and at times you were also a man. But it is not solely a question of being just a woman or a man for, moreover, you also went to womb of cattle – at times you also went[37] into being as cattle and you also went to the womb of other animals.[38] *The limit of this long past is thus not to be seen (evam etaṃ atītānaṃ pariyanto na dissati)*: the limit of this long past of existences – this aforesaid being a woman, being a man and being an animal and so on that you went into – is thus not to be seen, even to those looking very strenuously with the eye of knowledge. But this does not apply solely to you: indeed the limit of the existence of all beings who are wandering about in saṃsāra is not to be seen, is not revealed. For this reason the Lord said, 'Inconceivable, monks, is the beginning of this saṃsāra; the earliest point is not revealed of the running on, of the saṃsāra, of beings hindered by ignorance and fettered by craving.'*[39]

When she had thus heard Dhamma taught by that ascetic in which he made clear the influence of deeds[40] and the absence of any limit to saṃsāra, with agitation in her heart with respect to saṃsāra and with devotion in her heart for Dhamma, she came to lack the dart of grief and uttered these three verses making known her devotion and her lack of grief:

13 'I was truly ablaze, being like a fire fed with ghee; but now all my sorrow has been extinguished as if I had been sprinkled with water.

14 **[167]** Truly the dart, the grief,[41] that had pierced my heart has been drawn out. You have dispelled that grief, the grief for my husband which had overwhelmed me.

15 With dart withdrawn I am become tranquil and cool; since hearing you, great sage, I no longer grieve nor weep.'

The meaning of these is just as that given above.[42]

The Teacher then spoke four verses showing the behaviour of Ubbarī who now had agitation in her heart:

16 'When she heard these words of his, the well-spoken utterance of that recluse, she took robe and bowl and went forth into the homeless life.

*S ii 178 = iii 149 = 151 ≏ v 226.

17 And she, being one gone forth from home into the homeless life, cultivated a mind of friendliness leading to birth in the Brahmaloka,
18 Wandering from village to village, to market towns and royal cities; Uruvelā was the name of the village in which she died.
19 Having cultivated a mind of friendliness for the sake of arising in the Brahmaloka and having put aside a woman's thoughts she reached the Brahmaloka.'[43]

16 Herein *of his (tassa)*: of that ascetic. *Well-spoken utterance: subhāsitaṃ*[44] *=suṭṭhu bhāsitaṃ* (resolution of compound), meaning the Dhamma.
17 *One gone forth (pabbajitā)*: one gone into the homeless state. *Being: santā=samānā* (alternative grammatical form); or, after having become one gone forth, she is calmed (*santā*) in body and speech.[45] *A mind of friendliness (mettacittaṃ)*: a mind accompanied by friendliness. He speaks of the jhānas (attained by) friendliness which come under the heading of mind. *For the sake of arising in the Brahmaloka (brahmalokūpapittiyā)*: and in cultivating that mind of friendliness she did so for the sake of arising in the Brahmaloka, not with the purpose of establishing a basis[46] for insight (meditation).[47] Indeed, before the Buddha arose, ascetics and those gone forth who were cultivating the Brahmavihāras[48] and so on did so only in so far as for the sake of attaining an excellence of existence.[49]
18 [**168**] *From village to village (gāmā gāmaṃ)*: from one village to another village.
19 *Having cultivated (ābhāvetvā)*: having developed, having made to grow; some read *abhāvetvā*, the (prefix-)letter *a* being a mere particle for them. *Having put aside a woman's thoughts (itthicittaṃ virājetvā)*: having done away with the thoughts, dispositions and desires of womanhood[50] her mind became detached from femininity.[50] *She reached the Brahmaloka (brahmalokūpagā)*: she was one who reached the Brahmaloka by way of rebirth. The rest is quite self-evident since it has already been explained above.

When the Teacher had recounted this teaching on Dhamma and dispelled the grief of that layfollower, he afterwards gave her the Teaching on the Four (Noble) Truths at the end of which the layfollower became established in the sotāpatti-fruit. That teaching was (also) of benefit to the company assembled there.

The Exposition of the Ubbarī Peta Story is concluded – thus the exposition of the meaning of the second, Ubbarī, chapter, that is adorned with thirteen stories in this Peta Stories of the Khuddaka Nikāya is concluded.[51]

[1] The kingdom of Pañcāla was divided into a northern region (Uttara-Pañcāla) and a southern one (Dakkhiṇa-Pañcāla). It was situated between the Kuru country and Kosala and 'Pañcāla may be roughly identified with the tract north and south-east of Delhi from the foot of the Himalayas to the Chambal covering Budaun, Farukkhabad and adjoining districts', B. N. Chaudhury, *Buddhist Centres in Ancient India*, Calcutta 1969, p. 32; cp DPPN ii 108. Most sources agree that Kapila (often spelt Kampilla, Kāmpilya etc.) was in Dakkhiṇa-Pañcāla.

[2] His story is to be found in the Mahā-Ummagga Jātaka (No. 546); cp Uttarādhyayana xiii (SBE xlv 56–61) for a Jaina account.

[3] agatigamanaṃ, the four evils of desire (chanda), hatred (dosa), delusion (moha) and fear (bhaya). At Dial iii 220 n. 2 it is suggested that agatiṃ gacchati means 'literally, he goes to a not-going, or wrong going, or impasse'. Most common perhaps is the appearance of this expression in the phrase chandāgatiṃ gacchati which has seen various renderings: pursue the wrong path of impulse (GS i 67), goes to the no-bourn through desire (GS ii 19), goes astray from wish (GS iii 198), go astray through desire (GS iv 246), taking a wrong course through partiality (Dial iii 125; cp B of Disc v 111, 247), whilst at Vin Texts iii 25 agati is rendered 'does not walk'. Whatever the precise meaning of agati it is a conduct impossible of arahants (D iii 133 = A iv 370); its absence leads to heaven whilst its presence to suffering in hell (A ii 19) since the latter is a source of pāpakamma, wicked deeds (D iii 182). It cannot therefore be a 'no-bourn' in the sense of not gaining birth in one or other of the five bourns (pañcagati). Thus it would seem more a lack of a path altogether rather than either a wrong path or a lack of a destiny. That is, those who are distracted by any of the above four evils may be thought to lose their way and go astray in the sense that they are no longer going anywhere (in their spiritual development) – e.g. AA iii 22: chandāgatiṃ gacchatī ti chandena agatiṃ gacchati, akattabbaṃ karoti; due to desire he 'gets nowhere', he does what ought not to be done.

[4] dasa rājadhamme: almsgiving, morality, generosity, straightness, gentleness, self-restraint, non-anger, non-violence, forbearance and non-opposition (J iii 274; cp J i 260, 399, ii 400, iii 320, v 119, 378). They are said to guard against the ways of going astray (J i 176, v 510).

[5] Reading anupapīḷaṃ with Se Be for text's anupīḷaṃ.

[6] Reading bhattañ ca vetanañ ca with Se Be for text's vatthañ ca veṭhanañ ca.

[7] kattabbaṃ; Se Be omit.

[8] Reading bhattavetanaṃ vā with Se Be for text's vatthaṃ vā veṭhanaṃ vā.

[9] Reading jīvanūpāyaṃ with Se Be for text's jīvanupāyaṃ.

[10] Reading mā ukkaṇṭhasi with Se Be for text's mā khuṇḍali; cp PED sv khuṇḍali where a reading of ukkaṇṭhi is recommended.

[11] Cp PvA 74.

[12] Reading kassatthāyaṃ cāyaṃ with Se Be for text's kass' athāyaṃ.

[13] Reading paridevati with Se Be for text's paridevantī.

[14] muni.

[15] Reading bhaddante with Se Be for text's bhaddan te.

[16] Reading eko pi hi with Se Be for text's eko pi.

[17] Reading janapadikānaṃ with Be for text's janapadādhikānaṃ; Se -ādhikatānaṃ.

[18] Cp PvA 98, 265 for similar.

[19] Reading Ubbariyā ṭhitaṭṭhāne with Se Be for text's ubbhataṭṭhāne.

[20] Cp M i 32, 273, 354f., 471; S ii 218; A i 113f., ii 40, iv 108.

[21] He has faith (saddhā), shame (hirimā), a fear of blame (ottappī), is one who has heard much (bahussuta), his energy is stirred up (āraddha-viriya), his mindfulness is aroused (upaṭṭhita-sati) and possesses insight (paññavā). In detail at M i 356; cp also D iii 252, 282; M i 354, iii 23; A iv 108.

[22] Cp PvA 156.

[23] paraloka.

[24] Reading bhaddante with Se for text's Be bhaddan te.

[25] Cp M i 378 where through an act of ill will of mind on the part of rishis in the forests the (former) forests of Daṇḍaka, Kāliṅga, Mejjha and Mātaṅga became forests again just as in the same way fifty cities the size of Nālandā might be reduced to cinders.

[26] Cp Uttarādhyayana xiii 1f. (SBE xlv 57). We are not here told of the fate of Brahmadatta but in the Jaina account he ends up in hell.

[27] akāsi – so Se Be as a gloss on akārayi; text omits.

[28] Reading avisiṭṭhesu with Se Be for text's avasiṭṭhesu.

[29] Reading both here and below with our text's vll; all texts read āhu me.

[30] Reading itthibhūtāyā ti with Be for text's itthibhūtāya ti; Se reads itthibhūtā ti though later itthibhūtāya.

[31] Reading anussaraṇatthe with Se Be for text's anusaraṇatthe.

[32] Reading aparāpar' uppatti with Be for text's Se aparā 'va (Se ca) anuppatti.

[33] Reading yasmā with Be; Se reads tasmā whilst text omits.

[34] This is clearly a quotation from the preceding verse but no text adds ti.

[35] Dhammapāla was clearly facing a corrupt verse here. The translation can, given the nature of the text, be no more than provisional and several interpretations might be made at different places but these cannot be sustained with any consistency throughout the whole paragraph. The interpretation offered here is based both on how it seems Dhammapāla himself understood the verse and on the context in which the verse is found. The following verse seems to be answering a question raised by this present verse and this is the first of Dhammapāla's explanations. Given the second explanation we should however take the verse as:

> Oh, I myself remember that I was a woman for that long time, good sir, I of whom you speak as having been a woman often in saṃsāra

in which case v 12 no longer answers a question but rather corrects a faulty memory:

> You were (not only) a woman, you were (also) a man, you also went to womb of cattle. The limit of this long past is thus not to be seen.

[36] Reading ayaṃ niyamo saṃsāre n'atthi with Se Be for text's ayaṃ niyamo saṃsāren' atthi; PED sv niyama should be amended accordingly.

[37] Reading agamāsi with Be for text's Se āgamā.

[38] That is, 'cattle' in its widest sense of sheep, horses and so on. The Pali pasu, similarly defined at PvA 80 above, is here contrasted with tiracchāna, or animals in general.

[39] Though it is stated at M i 483 (cp MLS ii 161 n. 2) that the Buddha can (only) remember ninety-one aeons and though the stock passage concerning his knowledge of his former births states that he can (only) remember many aeons of such births – e.g. M i 22, 35; S ii 122, 213; A i 255; It 99 – D iii 134 states that he can do this as far back as he desires and It 121 that he can know anything that he desires. Similarly D iii 28 has the Buddha claiming, 'The ultimate beginnings of things I know, Bhaggava, and I know not only that, but much more than that.' See also the discussion at KS ii xi.

[40] kammassa kataṃ, literally deeds that have been done.

[41] Reading sokaṃ with Se Be for text's etaṃ.

[42] PvA 41.

[43] Cp 'It is impossible, it cannot come to pass that a woman could be a Sakka . . . a Māra . . . a Brahmā', M iii 65f.; A i 28 etc.

[44] Text wrongly reads subāsitaṃ here.

[45] Cp Dhp 378.

[46] Reading pādakādi with Se Be for text's pādakāpādakādi.

[47] vipassanā; the four Brahmavihāras, of which this mettacittaṃ is one, can lead to various degrees of jhāna and thus subsequent rebirth in the Brahmaloka, their cosmic counterpart. See e.g. M ii 78, 207f.; A ii 128ff., 184, iii 224ff.

[48] Cp D i 235–253.

[49] yāva-d-eva bhavasampatti-attham eva – so Be. Se does not separate the compound at all – yāvadevabhavasampattiyatthameva – whilst our text reads yāva devabhavasampatti attham eva in which case we might translate 'only in so far as for the sake of attaining the excellence of deva existence' which probably amounts to much the same thing.

[50] itthibhāve, literally being a woman.

[51] So Be.

Chapter III

SMALL CHAPTER
[Cūḷavagga]

III.1 EXPOSITION OF THE WITHOUT PARTING PETA STORY
[Abhijjamānapetavatthuvaṇṇanā]

'Without parting the water.' This was said when the Teacher was staying in the Bamboo Grove concerning a certain peta who had been a hunter.

It is said that across the Ganges to the west[1] of Benares as you go towards[2] the village of Vāsabha there was a hunter in a village named Cundaṭṭhila. He would slay a deer in the forest, eat the best meat which he had cooked over some embers and then bundle the remainder into a basket of leaves and take this on a pole to the village. When the young boys saw him at the village gate they would run up to him with outstretched hands saying, 'Give me some meat! Give me some meat!' Each time he would give them a little meat. Then one day he did not get any meat. **[169]** He bedecked himself with uddāla flowers[3] and taking many also in his hands he went to the village. When the boys saw him at the village gate they ran up to him with outstretched hands saying, 'Give me some meat! Give me some meat!' To each one of them he gave a spray of flowers. In due course he died and arose amongst the petas, naked, deformed and terrible to behold. Not knowing food or drink, not even in his dreams, and with bunches of garlands of uddāla blossoms tied on his head, he would go on foot upstream on the Ganges without parting the water, thinking, 'I will get something in the presence of my relatives in Cundaṭṭhila.' Now at that time the chief minister to king Bimbisāra, named Koliya, was returning after pacifying a disturbance on the border; having despatched his accompanying forces of elephants and horses and so on by road, he was himself coming by boat downstream the river Ganges when he saw that peta approaching in that manner and uttered this verse enquiring:

1 'You move along here without parting the water of the Ganges; you are naked yet your fore-half is unlike that of a peta, adorned, bearing garlands. Where are you going, peta, and where will be your abode?'

1 Herein *without parting (abhijjamāne)*: holding together without parting[4] at the setting down of the foot. *The water of the Ganges (vārimhi Gaṅgāya)*: the water of the river Ganges. *Here (idha)*: in this place. *Yet your fore-half is unlike that of a peta (pubbaddhapeto[5] va)*: your front half is unlike that of a peta – it is like that of a devaputta not belonging to the peta-womb. Why? *Adorned, bearing garlands (mālādhārī alaṅkato)* means the top of your head[6] is adorned, being bedecked with garlands. *Where will be your abode? (kattha vāso bhavissati)*: in which village or place will be your dwelling, meaning please tell (me) this.

Now to show what was said at that time by the peta and by Koliya those rehearsing the texts [**170**] spoke these verses:

2 ' "I am going to Cundaṭṭhila," the peta said, "between the village of Vāsabha, in the vicinity of Benares."

3 And when he saw him the chief minister, the famous Koliya, gave to the peta barley meal and food and a pair of yellow (clothes).

4 As his boat stopped he had (them) given to the barber; when they were given to the barber they were seen immediately (on the body) of the peta.

5 Thereupon (he became) dressed in fine clothes, adorned, bearing garlands; stood in that position the donation was of benefit to that peta – therefore one should give out of pity for the petas time and again.'

2 Herein *to Cundaṭṭhila (Cundaṭṭhilaṃ)*: to the village of that name. *Between the village of Vāsabha, in the vicinity of Benares (antare Vāsabhagāmaṃ Bārāṇasiyā santike)*: midway between the village of Vāsabha and Benares. Because of the preposition *antarā*[7] this (village of Vāsabha (*Vāsabhagāmaṃ*)) is in the accusative case (but) in the sense of the genitive,[8] for the village is in the vicinity of Benares. This is the meaning here:[9] 'Between (*antare*) the village of Vāsabha and Benares, not far from Benares, is a village named Cundaṭṭhila – I am going to this village.'

3 *The famous Koliya (Koliyo iti vissuto)*: with the well known name[10] of Koliya. *Barley meal and food: sattubhattañ ca=sattuñ c' eva bhattañ*[11] *ca* (resolution of compound). *Gave . . . and a pair of yellow (pītakañ ca yugaṃ adā)*: gave . . . and one pair of yellow, golden-coloured, clothes. In case (it should be asked), 'When did he give (this)?', he[12] said:

4 *As his boat stopped he had (them) given to the barber (nāvāya tiṭṭhamānāya kappakassa adāpayi)*: he halted his moving boat and there he had handed over to a bath-attendant[13] who was a layfollower; when the pair of clothes was given – this is how it should be construed. *Immediately: ṭhāne=ṭhānaso* (alternative grammatical form); at that very moment. *They were seen of the peta (petassa dissatha)*: they were perceived on the body of the peta; under and outer clothes came into being for him. For this reason he[12] said:

5 [**171**] *Thereupon dressed in fine clothes, adorned, bearing garlands (tato suvatthavasano mālādhārī alaṅkato)*: dressed in fine clothes and beautifully adorned with the garlands he wears.[14] *Stood in that position the donation was of benefit to that peta (ṭhāne ṭhitassa petassa dakkhiṇā upakappatha)*: that donation was, however, stood in the position of one worthy of donations since it was of benefit to that peta, since it came into his use. *Therefore one should give out of pity for the petas time and*

again (tasmā dajjetha petānaṃ anukampāya punappunaṃ) means one should give donations out of pity for the petas, on behalf of the petas, time and again.

Now the chief minister Koliya, feeling compassion for that peta, brought about that form of almsgiving and then came downstream and reached Benares at sunrise. The Lord, who had come through the air for the sake of helping[15] them, was standing on the bank of the Ganges. The chief minister Koliya disembarked from the boat and, overjoyed, invited the Lord saying, 'May the Lord accept out of pity my (invitation), Lord, for today's meal.' The Lord consented with his silence. When he learned of the Lord's acceptance he straightaway had erected on a delightful piece of ground a large pavillion of branches adorned above and on its four sides with numerous pieces of cloth that were decorated and dyed a variety of colours and then offered the Lord the seat he had had prepared therein. The Lord sat on the appointed seat. The chief minister then approached the Lord, honoured him with scents and flowers and so on, saluted him and, seated at one side, reported to the Lord what he had said and the peta's reply as mentioned above. The Lord determined, 'Let the order of monks come (here)!' Immediately he determined this the order of monks, instigated by the majesty of the Buddha, surrounded the King of the Dhamma as did the flock of golden swans (surround) Dhataraṭṭha, the king[16] of the (golden) swans.[17] The people gathered straightaway thinking, 'There is going to be a great teaching on Dhamma.' When he saw this the chief minister, with devotion in his heart, satisfied the order of monks with the Buddha at its head with drink and with foods both hard and soft. When he had finished his meal the Lord out of pity for the people concentrated his mind on the thought, 'Let those who dwell in the proximity of Benares gather (here)!' And all those peoples through the strength of his psychic power gathered (there). He then made great numbers of petas manifest and the people perceived them with their own eyes: some of them wore torn and shredded bits of rag; [172] some had what is shameful[18] covered only by their own hair; whilst some were naked as the day they were born,[19] overcome by hunger and thirst, with shrivelled skin and bodies that were mere bone and roaming about this way and that. The Lord then worked his psychic powers in such a way that they all gathered in the same place and declared to the people the wicked deed they had done.

Those rehearsing the texts spoke these verses elucidating the matter:

6 'Petas, some clad in ragged strips of cloth, others clothed by their hair, go off in search of food, going off in all directions.

7 Some run far away but turn back without having obtained anything, famished, fainting, staggering and sinking to the ground.

8 And some who fall there, sinking to the ground, tormented as though burnt by fire through not having done any lovely deeds in the past (said),

9 "In the past we were wicked-natured housewives and mothers of good family; though merit-offerings were at hand we made no refuge for ourselves.

10 Though there was abundant food and drink – so much so[20] that it was thrown away – yet we gave nothing to those who had reached the summit,[21] to those gone forth.

11 Desirous of doing what ought not to be done, lazy, desirous of sweet things[22] and gluttonous, we were givers[23] of morsels and lumps and abused the recipients.

12 Those houses and those servants and those ornaments of ours – these are now enjoyed[24] by others whilst our share is misery."

13 They will be basket-makers[25] who are held in contempt and insidious chariot-makers; they will be caṇḍālas[26] suffering great hardship and bath-attendants time and again.

14 [173] Whatever families are low and suffer great hardship – amongst these alone will they be born, this being the destiny of the selfish.

15 Whilst those unselfish givers who in the past did lovely deeds will fill heaven and light up Nandana.

16 When they have amused themselves in the Vejayanta[27] Palace and gratified all their desires they will be born in high-ranking, wealthy families as they fall from there.

17 In a pinnacled house and in a palace, on a couch strewn with long woollen fleeces,[28] with their limbs fanned[29] by those holding peacock (fans), to (such) a family they are born, knowing all life's comforts.

18 They travel from lap to lap adorned, bearing garlands; nurses[30] attend them morning and evening, striving after their comfort.

19 This carefree, charming Nandana,[31] great grove of the Thirty, is alone for those who have done meritorious deeds, not for those who have not done meritorious deeds.

20 For those who have not done meritorious deeds there is happiness neither here nor hereafter, whereas for those who have done meritorious deeds there is happiness right here as well as hereafter.

21[32] Many a skilled deed is to be done of those desiring their companionship for those who do meritorious deeds are provided with possessions and rejoice in heaven.'

6 Herein *clad in ragged strips of cloth (sāhundavāsino)*: clothed[33] in torn and shredded bits of rag. *Some: eke=ekacce* (alternative grammatical form). *Clothed by their hair (kesanivāsino)*: had what is shameful covered only by their hair. *Go in search of food (bhattāya gacchanti)*: whatever place they come to they go off in search of fodder thinking, 'Perhaps when we have gone from here we might get here or there some food that has been thrown away or vomited, or the impurities that accompanied child-birth and so on. *Going off in all directions (pakkamanti diso disaṃ)*: going off from one direction to another, to a place at an interval of countless yojanas.

7 *Far away (dūre)*: to a far away place. *Some (eke)*: some petas. *Run (padhāvitvā)*: run in search of fodder. **[174]** *But turn back without having obtained anything (aladdhā ca nivattare)*: but turn back without having obtained either fodder or drink. *Fainting (pamucchitā)*: they are in a faint condition due to the misery of hunger and thirst and so on. *Staggering (bhantā)*: reeling about. *Sinking to the ground (bhūmiyaṃ paṭisumbhitā)*: they get up in that same faint state and fall to the earth withered up[34] like cast out lumps of clay.

8 *There (tattha)*: the place to which they have gone. *Sinking to the ground (bhūmiyaṃ paṭisumbhitā)*: they fall to the ground as though falling down a precipice, being unable to stand on account of the misery of hunger and so on; alternatively the meaning is that they lose hope through their failure to obtain any fodder and so on there, at the place to which they have gone, and they fall (*paṭisumbhitā*) to the ground as though someone opposite (*paṭimukhaṃ*) had knocked them down (*sumbhitā*),[35] struck them down. *Through not having done any lovely deeds in the past (pubbe akatakalyāṇā)*: through not having done any skilled deeds in the previous life. *Tormented as though burnt by fire (aggidaḍḍhā va ātape)*: as though burnt by fire at some place tormented by the summer sun,[36] meaning they undergo great misery being burnt by the fire of hunger and thirst.

9 *In the past (pubbe)*: in a past life. *Wicked-natured (pāpadhammā)*: of a despicable character through being envious and mean. *Housewives (gharaṇī)*: mistresses of the house. *Mothers of good family (kulamātaro)*: mothers of boys of good family, or mothers of men of good family. *Refuge (dīpaṃ)*: support, meaning meritorious deeds. They are called a support through being a support for beings in the happy states.[37] *We made no: nākamha=na karimha* (alternative grammatical form).

10 *Abundant (pahūtaṃ)*: much. *Food and drink: annapānam pi=annañ ca pānañ ca* (resolution of compound). *So much so that it was thrown away (api ssu avakirīyati)*: *ssu* (untranslated) is a mere particle; *so much so*

that it was thrown away (api avakirīyati): even to the extent that it was thrown away, that it was discarded.[38] *To those who had reached the summit (sammaggate)*: to those who had rightly trodden,[39] to those who had rightly fared (*sammāpaṭipanne=sammāpaṭipannāya*); *to those gone forth: pabbajite=pabbajitāya* – this is the locative case in a dative construction; or, alternatively (if really locative), the meaning is 'Though those who had reached the summit,[40] those gone forth, were at hand, were available.'[41] *Yet we gave nothing (na ka kiñci adamhase)*: overcome with remorse they say that they gave not even so much as one merit-offering.

11 *Desirous of doing what ought not to be done (akammakāmā)*: (being) desirous of doing what ought not to be done is desiring (to do) unskilled deeds that should not be done by the virtuous; (being) desirous of doing what ought to be done is desiring (to do) skilled deeds that should be done by the virtuous. Desirous of doing what ought not to be done is not (being) desirous of what ought to be done, **[175]** meaning lacking proper effort as regards skilled states. *Lazy (alasā)*: indolent,[42] lacking energy in the pursuit of skilled states. *Desirous of sweet things (sādhukāmā)*: fond of pleasant and sweet things. *Gluttonous (mahagghasā)*: eating a lot. Both (expressions) indicate that though they obtained food both excellent and sweet they gave nothing to those in need and they themselves alone enjoyed it. *We were givers of morsels and lumps (ālopapiṇḍadātāro)*: we were those who give lumps of food no bigger than a morsel. *The recipients (paṭiggahe)*: those receiving[43] it. *Abused (paribhāsimhase)*: we spoke showing contempt,[44] meaning we disparaged and derided.

12 *Those houses (te gharā)*: where formerly we acted possessively thinking, 'This house is ours'; those houses continue to stand just the same[45] but they are now of no benefit to us whatsoever – this is the meaning. *And those servants and those ornaments of ours (tā ca dāsiyo tān' evabharaṇāni no)*: just the same is to be applied here too. Herein *of ours: no=amhākaṃ* (alternative grammatical form); *these (te)*: these houses and so on; *are now enjoyed by others (aññe paricārenti)*[46] means being made use of by way of enjoyment and so on. *Whilst our share is misery (mayaṃ dukkhassa bhāgino)*: they speak reproaching themselves saying, 'Formerly we were entirely given to the pursuit of playthings, being unaware that property had to be left behind when going (on to a new existence and that we were) to do that which would follow us in the next world; and now our share is this misery of hunger and thirst and so on.'[47] Now, since beings, though arising amongst human beings after falling from the peta-womb are, as a rule, of low birth and lead a life of great hardship due to the residual result[48] of that same deed, the two verses beginning: '(They will be) basket-makers' were therefore said to illustrate this point.

13 Herein *basket-makers who (veṇī vā)*: basket-makers by birth, meaning they will be workers in bamboo, workers in reeds. The word 'who' (*vā*) has the sense of a relative pronoun. *Are held in contempt (avaññā)*: should be held in contempt, that is to say, contemptible; an alternative reading is *despicable (vambhanā)*,[49] meaning those who are oppressed by others. *Chariot-makers (rathakārī)*: harness-makers.[50] *Insidious (dubbhikā)*: insidious to their friends, who oppress their friends. *Caṇḍālas (caṇḍālī)*: caṇḍālas by birth. *Suffering great hardship (kapaṇā)*: poor, [**176**] who have reached an extremely pitiful state. *Bath-attendants (nahāminī)*: barbers by birth; they will be (such) time and again in all places – this is how it should be construed; that is to say, they will arise in low families in successive (births).

14 *Amongst these alone will they be born (tesu tesveva jāyanti)*: whatever other families, such as hunters and refuse-clearers and so on, that suffer great hardship and are extremely despised, destinies of utmost misery, it is amongst these same low families that those who have arisen amongst the petas due to the stain of selfishness arise when they fall from there. For this reason he said, 'This being the destiny of the selfish.' The destiny of those who had not done meritorious deeds having thus been shown, the seven verses (beginning:) '(Whilst those unselfish givers who) in the past did lovely deeds' were said to show the destiny of those who had done meritorious deeds.

15 Herein *will fill heaven (saggan te paripūrenti)*: those givers who were without envy, who were without the stain of selfishness, who in the past, in their previous birth, did lovely deeds, took delight in meritorious deeds such as giving and so forth, will fill, will make full, heaven, the devaloka, with the very excellence of their beauty and with the excellence of their retinue. *And light up Nandana (obhāsenti ca Nandanaṃ)*: yet they do not quite fill it entirely for there is the wish-granting tree and so on also shining with their natural radiance alone; but they outshine and overpower this by the brightness of their clothes and ornaments and by the radiance of their own bodies and light up the Nandana Grove.

16 *Gratified all their desires (kāmakāmino)*: enjoyed themselves to their hearts' content amidst sense pleasures of their own choosing. *In high-ranking families (uccākulesu)*: in high ranking families such as kṣatriya families and so on. *Wealthy (sabhogesu)*: of great prosperity. *As they fall from there (tato cutā)*: as they fall from there, from that devaloka.

17 *In a pinnacled house and in a palace (kūṭāgāre ca pāsāde)*: both in a pinnacled house[51] and in a palace. *With their limbs fanned (vījitaṅgā)*: with their bodies being fanned.[52] *By those holding peacock (morahatthehi)*: by those holding fans adorned with peacock tail feathers. *Knowing all*

life's comforts (yasassino): possessing retinues, they amuse themselves – this is the meaning.

18 *They travel from lap to lap (aṅkato aṅkaṃ gacchanti)*: even in their childhood they travel just from the site of one lap to that of another of their relatives and nurses, not on the surface of the ground – this is the meaning. *Attend them (upatiṭṭhanti)*: take care of them. *Striving after their comfort (sukhesino)*: wishing for their comfort; [177] they attend them, sheltering them from the slightest discomfort, wondering, 'Is it (too) cold? Or is it (too) hot?' – this is the meaning.

19 *Not for those who have not done meritorious deeds (nay idaṃ akatapuññānaṃ)*: lacking things causing sorrow, this carefree, charming, delightful Nandana Grove, great grove, great park of the Thirty,[53] of the devas of the Thirty-three, is constantly for those who have done meritorious deeds, not for those who have not done meritorious deeds, meaning it is not able to be obtained by them.

20 *Here (idha)*: this is said with reference to the fact that it is especially in this world of men that meritorious deeds can be performed; or, alternatively, *here (idha)*: in this same life. *Hereafter (parattha)*: in the next world.

21 *Their (tesaṃ)*: with the aforementioned devas. *Of those desiring companionship (sahavyakāmānaṃ)*: by those wishing to be together (with them). *Are provided with possessions (bhogasamaṅgino)*: are endowed with possessions, meaning they rejoice at their possession of the five heavenly sense pleasures.

The rest is quite self-evident.

When those petas had thus generally made known the destiny of the deeds done by them and the destiny of meritorious deeds, the Lord taught Dhamma in detail, suiting the dispositions of the people gathered there, headed by the special adviser Koliya whose heart had been agitated thereby. At the end of this teaching insight into the Dhamma arose to eighty-four thousand beings.

[1] aparadisābhāge; this sense of apara is not listed by the PED.

[2] atikkamitvā; ati- must here have the sense of abhi- if there is to be no contradiction between this passage and v 2 and its cty below.

[3] uddālakapupphaṃ, Cassia fistula; cp VvA 43, 197.

[4] Reading abhijjamāne saṅghāte with Se Be for text's abhijjassamānasaṅghāte.

[5] Reading pubbaddhapeto with Se Be and verse for text's pubbadhapeto; it is hard to see how Gehman could have rendered this 'as though free from your former lot' given the cty.

[6] Reading alaṅkatasīsaggo with Se Be for text's -sīsattā.

[7] It seems Dhammapāla was reading antarā Vāsabhagāmaṃ in the verse rather than

antare Vāsabhagāmaṃ that is now the reading of all texts; it is possible that the present reading has been restored from the subsequent cty.

[8] Reading sāmyatthe with Se Be for text's sāmyatte.

[9] The text is badly punctuated and should be amended to read with Se Be as follows: . . . so gāmo ti; ayaṃ h' ettha attho: antare Vāsabhagāmassa. . . .

[10] Reading pakāsitanāmo with Se Be for text's pakāsananāmo.

[11] Text mis-spells bhattuñ here.

[12] So all texts but earlier it was said that these verses were spoken by those rehearsing the texts.

[13] Cp PvA 127.

[14] Following the preferable punctuation of Be, text should be amended by closing PvA 170 with Tenāha: and then starting a new paragraph on PvA 171 with the first line of verse 5, omitting the subsequent ti immediately before mālābharaṇehi.

[15] Cp PvA 196 for what this involves.

[16] Reading -rājaṃ with Se Be for text's -rājānaṃ.

[17] Cp J iv 425ff., v 333ff., 354ff.

[18] paṭicchāditakopīnā; for kopīnaṃ see note at PvA 88 above.

[19] yathā jātarūpā, literally of a form (or appearance) just like that possessed at birth. At Vism xvii 153f. Buddhaghosa asserts that petas may come into being through any of the four sorts of generation, viz egg-born, womb-born, moisture-born and of spontaneous arising (opapātika) (cp M i 73) but gives no examples of, say, petas born from eggs. More often, however, it has been supposed that petas are always of spontaneous arising and whilst these stories give no details of how the petas come into existence it seems to be assumed that they merely arise in the form required by their past deeds, no mention ever being made of their having to wait for adulthood and so forth. The odd references to petīs giving birth to children whom they subsequently devour need not entail that the children are themselves womb-born petas.

[20] Reading annapānam pi api ssu with Se Be for text's annapānaṃ hi api su.

[21] Reading sammaggate with Se Be for text's samaggate; this is an epithet of the arahant – see Dial i 73 n. 2; cp S i 76, It 87. The denial that there are such individuals amounts to wrong view – e.g. D i 55 = A iv 226 = v 265 – whilst its assertion to mundane (lokiya) right view – e.g. M iii 72; cp A i 269.

[22] Reading sādukāmā with Se Be for text's sādhukāmā.

[23] dātāro, both nominative and accusative plural. The preceding verse would suggest that it were accusative since they abused givers and recipients alike but the cty below takes it as nominative with the recipients (paṭiggahe) alone as objects of the abuse.

[24] Reading paricārenti with Be for text's Se parihārenti; cp II 3[21] and IV 14[1].

[25] Reading veṇī with Se Be for text's veṇiṃ; cp PED sv veṇa.

[26] caṇḍālī, the issue of the most unspeakable form of mixed marriage – female brahmin and śūdra or pañcama male.

[27] Gehman's adoption of vl is unnecessary. Se Be both read Vejayante, name of Sakka's famous palace in the Nandana Grove of the Thirty-three for a description of which see the Cūḷataṇhā Saṅkhayasutta (M-37) in which Sakka shows Moggallāna round it (M i 252-254). It was not Sakka's alone, however, but 'arose for the use of the multitude' (DhpA i 273; cp DA 698 and DPPN ii 915).

[28] Reading goṇakatthate with Se Be for text's goṇasaṇṭhite; Gehman p. 209 n. 2 mis-spells goṇākātthate.

[29] Reading vījitaṅgā with Se (Be bījitaṅgā) for text's vijitaṅgā; cp PED sv vijita.

[30] Reading dhātiyo with Se Be for text's jātiyo.

[31] The grove in the Thirty-three where the devas enjoy themselves. At J i 49 it is said that there is such a grove in all devalokas. It was also to the Nandana Grove that Sakka would send those devas who were about to fall and there they would

dissolve like snow or go out like a flame and arise elsewhere – cp KS i 9 n. 1; M i 505; S v 342; A iii 40.

[32] This verse appears without a number in the text.

[33] Reading -nivāsanā with Se Be for text's -mivāsanā.

[34] Reading vissussitvā with Be (Se visussitvā) for text's vissaṭṭhā.

[35] Quasi-etymology.

[36] Cp PvA 37.

[37] Reading sugatīsu patiṭṭhā bhāyato with Se Be for text's sugatisupatiṭṭhābhāvato.

[38] All texts disagree here. Se reads api avakirīyati chādīyati and Be api avakirīyati chaṭṭīyati. I follow our text's api avakirīyati yadi pi avakirīyati chaḍḍīyati.

[39] Reading sammā gate with Se Be for text's samāgate.

[40] Reading sammaggate with Se Be and verse for text's samaggate.

[41] The cty. is a little obscure here. Sammaggate and pabbajite of the verse are both locative. Having supplied two synonyms in the locative case – sammā gate and sammāpaṭipanne – for sammaggate, Dhammapāla then repeats the second of these in its dative form – sammāpaṭipannāya – and continues by glossing pabbajite with its dative form of pabbajitāya. Only then does he explain his reason, adding as an alternative what the phrase would mean if it were, after all, intended to be taken in the locative sense.

[42] Reading kusītā with Se Be for text's kusitā.

[43] Reading paṭigganhanake with Se Be for text's paṭiggāhake paṭigganhanake.

[44] Reading paribhavaṃ karontā with Se Be for text's paribhāsaṃ karontā.

[45] Reading yattha mayaṃ pubbe amhākaṃ gharan ti mamattaṃ akarimha tāni gharāni yathāṭhitāni with Se Be for text's tāni gehāni yattha mayaṃ pubbe amhākan ti mamakattaṃ akarimha tāni gharāni yathā ṭhitāni.

[46] Reading aññe paricārentī ti with Be for text's Se Aññe ti apare. Parihārentī ti paricaranti and in accordance with the vl adopted in the verse.

[47] Cp PvA 87.

[48] Reading vipākāvasesena with Se Be for text's vipākā 'va sesena; see S i 91–93 for another example of the residual result of a deed.

[49] So Se Be for text's 'vambhaṇā.

[50] Literally leather-workers.

[51] 'This refers to the high ridged, overhanging, barrel-vaulted roof characteristic of ancient India' – A. K. Warder, *Introduction to Pali*, London 1963, p. 78 n. 2; cp also III 2[21] and its cty.

[52] Reading vījiyamānadehā with Se (Be bījiya-) for text's vijjamānadehā; cp PED sv vījati.

[53] Reading tidasānaṃ with Se Be for text's ti dasānaṃ.

III.2 EXPOSITION OF THE SĀNUVĀSIN PETA STORY[1]
[Sānuvāsipetavatthuvaṇṇanā]

'The elder of the city of Kuṇḍi.' This was said when the Teacher was staying in the Bamboo Grove concerning some peta-relatives of the venerable elder of Sānuvāsin.

It is said that long ago in Benares the son of king Kitava was returning after sporting at some amusement in the park when he saw the Pacceka-buddha Sunetta leaving the city after going about in search of alms.[2] Drunk with the pride of authority and depraved in mind he thought, 'How dare that shaveling go by without paying me the añjali salute!' [178] He alighted from the elephant's back and, as he addressed him saying, 'Did you get any almsfood, I wonder?', he snatched his bowl from his hand, threw it on the ground and broke it. Then mocking him as he (stood) looking on with devotion in his heart, with eyes downcast, gentle, at ease and diffusing compassion,[3] unperturbed through having attained to Suchness[4] under all circumstances, he went away saying with a malevolence of mind due to his misplaced malice, 'What! Don't you know that I am the son of king Kitava? What can you do to me, just looking on (like that)?' But just as he was going away there arose a powerful heat about his body resembling the heat of hell fire. With his body overcome by that great torment, overcome by feelings of extremely intense misery, he died and arose in the Great Hell of Avīci. There he was boiled for eighty-four thousand years as he stood and turned about in many ways – on his right side, on his left side, lying face upwards and face downwards.[5] When he fell from there he underwent the misery of hunger and thirst and so on for an unlimited time amidst the petas. When he fell from there he arose in a village of fishermen near the city of Kuṇḍi during this Buddha-period. There arose to him the faculty of remembering former lives. Recollecting by this means the misery he had formerly undergone[6] in the past he would not go, through a fear of wicked deeds, to catch fish with his relatives, even though he was of age. As they were going he would hide, being unwilling to slaughter fish; whilst if he went[7] he would ruin the nets or take the living[8] fish and let them loose in the water. His relatives, disapproving[9] of his actions, threw him out of their home. One brother of his, however, held him in affection in his heart. Now at that time the venerable Ānanda was staying on Mount Sānuvāsin[10] close by to the city of Kuṇḍi and that fisherman's son who had been rejected by his relatives, roaming about this way and that, reached that place and approached the elder at the moment he was eating. When the elder questioned him he realised that he was in need of food and gave him a meal and, when the meal was over [179] he learned of the whole issue. When he knew that, just by means of a talk on Dhamma he had devotion in his heart (he asked), 'Do you wish to go forth, my friend?' (to which he replied), 'Yes, sir, I wish to go forth.' When the elder had had him go forth he went, together with him, into the presence of the Lord. The Teacher then said to him, 'Ānanda, you should have pity on this novice.' Since he had not done skilled deeds he received little (in the way of alms) so the Teacher, helping[11] him, urged him to fill the water-pots for the use of the monks. When they saw this the layfollowers provided him with a constant and plentiful supply of food. In due course he received ordination and attained arahantship and, after becoming an elder, dwelt on Mount Sānuvāsin together with twelve monks. As many as five hundred of his relatives, however. through the non-accumulation of skilled states and the accumulation of wicked states such as selfishness and so on, died and arose amongst the petas. His mother and father, however, would not approach him since they were embarrassed at the thought, 'This is the one we formerly cast out[12] of our home', and sent his brother who had held him in affection. He revealed himself at the time the elder entered the village in search of alms, kneeling[13] with his right knee on the ground and making the añjali salute, and spoke the verses beginning: 'Your mother and your father, sir'. However, the five verses beginning: 'The elder of the city of Kuṇḍi' and so on were inserted by those making a recension of the Dhamma with the aim of showing their context.

1 'The elder of the city of Kuṇḍi who dwelt upon Sānuvāsin, Poṭṭhapāda by name, was a recluse with developed faculties.

2 His mother, father and brother had gone to a miserable existence in the world of Yama. Having done wicked deeds they had gone from here to the world of the petas.

3 Gone to a miserable existence, needle-afflicted,[14] weary, naked and emaciated; terrified, in great terror and bloody-handed,[15] they would not reveal (themselves).

4 **[180]** His brother, transfixed, naked, alone on a single track, bent on all fours,[16] revealed[17] himself to the elder.

5 But the elder paid no attention[18] and passed by in silence, so he informed the elder, saying, "I am your brother, come as a peta;

6 Your mother and your father, sir, have gone to a miserable existence in the world of Yama. Having done wicked deeds they have gone from here to the world of the petas.

7 Gone to a miserable existence, needle-afflicted, weary, naked and emaciated; terrified, in great terror and bloody-handed, they will not reveal (themselves).

8 You are compassionate; please have pity – when you have given make that over to us (for it is) by means of alms given by you that the bloody-handed are sustained." '

1 Herein *the elder of the city of Kuṇḍi (Kuṇḍinagariyo thero)*: the elder who was born and grew up in the city of that name. An alternative reading is *Kuṇḍikanāgaro thero* but it means the same. *Who dwelt upon Sānuvāsin (Sānuvāsinivāsino)*: who dwelt upon Mount Sānuvāsin.

Poṭṭhapāda by name (Poṭṭhapādo ti nāmena): was known by the name of Poṭṭhapāda. *Was a recluse (samaṇo)*: had quieted (all) wickedness.[19] *With developed faculties (bhāvitindriyo)*: with the faculties of faith and so on developed through cultivation of the ariyan path, meaning an arahant.

2 *His (tassa)*: that Sānuvāsin elder's. *Had gone to a miserable existence (duggatā)*: had gone to a state of misery.

3 *Needle-afflicted (sūcik' aṭṭā)*:[20] afflicted[21] with putrid,[22] rough bodies;[23] an alternative reading is 'needle-gone' (*sūcigatā*).[24] They are afflicted, oppressed,[25] by hunger and thirst which have acquired the name 'the needle' (*sūcikā*) in the sense that they are piercing.[26] Some read *needle-throated (sūcikaṇṭhā)*, meaning the opening of their mouths are like the eyes of needles.[27] *Weary (kilantā)*: weary in mind and body. *Naked (naggino)*: unclothed, naked in appearance. *Emaciated (kisā)*: with emaciated bodies since they have bodies that are mere skin and bone. *Terrified (uttasantā)*: they become terrified due to a dread of reproach[28] thinking, 'This recluse was our son.' **[181]** *In great terror (mahātāsā)*: they are filled with great fear on account of the deeds done formerly by them. *Would not reveal (na dassenti)*: would not reveal themselves, would not go and confront him. *Bloody-handed (kurūrino)*: acting cruelly.

4 *His brother (tassa bhātā)*: the Sānuvāsin elder's brother. *Transfixed: vitaritvā=vitiṇṇo* (alternative grammatical form), meaning with fear and trembling at the dread of reproach. An alternative reading is *hastened (vituritvā)*:[29] was in haste, that is to say, hastening. *On a single track (ekapathe)*: on a road of single file. *Alone (ekako)*: alone, unaccompanied. *Bent on all fours (catukuṇḍiko bhavitvāna)*: he moves himself about with his four limbs bent[30] – (this is) bent on all fours; resting[31] and going about on two hands and on two knees, meaning having become as such. He acted in this manner so that what is shameful should be covered from the front. *Revealed himself to the elder (therassa dassayī 'tumaṃ)*: had himself be visible, let himself be visible, to the elder.[32]

5 *Paid no attention (amanasikatvā)*: paid no attention (*amanasikaritvā*, alternative grammatical form), took no notice, as to who he might be. *So he (so ca)*: so the peta. *I am your brother come as a peta (bhātā petāgato ahaṃ)*: he informed the elder saying, 'I was your brother in a past existence; now I have come here as a peta' – this is how it should be construed. The three verses beginning: '(Your) mother and (your) father' were said to show the manner in which he informed him of this.

6 Herein *your mother and your father: mātā pitā ca te=tava mātā pitā ca* (alternative grammatical form).

8 *Please have pity (anukampassu)*: please help (us), please be kind. *Make that over (anvādisāhi)*: assign that. *To us: no=amhākaṃ*[33] (alternative

grammatical form). *Given by you: tava dinnena=tayā dinnena* (alternative grammatical form).

(Those rehearsing the Dhamma) then uttered these verses to show the line of action taken[34] by the elder when he heard this:

9 'When the elder and the twelve other monks had been in search of alms they gathered at the same place with the purpose of sharing the meal.[35]

10 The elder said to them all, "Give to me as has been received; I will convert it into a meal for the Saṅgha[36] out of pity for my relatives."

11 [182] They handed it over to the elder and the elder invited the Saṅgha. When he had given the elder made it over to his mother, father and brother saying, "Let this be for my relatives! May my relatives be happy!"

12 Immediately he dedicated this food came into being – clean, choice, well-prepared and curried with many flavours, whereupon his brother had himself be visible,[37] handsome, strong and happy, saying,

13 "Abundant (is this) food, sir, but behold we are still naked. Please exert yourself,[38] sir, in such a manner that we might obtain clothes."

14 The elder gathered tatters from the rubbish heap. When he had made the rags into a garment he gave it to the Saṅgha of the four quarters.

15 When he had given the elder made it over to his mother, father and brother saying, "Let this be for my relatives! May my relatives be happy!"

16 Immediately he dedicated this clothes came into being, whereupon (his brother), dressed in fine clothes, revealed himself to the elder, saying,

17 "As many clothes as were in the whole of king Nanda's realm – still more than that, sir, are our clothes and coverings,

18 Of silk and wool, linen and cotton.[39] Many and costly are they – they even[40] hang down from the sky.

19 And we just put on whichever takes our fancy. Please exert yourself, sir, in such a manner that we might obtain a home."

20 [183] When the elder had built a hut of leaves he gave it to the Saṅgha of the four quarters. When he had given the elder made it over to his mother, father and brother saying, "Let this be for my relatives! May my relatives be happy!"

21 Immediately he dedicated this houses came into being – pinnacled-house residences[41] that are divided into equal portions.

22 "The like of such houses as ours here are not found amongst men; the houses such as ours here are like those found amongst the devas;

23 Dazzling, they shine forth thorughout the four directions. Please exert yourself, sir, in such a manner that we might obtain water."

24 When the elder had filled a water-pot he gave it to the Saṅgha of the four quarters. When he had given the elder made it over to his mother, father and brother saying, "Let this be for my relatives! May my relatives be happy!"

25 Immediately he dedicated this water came into being – deep, four-cornered and well laid out[42] lotus ponds,

26 With clear water and beautiful banks, cool and fragrant, covered with lotuses and water lilies, the water full of lotus filaments.

27 When they had bathed and drunk in them they appeared to the elder, saying, "Abundant (is this) water, sir, but our feet are painfully cracked.

28 Roaming about we limp on gravel and the thorny kusa[43] grass. Please exert yourself, sir, in such a manner that we might obtain a vehicle."

29 When the elder had obtained a sandal[44] he gave it to the Saṅgha of the four quarters. When he had given the elder made it over to his mother, father and brother saying, "Let this be for my relatives! May my relatives be happy!"

30 Immediately he dedicated this the petas came by carriage, saying, "You have shown pity, sir, by this food and clothing,

31 **[184]** This house and gift of water[45] – by both these and by this gift of a vehicle. We, sir, have come to salute the compassionate sage for the world." '

9 Herein *when the elder had been in search of alms (thero caritvā piṇḍāya)*: when the elder had gone about on his almsround.[46] *And the twelve other monks (bhikkhū aññe ca dvādasa)*: and the twelve other monks who were dwelling with the elder gathered together at the same place. If (it should be asked:) 'With what purpose?', *with the purpose of sharing the meal (bhattavissaggakāraṇā)*: with the purpose of taking their meal, for the sake of (eating) the food.

10 *To them (te)*: to those monks. *As has been received (yathā laddhaṃ)*: whatever has been received. *Give: dadātha=detha* (alternative grammatical form).

11 *They handed over (nīyātayiṃsu)*: they gave. *Invited the Saṅgha (saṅghaṃ nimantayi)*: invited the twelve monks to give that food by way of specifying it to be for the Saṅgha. *Made over (anvādisi)*: assigned;[47] to show to whom he dedicated it on that occasion, 'To his mother, father and brother saying, "Let this be for my relatives! May my relatives be happy!" ' was said.

12 *Immediately he dedicated this: samanantarānuddiṭṭhe=uddiṭṭha samanantaram eva*[48] (resolution of compound). *Food came into being (bhojanaṃ upapajjatha)*: food came into being for those petas. Of what sort? They said,[49] 'Clean' and so on. Herein *curried with many flavours (anekarasavyañjanaṃ)*: prepared with curries of a variety of flavours; or, alternatively, of many flavours and of many curries. *Whereupon (tato)*: after receiving the food. *His brother had himself be visible (uddassayī bhātā)*: the peta who had been his brother revealed himself to the elder. *Handsome, strong and happy (vaṇṇavā balavā sukhī)*: by means of receiving that food in that way he straightaway became endowed with beauty, endowed with strength and happy.

13 *Abundant food, sir (pahūtaṃ bhojanaṃ bhante)*: through the majesty of your gift, sir, abundant, plentiful food has been received by us. *But behold we are still naked (passa naggāmhase)*: observe, however, that we are still naked. Therefore please exert yourself, sir, please take it upon yourself, to act *in such a manner that we might obtain clothes (yathā vatthaṃ labhāmhase)*: by taking it upon yourself to act in such a way that [185] we might all obtain clothes, meaning please endeavour in this manner.

14 *From the rubbish heap (saṅkārakūṭato)*: from this and that dust heap. *Gathered (uccinitvāna)*: collected by way of seeking out. *Tatters (nantake)*: discarded bits of cloth that are torn at the edges; they are called 'rags' since they are in bits. Now the elder made a robe with these and gave it to the Saṅgha. For this reason they said,[49] 'When he had made the rags into a garment he gave it to the Saṅgha of the four quarters.' Herein *he gave it to the Saṅgha of the four quarters (saṅghe cātuddise adā)*: he gave it to the current[50] order[51] of monks of the four quarters. This is the locative case with the sense of the dative.[52]

16 *Dressed in fine clothes (suvatthavasano)*: dressed in beautiful clothes. *Revealed himself to the elder: therassa dassayī 'tumaṃ=therassa attānaṃ dassayī dassesi* (alternative grammatical forms), he became manifest.

17 They are 'clothes' (*paṭicchadā*) since in this case he clothes himself (*paṭicchādayati*)[53] (with them).

21 *Pinnacled-house residences (kūṭāgāranivesanā)*: those that are pinnacled houses and houses other than these that are known as residences; this is given with a distortion of gender.[54] *Divided (vibhattā)*: divided into shapes that are regular, rectangular, long, circular and so on. *Into equal portions (bhāgaso mitā)*: into measured portions.

22 *Ours: no=amhākaṃ* (alternative grammatical form). *Here (idha)*: in this world of the petas. *Amongst the devas (api dibbesu)*: *api* (untranslated)

is a mere particle; in the realms of the devas, meaning in the devalokas.[55]
24 *Water-pot (karakaṃ)*: a regulation water-pot.[56] *Filled (pūretvā)*: filled with water.
26 *The water full of lotus filaments (vārikiñjakkhapūritā)*: full in that the top of the water is covered all over with loads of hairy filaments of lotuses and water lilies and so on.
27 *Are cracked (phalanti)*: they blossom out, meaning the edges of their heels are split open.
28 *Roaming about (āhiṇḍamānā)*: wandering about. *We limp (khañjāma)*: [**186**] we go about limping. *On gravel and the thorny kusa grass (sakkhare kusakaṇṭhake)*: on pieces of ground that are full of gravel and the thorny kusa grass, meaning treading upon gravel and the thorny kusa grass. *A vehicle (yānaṃ)*: any vehicle such as a carriage or litter and so on.
29 *A sandal (sipāṭikaṃ)*: a single-soled sandal.
30 *Came by carriage: rathena-m-āgamuṃ=rathena āgacchiṃsu* (alternative grammatical form); (the words) are euphonically connected by the syllable *ma.*
31 *Both (ubhayaṃ)*: by both gifts – by that gift of the four requisites of food and so on and by this same gift of a vehicle. The gift of medicines is also included in this gift of water here. The rest is quite self-evident[57] since it has already been given above.

The elder raised the issue with the Lord. The Lord took the matter as an arisen need saying, 'Just like these here, so too in your immediately preceding existence were you a peta who underwent great misery', and, when begged by the elder, related the Thread Peta Story[58] and taught Dhamma to the company assembled there. When they heard this the people, full of agitation, became given to meritorious deeds such as the virtue of almsgiving and so on.

[1] This story may be compared with the version appearing at J ii 194f.
[2] Reading caritvā nagarato with Se Be for text's caritvāna gharato.
[3] Reading karuṇāvipphārasommasomanassanayananipātitapasannacittaṃ with Se for text's karuṇāvipphārasomanassanipātitapasannacittaṃ (Be -nipāta-).
[4] tādibhāvappattiyā.
[5] Cp IV 7[8].
[6] Reading anubhūtapubbaṃ with Se Be for text's anurūpaṃ bhūtaṃ.
[7] Reading gato with Be for text's Se tato.
[8] Reading jīvante vā with Se Be for text's jīvante.
[9] Reading arocantā with Se Be for text's ārocentā.
[10] Literally, Saturn's (Sānu) dwelling place (vāsin).
[11] See PvA 196.
[12] Reading nikkaḍḍhito with Se Be for text's nikkaḍḍito.
[13] Reading patiṭṭhāpetvā with Se Be for text's patiṭṭhapetvā.
[14] Reading sūcik' aṭṭā with Se Be for text's sūcikaṭṭhā.

[15] Not, as Gehman suggests, 'they did not appear ruthless', as the cty makes clear.
[16] Not, as Gehman suggests, 'like a waterpot'.
[17] Reading dassayī with Se Be for text's dassayi.
[18] Se reads just the opposite here – thero ca manasīkatvā – suggesting that the elder did pay attention.
[19] An edifying etymology of samaṇa, recluse; see also Dhp 265 and DhpA iii 84.
[20] All readings throughout this passage differ widely and are somewhat uncertain. I have selected those that seemed to make the most sense.
[21] Reading aṭṭitā as recommended by PED sv for text's aṭṭhikā; Be reads aṭṭakā and Se aṭṭikā.
[22] pūtinā, so text and Be; Se reads sūcinā.
[23] Reading lūkhagattā with Be for text's lūkhavantādinā; Se reads lukhavatthādinā, presumably with rough clothes and so on, though earlier they were said to be naked, a fact also confirmed further on.
[24] Se reads sūciggatā, Be omits; the meaning is unclear.
[25] Reading aṭṭā pīḷitā with Be for text's ajjhāpīḷitā; Se reads aṭṭitā pīḷitā.
[26] vijjhanatthena, Be omits.
[27] All texts.
[28] ottappena; for a discussion of this term see Buddhist Psych. Ethics p. 20 n. 1.
[29] Reading vituritvā ti vā pāṭho with Se Be for text's vitaritvā ti vā.
[30] Reading kuṇḍeti with Se Be for text's kuṇḍo ti.
[31] Reading tiṭṭhanto ca with Be (Se tiṭṭhanto ti) for text's ti ca.
[32] therassa attānaṃ uddisayi uddisesi; so text and Se. Be has . . . uddisayi dassesi. CPD sv ud-dasseti recommends reading . . . uddassayi uddassesi.
[33] Reading Anvādisāhī ti ādisa. No ti amhākaṃ with Se Be for text's Anvādisāhi no ti ādisa no ti amhākaṃ.
[34] Reading yathā paṭipajji taṃ dassetuṃ with Se Be for text's gāthā paṭipajji. Taṃ dassetuṃ. . . .
[35] Reading bhattavissaggakāraṇā with Se Be for text's -vissatta-; cp PED sv bhatta.
[36] saṅghabhattaṃ karissāmi; see Vin i 58 where this is distinguished from a meal for a special person, meals made from scraps and those got by invitation and so on; cp PvA 81 and v 14 below. It would seem to be another case of making a gift saṅghika.
[37] Reading uddassayī with Be for text's uddissati; Se reads uddissayī.
[38] Parakkāma, not exert desire, as Gehman suggests, but from para + $\sqrt{}$kram; cp PED sv.
[39] Reading khomakappāsikāni with Se Be and II 1[17] for text's -kappāsiyāni.
[40] Reading p' ākāse with Se Be and II 1[18] for text's c' ākāse.
[41] Reading kūṭāgāranivesanā with Se Be for text's kūṭāgārā nivesanā.
[42] Reading sunimmitā with Se Be and II 1[19] for text's sanimmitā.
[43] Poa cynosuroides.
[44] Reading sipāṭikaṃ with Se Be for text's sipātikaṃ; see PED sv sipāṭikā which misquotes the cty here and which should be amended to read ekapaṭalaṃ upāhanaṃ.
[45] Reading pānīyadānena with Be and cty below for text's Se pānadānena.
[46] Reading thero piṇḍapātacārikāya caritvā with Se Be for text's piṇḍapātacārikāya.
[47] Reading Anvādisī ti ādisi; tattha . . . with Se Be for text's Anvādisī ti tattha . . .
[48] So Se Be and PvA 50 for text's uddissa samanantaram eva ca.
[49] All texts read āha, he said, here.
[50] Cp CPD sv āgata and Vin i 305, ii 147, 164; J i 93.
[51] Saṅgha.
[52] Cp PvA 174.
[53] Reading Paṭicchādayati etthā ti paṭicchadā with Se Be for text's Paṭicchadā ti paṭicchādayati; cp cty at PvA 76. The usual meaning of these words is covering, concealing etc.
[54] Masculine/feminine plural for neuter plural.

[55] Reading dibbesu bhavanesu devalokesū ti attho with Se for text's dibbesū ti etesu devalokesū ti attho; Be reads devalokesū ti attho alone.

[56] dhammakarakaṃ, the regulation water-pot issued to monks provided with a strainer (parissāvana) to prevent injury to living things; see Vin i 209, ii 118f., 177, 302.

[57] Reading uttānaṃ with Se Be for text's vuttānaṃ.

[58] II 11.

III.3 EXPOSITION OF THE RATHAKĀRA PETA STORY
[Rathakārapetavatthuvaṇṇanā]

'Beryl-pillared, gleaming, radiant.' This was said when the Teacher was staying at Sāvatthī concerning a certain petī.

It is said that long ago, at the time of Lord Kassapa, there was a certain woman who was endowed with good conduct and who found faith in the Teaching through association with a lovely friend.[1] She built a dwelling that was extremely lovely to behold being well apportioned with decorated walls, pillars, stairways and ground floor.[2] She had the monks be seated there, waited upon them with the choicest food and presented it to the order of monks. She died in due course and, due to a different, wicked deed she had performed, arose as a vimānapetī near lake Rathakāra[3] on the Himālaya, the king of mountains. Through the power of her meritorious deed of her gift of that dwelling to the Saṅgha there arose, amidst a lotus pond and embellished like the Nandana Grove, a lofty mansion made entirely of jewels and on all sides extremely charming, captivating and delightful, [187] whilst she herself was of a golden complexion, beautiful, lovely to behold and charming. There she dwelt, enjoying heavenly excellence, but in the absence of any men. Discontent arose to her at dwelling without men for that long time. She became dissatisfied and thinking, 'This will do the trick!', she lowered some ripe heavenly mangoes into the river. Everything is to be understood in the same manner as was handed down in the Kaṇṇamuṇḍa Peta Story.[4] Here, however, a young man who was a resident of Benares saw one of those mango fruits in the Ganges. In due course he set out looking for where it had come from, saw that river[5] and by following this came to her dwelling place. When she saw him she led him to her dwelling place and, making him welcome, sat down. When he saw the excellence of her dwelling place he spoke these verses enquiring (about it):

1 'Beryl-pillared,[6] gleaming, radiant and possessing countless paintings is the mansion to which you have ascended; and there you rest, O devī of great majesty, like the moon in mid-career on the fifteenth day.[7]

2 And your complexion resembles molten gold, your glowing appearance is exceedingly[8] lovely to behold, but you are seated alone on your excellent couch beyond compare; (it would seem) you have no husband.

3 And you have on all sides these lotus ponds, abundant in flowers, with many lotuses and entirely spread with gold dust, mud and duckweed[9] not being known there.

4 These swans, delightful and lovely to behold, [188] glide about on the water at all times and, flocking together, they all beautifully sing out with full voice[10] like the sound[11] of kettle-drums.

5 Dazzling, resplendent in your glory, you rest reclining in your boat, with thick eyelashes, merry and speaking pleasantly;[12] lovely in every limb, you are exceedingly brilliant.

6 This mansion is flawless and stands level; possessing parks enhancing your delight and pleasure. I wish, O lady of supreme beauty, that I might enjoy myself with you here amidst this pleasure.'[13]

1 Herein *there (tattha)*: in that mansion. *You rest (acchasi)*: you sit, you dwell, at whatever time you so desire. *O devī (devi)*: he is addressing her. *Of great majesty (mahānubhāve)*: endowed with great heavenly majesty. *In mid-career (pathaddhani)*: journeying on its own path, meaning on its course through the expanse of the heavens. *Like the moon on the fifteenth day (pannarase va cando)* means shining like the moon's fully rounded orb on the night of the full moon.

2 *And your complexion resembles molten gold (vaṇṇo ca te kanakassa sannibho)*: your complexion is extremely captivating, being similar to molten gold. For this reason he said, 'Your glowing appearance[14] is exceedingly lovely to behold.' *Beyond compare (atule)*: of great value; or, alternatively (we should read:) *O one beyond compare (atule)*, it being his way of addressing the devatā, meaning 'O one of matchless beauty.' *You have no husband: n'atthi ca tuyhaṃ sāmiko=sāmiko ca tuyhaṃ n'atthi*[15] (alternative grammatical form).

3 *Abundant in flowers (pahūtamālyā)*: they possess many and various flowers such as the lotus and the blue water lily and so on. [189] *With gold dust (suvaṇṇacuṇṇehi)*: with golden[16] sands. *Entirely spread (samant' otatā)*: entirely strewn. *There (tattha)*: in those lotus ponds. *Mud and duckweed (paṅko paṇṇako ca)*: neither mud nor slime[17] is known.

4 *These swans, delightful and lovely to behold (haṃsā pi me dassanīyā manoramā)*: these swans, delightful and pleasant looking. *Glide about (anupariyanti)*: wander up and down. *At all times (sabbadā)*: in all seasons. *Flocking together (samayya)*: coming together. *Beautifully (vaggu)*: sweetly. *Sing out (upanadanti)*: coo. *With full voice (bindussarā)*: with uninterrupted voice, with rounded voice. *Like the sound of kettle-drums (dundubhīnaṃ va ghoso)* means that by nature of their beautiful, full voice the sound of the swans on your lotus pond is like that of kettle-drums.

5 *Dazzling (daddaḷhamānā)*: brilliantly blazing forth. *In your glory (yasasā)*: with the psychic power of a deva. *In your boat (nāvāya)*: in your coracle;[18] he said this having thus seen the petī[19] enjoying herself on the water seated on her couch of great value in a golden, lotus-like[20] boat on the lotus pond. *Reclining: avalamba=olambitvā* (alternative grammatical form); leaning against for support.[21] *You rest (tiṭṭhasi)*: this is the opposite expression to motion[22] due to the implication of a cessation of motion of the word '(being at) rest'. An alternative reading is *nisajjasi*; its meaning should be regarded just as 'you are seated'. *With thick eyelashes (āḷārapamhe)*: with long, black, curved eyelases. *Merry (hasite)*: full of merriment, with a merry face. *Speaking pleasantly (piyaṃvade)*: talking pleasantly. *Lovely in every limb (sabbaṅgakalyāṇi)*: beautiful in every limb, meaning beauteous in every limb, both large and small. *You are brilliant (virocasi)*: you glare.

6 *Flawless (virajaṃ)*: without a flaw, faultless. *Stands level (same ṭhitaṃ)*: stands on a level portion of ground (*sama bhūmibhāge*); or, alternatively, on account of its beauty on (all) four (sides)[23] it stands in equal proportion (*samabhāge*), meaning perfect all round. *Possessing parks (uyyānavantaṃ)*: similar to the Nandana Grove. *Enhancing your delight and pleasure (ratinandivaḍḍhanaṃ)*: it is 'enhancing your delight **[190]** and pleasure' since it enhances your delight and pleasure, meaning causing your happiness and joy to grow. *O lady (nāri)*: this is his way of addressing her. *Of supreme beauty (anomadassane)*: blameless looking through being perfect in every limb, both large and small.[24] *Amidst this pleasure (nandane)*: amidst what produces pleasure. *Here (idha)*: in this 'Nandana Grove' or in your mansion. *That I might enjoy myself (moditum)*: I wish that I might indulge in the pleasures of love – this is how it should be construed.

When the young man had spoken thus the vimānadevatā,[25] answering him, uttered this verse:

7 'Perform a deed to be experienced here and let your mind be bent[26] on here; when you have performed a deed to be experienced here you will thus obtain me who will gratify all your desires.'

7 Herein *perform a deed to be experienced here (karohi kammaṃ idha vedaniyaṃ)*: perform, you should pursue, a skilled deed which will ripen and yield its result here in this heavenly place. *Bent on here (idha nataṃ)*: sloping towards here; an alternative reading is *sliding towards here (idha ninnaṃ)* meaning let your mind be, allow it to be, sliding, tending, inclining[27] towards this place. *Me: mamaṃ=maṃ* (alternative grammatical form). *You will obtain: lacchasi=labhissasi* (alternative grammatical form).

When the young man heard what the vimānapetī had to say he went from there to the ways of men; he kept his mind intent on that place and performed the appropriate meritorious deed and, dying not long afterwards, arose there in the company of that petī.[28] Those rehearsing the texts uttered the concluding verse explaining the matter:

8 'He gave her his consent saying, "Very well", and performed a deed to be experienced there;[29] when he had performed a deed to be experienced there the young man arose in her company.'

8 **[191]** Herein *very well (sādhu)*: this is a particle denoting agreement. *Her (tassā)*: that vimānapetī. *He gave his consent (paṭisuṇitvā)*: he agreed with what she had to say. *To be experienced there (tahiṃ vedanīyaṃ)*: a skilled deed resulting in happiness that is to be experienced with her in that mansion. *In company (sahavyataṃ)*: together with; the young man arose in her company – this is how it should be construed.

When they had thus been enjoying heavenly excellence there for a long time the man died through the exhaustion of that deed but the woman dwelt there for one full Buddha-interval through her meritorious deed being gone to the field.[30] Then when our Lord had arisen in the world and had set rolling the Wheel of the Noble Dhamma and was in due course staying in the Jeta Grove, the venerable Mahāmoggallāna when wandering one day in the mountains saw that mansion and the vimānapetī and questioned her with the verses that begin: 'Beryl-pillared, gleaming, radiant.' She reported the whole incident to him right from the beginning and when he had heard this the elder went to Sāvatthī and raised (the issue) with the Lord. The Lord took the matter as an arisen need and taught Dhamma to the company assembled there. When they heard this the people performed meritorious deeds such as almsgiving and so on and became given to the Dhamma.

[1] kalyāṇamitta, the technical term for a spiritual guide or adviser.

[2] Reading suvibhattavicitrabhittithambhasopānabhūmitalaṃ with Be (Se omits -bhitti-) for text's suvibhattavicittathambasopāṇabhūmitalaṃ.

[3] One of the seven great lakes – see PvA 152 above.

[4] II 12.

[5] Reading nadiṃ with Se Be for text's na.

[6] Reading -thambhaṃ with Se Be for text's thambaṃ.

[7] Reading pannarase with Se Be and cty below for text's pannasare.

[8] Reading bhusa with Se Be for text's bhūsa; the PED entry sv bhūsa should be deleted. Cp J v 203.

[9] paṇṇaka; I follow Ñāṇamoli, Path of Purification, p. 280. Cp S v 122; A iii 187, 232, 235; J iv 71; Miln 35; Vin iii 177.

[10] Reading bindussarā with Se Be for text's vindussarā; cp Sn 350, Thag 1270 and D ii 211 where it is one of the eight qualities of the voice of Brahmā Sanaṃkumāra whose steed is the swan (haṃsa).

[11] PED sv ghosa wrongly attributes this sound to the petas suggesting it should be rendered as 'wailing'.

[12] Reading piyaṃvade with Se Be for text's piyavade.

[13] nandane, an allusion to the Nandana Grove in Sakka's heaven; cp III 1[19]. We could alternatively translate as 'amidst this "Nandana" '.

[14] Reading uttattarūpo with Se Be and v 2 for text's uggatarūpo.

[15] Se Be read n' atthi ca tuyha-sāmiko=tuyhaṃ sāmiko ca n' atthi; the meaning remains the same.

[16] Reading suvaṇṇa- with Se Be for text's suvanna-.

[17] Reading udakapicchilo with Se (Be -picchillo) for text's udakacchikkhalo, water and swamp (cp PvA 102, 225), since it would seem here to be something that pollutes a pond.

[18] doṇiyaṃ; PED sv doṇī states this to be 'a trough-shaped canoe (cp Marāthi ḍon "a long flat-bottommed boat made of unḍiwood" and Kanarese ḍoni "a canoe hallowed (sic) from a log")'. With this we may compare the English 'dinghy' (from Hindi ḍeṅgi). Here however the vessel is said to resemble a lotus bud and the other sense of doṇī, that of a hollow (cp Skt droṇa, a tub or bucket etc.), is probably predominant.

[19] Se Be add petiṃ here.

[20] Reading paduminiyaṃ suvaṇṇanāvāya with Se Be for text's paduminisuvaṇṇanāvāya.

[21] Reading apassenaṃ with Se Be for text's apassena.

[22] Reading gatiyā with Be for text's Se gatiyā ca.

[23] Reading caturassa sobhitatāya with Se Be for text's caturaṃsaso hitāya.

[24] Reading paripuṇṇaṅgapaccaṅgatāya aninditadassane with Se Be for text's paripuṇṇaṅgatāya nandanadassane; cp Sn 548 and SnA 452. Perfection in body was often considered the result of meritorious and skilled deeds as indeed were the thirty-two marks on the body of the Buddha – cp D iii 142ff.

[25] So our text and Se; Be reads vimānapetidevatā. Earlier she was called a vimānapetī.

[26] nataṃ; Se Be read nihitaṃ whilst Pv has nītaṃ.

[27] Cp M i 493 for a parallel use of these terms.

[28] The text's punctuation should be amended to read, in accordance with Se Be, as follows: . . . tattha nibbatti tassā petiyā sahavyataṃ. Taṃ. . . .

[29] Reading tahiṃ vedanīyaṃ with Se Be and cty below for text's sahavedaniyaṃ; PED has no entry for tahiṃ.

[30] That is, the world's unsurpassed merit-field of I 1 above.

III.4 EXPOSITION OF THE CHAFF PETA STORY
[Bhusapetavatthuvaṇṇanā][1]

'One the chaff of paddy whilst again another.'[2] This was said when the Teacher was staying at Sāvatthī concerning four petas.

It is said that there was in a certain village not far from Sāvatthī a dishonest trader who made his living by giving false measure and so on. He would take some paddy husks,[3] add brown clay to increase the weight and then mix this with the red paddy that he then sold. His son became angry thinking, 'He does not act honourably towards my friends and well-wishers coming to the house', and seized a leather yoke-pad[4] and gave his mother a blow on the head. His **[192]** daughter-in-law ate by stealing meat that had been appointed for the use of all and being called upon once more by them to account for herself made an oath saying, 'If that meat were eaten by me then may I devour the flesh that I have cut from my back in life after life!' His wife said to those begging any means of livelihood whatsoever that there was none and on being pressed by them she made an oath by lying, 'If there should be something when I say there is none then may I feed on excrement wherever I am born!' In due course these four people died and arose as petas in the Viñjha forest.[5] There the dishonest trader would, as the fruit of his deeds, take blazing chaff in both hands and scatter it over his head and (thereby) underwent great misery. His son would split his own head all by himself with hammers made of iron and suffer untold misery. His daughter-in-law, as the fruit of her deeds, underwent unlimited misery devouring the flesh she continually gouged from her back with her well-sharpened and extremely long great nails; whilst no sooner had a meal of fragrant and well-cleansed rice from which the black grains had been removed been presented to his wife than it would become the most foul-smelling and loathsome excrement riddled with various kinds of species of worms which she would grasp with both hands and experience great misery eating it.

Now when these four people had arisen amongst the petas and were suffering great misery the venerable Mahāmoggallāna who was wandering in the mountains one day reached that spot and saw them. He enquired about the deeds they had done with this verse:

1 'One the chaff of paddy whilst again another; and this woman her own flesh and blood; whilst you eat this filthy and disgusting excrement – of what is this the result?'

1 Herein *chaff (bhusāni)*: husks.[6] *One (eko)*: alone.[7] *Of paddy: sāliṃ= sālino*; this is the accusative case with the force of the genitive: **[193]** he

would scatter the blazing husks of paddy over his head – this is the meaning. *Again another: punāparo=puna aparo* (resolution of compound); he who struck his mother's head ended up with his own head split open after striking his head with iron hammers – it is with reference to this that he speaks.[8] *Her own flesh and blood (sakamaṃsalohitaṃ)*: she eats the flesh and blood from her back – this is how it should be construed. *Disgusting (akantikaṃ)*: unpleasant, disagreeable, loathsome. *Of what is this the result? (kissa ayaṃ vipāko)* means of what wicked deed is this the fruit that is now being suffered by you?

When the elder had thus enquired about the deeds they had done, the wife of that dishonest trader then spoke these verses explaining the deeds done by them all:

2 'This one in the past injured his mother whilst this one was a dishonest trader; this one ate meat and deceived by lying.

3 When I was a human being, in the world of men,[9] I was a housewife and mistress of the whole family; though at hand, I concealed this and gave not one bit of it, covering myself by lying, "There is none of this in my house; if there should be and I have hidden it then may my food be excrement!"

4 It is both as a result of that deed and due to the fact that I lied that this meal of fragrant rice turns into excrement for me.

5 Deeds are not barren nor perishes any deed, for I must eat and drink this foul-smelling excretion of worms.'

2 Herein *this one (ayaṃ)*: she speaks pointing to her son. *Injured (hiṃsati)*: he attacked with force, meaning he struck with a hammer.[10] *A dishonest trader (kūṭavāṇijo)*: a scoundrel[11] of a trader, meaning one who conducts his trade by fraud. [194] *Ate meat (maṃsāni khāditvā)*: ate, all by herself, meat provided for the general use of others and deceived by lying, saying that she had not eaten it.[12]

3 *A housewife (agāriṇī)*: mistress of the house. *Though at hand (santesu)*: though the means of livelihood begged by others were available. *I concealed this (parigūhāmi)*: I covered this over; this is said with a distortion of tense.[13] *And gave not one bit of it (mā ca kiñci ito adaṃ)*: gave not even the slightest bit of it, of my property, to others who were in need. *Covering myself (chādemi)*: she covered herself by lying, 'There is none of this in my house.'

4 *Turns into excrement for me (gūthaṃ me parivattati)*: this meal of fragrant rice turns into, changes into, excrement on account of that deed of mine.

5 *Are not barren (avañjhāni)*: are not in vain, are not without fruit.

Nor perishes any deed (na hi kammaṃ vinassati): nor perishes any deed, as accumulated,[14] without having given their fruit. *Of worms (kimīnaṃ)*: possessing worms, full of (whole) families of worms. *Excretion (mīḷhaṃ)*: excrement. The rest is quite self-evident since it has already been given above.

When the elder had thus heard what the petī had to say he raised the issue with the Lord. The Lord took it as an arisen need and taught Dhamma to the company assembled there. That teaching was of benefit to those people.

[1] So Se Be; text reads Bhūsa- here and throughout.

[2] Reading punāparo with Se Be and v 1 for text's punāpare.

[3] Reading sālipalāpe with Se Be for text's sālipalāse.

[4] Reading yugacammaṃ with Be for text's Se yoggacammaṃ; cp SED sv yuga where it is suggested that yugacarman is a leather pad attached to a yoke.

[5] See PvA 244.

[6] Reading palāpāni with Se Be for text's palāsāni both here and below; the entry in PED sv palāsa should be amended accordingly.

[7] Reading ekako with Se Be for text's ekato.

[8] The text is poorly punctuated here and should read with Se Be as follows: sīsabhedaṃ pāpuṇāti taṃ sandhāya vadati. Sakamaṃsalohitan ti. . . .

[9] ahaṃ manussesu manussabhūtā: cp the remarks at MLS iii 249 n. 1 concerning the similar expression manussānaṃ yeva sataṃ manussabhūtānaṃ. This latter expression recurs at S ii 188 where it seems to be merely a gloss, probably for the sake of emphasis as perhaps here.

[10] In the introductory story this was said to be a leather yoke-pad.

[11] Reading khalavāṇijo with Se Be for text's bāla-; this adjectival sense of khala is not listed by PED though it was given in Childers.

[12] It may be noted that it is the theft (or greed) that is the offending deed and not the eating of the meat as such; the Buddha at no time forbade the eating of meat, given certain conditions.

[13] Present indicative for aorist.

[14] Reading yathūpacitaṃ with Be for text's Se hetupacitaṃ.

III.5 EXPOSITION OF THE BOY PETA STORY
[Kumārapetavatthuvaṇṇanā]

'The Sugata's[1] knowledge is wonderful.' This is the Boy Peta Story. How did it originate?

It is said that at Sāvatthī many layfollowers organised themselves into a body of Dhamma-followers and had built in that city a large pavillion and adorned it with cloths of various colours. Early in the morning they invited the Teacher and the order of monks and had that order of monks with the Buddha at its head be seated on seats spread with costly coverings of the highest quality, honoured them with scent and flowers and so on [**195**] and inaugurated a great almsgiving. When he saw this a certain man, whose heart was possessed by the stain of selfishness, unable to bear such worship said, 'It would be better if all this were thrown on the rubbish-heap rather than given to these shavelings.' When they heard this the layfollowers, their hearts agitated, reflected, 'Grave indeed is the wicked deed pursued by this man with which he offended the order of monks with the Buddha at its head.' They reported the matter to his mother and said, 'You should go and apologise to the Lord and his Sāvakasaṅgha.' 'Very well', she agreed and having remonstrated with her son, threatening him, she approached the Lord and the order of monks and apologised, confessing the transgression her son had committed, and paid honour to the Lord and the order of monks for seven days with gifts of rice-gruel. Her son died not long afterwards and arose in the womb of a harlot who made her living by impure deeds. Now she realised that he was a boy just as soon as he was born and had him abandoned in the cemetery.[2] He was there taken into protection by the power of his meritorious deeds and, unmolested by anyone, slept happily as though on his mother's lap. They say that the devatās took him into their protection. Then when, towards dawn, the Lord had emerged from the meditation of great compassion[3] and was surveying the world with his Buddha Eye, he saw the boy abandoned in that charnel ground and went at sunrise to that charnel ground. The people gathered saying, 'The Teacher has come here; he must have some purpose here.' The Lord spoke to the company that had gathered saying, 'This boy is not to be despised; even though he is now abandoned in this cemetery in this helpless state, he will, in future, obtain the highest excellence both in this same life and in the life to come.' Asked by those people, 'What Lord, was the deed done by him in his previous birth?', he explained the deed done by the boy and the excellence he was to attain in the future with (the verses) that begin:

> 'The highest honour was being paid by the people to the order of monks with the Buddha at its head when he had a mental aberration and spoke harsh, discourteous words.'

taught Dhamma suiting the dispositions of the company gathered there and afterwards gave that Teaching on Dhamma which (the Buddhas) have themselves discovered (: ill, uprising, stopping, the way).[4] At the end of that teaching [**196**] insight into the Dhamma arose to eighty-four thousand beings. And in the presence of the Lord a man of property worth eighty koṭis adopted that boy saying, 'He will be my son.'[5] The Lord said, 'This boy is protected by such great (wealth) and help has been rendered to the people',[6] and went to his vihāra. In due course, when the man of property died, he came into the wealth bequeathed by him and, setting up an establishment,[7] he became a householder of great prosperity in that same city and was given to meritorious deeds such as giving and so on. Then one day the monks began to talk amongst themselves in the Dhamma-hall saying, 'It is indeed wonderful how the Teacher possesses pity for beings; indeed that same boy even who at that time was in that helpless state now enjoys great excellence and performs lofty meritorious deeds.' When he heard this the Teacher answered, 'This, monks, is not the whole extent of his excellence for indeed at the end of his life he will arise as the son of Sakka, king of devas, in the realm of the Thirty-three and obtain great heavenly excellence.' When they heard this the monks and the people praised the unique knowledge of the Teacher saying,[8] 'It is said that when the far-seeing Lord saw what had to be done he went there and rendered assistance to him who had been abandoned in that fetid cemetery just as soon as he was born', and would speak about that incident concerning him during their lifetime.[9] Those rehearsing the texts spoke six verses elucidating this matter:

1 'The Sugata's knowledge is wonderful; the Teacher answers according to the individual: though overflowing with merit some become [low born] whilst though of limited merit some become [lofty].[10]

2 This boy, abandoned in the charnel ground, subsisted during the night on the moisture of the thumb: neither yakkha-demons nor reptiles might harass[11] a boy who has done meritorious deeds.[12]

3 Dogs, moreover, licked his feet whilst crows and jackals circled him; [197] flocks of birds removed the impurities of childbirth whilst crows removed the matter from his eyes.

4 No one provided him protection nor provided medicine or a mustard fumigation; nor did they even take note of the planetary conjunctions or scatter all the grains even.

5 Fallen into such utter wretchedness as to be taken at night and abandoned in the charnel ground and, quivering like a knob of fresh butter, dubious yet with life remaining –

6 The one honoured by devas and men saw him; as soon as he saw him the Extremely Wise One declared. "This boy will become a member of the highest family of this city through his wealth." '

7 'What was his observance, now what his Brahmafaring;[13] of what good conduct is this the result that, having come to such a plight, he could go on to enjoy such potency as this?'[14]

1 Herein *wonderful (accherarūpaṃ)*: of a wonderful nature. *The Sugata's knowledge (Sugatassa ñāṇaṃ)*: the knowledge of the Perfect Buddha is not shared by others – it is said with respect to his omniscience, such as his knowledge of one's inclinations and dispositions and so on. How is it that this knowledge is not within the reach of others? They said, 'The Teacher answers according to the individual.' This indicates that it is only[15] through the teaching of the Teacher that the wonderful nature of his knowledge becomes apparent. Then illustrating this (method of) answering they said,[16] 'Though overflowing with merit some become [low born] whilst though of limited merit some become [lofty].' This is the meaning: though overflowing with skilled states, some individuals here **[198]** become low in matters of birth and so on by way of an act of demerit of that kind which has been conserved whilst though of limited merit, though of fewer meritorious states, some beings, on account of their successful attainment of the field and so on,[17] become lofty due to the great splendour of that merit.

2 *In the charnel ground (sīvathikāya)*: in the cemetery. *On the moisture of the thumb (aṅguṭṭhasnehena)*: on the moisture that comes from the thumb, meaning on the milk that flows from the thumb of a devatā. *Neither yakkha-demons nor reptiles (na yakkhabhūtā na siriṃsapā vā)*: neither pisāca-demons nor yakkha-demons nor reptiles nor any who creep when moving about.[18] *Might harass (na viheṭhayeyyuṃ)*: might oppress.

3 *Licked his feet (palihiṃsu pāde)*: licked his feet with their tongues.[19] *Crows (dhaṅkā)*: crows (*kākā*). *Jackals circled him (siṅgālā parivattayanti)*: circled him continuously[20] protecting him in order to maintain his state of health thinking, 'Let no one harm this boy!' *The impurities of childbirth (gabbhāsayaṃ)*: the stains of childbirth. *Flocks of birds (pakkhigaṇā)*: flocks of birds such as vultures and hawks and so on. *Removed (haranti)*: took away. *The matter from his eyes (akkhimalaṃ)*: what had been excreted by his eyes.

4 *(No) one (keci)*: (no) one who was human for non-human beings did afford protection. *Medicine (osadhaṃ)*: antidotes bringing health both at that time and in the future.[21] *Or a mustard fumigation (sāsapadhūpanaṃ vā)*: the fumigation that they perform with mustard for the sake of protecting a newborn boy; they elucidate that there were none doing even this for him. *Nor did they even take note of the planetary conjunctions: nakkhattayogaṃ pi na uggahesuṃ=nakkhattayuttaṃ pi na uggaṇhiṃsu* (alternative grammatical form), meaning no one cast his horoscope even in a manner such as, 'This one was born under such and such a sign of the zodiac, under such and such a planet, on such and such a lunar day and at this precise time.' *Or scatter all the grains even (na sabbadhaññāni pi*

ākiriṃsu): they would scatter grain such as paddy and so on mixed with mustard oil when performing an auspicious act as an antidote to disease, meaning they did not do even this for him.

5 *Such (etādisaṃ)*: [**199**] like that. *Fallen into utter wretchedness (uttamakicchapattaṃ)*: met with the utmost wretchedness, fallen into extreme misery. *As to be taken at night: rattābhataṃ=rattiyaṃ ābhataṃ* (resolution of compound). *Like a knob of fresh butter (nonītapiṇḍaṃ viya)*: similar to a knob of fresh butter; this is said on account of his being a mere lump of flesh. *Quivering (pavedhamānaṃ)*: trembling on account of his weak condition. *Dubious (sasaṃsayaṃ)*: full of doubt due to the uncertainty as to whether he will live or not.[22] *Yet with life remaining (jīvitasāvasesaṃ)*: yet with but the slightest life remaining due to the absence of materials that are for beings the means[23] of maintaining life.

6 *Will become a member of the highest family through his wealth (aggakuliko bhavissati bhogato)* means he will become a member of the highest family, of the best of families, on account of his wealth, by way of his wealth. The verse (beginning:) 'What was his observance' was said by layfollowers who were standing in the Teacher's presence as a means of enquiring about the deed done by him, by those who had gathered in the charnel ground – this is how it should be understood.

7 Herein *what was his?: ki' ssa=kim assa* (resolution of compound). *Observance (vataṃ)*: undertaking of an observance. Once again *of what? (kissa)*: of what sort of good conduct, observance and Brahmafaring? – this is how it should be construed, its inflection having been altered.[24] *Such (etādisaṃ)*: such as arising in the womb of a harlot and being abandoned in a cemetery. *A plight (vyasanaṃ)*: misfortune. *Such (tādisaṃ)*: so great a, meaning in the manner stated, namely, 'subsisted during the night on the moisture of the thumb' and so on as well as 'this boy will become a member of the highest family of this city' and so forth. *Potency (iddhiṃ)* refers to the heavenly excellence of a deva's psychic power.

Now the Lord, questioned in that manner by those layfollowers, answered accordingly; those rehearsing the texts spoke four verses illustrating this:

8 'The highest honour was being paid by the people to the order of monks with the Buddha at its head when he had a mental aberration and spoke harsh, discourteous words.

9 When he had dispelled that thought and had afterwards gained joy and devotion [**200**] he waited for seven days with rice-gruel on the Tathāgata who was staying in the Jeta Grove.

10 That was his observance, now that his Brahmafaring; of that good

conduct is this the result that, having come to such a plight, he could go on to enjoy such potency as this.

11 After remaining right here for a hundred years provided with all he desires he will, at the breaking up of the body, go into the company of Vāsava in the life to come.'

8 Herein *by the people (janatā)*: by the collection of people forming that body of layfollowers – this is the meaning. *When (tatra)*: at that paying of honour.[25] *He (assa)*: that boy. *Had a mental aberration (cittassa ahu aññathattaṃ)*: in a previous life his mind was of an aberrant nature and he lacked respect, reverence and trust. *Discourteous (asabbhiṃ)*: he spoke harshly and in a manner not fit to be heard in a court of the virtuous.[26]
9 *He (so)*: this one (just mentioned). *That thought (taṃ vitakkaṃ)*: that wicked thought. *Had dispelled (paṭivinodayitvā)*: had dissipated due to the remonstrance from his mother. *Had gained joy and devotion (pītipasādaṃ paṭiladdhā)*: had gained, had given rise to, joy and devotion.[27] *He waited with rice-gruel on (yāguyā upaṭṭhāsi)*: he waited with gifts of rice-gruel on. *For seven days (sattarattaṃ)*:[28] for seven days.
10 *That was his observance, now that his Brahmafaring (ta' ssa vataṃ taṃ pana brahmacariyaṃ)*: that devotion of heart and the gift in the manner stated by me above was the observance of this person, together with his Brahmafaring, meaning there is nothing other (than this).
11 *After remaining (ṭhatvāna)*: after he has remained right here, in this world of men, until the end of his life. *In the life to come (abhisamparāyaṃ)*: in his next existence. *He will go into the company of Vāsava (sahavyataṃ gacchati Vāsavassa)*: he will go into companionship with Sakka,[29] lord of devas, [**201**] as his son; this is a present tense statement with the sense of the future (tense). The rest is quite self-evident throughout.

[1] An epithet of the Buddha, sometimes rendered Well-gone.

[2] This was apparently the custom – see H. Kern, *A Manual of Indian Buddhism*, Delhi 1974, p. 29.

[3] Cp PvA 61.

[4] See note at PvA 38 above.

[5] The text's punctuation should be amended to read with Se Be as follows: . . . Bhagavato sammukhā 'va 'mama putto' ti aggahesi.

[6] The help (anuggaho) is the insight into Dhamma that they have been granted and is being contrasted here with the mundane protection (rakkhito) afforded the boy; Gehman seems to have entirely misunderstood this.

[7] kuṭumbaṃ saṇṭhapento, so PED; perhaps a family business is meant.

[8] The text's punctuation should be amended to read with Se Be as follows: Taṃ sutvā bhikkhū mahājano ca: 'idaṃ kira kāranaṃ disvā dīghadassī Bhagavā . . .'.

[9] Reading attabhāve with Se Be for text's atthabhāve.

[10] This verse is corrupt and, as it stands, cannot mean what Dhammapāla says it

means. However, since it seems that Dhammapāla was himself facing a corrupt verse I have inserted extractions from the cty that follows in square brackets merely in an attempt to give some sense to the verse.

[11] Reading viheṭhayeyyuṃ with Se Be for text's na heṭhayeyyuṃ.

[12] From here onwards I follow the division of the verses found in Se Be, this being neither that of our text nor of Pv.

[13] The verse should read ki' ssa . . . kissa . . . in accordance with the cty below and not kissa . . . ki' ssa. . . .

[14] Cp Vv 84[24].

[15] Reading eva with Se Be for text's evaṃ.

[16] āha, literally he said.

[17] Cp PvA 191 above.

[18] So all texts; however a vl of Be may be preferable: na yakkhabhūtā ti yakkhā vā bhūtā vā. Na sarīsapā vā ti ye keci sarantā gacchanti which would give: *neither yakkhas nor demons: na yakkhabhūtā=yakkhā vā bhūtā vā* (resolution of compound). *Nor reptiles (sarīsapā vā)*: nor those who creep when moving about. It may be noted that sarīsapa, here rendered reptile, means crawling, creeping or gliding and by extension one doing this; cp the similar etymology of 'reptile'.

[19] Reading Palihiṃsu pāde ti attano jivhāya pāde lihiṃsu with Be (≏ Se) for text's Palahiṃsu pāde ti attano jīvhāya pāde palahiṃsu.

[20] Reading aparāparaṃ with Se Be for text's apāraparaṃ.

[21] Cp GS ii 55 n. 1 where this is referred to.

[22] Reading na nu with Se Be for text's nanu.

[23] Reading hetabhūtānaṃ with Se Be for text's hetu bhūtānaṃ.

[24] That is, the preceding nominative kiṃ is here dative/genitive kissa.

[25] Reading tassaṃ pūjāyaṃ with Se Be for text's tassa pūjāyaṃ.

[26] Reading sādhusabhāya with Se Be for text's sādhu sabhāya. Sabhā, usually rendered assembly hall is here given as 'court' in order to emphasise the fact that asabbhiṃ is derived from sabhā together with the negative prefix a- and hence means uncourtly, discourteous, not consistent with good manners – see PED sv asabbha. Se Be read asabbhaṃ here.

[27] Se Be add pītiṃ pasādañ ca here; text omits.

[28] Literally for seven nights.

[29] S i 229 states that he acquired the name Vāsava through having given dwelling places (āvasatham adāsi) in a previous life and is thus Vāsava, house-owner – cp DhpA i 264; whilst D ii 260 says that he is so called because he is chief of the Vasū (Vasūnaṃ seṭṭho) which Buddhaghosa takes as a class of devatās (Vasudevatānaṃ DA 690): see DPPN ii 857f. for further details.

III.6 EXPOSITION OF THE SERINĪ PETA STORY
[Serinīpetavatthuvaṇṇanā]

'Naked and of hideous appearance are you.' This was said when the Teacher was staying in the Jeta Grove concerning the petī Serinī.

It is said that at Hatthinipura[1] in the kingdom of the Kurus there was a harlot named Serinī. Now monks from here and there gathered there for the purpose of holding the Uposatha[2] and a large assembly of monks took place. When they saw this the people prepared abundant alms materials such as sesame and rice and so on, ghee, fresh butter and honey and so forth and inaugurated a great almsgiving. Now at that time that prostitute had neither faith nor devotion and her heart was possessed of the stain of selfishness. Although the people urged her saying, 'Do come and show your appreciation at this almsgiving!', she demonstrated her complete lack of devotion saying, 'What is the use of giving to these shaveling recluses? Why should I give away a mere trifle even?' She died in due course and arose as a petī in the moat of a certain border city. Now a certain lay-follower of Hatthinipura had gone to that city in order to trade and during the night, towards dawn, he went to that moat on such an undertaking. When she saw him there she recognised him and, standing not far away, revealed herself, naked and with a body with only its skin and bones remaining, an extremely disgusting sight. When he saw her he questioned her with this verse:

1 'Naked and of hideous appearance are you, emaciated and with prominent veins. You thin one, with your ribs standing out, now who are you, you who are stood here?'

She made herself known to him also with a verse:

2 'I, sir, am a petī gone to a miserable existence in the world of Yama. Having done a wicked deed, I have gone from here to the world of the petas.'

He questioned her once more about the deed she had done with this verse:

3 'Now what evil deed was done by you, by body, speech or mind? As a result of which deed have you gone from here to the world of the petas?',

[202] and she then told him about the deed she had done and, further, what was to be done by him for her benefit, with these six verses:

4 'At public bathing places I searched for small coins; though merit-offerings were at hand I made no refuge for myself.
5 I approach the river parched but it becomes empty; amidst the heat I approach the shade but it becomes scorched by the sun.
6 And a wind like fire blows on me, burning me, but I deserve this, sir, and other (misery) more terrible than this.
7 When you go to Hatthinipura you should say to my mother, "I have

seen your daughter gone to a miserable existence in the world of Yama. Having done a wicked deed, she has gone from here to the world of the petas.

8 There is here what was laid up but not announced by me – some four hundred thousand beneath the couch.

9 From this she should give alms for me; may it also provide her livelihood. And when she has given the alms my mother should assign the donation to me – then I will be happy and richly endowed with all I desire." '

4 Herein *at public bathing places (anāvaṭesu titthesu)*: at bathing places such as rivers and pools and so on that are uncontrolled[3] by anyone, at such places where people bathe and wash themselves. *I searched for small coins (vicini addhamāsakaṃ)*: overcome with greed I searched for, I sought out, even the smallest of coins[4] thinking, 'Here perhaps I might find something that people have put down and then forgotten.' Or, alternatively, *at public bathing places (anāvaṭesu titthesu)*: where recluses and brahmins are to be found – those 'bathing places' that are uncontrolled by the approach of anyone and that provide the means of purification of the behaviour and inclinations of beings. *I searched for small coins (vicini addhamāsakaṃ)*: with a heart possessed of the stain of selfishness and not giving anything to anyone I specifically searched even for small coins and did not accumulate any merit. For this reason she said, 'Though merit-offerings were at hand I made no refuge for myself.'

5 *Parched (tasitā)*: thirsty. *Empty (rittakā)*: though a flowing river, full to overflowing so that a crow could drink from it, it becomes empty and devoid of water, becomes mere sand, on account of my wicked deed. **[203]** *Amidst the heat (uṇhesu)*: at times when it is hot. *It becomes scorched by the sun (ātapo parivattati)*: a shaded place, when approached by me, becomes scorched by the sun.

6 *Like fire (aggivaṇṇo)*: like fire to the touch. For this reason it was said, 'Blows (on me) burning (me).' *But I deserve this, sir (etañ ca bhante arahāmi)*: she speaks respectfully to that layfollower addressing him as 'sir'. But I deserve to undergo this aforesaid misery of thirst and so on, sir, and other misery more terrible, more severe, than this, on account of having done such a wicked deed – this is the meaning.

7 *You should say: vajjesi=vadeyyāsi* (alternative grammatical form).

8 *Here what was laid up (but) not announced (ettha nikkhittaṃ anakkhātaṃ)*: the extent of what was laid up was not spoken of. She then said, 'Some four hundred thousand beneath the couch', indicating the

amount and the place where it had been put. Herein *the couch (pallaṅkassa)*: the couch on which she formerly slept.

9 *From this (tato)*: take a portion from that laid down wealth and give alms on my behalf. *Her (tassā)*: my mother's.

When that petī had thus spoken the layfollower agreed to what she had said. He completed his business there, went to Hatthinipura and reported the matter to her mother. Indicating this fact those rehearsing the texts said:

10 ' "Very well", he consented and went to Hatthinipura (and said), "I have seen your daughter gone to a miserable existence in the world of Yama. Having done a wicked deed, she has gone from here to the world of the petas.

11 She urged me at that time, saying, 'You should say to my mother, "I have seen your daughter gone to a miserable existence in the world of Yama. Having done a wicked deed, she has gone from here to the world of the petas.

12 There is here what was laid up but not announced by me – some four hundred thousand beneath the couch.

13 [**204**] From this she should give alms for me; may it also provide her livelihood. And when she has given the alms my mother should assign the donation to me – then I will be happy and richly endowed with all I desire." ' "

14 She thereupon gave alms and assigned the donation to her – and that petī became happy and with a body that was beautiful to behold.'[5]

These can be easily understood.

When she heard this her mother gave alms to the order of monks and assigned these to her. Established in the excellence of the means of livelihood that she had received in this way, she revealed herself to her mother and explained its cause. Her mother informed the monks and the monks raised the issue with the Lord. The Lord took the matter as an arisen need and taught Dhamma to the company assembled there. That teaching was of benefit to those people.

[1] Hastinapur, capital city of the famous Kaurava dynasty who formed one of the two opposing families in the Mahābhārata war.

[2] The Uposatha ceremony of the layman that is tied to the phases of the moon. Just as the moon, on full moon nights, may be thought to imitate the sun, so does the layman, dressed in white, on such occasions imitate the monk (though formerly the arahant) dressed in yellow, by taking upon himself extra precepts; cp A i 211f., iv 388ff.

[3] anivāritesu; PED sv nivārita erroneously suggests nivārita to mean 'unobstructed' whereas this latter is the meaning of its negative form, as here.

[4] For details of this coin see PED sv māsaka. Gehman's rendering of this verse is quite wrong.

[5] Be reads here: petī ca sukhitā āsi tassā c' āsi sujīvikā, and that petī became happy and her (mother) had a life of ease.

III.7 EXPOSITION OF THE DEER-HUNTER PETA STORY [Migaluddapetavatthuvaṇṇanā]

'You are youthful and honoured by men and women.' This was said when the Lord was staying in the Bamboo Grove concerning a peta who had been a deer-hunter.

It is said that in Rājagaha a certain hunter made his living by shooting and slaying deer by both day and night. He had a friend who was a lay-follower who, though unable to dissuade him from his wicked deeds all the time, roused him (to behave) meritoriously by night saying, 'Come on, my friend, refrain from destroying living beings by night.' He would refrain from this at night and would destroy living beings only during the day. He died in due course and arose as a vimānapeta near to Rājagaha undergoing great misery during the daytime but would gratify himself,[1] endowed and provided with the pleasures of the five senses, by night. When he saw him the venerable elder Nārada questioned him with this verse:

1 **[205]** 'You are youthful and honoured by men and women; you look splendid with the pleasures of the senses amidst the enticing but by day you undergo torture – what did you do in your previous life?'

1 Herein *honoured by men and women (naranāripurakkhato)*: honoured by, attended by, devaputtas and devadhītās[2] as attendants. *Youthful (yuvā)*: young. *Amidst the enticing (rajanīye)*: with those things that entice, that are apt to arouse lust. *With the pleasures of the senses (kāmaguṇehi)*: with what is sensual. *You look splendid (sobhasi)*: you are brilliant by night due to your being provided with these – this is the meaning. For this reason he said: *but by day you undergo torture (divasaṃ anubhosi kāraṇaṃ)*: but during the daytime you suffer various sorts of torture, destruction. Or alternatively (we should read:) *at night (rajanī)*: by night (*rattīsu*), *ye* being a mere particle. *What did you do in your previous life?*

(kiṃ akāsi purimāya jātiyā): what was the deed that you did in your life previous to this conducing to such happiness and misery, meaning please tell me this.

When he heard this the peta spoke these verses telling the elder of the deeds he had done:

2 'In beautiful Rājagaha, that delightful Giribbaja,[3] I was in the past a deer-hunter, cruel and bloody-handed.

3 Depraved in mind, I roamed about unrestrained, always bent on harming others and extremely cruel as regards harmless living beings, creatures far and wide.

4 I had a kind hearted companion, a layfollower possessing faith, and he, feeling pity, warned me time and again saying,

5 "Do not perform wicked deeds, my friend, do not go to a state of misery; if you should wish for happiness after death,[4] refrain from this unrestrained slaughter of living beings."

6 I listened to these words of him desirous of my happiness and anxious for my welfare yet I, being so long given to wickedness and lacking insight, did not follow his advice to the full.

7 Once more that extremely wise one, out of pity, admonished me to show restraint saying, "If by day you must kill living beings then please show restraint at night."

8 **[206]** So I killed living beings by day but, restrained, at night refrained therefrom – and at night I gratify myself whilst by day I have a miserable existence and am devoured.

9 On account of that skilled deed I enjoy at night non-human (pleasures) whilst by day aggressive hounds fall upon me from all sides to devour me.

10 Now those who continually apply themselves to, and who are constantly intent on, the teaching of the Sugata – these alone, methinks, will reach the Deathless, the unconditioned place.'

2 Herein *hunter (luddho)*: (one who is) cruel. *Bloody-handed (lohitapāṇi)*: with hands that are smeared with blood by the repeated destruction of beasts. *Cruel (dāruṇo)*: savage, meaning one harming creatures.

3 *Harmless: avirodhakaresu=avirodhaṃ karontesu* (resolution of compound); such as deer and birds and so on.

5 *Unrestrained (asaṃyamaṃ)*: uncontrolled, of an evil nature.

6 *His advice to the full (sakalānusāsaniṃ)*: his whole advice, meaning abstention from wicked deeds at all times. *Being so long given to wickedness (cirapāpābhirato)*: being given to wickedness for so long a time.

7 *Restraint (saṃyame)*: good conduct. *Admonished: nivesayi=nivesesi*

(alternative grammatical form). *If by day you must kill living beings then please show restraint at night (sace divā hanasi pāṇino atha te rattiṃ bhavatu saṃyamo)*: this shows the manner in which he was admonished. It is said that even at night he applied himself to the slaughter of living beings in that he was setting stakes and snares and so on.

8 *By day I have a miserable existence and am devoured (divā khajjāmi duggato)*: I have now gone to a state of misery, have come to great misery, and am devoured during the daytime. It is said that this fruit of his deed was in accordance with his deed in that he had dogs devour the deer by day – (thus) during the daytime huge, great dogs would fall upon him and reduce his body so that nothing but the skeleton remained, whilst when night approached, however, he would regain his former condition and enjoy heavenly excellence. For this reason it was said: [207] 'On account of that skilled deed I enjoy at night non-human (pleasures) whilst by day aggressive hounds fall upon me from all sides to devour me.'

9 Herein *aggressive (paṭihatā)*: in an aggressive mood as though destruction-bound. *From all sides to devour me (samantā khādituṃ)*: they fall upon me from all sides to devour my body; this is said with reference to the time during which they approach which causes him extreme fear. When they have fallen upon him and have reduced his body so that nothing but the bones remain, however, they go on their way.

10 *Now those who continually apply themselves (ye ca te satatānuyogino)*: this is the meaning in brief of the concluding verse: even though I, indeed, enjoy such excellence through having refrained merely from the slaughter of living beings by night, those men, however, who are constantly intent on, firmly intent on, continually, at all times, applying themselves to the teaching of the Sugata, of the Lord Buddha, to that higher morality and so on[5] – these meritorious ones alone, methinks, will reach the Deathless, the so-called unconditioned place[6] that is not to be confused with mundane happiness – there is nothing that could be a fetter in their attainment of this.

When he had thus spoken the elder raised the issue with the Teacher. The Teacher took the matter as an arisen need and taught Dhamma to the company assembled there. Everything is just as given above.

[1] Reading paricāreti with Se (Be paricāresi) for text's pariharati.

[2] The true meaning of devaputta, in contrast with other terms such as devatā and deva and so on, is still in need of urgent investigation. It is of interest to note its use here as, literally at least, deva-sons and deva-daughters. Cp PvA 147.

[3] Giribbaja, another name for Rājagaha which was in a valley surrounded by hills. Many of these hills acquired a religious significance, such as the Vulture Peak on

which the Buddha is said to have delivered many (mainly Mahāyāna) sūtras. Others became sacred to the Jainas and are today important places of pilgrimage. The Bamboo Grove, where many of the stories in this collection are said to have been told, is thought to have been located in this valley. Cp DPPN ii 721 for its history and also MLS i 39 n. 3 for one etymology of Giribbaja.

[4] pecca.

[5] Reading adhisīlādike with Se Be for text's adhisīlādhike.

[6] Reading asaṅkhataṃ padan ti with Se Be and v 10 for text's asaṅkhatan ti.

III.8 EXPOSITION OF A SECOND HUNTER PETA STORY
[Dutiyaluddhapetavatthuvaṇṇanā]

'In a pinnacled house and in a palace.' This was said when the Lord was staying in the Bamboo Grove concerning another peta who had been a deer-hunter.

It is said that at Rājagaha a certain young deer-stalker who though being endowed with wealth abandoned the comforts of his possessions and roamed about day and night killing deer. A layfollower who was a companion of his, out of kindness, gave him this advice, 'Please refrain from destroying living beings, my friend, lest for a long time there be woe and misery for you', [208] but he took no notice. That layfollower then begged a certain elder who had developed the mind[1] and had destroyed the āsavas, saying, 'Please teach Dhamma, sir, to such and such a man in such a way that he might refrain from destroying living beings.' So one day that elder, whilst going round Rājagaha in search of alms, stood at the door of his house. When he saw him the deer-stalker, full of veneration, went out to meet him, had him enter the house and offered him the appointed seat. The elder sat down on the appointed seat. When he had approached the elder and also sat down the elder told him of the disadvantages of destroying living beings and then explained the advantages of refraining but when he heard this he was unwilling to refrain therefrom. The elder then said to him, 'If you, my friend, are unable to refrain completely, please refrain during the night at least.' 'Very well, sir, I will refrain', he replied and refrained at night. The rest is similar to the story immediately preceding except that where the verses are concerned the elder Nārada questioned him with these three[2] verses:

1 'In a pinnacled house and in a palace,[3] on a couch strewn with long woollen fleeces,[4] you delight to the sweet sound of the fivefold instrumental music.[5]

2 Then at the end of the night, towards sunrise, you are removed[6] to the cemetery where you undergo much misery.

3 Now what evil deed was done by you by body, speech or mind? As a result of which deed do you undergo this misery?'

That peta then explained the matter to him:

4 'In beautiful Rājagaha, that delightful Giribbaja, I was in the past a deer-hunter, I was cruel[7] and unrestrained.

5 I had a kind hearted companion, a layfollower possessing faith [209] and a monk, a sāvaka of Gotama, was dependent upon his family for alms; though he, feeling pity, warned me time and again saying,

6 "Do not perform wicked deeds, my friend, do not go to a state of misery; if you should wish for happiness after death, refrain from this unrestrained slaughter of living beings."

7 I listened to these words of him desirous of my happiness and anxious for my welfare yet I, being so long given to wickedness and lacking insight, did not follow his advice to the full.

8 Once more that extremely wise one, out of pity, admonished me to show restraint saying, "If by day you must kill living beings then please show restraint at night."

9 So I killed living beings by day but, restrained, at night refrained therefrom – and at night I gratify myself whilst by day I have a miserable existence and am devoured.

10 On account of that skilled deed I enjoy at night non-human (pleasures) whilst by day aggressive hounds fall upon me from all sides to devour me.

11 Now those who continually apply themselves to, and who are constantly intent on, the teaching of the Sugata – these alone, methinks, will reach the Deathless, the unconditioned place.'

The meaning of these is just as that already given above.

[1] manobhāvanīyaṃ; cp M iii 261, S iii 1, A iii 317, v 55, Vv 34[13] and also notes at MLS iii 312 n. 2, GS iii p. xii, 225 n. 1, v 38 n. 1. Here we must assume the process to have been completed.

[2] Text wrongly reads Tīhi for tīhi.

[3] Reading kūṭāgāre ca pāsāde with Se Be and III 1[17] above for text's kūṭāgāre 'va pāsāde.

[4] Reading goṇakatthate – see note at III 1[17] above.

[5] pañcaṅgikena turiyena; cp S i 131, Thag 398, Thig 139, Vv 5[4], 36[4], 39[1], VvA 37, 181, 183, 210, 257, DhA i 274, 394 etc. These five instruments were: (1) ātataṃ; (2) vitataṃ; (3) ātata-vitataṃ; (4) ghaṇaṃ; (5) susiraṃ – drums with leather on one

side, two sides, all over, a cymbal or tambourine and a wind instrument respectively – SA i 191; cp EV i 188.

[6] Reading apaviddho with Se Be for text's apaviṭṭho; cp PED sv.

[7] luddho, usually rendered hunter but here perhaps adjectival.

III.9 EXPOSITION OF THE FALSE DECLARATION PETA STORY [Kūṭavinicchayikapetavatthuvaṇṇanā]

'Garlanded, crowned[1] and bangled.' This was said when the Teacher was staying in the Bamboo Grove concerning a peta who had made a false declaration.

At that time the great king Bimbisāra used to observe the Uposatha for six days a month and following his example many people (also) observed the Uposatha. The king would ask all those who came into his presence, 'Well, now, did you or did you not observe the Uposatha?' Then a man appointed to his administration who was of slanderous speech, fraudulent, given to taking bribes and to acts of violence, said, 'I did observe it, your majesty', being afraid to say that he had not observed it. Then as he was leaving the king's presence a companion said to him, 'Well, now, my friend, did you observe it today?' 'I said so through fear, my friend, when face to face with the king but I am not observing it.' Then his companion said to him, 'Even so, you can still observe a half-day Uposatha for today, so undertake the Uposatha vows.' 'Very well', he said, agreeing with what he said and went home and, without eating, rinsed his mouth and kept the Uposatha.[2] That night, when he had gone to bed, **[210]** sharp, acute pains that were caused by the strong wind arising from his empty condition[3] cut short his span of life[4] and he arose, immediately after falling, as a vimāna-peta in the interior of a mountain. Through keeping a mere half-day Uposatha for one night he received a mansion[5] with a retinue of ten thousand maidens[6] and enjoyed great heavenly excellence; but on account of his false declaration and slanderousness he devoured the flesh he had gouged from his own back. The venerable Nārada, descending from the Vulture Peak,[7] saw him and the elder questioned him with four verses after which he gave answer on this matter also with four verses:

1 'You are garlanded, crowned and bangled and your limbs are covered with sandal;[8] your features are clear and you shine just like the sun.

2 These who are your attendants,[9] these non-human members of your

company (and) these who are your maid-servants,[10] these ten thousand maidens,

3 They wear bracelets and bangles and their heads are adorned with chaplets of gold[11] – you possess great majesty and your appearance is hair-raising.

4 Yet you devour the flesh that you yourself have gouged[12] from your back: now what evil deed was done by you by body, speech or mind? As a result of which deed do you devour the flesh from your back?'

5 'In the world of the living I acted to my own ruin with slanderous and lying speech and with fraud and deceit.

6 When I had approached a company there and the time came to speak the truth I rejected what was right[13] and in my interests and followed a wrong course.[14]

7 Just as I today devour the flesh from my own back, even so will he who is a backbiter have to devour himself.

8 [211] You yourself have seen this, Nārada. Those who possess pity and are skilled would say, "Neither slander nor tell lies and do not be a backbiter!" '

1 Herein *garlanded (mālī)*: wearing garlands adorned with heavenly flowers – this is the meaning. *Crowned (kirīṭī)*: with the head turbaned. *Bangled (kāyūrī)*: possessing bangles, meaning with one's arms adorned with ornaments. *Your limbs (gattā)*: the members of your body. *Are covered with sandal (candanussadā)*: are anointed with the essence of sandal-wood. *You shine just like the sun (suriyavaṇṇo va sobhasi)*: you are brilliant, being in appearance just like the newly arisen sun. Or, alternatively, the text reads, 'You are beautiful like the dawn sun' (*aruṇasadisavaṇṇavā*); *the dawn sun (aruṇaṃ)*:[15] similar in appearance to the Araṇiya devas, meaning[16] having an ariyan appearance.

2 *Members of your company (pārisajjā)*: those belonging to his company, meaning his personal attendants.[17]

3 *You: tuvaṃ=tvaṃ* (alternative grammatical form). *Your appearance is hair-raising (lomahaṃsanarūpavā)*: your appearance is fit to make the hair raise of those seeing you; this is said on account of his great majesty and power.

4 *You have gouged: ukkantvā=ukkantitvā* (alternative grammatical form), meaning you have cut.

5 *I acted: acārisaṃ=acariṃ* (alternative grammatical form), I took a line of action. *With slanderous and lying speech: pesuññamusāvādena=pesuññena musāvādena ca* (resolution of compound). *And with fraud and deceit: nikativañcanāya ca=nikatiyā vañcanāya ca* (resolution of

compound), with machination and deceit that appear genuine to others.
6 *When the time came to speak the truth (saccakāle)*: when the time came at which it was proper to speak the truth. *What was in my interests (atthaṃ)*: the kinds of things that are of benefit in the same life and so on. *What was right (dhammaṃ)*: my duty, right conduct. *I rejected (niraṅkatvā)*: I separated myself from, I abandoned.
7 *He (so)*: that creature who acts slanderously and so on.

All the rest is just as already given above.

[1] kirīṭī; this sense is not listed by PED but see SED sv kirīṭa and kirīṭin.

[2] Gehman's 'devoted himself to the feast' conjures up exactly the reverse of what is involved here – it is as if one were to say the same of Lent.

[3] Gehman is not correct in taking this as 'when he reached his dwelling, his span of life was cut short by a stake blown down from his poor abode through a high wind'.

[4] āyusaṅkhāro, that is, the span of life he would have enjoyed in accordance with his kamma had this not been interrupted or cut short by this wicked deed; cp D ii 106 (and Dial ii 113 n. 1); M i 295; S ii 266; A iv 311; Ud 64.

[5] Reading vimānaṃ with Se Be for text's vipākaṃ.

[6] kaññā.

[7] Cp PvA 205.

[8] Cp Thag 267.

[9] Reading te 'me paricārakā with Se Be for text's te me parivārikā.

[10] Reading te 'me paricārikā with Se Be for text's temā paricārikā; cp II 12[6].

[11] kañcanāveḷabhūsitā; cp II 12[6].

[12] All texts differ here: text reads ukkantvā, Se ukkaḍḍha whilst Be ukkacca.

[13] dhammaṃ.

[14] adhammaṃ.

[15] Cp Skt Aruṇa, charioteer of the sun and 'appointed to go before the sun on his rising, thus protecting the world from excessive heat' – E. Washburn Hopkins, *Epic Mythology*, Delhi 1974, p. 84.

[16] Reading araṇiyehi devehi sadisavaṇṇo, ariyāvakāso ti attho with Be for text's araṇiyehi devehi sadisavaṇṇa-ariyāvakāso ti attho (Se reads araṇiyehi devehi sadisavaṇṇo; ariyāva kāsatī ti attho).

[17] Reading upaṭṭhākā with Se Be for text's upaṭṭhakā.

III.10 EXPOSITION OF THE CONTEMPT FOR THE RELICS PETA STORY
[Dhātuvivaṇṇapetavatthuvaṇṇanā]

[212] 'Standing in the air.' This is the Contempt for the Relics Peta Story.

When the Lord had attained Parinibbāna between the twin sāla-trees[1] in the Mallas' Upavattana Sāla Grove at Kusinārā and his relics had been divided, king Ajātasattu took his share of the relics and, recollecting the Buddha's virtues, inaugurated a great (ceremony in his) honour lasting seven years, seven months and seven days, during which incalculable and innumerable people became devoted in heart and reached heaven. However, as many as eighty-six thousand men were corrupt through having for a long time been without faith and of wrong outlook and, though amidst conditions that should inspire devotion, became of defiled mind and arose amongst the petas. In that same Rājagaha,[2] the wife, daughter and daughter-in-law of a certain man of property, who was endowed with wealth, with devotion in their hearts thought, 'Let us pay honour to the relics', and took some scent and flowers and so on and set out to go to the place where the relics were situated. That man of property showed his contempt for the honour of relics and scoffed at them saying, 'What's the good of honouring bones?' They took no notice of what he said and went to that place and paid honour to the relics and, having returned home, they became afflicted with such illness[3] that not long afterwards they died, arising in the devaloka (on account of that meritorious deed). He, however, was overcome by anger and not long afterwards died, arising amongst the petas on account of that wicked deed. Then one day the venerable Mahākassapa, out of pity for beings, worked his psychic powers in such a way that people could see both petas and devatās. When he had done this he stood in the precincts of that cetiya[4] and questioned the peta who had shown contempt for the relics with three verses to which the peta then replied:

1 'Standing in the air you emit a foul, putrid smell and worms devour your putrid smelling mouth – what deed did you do in the past?[5]

2 Thereupon they take their knives and carve you time and again; they spray you with alkaline and then carve you (yet) time and again.

3 Now what evil deed was done by you by body, speech or mind? As a result of which deed do you undergo this misery?'

4 [213] 'In beautiful Rājagaha, that delightful Giribbaja, good sir, I was lord of very abundant wealth and grain.

5 I (tried to) obstruct this wife and daughter and daughter-in-law of mine who were taking tamāla[6] (blossoms), blue lotuses and costly ointments to the stūpa – this was the wicked deed done by me.

6 We eighty-six thousand separately suffering,[7] having shown contempt for honouring the stūpa, we are boiled[8] intensely in hell.

7 You should separate therefrom those who make known the disadvantages when a great (ceremony of) honouring the stūpa of the Arahant is in progress.

8 And behold these approaching, wearing garlands and adorned, enjoying the result of flowers – they are magnificent, resplendent.[9]

9 And when they have seen this marvellous, amazing and hair-raising (fact) the wise will praise and salute you, great sage.

10 Now when I have gone from here and regained the human womb, I will diligently pay honour at the stūpa time and again.'

1 Herein *a foul smell (duggandho)*: a disagreeable smell, meaning smelling with the stench of a rotting corpse. For this reason he said, 'You emit a putrid (smell).'

2 *Thereupon (tato)*: after emitting that foul smell and being fit to be devoured by worms. *They take their knives and carve you time and again (satthaṃ gahetvāna okantanti punappunaṃ)*: creatures driven on by kamma[10] take sharp-edged knives and carve your mouth[11] time and again. *They spray you with alkaline and then carve you time and again (khārena paripphositvā okantanti punappunaṃ)*: they sprinkle the places where they carved you with an alkaline solution and then carve you time and again.[12]

4 *I was lord of very abundant wealth and grain (issaro dhanadhaññassa supahūtassa)*: [214] I was lord of, owner of, extremely abundant, of enormous, wealth and grain, meaning I was rich and wealthy.

5 *This wife and daughter and daughter-in-law of mine (tassāyaṃ me bhariyā ca dhītā ca suṇisā ca)*: this wife of mine in my previous existence, this daughter, this daughter-in-law; he speaks pointing to the deva-beings[13] that are stood in the sky. *Costly (paccagghaṃ)*: fresh. *I (tried to) obstruct . . . who were taking . . . to the stūpa (thūpaṃ harantiyo vāresiṃ)*: showing contempt for the relics, I opposed . . . who were carrying . . . to honour the stūpa. *This was the wicked deed done by me (taṃ pāpaṃ pakataṃ mayā)*: he speaks with remorse saying, 'This wicked deed of showing contempt for the relics was done, was pursued, by me.'[14]

6 *Eighty-six thousand (chaḷāsītisahassāni)*: as many as eighty thousand and six thousand more besides. *We (mayaṃ)*: he speaks including those petas together with himself. *Separately suffering (paccattavedanā)*: this indicates that the suffering of great misery is being experienced separately, individually by each one himself. *In hell (niraye)*: he says this, likening the peta-plane to hell on account of its intense misery.

7 *Those who . . . when a great (ceremony of) honouring the stūpa of the Arahant is in progress (ye ca kho thūpapūjāya vattante arahato mahe)*: he clarifies his own great loss allegorically saying, 'You should separate, you should have separated, you should consider as outsiders, therefrom, from that meritorious deed, those persons who, like me, make known the

disadvantages of, the faults with, honouring the stūpa when a great (ceremony of) honour with respect to the stūpa of the Arahant, the Perfect Buddha, is in progress.'

8 *Approaching (āyantiyo)*: coming through the sky. *The result of flowers (mālavipākaṃ)*: the result, the fruit,[15] of having paid honour with flowers at the stūpa. *Magnificent (samiddhā)*: magnificent with heavenly excellence. *They are resplendent (tā yasassiniyo)*: they possess a retinue.[16]

9 *And when they have seen this (tañ ca disvāna)*: when they have seen the marvellous, amazing, hair-raising, extremely fine and extraordinary result of that extremely limited meritorious deed of honour. *The wise will praise and salute you, great sage (namo karonti sappaññā vandanti taṃ mahāmuni)*: these women, Kassapa sir, will salute, will prostrate themselves before, you, the utmost merit-field, meaning they will praise, pay homage to,[17] you.

[215] Then that peta, his heart agitated, uttered the verse (beginning:) 'Now when I', showing what he was to do in the future consistent with that agitation. The meaning of this is quite self-evident.

Mahākassapa took as an arisen need the matter that had thus been spoken of by the peta and taught Dhamma to the company assembled there.

The Contempt for the Relics Peta Story is concluded – thus the exposition of the meaning of the third, Small, chapter that is adorned with ten stories in these Peta Stories of the Khuddaka Nikāya is concluded.[18]

[1] Shorea robusta.

[2] Ajātasattu's capital.

[3] Reading tādisena rogena with Se Be for text's tādisena puññakammena rogena, although it would seem nevertheless that this death of theirs were due to this meritorious deed cutting short their span of life in order that they might reap the splendour to which they are now due; cp PvA 210 above. It could be that the text originally read puññakammena devaloke nibbattiṃsu in parallel with the following sentence.

[4] The stūpa in which the relics were housed.

[5] Reading kiṃ kammam akāsi pubbe with Se Be as part of v 1; cp I 3[1].

[6] Xanthochymus pictorius.

[7] paccattavedanā; cp M i 337 where one of three appellations of hell is 'The Separate Feelings', paccattavedaniyo.

[8] Reading paccāma with Se Be for text's paccāmi.

[9] Reading yasassiniyo with Se Be for text's yasassiyo.

[10] It is unclear whether this kamma is their own or that of the peta.

[11] Be reads vaṇamukhaṃ, the openings of your sores, here, such sores perhaps being the source of the foul smell.

[12] Reading punappunaṃ with Se Be for text's puna.

[13] Reading tā devabhūtā with Se Be for text's tāva-d-eva bhūtā.

[14] Reading taṃ pāpaṃ pakataṃ mayā ti taṃ dhātuvivaṇṇanapāpaṃ kataṃ with Se Be for text's taṃ pāpan ti dhātuvivaṇṇapāpaṃ. Pakataṃ. . . .

[15] Reading vipākaṃ phalaṃ with Be for text's Se vipākaphalaṃ.

[16] Reading tā parivāravantiyo with Be (Se omits tā) for text's paricāriniyo.

[17] namakkāraṃ, not listed by PED.

[18] So Be.

Chapter IV

GREAT CHAPTER
[Mahāvagga]

IV.1 EXPOSITION OF THE AMBASAKKHARA PETA STORY
[Ambasakkharapetavatthuvaṇṇanā]

'There is a Vajjian city named Vesāli.' This is the Ambasakkhara Peta Story. How did it originate?

When the Lord was staying in the Jeta Grove the Licchavi king named Ambasakkhara, who was of wrong view and who held the natthika doctrine,[1] ruled at Vesāli. Now there was in the city of Vesāli at that time a stretch of mud near the shop of a certain trader[2] which inconvenienced many people passing by[3] there who had to jump over it, some getting splashed with mud. When he saw this the trader thought, 'These people should not have to walk through mud', and had the skull of an ox[4] that was free of unpleasant smells and similar in colour to mother-of-pearl[5] fetched and laid down there. He was virtuous by nature, not given to anger, and of gentle speech and would praise the virtues of others for what they were.[6] Then one day when his companion was bathing and carelessly not watching he hid his clothes in fun, giving them (back only) after causing him misery. His nephew, however, brought goods stolen from other houses and deposited them in his shop. The owners of those goods who had been tracing (their goods) presented him and his nephew, along with those goods, before the king. The king ordered, 'Cut off this one's head but impale his nephew!', and the king's men did as they were commanded. When he died he arose amongst the terrestrial devas, receiving a heavenly white thoroughbred horse, as swift as thought, for having made that bridge with the ox's head **[216]** and a heavenly scent exuded from his body due to his remarks in praise of those possessing virtue but he was naked on account of having hidden the cloak. It was as a consequence of his looking back on these deeds he had done in the past that he saw his impaled nephew. His heart stirred with compassion, he would mount his horse that was swift as thought and go at midnight to the place where (his nephew) was impaled and, standing not far away, would say each day, 'Stay alive, my friend, for being alive is better.'

Now at that time king Ambasakkhara was circumambulating the city by the right mounted on the back of the most stately elephant. He saw a woman who had opened a window in a certain house and who was watching the royal glory. He fell in love with her and signalled to a man seated nearby as if to say, 'You see that house and that woman', and in due course entered the royal residence and despatched that man saying, 'Go and find out, I say, whether that woman has a husband or not!' He went and when he found that she had a husband he informed the king. The king, thinking of some means by which he could make her his wife,[7] sent for her husband and said, 'Come, I say, and enter my service!' Out of fear he reluctantly agreed to serve the king, thinking that if he did not do what the king said the king would punish him, and went daily to serve the king. The king had food and remuneration be given him and, when a few days had passed, he said to him as he came for service early in the morning, 'You should go, I say, to such a place as where there is a lotus pond and fetch from there some red clay and red water lilies; if you do not return this very day you will lose your life!' When he had gone he told the gate-keeper, 'All the gates are to be closed just before the sun sets.' Now that lotus pond was at least three yojanas from Vesāli but even so that man, spurred on by the fear of death, reached the lotus pond with the speed of wind that same forenoon. Because he had earlier heard[8] that the lotus pond was haunted by beings other than human he went fearfully all round it wondering, 'Is there any danger here?' [217] When he saw him the guardian spirit[9] of the lotus pond felt pity for him and approached him in human form saying, 'For what purpose have you come here, my good man?' He related his story to him. 'If that be so then take whatever you need', he said and disappeared after revealing his heavenly form. He collected some red clay and red water lilies there and reached the city gate just before the sun set. The gate-keeper saw him and closed the gate just as he was calling out. Unable to gain entry at the closed gate he called upon the man who was impaled close by that gate to be his witness saying, 'When I came just before the sun set they closed the gate just as I was calling out. Be it known to you that I came just in time and that there is no fault on my part.' When he heard this he said, 'I am facing death, having been executed by impalement – how can I be your witness? There is, however, a peta of great psychic power who will be coming close by me – you should call upon him as your witness.' 'But how could I see him?' 'If you stay right here you will see him for yourself.' He stayed there and saw that peta come during the middle watch of the night and called upon him as his witness. At daybreak when the king said, 'You went against my command – as king I will therefore have to punish you', he said, 'Your majesty, I did not go against your command; I came here before the sun had set.' 'Who is your witness?' He pointed out that his witness was a naked peta that came into the presence of the impaled man and, when the king said, 'How are we to believe this?', he said, 'This same night send along with me a man whom you trust.' When he heard this the king himself went along with him and stood at that place. When the peta came and said, 'Stay alive, my friend, for being alive is better', he questioned him with the five verses beginning: 'There is for him no lying or sitting.' Before this, however, the verse (beginning:) 'There is a Vajjian city named Vesāli' was inserted by those rehearsing the texts with the purpose of showing their context.

1 [218] 'There is a Vajjian city named Vesāli; it was there that the Licchavi Ambasakkhara, having seen a peta outside the city, questioned him right there, desiring to know his reason.'

2 'There is for him no lying or sitting nor is there stepping forwards or backwards; there is for him[10] not even the pleasure of the enjoyment of clothes and (foods that) are eaten, drunk and chewed.

3 Those in the past who were his relatives, his well-wishers possessing pity who were seen and heard with him – these are now unable even to see him,[11] his state is that of being discarded[12] by those people.

4 Those who have fallen have no friends – friends forsake you when they learn of your lack;[13] whilst they surround you when they see your prosperity – those who flourish have many friends.

5 Having lost all his possessions, in distress,[14] smeared and with his body all broken up, like a dew-drop hanging,[15] the end of his life (will come) today or tomorrow.

6 Having come to such utter distress as to be impaled on a stake of nimba wood[16] – by what token, then, yakkha, can you say, "Stay alive, my friend, for being alive is better"?'

1 Herein *there (tattha)*: in that Vesāli. *Outside the city (nagarassa bāhiraṃ)*: who was outside the city; it occurred, happened, took place, just outside the city of Vesāli.[17] [219] *Right there (tatth' eva)*: right there at the place where he saw him. *Him (taṃ)*: that peta. *Desiring to know his reason (kāraṇatthiko)*: desiring to know the reason for his having said,[18] 'Stay alive, my friend, for being alive is better.'

2 *There is for him no lying or sitting (seyyā nisajjā nayimassa atthi)*: there is for the person impaled no lying, the distinguishing characteristic of which is reckoned to be being stretched out on one's back,[19] or sitting of which the distinguishing characteristic is sitting cross-legged and so on. *Nor is there stepping forwards or backwards (abhikkamo n' atthi paṭikkamo vā)*: nor is there for him even the slightest[20] movement of which the distinguishing characteristic is stepping forwards. *Even the pleasure (paricārikā sā pi)*:[21] there is for him not even the pleasure of the senses,[22] the distinguishing characteristic[23] of which is enjoying the use of clothes and (foods that) are eaten, drunk and chewed[24] and so on. An alternative (reading)[25] is *even maintenance (pariharaṇā sā pi)*: there is for him not even maintenance of the faculties[22] by way of enjoying the use of (clothes and foods that) are eaten and so on, meaning[26] he is deprived of life. Some read 'even attention to' (*paricāraṇā sā pi*).

3 *Those in the past who were his well-wishers possessing pity that were seen and heard with him (diṭṭhasutā suhajjā anukampakā yassa ahesuṃ pubbe)*: those in the past who were his friends possessing kindness, both those companions who were seen together with him and those companions who were not (so) seen. *Even to see (daṭṭhum pi)* means that these are unable even to see[27] (him), let alone dwell (with him). *His state is that of being discarded (virājitatto)*: his condition is one of having been rejected. *By those people (janena tena)*: by those people who were his relatives and so on.
4 *Those who have fallen have no friends (na oggatattassa bhavanti mittā)*: those who are dead, those whose consciousness has departed, indeed have no friends on account of their having gone beyond the stage where anything could be done by their friends. *Friends forsake you when they learn of your lack (jahanti mittā vikalaṃ viditvā)*: friends abandon you thinking, 'Nothing is to be gained from this one', when they learn that a man lacks possessions even when he is living, let alone one that is dead. *Whilst they surround you when they see your prosperity (atthañ ca disvā parivārayanti)*: but they surround you with affectionate talk and watch your every look[28] when they see your property, prosperity and wealth. *Those who flourish have many friends (bahū mittā uggatattassa honti)*: **[220]** those who are endowed with wealth, whose nature is to flourish and who are successful have many and numerous friends, meaning this is the way of the world.
5 *Having lost all his possessions (nihīnattho sabbabhogehi)*: having become wanting in all possessions, large and small. *In distress (kiccho)*: in misery.[29] *Smeared (sammakkhito)*: with his body smeared with blood. *With his body all broken up (samparibhinnagatto)*: with his body torn inside by the stake. *Like a dew-drop hanging (ussāvabindu va palimpamāno)*: similar to a dew-drop hanging on the tip of a blade of grass. *Today or tomorrow (ajja suve)*: the end, the cessation, of this man's life (will) indeed (come) either today or tomorrow, meaning it will cease to continue thereafter.
6 *To be impaled (uttāsitaṃ)*: to be strung upon, to be put on. *On a stake of nimba wood (picumandassa sūle)*: on a stake made from the stem of the nimba tree. *By what token? (kena vaṇṇena)*: for what reason? *Stay alive, my friend, for being alive is better (jīva bho jīvitam eva seyyo)*: stay alive, my good man. Why? Being alive is for you, even though impaled here, still a hundred times, a thousand times, better, finer, than the life (that awaits you) when you have fallen from here.

When questioned thus by the king the peta spoke four verses explaining what he meant:

7 'He was my blood-relation, I remember, in my previous life. When I

saw him I had compassion for him thinking, "Do not let that wicked character fall into hell."

8 When he falls from here, O Licchavi, this man, this doer of evil deeds,[30] will arise in the terrible and crowded hell that is extremely hot, severe and frightful.

9 This stake is countless times better than that hell – do not let him fall into that exceedingly miserable, severe and frightful, that exceedingly painful, hell.

10 **[221]** Now if he were to hear these words of mine he would be made miserable and might give up his life's breath. Therefore I do not speak in his presence lest the end of his life (should come) through me alone.'

7 Herein *blood-relation (sālohito)*: being of the same blood, connected in that he is related by birth, meaning a relative. *In my previous life (purimāya jātiyā)*: in my previous existence. *Do not let that wicked character fall into hell (mā pāpadhammo nirayaṃ patāyaṃ)*: when I saw him I had compassion for him thinking, 'Do not let this man of wicked character fall into hell, do not let him arise in hell' – this is how it should be construed.

8 *Crowded (sattussadaṃ)*: crowded with beings who were doers of wicked deeds. Or, alternatively it means crowded with, heaped up one after the other with,[31] the seven grievous tortures beginning with the fivefold pinion, to wit, the fivefold pinion,[32] the pouring of glowing copper into the mouth,[33] being set upon the mountain of live embers,[34] being hurled into the Iron Cauldron,[35] being made to enter the Sword-leafed Forest,[36] having to descend into the Vetaraṇī,[37] and then be hurled back into the Great Hell. *Extremely hot (mahābhitāpaṃ)*: tortuously heated by the great fire. *Severe (kaṭukaṃ)*: disagreeable. *Frightful (bhayānakaṃ)*: causing fear.

9 *Countless times (anekabhāgena guṇena)*: countless times (more) to your advantage. *This stake . . . than that hell (ayam eva sūlo nirayena tena)*: this stake is better than that hell which is the place where he will afterwards arise. This is the instrumental case in an ablative (sense). *Exceedingly painful (ekantatippaṃ)* means of exceeding and acute misery, of positively immense misery.

10 *Now if he were to hear these words of mine (idañ ca sutvā vacanaṃ mam' eso)*: what he has said, beginning with 'When he falls from here'; if he were to hear these words of mine this man would be made miserable, would become as though made to suffer the misery of hell by these words of mine. *Might give up his life's breath (vijaheyya pānaṃ)*: might renounce[38]

his life. *Therefore (tasmā)*: for that reason. *Lest through me alone (mā m' ekato)*: I do not speak these words in his presence lest the end of this man's life (should come) through me alone. [222] Rather I just say, 'Stay alive, my friend, for being alive is better' – this is the meaning.

When the peta had thus explained what he meant the king uttered this verse asking permission to question the peta once more on the issue:

11 'The facts about this man are known; we wish to question you also about other things. If you will give us your permission we will ask you but you are not to become angry with us.'

12 'Surely I gave my consent[39] then – there is no discussion[40] with one not trusted. Reluctantly assuming you to be one whose word can be believed, acting thus, you may ask me what you desire and if possible (I will answer).'

These verses are the exchange of conversation between the king and the peta.

11 Herein *are known (aññāto)*: are understood. *We wish: icchāmase= icchāma* (alternative grammatical form). *Us: no=amhākaṃ* (alternative grammatical form). *But you are not to become angry (na ca kujjhitabbaṃ)*: you are not to get angry thinking, 'Whatever is it that these people are asking?'

12 *Surely (addhā)*: certainly. *I gave my consent (paṭiññā me)*: I gave my consent saying you might ask for information, meaning I gave my permission.[41] *Then (tadā ahu)*: at the time that I first saw you. *There is no discussion with one not trusted (nācikkhanā[42] appasannassa hoti)*: there is no talking with one not trusted. The trusted will only talk about anything with those they trust. However you had no trust in me then nor I in you. For this reason, having admitted this, there was no desire to talk.[43] But now, reluctantly assuming you to be one whose word can be believed, quite reluctantly assuming what you say is to be believed. *Acting thus (iti katvā)*: for this reason. [223] *You may ask me what you desire and if possible (pucchassu maṃ kāmaṃ yathā visayhaṃ)*: you may ask me about whatever matter you wish and if possible, if I am at all able, I will, however, answer in accordance with the extent of my knowledge – this is the meaning.

Having thus been given permission by the peta to question him the king uttered this verse:

13 'Whatever I may see with my eyes – may I believe all that. Should I see something and yet still not believe[44] it then you should help[45] me, yakkha.'

13 This is the meaning: whatever I may see with my eyes, may I believe, may I admit, all that just as it is. Should, however, I see something and yet still not believe what you say then you should help me, yakkha, you should rebuke[46] me. Or, alternatively *whatever I may see with my eyes (yaṃ kiñcāhaṃ cakkhunā passissāmi)*: whatever I may see with my eyes due to its being out of sight to another who is without eyes. *May I believe all that (sabbam pi tāhaṃ abhisaddaheyyaṃ)*: may I believe all that I see, hear or come to know for such is the trust that I have in you – this is the meaning. The meaning of the last (two) lines, however, is exactly as stated.

When he heard this the peta uttered this verse:[47]

14 'Let me have your solemn promise that having heard Dhamma you will acquire proper devotion.[48] As you are anxious to know and your heart is not depraved I will proclaim all the Dhamma, exactly as discerned, whether you have heard it or not.'[49]

[224] From here onwards[50] are the verses of the exchange of conversation between them both:

15 'On a white caparisoned horse you go up to the one who has been impaled; this mount is marvellous and lovely to behold – of what deed is this the result?'

16 'In the centre of the city of Vesāli there was a hole in a muddy road; with devotion in my heart I took the white[51] head of an ox and laid it down in that hole.

17 By placing our feet on this both we and others could get past; this mount, marvellous and lovely to behold – of that same deed is this the result.'

18 'Now your complexion is radiant in all directions and your fragrance pervades all directions; you possess great majesty and have attained this psychic power of a yakkha yet you are naked – of what is this the result?'

19 'Free from anger and with devotion constantly in my heart, I approached people with gentle speech; my heavenly complexion is continually radiant – of that same deed is this the result.

20 When I saw the fame and celebrity of those established in the Dhamma I proclaimed (them) with devotion in my heart; my heavenly fragrance continually pervades – of that same deed is this the result.

21 Whilst my companions were bathing at the bathing place I playfully and with no depravity of mind took their garments and hid them on some raised ground – for this reason I am naked and lead a troubled life.'

22 [225] 'Of him who performs a wicked deed for fun, such is the result of that deed of his; but of him who does it not for fun, what do they say is the result of that deed of his?'

23 'Those people of depraved purpose and mind and tarnished in body and speech – their lot at the breaking up of the body is, without doubt, that they go to hell.

24 But those others who, longing for a happy state, delight in giving and are of a sympathetic nature[52] – their lot at the breaking up of the body is, without doubt, that they go to a happy state.'

14 Herein *let me have your solemn promise (saccappaṭiññā tava me sā hotu)*: let this promise of yours to me be a solemn one. *That having heard Dhamma you will acquire proper devotion (sutvāna dhammaṃ labha suppasādaṃ)*: that having heard this Dhamma of which I am speaking you will acquire true devotion. *Anxious to know (aññatthiko)*: anxious of understanding. *Exactly as discerned (yathā pajānaṃ)*: exactly as another also would discern it; or, alternatively *exactly as discerned (yathā pajānaṃ)* means just as it has been realised by me.
15 *Of what deed is this the result? (kiss' etaṃ kammassa ayaṃ vipāko)*: of what is this, of what indeed is this? Of what deed is this the result? Or, alternatively *etaṃ* (untranslated) is a mere particle; of what deed – this is how it should be construed.[53] Some read *kissa te* (the meaning remaining unaltered).
16 *In a muddy road (cikkhallamagge)*:[54] in a path full of mud. *A hole (narakaṃ)*: a pit. *I (took) the: ekāhaṃ=ekaṃ ahaṃ* (resolution of compound). *Laid it down in that hole (narakasmiṃ nikkhipiṃ)*: set it down in that muddy pit so that the mud need not be trodden on.
17 *Of that (tassa)*: of making that bridge with that head of an ox.
20 *Of those established in the Dhamma (dhamme ṭhitānaṃ)*: of those who were Dhamma-farers, of those who were even-farers.[55] *I proclaimed (mantemi)*: I spoke about, I celebrated.
21 [226] *Playfully (khiḍḍatthiko)*: intending it as a joke. *And with no depravity of mind (no ca paduṭṭhacitto)*: with no malevolence of mind as regards the owner of the garment, meaning there was no intention of stealing nor any intention to cause loss.[56]
22 *Not for fun (akīḷamāno)*: not intending it playfully, with the malevolence of mind due to greed[57] and so on. *What do they say is the result of that deed of his? (kiṃ tassa kammassa vipākam āhu)*: how severe do the wise say is the resulting misery of that wicked deed of his done in that way?[58]
23 *Of depraved purpose and mind (duṭṭhasaṅkappamanā)*: with thoughts

that are malevolent due to purposes involving sense desires and so on – in this way he speaks of evil conduct of mind. *And tarnished in body and speech (kāyena vācāya ca saṅkiliṭṭhā)*: stained in body and speech by way of the destruction of living beings and so on.

24 *Longing for (āsamānā)*: hoping for, wishing for.

When the fruition of deeds had thus been demonstrated with this analysis in brief by the peta the king uttered this verse, disbelieving what he had heard:

25 'How can I know this for certain, that this is the result of lovely and wicked deeds? Or what have I seen that I should believe? Or who, even, might make me believe this?'

25 Herein *how can I know this for certain (taṃ kin ti jāneyyaṃ ahaṃ avecca)*: how, for what reason, can I believe this for certain, without having to rely on others, this result of lovely and wicked deeds spoken of and analysed by you by way of, 'Those people of depraved purpose and mind and tarnished in body and speech' and so on and 'But those others who, longing for a happy state' and so forth. *Or what have I seen that I should believe? (kiṃ vā 'haṃ disvā abhisaddaheyyaṃ)*: or what sort of evidence have I seen with my own eyes that I should lend my consent? *Or who, even, might make me believe this? (ko vā pi maṃ saddahāpeyya etaṃ)*: or what learned man, what wise man, might make me believe this matter, meaning please tell me this.

[227] When he heard this the peta spoke these verses explaining the matter to him in a reasoned fashion:

26 'When you have seen and heard you must believe that this is the result of lovely and wicked deeds; were both lovely and wicked deeds not to exist how could beings have happy or miserable existences?

27 And were mortals not to do deeds here, lovely and wicked deeds in the world of men, there would be no beings having happy or miserable existences, (none) low and high in the world of men.

28 But since mortals do do deeds, lovely and wicked deeds in the world of men, therefore (there are) beings having happy or miserable existences, (who are) low and high in the world of men.

29 At present they say the result of deeds is twofold – those to be experienced as happiness and those as misery; the devatās gratify themselves[59] whilst fools who do not see the duality are boiled.'[60]

26 Herein *when you have seen (disvā)*: when you have also seen with your own eyes. *Heard (sutvā)*: (when you have) heard the Dhamma you

can draw your own conclusion, make your own judgement in accordance therewith. *Of lovely and wicked deeds: kalyāṇapāpassa=kalyāṇassa pāpassa* (resolution of compound); you must believe that this happiness and this misery is the result of skilled and unskilled deeds. *Were both not to exist (ubhaye asante)*: were the two kinds of deeds, lovely and wicked deeds, not known. *How could beings have happy or miserable existences? (siyā nu sattā sugatā duggatā vā)* means how could, how[61] might, it be a fact that these beings have gone to a happy state or to a miserable state, or that the rich are in a happy state and the poor in a miserable state? [228] He[62] now explains the matter in accordance with, and in addition[63] to, what has been said already by means of the two verses (beginning:) 'And (were mortals) not (to do) deeds here' and 'But since (mortals do do) deeds.'

28 Herein *low and high (hīnā paṇītā)*: low and lofty in family, appearance, health, retinue and so on.

29 *At present they say the result of deeds is twofold (dvay' ajja kammānaṃ vipākam āhu)*: at present, now, they speak of, they talk of, the result of deeds of good and bad conduct as being twofold, of two kinds. What were they? He said,[64] *those to be experienced as happiness and those as misery (sukhassa dukkhassa ca vedanīyaṃ)*: those suitable for experiencing what is agreeable and what is disagreeable.[65] *The devatās gratify themselves (tā devatāyo paricārayanti)*: those who by virtue of their superiority acquire a result to be experienced as happiness become devatās in the devaloka[66] and, endowed with heavenly happiness, gratify their senses.[67] *Whilst fools who do not see the duality are boiled (paccanti bālā dvayataṃ apassino)*: whilst those fools who, not seeing and not believing the twofold (aspect of the) deed and the fruition of the deed, pursue wicked deeds and, on account of those deeds, are boiled, meet with misery, in the hells and so on experiencing results to be experienced as misery.

With reference to (the king's) question, 'But why do you, believing thus in the fruition of deeds, suffer such misery?', he then uttered this verse:

30 'There are no deeds of mine done by myself nor is there even he who, having given, would assign to me that clothing, bed and food and drink – for this reason I am naked and lead a troubled life.'

30 Herein *there are no deeds of mine done by myself (na m' atthi kammāni sayaṃ katāni)*: since there are no meritorious deeds of mine, since none are known, done in the past by me myself by which I might now obtain clothing and so on. *Nor is there even he who, having given, would assign to me (datvā pi me n' atthi so ādiseyya)*: nor is there he who, having given a gift to recluses and brahmins, would assign, would

dedicate, it to me saying, 'Let this be for that particular peta.' *For this reason I am naked and lead a troubled life (ten' amhi naggo kasirā ca vutti)*: for these two kinds of reason [229] I am now naked, unclothed, and lead a troubled and miserable life, existence.

When he heard this the king, wishing him to obtain clothing and so on, uttered this verse:

31 'Could there be some means, yakkha, by which you could obtain clothing? Tell me if there is any condition for we will listen to any statement of conditions that is credible.'

31 Herein *by which (yena)* means could there be, might there be, some means by which you could obtain, you might obtain, clothing? *If there is: yadatthi=yadi atthi* (resolution of compound).

Then that peta spoke these verses telling him of the means:

32 'There is here a monk named Kappitaka, a meditative, of good morality, an arahant, freed, with well guarded senses, restrained by the Pātimokkha rules, who has become cool and arrived at the utmost view;

33 Kindly spoken, affable, well spoken, with a kind face, well versed and one who speaks very amiably, a merit-field, one dwelling in peacefulness and one worthy of donations from devas and men;

34 Tranquil, fumeless, untroubled, free from desire, emancipated, dart-free, egoless, upright, without substrata, one who has destroyed all obstacles, one who has attained the three knowledges,[68] brilliant;

35 Unknown and not easily recognised even when seen, amongst the Vajjians they call him "sage"; yakkhas know him as free of passion, roaming about the world with a lovely nature.

36 [230] If you were to give him a pair or two, dedicating this to me, and these were to be accepted you would see me fitted out with garments.'

32 Herein *named Kappitaka (Kappitako nāma)*: he speaks with reference to the preceptor of the venerable elder Upāli, the (one time) leader of a thousand matted-hair ascetics.[69] *Here (idha)*: nearby this Vesāli. *A meditative (jhāyī)*: a meditative on account of the jhāna associated with the topmost fruit.[70] *Who has become cool (sītibhūto)*: who has attained the cool state by allaying the feverish distress of all the defilements. *Arrived at the utmost view (uttamadiṭṭhipatto)*: arrived at the utmost, at the topmost fruit, at right view.[71]

33 *Kindly spoken (sakhilo)*: gentle. *Well spoken (suvaco)*: meek. *Well versed (svāgamo)*: one to whom the tradition has been properly handed

down.[72] *And one who speaks very amiably (suppaṭimuttako ca)*: one who is very amiably spoken, meaning one speaking in moderation.[73] *One dwelling in peacefulness (araṇavihārī)*: one dwelling in loving kindness.

34 *Tranquil (santo)*: with the defilements calmed. *Fumeless (vidhūmo)*: lacking the fumes of wrong thoughts.[74] *Untroubled (anīgho)*: free of misery. *Free from desire (nirāso)*: free of craving. *Emancipated (mutto)*: freed from all (future) becoming.[75] *Dart-free (visallo)*: lacking the dart of lust and so on. *Egoless (amamo)*: rid of egotistic assertion. *Upright (avaṅko)*: rid of crooked ways such as crooked (deeds) in body and so on. *Without substrata (nirupadhi)*: one who has given up the substrata such as the defilements and accumulations and so on.[76] *One who has destroyed all obstacles (sabbapapañcakhīṇo)*: one who has exhausted obstacles such as craving and so on. *Brilliant (jutimā)*: brilliant with the unsurpassed brilliance of knowledge.

35 *Unknown (appaññāto)*: not well known due to his absolutely minimum needs and his virtues being hidden.[77] *Not easily recognised (na sujāno)*: due to his profound nature he is not easily ascertained to be of such virtue, of such a nature and of such wisdom, even when seen. *Yakkhas know him as free of passion (jānanti taṃ yakkhabhūtā anejaṃ)*: and yakkhas know him as free of passion, free of craving and an arahant. *With a lovely nature (kalyāṇadhammaṃ)*: with good qualities of virtue and so on.

36 *To him (tassa)*: to that senior elder Kappitaka. *A pair (ekaṃ yugaṃ)*: a pair of garments. *Or two (duve vā)*: or two pairs of garments. *Dedicating this to me: mam uddisitvāna=mamaṃ uddisitvā*[78] (alternative grammatical form). [231] *And these were to be accepted (paṭiggahitāni ca tāni c' assu)*: if these pairs of garments were to be, should be, accepted by him. *Fitted out with garments (sannaddhadussaṃ)*: my fitting out with garments completed, meaning clothed and covered with garments, with the clothes he had received.[79]

The king then enquired about the dwelling place of the elder:

37 'At what place is that recluse dwelling to which we might now go and see him who today might dispel my doubt and uncertainty, this wriggling of (wrong) view?'

37 Herein *at what place? (kasmim padese)*: in which place? *Who today: yo m' ajja=yo ajja*; (the words) are euphonically connected by the syllable *ma.*[80]

The peta then said:

38 'He is seated at Kapinaccanā surrounded by many devatās; the truly named is giving a talk on Dhamma, heedful as to (the teachings of) his own teacher.'[81]

38 Herein *at Kapinaccanā (Kapinaccanāyaṃ)*: at the place that commonly goes by the name Kapinaccanā because of the monkeys' (*kapīnaṃ*), the forest-folk's,[82] dancing (*naccanena*). *The truly named (saccanāmo)*:[83] correctly named, named exactly in accordance with his named qualities – 'a meditative, of good morality, an arahant, freed' and so on.

When the peta said this the king uttered this verse, desiring to visit that elder immediately:

39 'I will now go and do what you suggested; I will clothe that recluse with a pair and if these are accepted we will see you fitted out with garments.'

39 [232] Herein *I will now do: kassāmi=karissāmi* (alternative grammatical form).

Then the peta uttered this verse showing that since the elder was teaching Dhamma to those devatās[84] it was not therefore the time to approach him:

40 'Do not approach one gone forth when it is untimely – please, O Licchavi, this is not the custom[85] for you. Approach him afterwards, at the proper time,[86] and see him right there seated in solitude.'

40 Herein *please (sādhu)* is a particle of entreaty. *O Licchavi, it is not the custom for you (vo Licchavi n' esa dhammo)*: O Licchavi king, this is not the custom for you kings, approaching at an improper time. *Right there (tatth' eva)*: at that same place.

When the peta said this the king agreed saying, 'Very well', and returned to his residence. When the proper time had once more arrived he approached the elder having eight pairs of clothes carried along. Seated at one side he extended him a friendly greeting and said, 'Please accept these eight pairs of clothes, sir.' When he heard this the elder, in order to begin conversation with him, asked, 'Great king, you previously lacked the virtue of giving and oppressed recluses and brahmins. How come you now desire to give these excellent clothes?' When he heard this the king told him the reason, reporting to the elder his meeting with the peta and all that they each had said, and then gave him the clothes and dedicated them to the peta. By means of this the peta appeared before the elder and the king, dressed and adorned, wearing heavenly clothes and mounted on a horse. When he saw him the king was very pleased, delighted and full of joy and happiness and said, 'I have certainly seen with my own eyes the fruition of deeds. I will not now do wicked deeds, I will do only meritorious deeds', and called upon that peta to be his witness. The peta said, 'If you, O Licchavi king, henceforward abandon unrighteous ways[87] and conduct yourself in accordance with the Dhamma, then only will I be your witness and come into your presence. Quickly release the impaled man from the stake. Having thus regained his life and conducting himself in accordance with the Dhamma he may yet escape the misery (awaiting him). Approach the elder from time to time and listen to Dhamma; do meritorious deeds!', [233] and then departed. The king then saluted the elder and entered the city. He very quickly called together the Licchavi people and, with their consent, released the man from the stake and ordered his physicians to make him well again. He approached the elder and asked, 'Is it possible that for one who has done a deed that would take one to hell, sir, there might still be escape from hell?' 'It is possible, great king. If he does lofty, meritorious deeds he can escape', replied the elder and then established the king in the Refuges and the Five Precepts. Thus established therein and set firm in the elder's exhortation he became a sotāpanna. The impaled man, however, became well again and, filled with agitation, went forth amongst the monks and not long afterwards attained arahantship. Those rehearsing the texts spoke these verses, illustrating this fact:

41 'Saying, "So be it", he left that place and surrounded by a group of slaves the Licchavi approached the city and went to bed in his own residence.

42 Then in the morning, when he had attended to his household duties, he bathed and drank; when the proper time arrived he chose eight pairs from a chest and that Licchavi had them carried along by the group of slaves.

43 He approached that place and saw the recluse who had become cool, seated tranquil in heart at the foot of a tree, being got back, returned from his search for food.

44 He approached him and said this to him, enquiring about his health and well being, "I am a Licchavi from Vesāli, good sir; they know me as the Licchavi Ambasakkhara.

45 [234] Please accept, sir, these eight beautiful pairs of mine; I offer them to you – it is for this purpose alone that I have come here and I would be delighted if you would do so."

46 "From afar recluses and brahmins avoid your residence; in your residence their bowls are broken and even their robes torn up.

47 Moreover, recluses are tripped up[88] and made to fall head first – such is the harassment caused by you to recluses and those gone forth.

48 You gave no oil, not even with a blade of grass, nor did you show the way to those who had gone astray; you yourself would seize the

stick from a blind man, so miserly and unrestrained were you. Now for what reason, just what have you seen that you now share these with us?"

49 "I admit to what you say, sir; I harassed recluses and brahmins. Yet even this same evil deed of mine was done playfully and with no depravity of mind.

50 A yakkha,[89] having pursued wicked deeds in play, experiences misery, his enjoyment being incomplete. [235] He has a boyish youthfulness but his own nakedness is his lot – now what could be more miserable for him than that?

51 When I saw him I became agitated, sir – that is the reason that I am offering this gift. Please accept these eight pairs of clothes, sir, and may this donation reach that yakkha."

52 "For surely a gift is praised in many ways; now may this be of an inexhaustible nature for you who gives it. I accept your eight pairs of clothes – may this donation reach that yakkha."

53 Then the Licchavi performed the ablution and gave the elder the eight pairs saying, "May these be accepted" (whereupon the elder said), "Now behold the yakkha, fitted out with garments!"

54 He saw him, anointed with the choicest sandalwood, mounted on a thoroughbred, with the finest complexion, adorned, clothed in respectable garments, surrounded, attained to the great psychic power of a yakkha.

55 When he saw him he was delighted, elated, his heart bristling with joy, radiant; he saw his deed and its actual, great result with his eye, saw this with his own eyes.

56 He approached him and said this to him, "I will give gifts to recluses and brahmins for there is nothing of mine I would not give. You have been a great help to me, yakkha."

57 "And you gave partial alms on my behalf, Licchavi – this was not in vain; [236] I will be your witness,[90] a non-human with a human."

58 "You are my destiny, kinsman, support and friend and, moreover, my devatā. I beg you with the añjali salute as I wish to see you again, yakkha."

59 "If you become one lacking faith, appear miserly or possess an erring heart, you will not be allowed to see me at all, whilst even if I see you I will not address you.[91]

60 But if you develop respect for the Dhamma, delight in giving, are of a sympathetic nature and become a welling spring for recluses and brahmins, you will in this way be allowed to see me and when I see you I will address you, good sir.[92]

61 Now quickly free this (man) from the stake on account of whom I became your witness;[93] it is by reason of the one impaled, I think, that we have become each other's witness.[93]

62 And if this (man) is quickly freed from the stake he may yet, duly engaging in (skilled) states,[94] escape hell and[95] that deed become one to be experienced elsewhere.

63 [237] Having approached Kappitaka at the proper time and shared with him (what you have) sit down close by and ask him face to face and he will proclaim on this subject.

64 Just approach that monk and ask him. As you are anxious to know[96] and your heart is not depraved he will proclaim all the Dhamma,[97] exactly as discerned, whether you have heard it or not."[98]

65 When he had secretly conversed there with that non-human and made him his witness he departed and in the presence of the Licchavis he spoke to the company seated together saying,

66 "Listen, good sirs, to but one word of mine[99] – I seek from you a boon by which I will obtain benefit. That man of cruel deeds has been impaled, has had punishment applied[100] and has had the form of one who has incurred (the king's sentence),

67 For as many as twenty days now with the result that that impaled (man) is now neither quite alive nor dead. I wish now to release him – may the company permit (me to act) as I think fit."

68 "Quickly free this one and others – who would speak against you acting in that way? You should do what you deem necessary – the company permits (you to act) as you think fit."

69 [238] He approached that place and quickly released the one impaled; "Have no fear, my friend", he said to him and had his physicians nurse him.

70 He then approached Kappitaka at the proper time and shared with him (what he had); sitting down close by the Licchavi asked him right there, face to face, anxious for some means,

71 "That man of cruel deeds had been impaled, had had punishment applied[101] and appears to have incurred this for as many as twenty days with the result that that impaled (man) was neither quite dead nor alive.

72 But now I have gone and released him, sir, for this was the word of that yakkha. Could there be any means at all by which he might not go to hell?

73 Tell (me), sir, if there is any condition for we will listen to any statement of conditions[102] that is credible. Can there be no destruction of those deeds, no making an end of them here without their being experienced?"[103]

74 "If he should duly engage in (skilled) states, with diligence both day and night, he may yet escape hell and[104] that deed become one to be experienced elsewhere."

75 "The facts about this man are known. Please have pity on me too now,[105] sir. Advise me, exhort me, Extremely Wise One, in such a way that I might not go to hell."

76 "You should go for refuge this very day to the Buddha, [239] the Dhamma and the Saṅgha with devotion in your heart; likewise you should undertake the Five Precepts, unbroken and in their entirety.

77 You should forthwith refrain from destroying living beings and shun in this world what is not given; you should not be one to drink intoxicating drinks nor should you speak a lie, whilst you should be content with your own wife.[106]

78 And you should undertake these skilled deeds leading to happiness that are ariyan and fulfilled by means of the eightfold vow:[107]

79 To the upright you should give with a devout heart robes and almsfood, requisites and lodging, food and drink, solid food, clothing and lodging,

80 And you should satisfy with food and drink monks who are endowed with virtue, free of lust and learned – merit continually grows up.

81 Duly engaging thus in (skilled) states, with diligence both day and night, you may yet escape hell and that deed become one to be experienced elsewhere."

82 "I will go for refuge this very day to the Buddha, the Dhamma and the Saṅgha with devotion in my heart; likewise I will undertake the Five Precepts, unbroken and in their entirety.

83 I will forthwith refrain from destroying living beings and shun in this world what is not given; I will not be one to drink intoxicating drinks, nor will I speak a lie, whilst I will be content with my own wife.

84 I will undertake skilled deeds leading to happiness that are approached by way of the ariyan eightfold vow:

85 [240] Robes and almsfood, requisites and lodging, food and drink, solid food, clothing and lodging will I give, without faltering and devoted to the Teaching of the Buddhas, to monks who are endowed with virtue, free of lust and learned."

86 Such a one is the Licchavi Ambasakkhara – a layfollower in Vesāli who possesses faith, who is gentle and helpful and who now supports the order of monks with due care.

87 And the one impaled became well again and of his own accord happily went into the homeless state; on account of Kappitaka, the

noblest of monks, both attained the fruits that result from the life of a recluse.[108]

88 Association with good and discerning worthy men is of such great fruit that the one impaled reached the topmost fruit whilst Ambasakkhara a lesser fruit.'

41 Herein *went to bed: vās' upagañchittha=vāsaṃ upagañchi* (resolution of compound in alternative grammatical form).
42 *His household duties (gihikiccāni)*: duties concerning the family property and estates that have to be attended to by one residing at home. *He chose (viceyya)*: he chose in order to take the finest clothes.
43 *Got back (paṭikkantaṃ)*: got back from his almsround. For this reason he said, 'returned from his search for food'.
44 *Said (avoca)*: said, 'I am a Licchavi from Vesāli, good sir', and so on.
46 *Torn up: vipātayanti=viphālayanti*[109] (alternative grammatical form).
47 *Are tripped up (pādak' udārikāhi)*: with axes (*kuṭhārīhi*) known as feet (*pādasaṅkātāhi*).[110] *Made to fall (pātayanti)*: caused to fall down.[111]
48 [**241**] *With a blade of grass (tiṇena)*: not even with the tip of a blade of grass. *Nor did you show the way to those who had gone astray (mūḷhassa maggaṃ pi na pāvadāsi)*: nor did you tell the way to those who had lost their way but thought, 'Just let that man wander about here and there'; this king is indeed unreliable. *You yourself would seize (sayam ādiyāsi)*: you yourself would snatch and take the staff from the hand of a blind man. *You now share (saṃvibhāgaṃ karosi)*: you now share, giving some of the things meant for your own use.
49 *I admit to what you say, sir (paccemi bhante yaṃ tvaṃ vadesi)*: I agree with what you say such as '(in your residence) their bowls are broken' and so on. He points out that all those things were done or caused to be done by him. *Yet even this (etam pi)*: yet even this was done, being meant to be playful.
50 *In play: khiḍḍā=khiḍḍāya* (alternative grammatical form). *Having pursued (pasavitvā)*: having accumulated. *Experiences (vedeti)*: undergoes. *His enjoyment being incomplete (asamattabhogī)*: his enjoyment lacking fulfilment; to show this same lack of fulfilment in his enjoyment 'He has a boyish youthfulness' and so on was said. *His own nakedness (nagganiyassa)*: his state of nakedness. *Now what could be more miserable for him than that? (kiṃ su tato dukkhatar' assa hoti)*: now what indeed could be more miserable for that peta than that state of nakedness?
51 *May this donation reach that yakkha (yakkhass' im' āgacchantu dakkhiṇāyo)*: may this donation of clothes that I am giving be of benefit to that peta.

52 *Is praised in many ways (bahudhā pasaṭṭhaṃ)*: is extolled in various ways by Buddhas and so on. *May this be of an inexhaustable nature (akkhayadhammam atthu)*: let this be of an indestructible nature.
53 *Performed the ablution (ācamayitvā)*: rinsed his mouth, having previously washed his hands and feet.
54 *Anointed with the choicest sandalwood (candanasāralittaṃ)*: anointed with the essence of sandalwood. *With the finest complexion (uḷāravaṇṇaṃ)*: with an excellent appearance. *Surrounded (parivāritaṃ)*: surrounded by attendants with agreeable habits. *Attained to the great psychic power of a yakkha (yakkhamahiddhipattaṃ)*: standing[112] having attained the great psychic power of a yakkha, the (great) psychic power of a deva.
56 *Said this to him: tamenamavoca*[113]*=tam enam avoca* (resolution of compound).
57 *You gave partial alms (ekadesaṃ adāsi)*: he speaks with reference to the gift of clothes which forms a part of the four requisites. *Witness (sakkhiṃ)*: of the nature of a witness.
58 [242] *You are my: mamāsi=me āsi* (resolution of compound in alternative grammatical form). *My devatā (devatā me)*: you are my devatā – this is how it should be construed.
59 *Possess an erring heart (vippaṭipannacitto)*: with a heart following wrong views, meaning following a wrong path after abandoning the right[114] path.
61 *On account of whom (yato nidānaṃ)*: because of whom, by reason of coming into whose presence.
63 *Shared (saṃvibhajitvā)*: shared as a gift. *Sit down close by and ask him face to face (sayaṃ mukhena upanisajja puccha)*: without sending other men, sit down close by and just ask him to his face.
65 *Seated together (sannisinnaṃ)*: seated after coming together.
66 *I will obtain benefit (labhissāmi atthaṃ)*: I will obtain the benefit I desire. *Has had punishment applied (paṇihitadaṇḍo)*: has had physical punishment rendered. *Has had the form of one who has incurred (anupattarūpo)*: has been in the condition of one who has incurred the king's sentence.
67 *As many as twenty days (vīsatirattimattā)* means that as many as twenty days have passed.[115] *I . . . him: tāhaṃ=taṃ ahaṃ* (resolution of compound). *As I think fit (yathā matiṃ)*: exactly as it pleases me.
68 *This one and others (etañ ca aññañ ca)*: this impaled man and those others to whom the king's punishment has been applied.[116] *Quickly free (lahuṃ pamuñca)*: release forthwith. *Who would speak against you? (ko taṃ vadetha)*: who in this kingdom of Vajjī might say, 'Do not[117] set him free', to one acting in such a just way[118] as that, meaning no one would be allowed to speak like this.

69 *And (had) his physicians: tikicchakānañ ca=tikicchake ca* (alternative grammatical form).
72 *This was the word of (that) yakkha (yakkhassa vaco)*: this was what the peta had to say. He points out, 'I acted thus, in accordance with what that peta had to say, sir.'
74 *(Skilled) states (dhammāni)*: meritorious states[119] able to overcome previously done wicked deeds. *That deed become one to be experienced elsewhere (kammaṃ siyā aññatra vedanīyaṃ)*: the wicked deed that was to be experienced on arising become an *ahosi* deed, whilst that that was to be experienced in some other mode become one whose fruit is to be experienced elsewhere, in some (still) other mode, meaning (only) when saṃsāra continues to roll (for him).[120]
78 [243] *And . . . these (imañ ca)*: this is said with reference[121] to what is near or in sight due to its being said by him himself. *That are ariyan and fulfilled by means of the eightfold vow (ariyaṃ aṭṭhaṅgavaren' upetaṃ)*: the highest Uposatha precepts that are fulfilled, engaged in, by means of the eightfold (vow of) refraining from destroying living beings and so on and that are ariyan in the sense that they are pure. *Skilled deeds (kusalaṃ)*: blameless deeds. *Leading to happiness (sukhundriyaṃ)*: resulting in happiness.
80 *Merit continually grows up (sadā puññaṃ pavaḍḍhati)*: when one has done a meritorious deed only once one does not become wholly satisfied[122] thinking, 'To that extent it is enough', and whilst one is fulfilling good conduct again and again one's merit is increasing all the time. Alternatively the meaning is that while one is fulfilling good conduct again and again the fruits of one's meritorious deeds, the merit so called, grow, are added to, one after the other.

When the elder had thus spoken the king was terrified by the misery of the states of woe[123] and with an increasing devotion in the Three Jewels and in meritorious states he said, 'I will go for refuge this very day to the Buddha' and so on, henceforward undertaking the Refuges and the Precepts.
86 Herein *such a one (etādiso)*: such as the aforesaid kind. *A layfollower in Vesāli (Vesāliyaṃ aññataro upāsako)*: he has become a layfollower amongst countless thousands in Vesāli. *Who possesses faith (saddho)* and so on:[124] this is said to show the difference from his earlier nature in that he (now) sits down together with a lovely friend and so on; for previously he lacked faith, was rough and insulting to monks and did not support the Saṅgha, whereas now he possesses faith and is gentle and now supports the order of monks with due care. In this connection *helpful (kārakaro)*: one who renders a service.
87 *Both (ubho pi)*: the two, the one impaled and the king. *Attained the*

fruits that result from the life of a recluse (sāmaññaphalāni ajjhaguṃ): attained the fruits that result from the life of a recluse in accordance with their deserts.[125] It was to show this accordance with their deserts[125] that 'the one impaled reached the topmost fruit whilst Ambasakkhara a lesser fruit' was said.

88 Herein *a lesser fruit (phalaṃ kaniṭṭhaṃ)*: he spoke with reference to the sotāpatti-fruit.

That which has not here been analysed as to its meaning is, however, quite easily understood.

The venerable Mahākappitaka proceeded to Sāvatthī to salute the Teacher and raised with the Lord the issue of what had thus been said between the king,[126] the peta and himself. [244] The Teacher took the matter as an arisen need and taught Dhamma to the company assembled there. That teaching was of benefit to those people.

[1] Cp PvA 99.
[2] Reading vāṇijassa āpaṇasamīpe with Se Be for text's vāṇijassāpaṇasamīpe.
[3] Reading atikkamantā with Se Be for text's atikkamanto.
[4] gosīsaṭṭhiṃ, not an excellent kind of sandalwood as suggested by PED.
[5] saṅkhavaṇṇasannibhaṃ; cp M i 58 = A iii 324; J iii 477.
[6] yathābhūtaṃ.
[7] Cp KS i 102 n. 1 for similar royal designs on other men's wives.
[8] Reading sutattā bhayena with Se Be for text's sutatthābhayena.
[9] amanusso, literally non-human.
[10] Reading imassa with Se Be for text's tam assa.
[11] Reading daṭṭhum pi te 'dāni na taṃ labhanti with Se Be for text's daṭṭhum pi dāni na labhanti taṃ pi.
[12] Reading virājitatto with Be for text's Se virādhitatto.
[13] vikalaṃ; PED sv should be amended to read 'Pv IV.1[4] (=bhoga- PvA 219)'.
[14] Reading kiccho with Se Be for text's kicco.
[15] palimpamāno, so all texts but cp PED sv palippati.
[16] picumandassa (Se Be pucimandassa), the margosa, Azadirachta Indica; PED sv picu mis-spells Azadizachta.
[17] Reading nagarassa bahi bhavaṃ . . . jātaṃ pavattaṃ sambandhaṃ with Se Be for text's nagarassa bāhirabhāgaṃ . . . jātaṃ pavattaṃ.
[18] Reading vutta-atthassa with Be for text's vutte atthassa; Se reads vuttassa atthassa.
[19] Cp A ii 244f. where this is said to be the way in which petas lie.
[20] Reading appamattakam pi with Se Be for text's appamattam pi.
[21] Reading imassa natthi. Paricārikā sā pī ti yā asita- with Se Be for text's imassa natthi paricārikāsāmītiyā. Asita-.
[22] indriyānaṃ.
[23] Reading -lakkhaṇā indriyānaṃ with Se Be for text's -lakkhaṇa-indriyānaṃ.
[24] Reading -khāyita- with Se Be and verse for text's -khādita-.
[25] Be adds pāṭho here.
[26] Text wrongly begins a new sentence with vigatajīvitattā.
[27] Reading passitum pi na labhanti kuto with Se Be for text's passitum pi. Na labhantī ti kuto.

[28] mukhullokikā; cp D i 60.

[29] Reading parihīnattho. Kiccho ti dukkhitowith Se Be for text's parihīnattho kicco.

[30] Reading dukkatakammakārī with Se (Be -kaṭa-) for text's dukkhaṭakammakārī.

[31] These tortures are to be endured one after the other in an endless cycle; cp M iii 184ff.

[32] Cp M iii 183: they drive a red-hot iron stake through each hand and foot and a red-hot iron stake through the middle of his breast.

[33] Reading pañcavidhabandhanaṃ, mukhe tattalohasecanaṃ with Se Be for text's pañcavidhabandhanamukhe tatta-.

[34] Cp Miln 303.

[35] See PvA 280 and cp J iii 22, 43, iv 493, v 268; SnA 59, 480.

[36] Cp J vi 250; see also Mārk. Pur. xii 24f., MBh xii 321, Manu iv 90, xii 75.

[37] A river of caustic water; see MLS iii 229 n. 1.

[38] Reading pariccajeyya with Se Be for text's parivajjeyya.

[39] Reading paṭiññā with Se Be for text's patiññā.

[40] Reading nācikkhanā with Se Be for text's nacikkhanā.

[41] Reading paṭiññā me ti ñāṇavasena mayhaṃ pucchassū ti paṭiññā okāsadānan ti attho with Se Be for text's patiññā ti ñātavasena mayhaṃ pucchassu ti, okāsadānan ti attho.

[42] Text wrongly reads acikkhanā here.

[43] This episode seems wanting in the narrative above.

[44] Reading saddaheyyaṃ with Se Be for text's saddaheyya.

[45] Reading nissayakammaṃ as recommended by PED sv niya for all texts' niyassa kammaṃ; cp A i 99, Vin i 49. PED sv nissaya wrongly refers to this as v 1.

[46] Reading niggahakammaṃ with Se Be for text's niggata-.

[47] Reading Taṃ sutvā peto gāthaṃ āha with Be for text's Se Taṃ sutvā peto.

[48] Reading labha suppasādaṃ with Be for text's labhassu pasādaṃ (Se labhassuppa-).

[49] Reading c' āpi with Se Be for text's vā pi.

[50] Reading ito paraṃ with Be; text Se omit.

[51] Reading setaṃ with Se Be for text's setuṃ.

[52] saṅgahitattabhāvā, cp v 60; see also Vv 11[6] and VvA 59.

[53] This sense has been followed in the verse.

[54] Text wrongly reads cikkhallapathe here.

[55] See e.g. M i 285ff.

[56] Reading dussasāmike na dūsitacitto na avaharaṇādhippāyo n' āpi vināsādhippāyo with Be (≏ Se) for text's dussasāmikena dūsitacittena apaharaṇādhippayo nāpi vināsādhippāyo.

[57] lobha which together with dosa, ill will, and moha, delusion, forms the three akusalamūlas, the roots of unskilled deeds.

[58] Reading tassa tathā katassa pāpakammassa with Be (≏ Se) for text's tassa yathā mayā katassa pāpakammassa.

[59] Reading devatāyo paricārayanti with Se Be for text's devatā parivārayanti.

[60] paccanti; Se Be read paccenti here.

[61] Text wrongly beings a new sentence here.

[62] The words Idāni yathā vuttam atthaṃ at the foot of PvA 227 are to be read as the opening words of the sentence at the top of the following page.

[63] Reading vyatirekato with Se Be for text's vyātirekato.

[64] Reading Kin tan ti. Āha: with Se Be for text's Kin tan ti āha.

[65] Cp PvA 152 and Nett 28 (quoted PED sv anubhavana).

[66] Se Be add devaloke tā here.

[67] Reading paricārenti with Be (Se paricārayanti) for text's parivārenti.

[68] i.e. knowledge of one's former lives, knowledge of the kammically conditioned rebirth of others and the knowledge as to the certainty of one's liberation; see e.g. M i 22f.

[69] Jaṭilasahassassa abbhantare; cp PvA 21, VA iv 937 and DPPN i 524.
[70] i.e. arahantship; cp Asl 12.
[71] Reading sammādiṭṭhiṃ patto with Se Be for text's sammādiṭṭhipatto.
[72] suṭṭhu āgatāgamo; cp discussion at B of Disc iii 71 n. 1.
[73] Text reads suṭṭhu paṭimuttabhāṇī ti attho; Be reads suṭṭhu paṭimuttakavāco muttabhāṇī ti attho; whilst Se has suṭṭhu paṭimuttakatho mattabhāṇī ti attho. I take paṭimuttaka as a variant of paṭimantaka (found at M i 386) and muttabhāṇī/mattabhāṇī as equivalent to mantabhāṇī (cp Thag 2 and cty at EV i 117). I follow Be here. PED entry sv paṭimutta is wrong and both Jātaka references cited mean 'put on (of clothes, ornaments)'.
[74] vigatamicchāvitakkadhūmo.
[75] sabbabhavehi vimutto; cp A ii 133f. where bhava, becoming, is apparently distinguished from uppatti, arising.
[76] kilesābhisaṅkhārādi-upadhippahāyī; probably the four listed at SnA 44, 436 are intended here, that is, the kāma-, khandha-, kilesa- and abhisaṅkhāra-upadhis.
[77] Reading paṭicchannaguṇatāya ca na pākaṭo with Se Be for text's -guṇattāya na pākaṭo ca.
[78] So Se Be; text mis-spells udisitvā.
[79] Reading laddhavatthaṃ nivatthapārutadussan ti attho with Se Be for text's laddhavatthaṃ hutvā. Nivattha-.
[80] It might therefore be better to transliterate as yo-m-ajja.
[81] Reading ācerake with Be for text's averake; not listed by PED which, sv ācera, claims this contracted form is peculiar to the Jātakas but see also Vin i 359. (Se reads accherake.)
[82] Reading vānarānaṃ with Se Be for text's vā narānaṃ. The reading of our text may have misled Malalasekera to suppose that men also danced there; see DPPN i 513 where it is suggested that Kapinaccanā may have been a name for the cemetery near Vesāli where Kappitaka lived. Cp Vin iv 308.
[83] Cp EV i 207 on Thag 533.
[84] Reading atha peto devatānaṃ thero dhammaṃ deseti tasmā with Se Be for text's atha petānaṃ thero dhammaṃ desesi. Tasmā.
[85] dhammo.
[86] kāle, which also means early in the day and the proper time according to v 42.
[87] adhammaṃ.
[88] Readings are uncertain here. Text reads pādakudārikāhi whereas Se Be read -kuṭhārikāhi, similar discrepancies recurring in the cty. In the copy of the text used by me F. L. Woodward had written a note suggesting it be taken as pādak' udārikāhi, (are made to fall) by means of lifted feet, that is, tripped up. The expression pādakudārikāhi avaṃsirā may be compared with the more common uddhaṃpādaṃ avaṃsiraṃ – feet up, head down – at such places as Vv 52[25], J i 233, Nd[1] 404 etc. If in the cty one reads with the gloss of Be, pādasaṅkhātāhi kuṭhārīhi, with axes known as feet, it is possible to detect a pun in which the tripping up of recluses (with the feet) is likened to the felling of trees (with axes).
[89] Se Be read khiḍḍāya yakkho for text's khiḍḍāya kho whereas all read khiḍḍā ti khiḍḍāya in the cty; perhaps we should therefore read khiḍḍā yakkho here – cp following verse.
[90] Gehman seems to have misread sakkhiṃ, here and throughout, as sakhiṃ.
[91] Reading tvaṃ n' eva maṃ lacchasi dassanāya disvā ca taṃ no pi ca ālapissaṃ with Be for text's (≏ Se) ten' eva maṃ lacchasi dassanāya disvā ca taṃ nāpi ca ālapissaṃ.
[92] Reading bhadante with Be (Se bhaddante) for text's bhaddan te; Se Be read this line with the following verse.
[93] Gehman has 'formed intimate relations' and 'made mutual friendship' respectively here; cp n. 90.

[94] dhammāni samācaranto.

[95] Reading ca with Se Be for text's 'va.

[96] Reading aññatthiko with Se Be for text's puññatthiko; cp v 14.

[97] Text erroneously transposes dhammaṃ sabbaṃ of Se Be and v 14.

[98] Se adds suto ca dhammaṃ sugatiṃ akkhissa here as do some vll of text, except that they read sato for suto.

[99] Cp D ii 166.

[100] Reading paṇihitadaṇḍo with Se Be for text's paṇītadaṇḍo.

[101] Reading paṇihitadaṇḍo with Se for text's Be paṇītadaṇḍo.

[102] Reading hetuvaco with Se Be and v 31 for text's hetu vo.

[103] Not, as Gehman suggests, although we do not understand it.

[104] Reading mucceyya so nirayā ca with Se Be and v 62 for text's muñceyya so nirayā 'va.

[105] Reading pī 'dani for text's pīdāni.

[106] Vv 76–77 recur at Vv 83[17–18]; v 77 also at IV 3[50] below except that the latter reads abhaṇi for abhāsi here, whilst Se reads abhāsi and Be abhāṇi at both places.

[107] Reading aṭṭhaṅgavaren' upetaṃ with Se Be for text's aṭṭhaṅgavaraṃ upetaṃ here and at v 84.

[108] sāmaññaphalāni; cp the Sāmaññaphala Sutta (D i 47ff.) which is devoted to this subject and where such fruits are those connected with arahantship. Elsewhere mention may be found of four such fruits, those of becoming a sotāpanna, once-returner (cp VvA 71), non-returner and arahant – D iii 227, 277; S v 25; Miln 344, 358 etc. Whilst the cty below states Ambasakkhara became a sotāpanna, it is not clear that he ever went forth and thus was no recluse.

[109] So Se for text's vipātayanti=vipāṭiyanti; Be reads vidālayanti=viphālayanti. Cp PED sv vipāṭeti and vipphalati.

[110] See n. 88.

[111] Reading paripātayanti with Se Be for text's pasāriyanti.

[112] ṭhitaṃ, or perhaps stationed, since the verse claims he is on a horse.

[113] Be alone retains the compound unresolved; Se reads tamenaṃ avoca and text separates completely when giving this in the verse itself.

[114] dhammiyaṃ, in accordance with the Dhamma, here contrasted with the wrong path, adhammiyaṃ.

[115] Text wrongly begins a new sentence with ativattā.

[116] Reading paṇihitā with Se Be for text's paṇītā.

[117] Reading na pamocehi with Se Be for text's pamocehi.

[118] dhammiyakammaṃ.

[119] Reading puññadhamme with Se Be for text's aññadhamme.

[120] M iii 214 says of a person committing a given deed that he 'undergoes its fruition which arises here and now or in another mode (diṭṭhe va dhamme vipākaṃ paṭisaṃvedeti uppajjaṃ (vl uppajje) vā apare vā pariyāye)'. A iii 415, however, seems to say that such fruition is threefold: 'Monks, I say that the fruition of deeds is threefold (tividhāhaṃ bhikkhave kammānaṃ vipākaṃ vadāmi)' but then continues: diṭṭh' eva dhamme upapajje (vl uppajjaṃ) vā apare vā pariyāye, more reminiscent of the apparently twofold fruition above. Hare notes (GS iii 294 n. 3) that 'S.e. for eva reads vā. But if tividha, we must read pariyāye vā (?)'. It is worth noting that the reading tividhāhaṃ was not one supported by all MSS. and that the vl uppajjaṃ may have been the more authentic, especially given the Majjhima passage. The later tradition came to understand such fruition as threefold and this no doubt accounts for the Se vl of vā for eva since such fruition was now thought to arise either (1) diṭṭhe vā dhamme, here and now, in this same life; (2) uppajje vā, upon arising in the next life; or (3) apare vā pariyāye, in some other mode, usually a still later life. This was in turn combined with the theory of volitions being divisible into seven javana-moments. A deed performed during the first of these javana-moments was known as a

diṭṭhadhamma-vedanīya-kamma, a deed to be experienced in this same life; during the last javana-moment as an upapajja-vedanīya-kamma, a deed to be experienced upon arising in the next life; whilst during the five intervening javana-moments as an aparāpariya-vedanīya-kamma, a deed to be experienced in still later lives (or in some other mode). The strength of the first and last of these javana-moments is weaker than that of the other five with the result that if a deed should for some reason or other not find the conditions necessary for its fruition during the period stipulated, that deed becomes ahosi, or lapsed, and no longer capable of fruition. This does not, however, apply in the case of an aparāpariya-vedanīya-kamma which can never become ahosi. Dhammapāla's point here is that a meritorious or skilled deed may have the consequence of preventing the conditions necessary for the fruition of a wicked deed of types (1) and (2) from prevailing during the period stipulated for its fruition, thereby rendering that deed ahosi and incapable of fruition either then or in the future. Similarly a meritorious or skilled deed may postpone, or alter the mode of experience of, a deed of type (3) but cannot prevent its fruition entirely except when a person attains liberation during such postponement. See Vism xix 14; Compendium p. 44f., 144f.; Encyclopedia of Buddhism sv ahosi, aparāpariya etc.

121 Reading paccakkhaṃ vā ti with Se Be for text's paccakkhaṃ vā.

122 Reading aparituṭṭho with Be for text's acchrituṭṭho (Se acchariyatuṭṭho); none of these are listed by PED, CPD or Childers.

123 Reading apāyadukkhato with Se Be for text's upāyadukkhato.

124 Reading saddho ti ādi kaly- with Se Be for text's saddho ti ādikaly-.

125 Reading yathārahaṃ for text's yathā rahaṃ.

126 Reading raññā with Se Be for text's rañño.

IV.2 EXPOSITION OF THE SERISSAKA PETA STORY [Serissakapetavatthuvaṇṇanā][1]

'Listen[2] (where the meeting) between the yakkha and the traders.' This is the Serissaka Peta Story.

Since there is no difference between this and the Serissaka Mansion Story,[3] what was to be said herein with respect to the arisen need and to the verses is therefore just as that already given in the Exposition of the Mansion Stories (section) of this Clarification[4] of the Intrinsic Meaning. It should therefore be understood exactly as already given therein.

1 Be alone reads Serīsaka-.

2 suṇātha, so text Se; Be Vv VvA all read suṇotha.

3 Vv 84; Stories of the Mansions pp. 147–154.

4 Paramatthavibhāvaniyaṃ; Se Be both read -dīpaniyaṃ, as does text at PvA 257, but see the remarks at p. iv of Stories of the Departed, 1974 edition.

IV.3 EXPOSITION OF THE NANDAKA PETA STORY
[Nandakapetavatthuvaṇṇanā]

'The king named Piṅgalaka.' This is the Nandaka Peta Story. How did it originate?

After a lapse of two hundred years from the Teacher's Parinibbāna[1] there was in the realm of Suraṭṭha[2] a king named Piṅgala. His general, named Nandaka, was of wrong view and perverted outlook and went around professing the misconception that 'There is no such thing as alms . . .'[3] and so on. His daughter, named Uttarā, was a layfollower and had been given (in marriage) to a suitable family. Now when Nandaka died he arose as a vimānapeta in a huge banyan tree in the Viñjha forest.[4] At his death Uttarā gave to an elder in whom the āsavas were destroyed a plate full of lovely scented and tasty cakes made from junket and a water-pot that was filled with clean, cool and fragrant water and dedicated them saying, 'May this donation be of benefit to my father.' By means of that gift there appeared to him heavenly water and an unlimited quantity of cakes. When he saw these he thought, 'I surely did a wicked deed in making the people adopt the misconception that "There is no such thing as alms . . ." and so on. However king Piṅgala has now gone to give advice to king Dhammāsoka[5] and will return when he has given this to him. Well then, I had better dispel that natthika view.' Not long afterwards, as king Piṅgala was going along the road, returning after having given advice to king Dhammāsoka, [**245**] the peta brought it about that the road led towards his dwelling place. The king went along that road about noon. As he went along the road before him could be seen but behind him it disappeared. When the man who was hindmost of all saw the road had disappeared he was frightened and, crying out in distress,[6] ran and informed the king. When he heard this the king, frightened and his heart agitated, stood on the back of his elephant surveying the four directions. When he saw the peta's banyan tree dwelling he went towards it accompanied by the four divisions[7] of his army. When in due course the king reached that place the peta, all decorated and adorned, approached the king and extended him a friendly greeting and had cakes and water served to him. The king and his servants bathed, ate the cakes and drank the water and when his fatigue from the journey had subsided[8] he asked the peta, 'Are you a devatā, a gandhabba?' and so on.[9] When the peta had told him his story right from the beginning and had rid the king of his wrong outlook he established him in the Refuges and the Precepts. To illustrate this those rehearsing the texts uttered these verses:

1 'The king named Piṅgalaka, who was ruler of the Suraṭṭha people,

was returning once more to Suraṭṭha after having gone in attendance on the Moriyas.[10]

2 In the noonday heat the king came upon a mire and saw a delightful road, that peta's sandy path.[11]

3 The king addressed his coachman saying, "This road is delightful, peaceful, safe and augurs well – coachman, let us go along this from here to the vicinity of the Suraṭṭhas."[12]

4 The Soraṭṭha set out this way together with the four divisions of his army. A man who appeared flurried[13] said this to the Soraṭṭha,

5 **[246]** "We have taken a wrong path that is dreadful and hair-raising – in front the road can be seen but behind it is not to be seen.

6 We have taken a wrong path into company with Yama's men; a non-human stench blows and a frightful wailing is to be heard."

7 The Soraṭṭha king, agitated, said this to his coachman, "We have taken a wrong path that is dreadful and hair-raising – in front the road can be seen but behind it is not to be seen.

8 We have taken a wrong path into company with Yama's men; a non-human stench blows and a frightful wailing is to be heard."

9 He climbed onto an elephant's back and, surveying the four directions, he saw a banyan tree, a "leg-drinker", that was full of shade, similar in appearance to a black cloud, resembling the majesty of a thunder cloud.[14]

10 The king addressed his coachman saying, "What is this huge thing that is seen, similar in appearance to a black cloud, resembling the majesty of a thunder cloud?"

11 "It is a banyan, great king, a 'leg-drinker', that is full of shade, similar in appearance to a black cloud, resembling the majesty of a thunder cloud."

12 The Soraṭṭha set out in the direction in which that huge thing was seen, similar in appearance to a black cloud, resembling the majesty of a thunder cloud.

13 The king got down from the elephant's back and went towards the tree and sat down at the foot of the tree together with his adviser and attendants and saw a full water-pot and some delicious cakes.

14 A man with the appearance of a deva, all decorated and adorned, approached and said this to the Soraṭṭha king,

15 "You are welcome, great king, you are truly not ill-come;[15] drink the water, your majesty, and eat the cakes, O tamer of your enemies."

16 The king together with his adviser and attendants drank the water and ate the cakes; after drinking the Soraṭṭha said this,

17 [247] "Are you a devatā, a gandhabba or Sakka Purindada?[16] Not recognising you we ask you how we might recognise you."

18 "I am no deva, nor gandhabba, nor even Sakka Purindada[17] – I am a peta, great king, come here from Suraṭṭha."

19 "What was your behaviour, what your conduct, when formerly in Suraṭṭha – by means of what Brahmafaring comes this majesty of yours?"

20 "Hear this, great king, O tamer of your enemies and extender of the realm, and also you advisers, attendants and that brahmin, that chief priest:

21 I am of Suraṭṭha, your majesty, and was a man with a wicked mind, being of wrong views and badly behaved, miserly and abusive.

22 I had the habit of obstructing many people who were giving and performing – whilst others were giving I acted as an obstacle (saying),

23 'There is no result from giving; from where would come the fruit of self-restraint? There is indeed no Teacher, so who will tame the untamed?

24 All beings are exactly the same – why then honour one's superiors? There is no power or effort, so what is the use of man's exertion?

25 There is indeed no fruit from giving – one bearing hostility cannot be cleansed; the mortal gets what is his to get through the vicissitudes of fate.[18]

26 There is neither mother, father nor brother; there is no world beyond this one. There is no given, there is no sacrificial offering – nothing well laid down is known.

27 If one should kill a man or cut off another's head it is not a case of someone killing somebody – (a sword has only penetrated) into the interval between seven (elementary substances).[19]

28 Indestructible and indivisible is the soul; it is octagonal, or spherical like a ball, and five hundred yojanas (high) – who is then capable of destroying the soul?

29 [248] Just as a ball of thread when cast forth runs on unwinding itself, even so in that same way does the soul run on unwinding itself.

30 Just as one leaves one village and enters another village, even so in that same way does the soul enter another body.

31 Just as one leaves one house and enters another house, even so in that same way does the soul enter another body.

32 For eighty-four hundred thousand great aeons both the foolish and the wise are cast about in saṃsāra before they make an end of misery.[20]

33 Happiness and misery are measured by the doṇa and the basket; the Conqueror knows all whilst other people are bewildered.'

34 I was in the past of such a view;[21] I was bewildered and enveloped by delusion, being of wrong views and badly behaved, miserly and abusive.

35 This side of six months will come my death and down to the exceedingly severe and terrible hell will I fall.

36 Four-cornered and with four gates, it is divided into equal portions, encircled by an iron wall, with a roof of iron above.

37 Its incandescent floor is made of glowing iron; all around a hundred yojanas it spreads, forever standing.

38 After a hundred thousand years a sound is straightway heard – this is a lakkha,[22] great king, after one hundredth of a koṭi of years.

39 For a hundred thousand koṭis people who are of wrong views, who are badly behaved and who are scoffers at the ariyans are boiled in hell.

40 There for a long time I will experience painful feelings as the fruit of my wicked deeds – for this reason I am exceedingly sorrowful.

41 [249] Hear this, great king, O tamer of your enemies and extender of the realm, my blessings be to you. I have a daughter Uttarā, great king,

42 Who does auspicious deeds and who is devoted to the Precepts and Uposatha, restrained, open-handed, affable and unselfish.

43 She undertakes the Precepts unbroken and is a daughter-in-law to those of another family. She is a layfollower of the Sakyan Sage, the Buddha, the Glorious One.

44 A monk endowed with virtue, with downcast eyes, possessing mindfulness, his (sense-)doors guarded, well controlled, entered the village in search of alms on an uninterrupted almsround and came to her dwelling.

45 My blessings be to you, great king. When Uttarā saw him she gave him a full water-pot and some delicious cakes saying, 'My father has died, sir; may this be of benefit to him.'

46 Immediately she dedicated this the result came into being – I enjoy the gratification of all my desires just like king Vessavaṇa.[23]

47 Hear this, great king, O tamer of your enemies and extender of the realm – you, O tamer of your enemies, and your family should go for refuge to the Buddha, the Buddha who in this world together with its devas is pronounced supreme.[24]

48 You, O tamer of your enemies, and your family should go for refuge to the Dhamma, the eightfold path by means of which they reach the Deathless.[25]

49 You, O tamer of your enemies, and your family should go for refuge to the Saṅgha, the four who have entered on the paths and the four who stand in their fruition,[26] this being the Saṅgha of the upright who are settled in virtue and insight.

50 You should forthwith refrain from destroying living beings and shun in this world what is not given; **[250]** you should not be one to drink intoxicating drinks nor should you speak a lie, whilst you should be content with your own wife."

51 "You desire my good, yakkha, you desire my welfare, devatā; I will do what you say – you are my teacher.

52 I will go for refuge to the Buddha, to the Dhamma and I will also go for refuge to the unsurpassed Saṅgha for deva and man.

53 I will forthwith refrain from destroying living beings and shun in this world what is not given; I will not be one to drink intoxicating drinks nor will I speak a lie and I will be content with my own wife.

54 I will shake off, as into a strong wind or into a swiftly flowing river, I will reject that wicked view, being devoted to the Teaching of the Buddhas."

55 When the Soraṭṭha had said this, he renounced his wicked outlook, paid homage to the Lord and climbed into his carriage facing east.'[27]

1 Herein *the king named Piṅgalaka, who was ruler of the Suraṭṭha people (rājā Piṅgalako nāma Suraṭṭhānaṃ adhipati ahu)*: the king who was lord of the region of Suraṭṭha was commonly known by the name of Piṅgala due to the redness (*piṅgala*) of his eyes. *On the Moriyas (Moriyānaṃ)*: on the Moriyan kings; it is said with reference to Dhammāsoka. *Was returning once more to Suraṭṭha (Suraṭṭhaṃ punar*[28] *āgamā)*: he was returning on the road leading to Suraṭṭha, in the direction of the realm of Suraṭṭha.
2 *A mire (puṅkaṃ)*: soft ground. *Sandy path (vaṇṇupathaṃ)*: the road the peta had created over that soft ground.
3 *Peaceful (khemo)*: free of danger. *Safe (sovatthiko)*: providing a state of security. *Augurs well (sivo)*: free of misfortune.[29] *From here to the vicinity of the Suraṭṭhas (Suraṭṭhānaṃ santike ito)*: going along this road we (will come) quite near to the realm of Suraṭṭha.
4 *The Soraṭṭha (Soraṭṭho)*: the ruler of Suraṭṭha. *Who appeared flurried (ubbiggarūpo)*: who was in a terrified state.
5 *Dreadful (bhiṃsanaṃ)*: **[251]** causes fear. *Hair-raising (lomahaṃsanaṃ)*: causes the hair to bristle on account of its dreadful nature.[30]
6 *Into company with Yama's men (Yamapurisānaṃ santike)*: we are faring amidst the petas. *A non-human stench blows (amānuso vāyati gandho)*: the bodily stench of the petas blows. *A frightful wailing is to be*

heard (ghoso sūyati dāruṇo): a more terrible sound is to be heard (only) from the creatures who are being punished in the separate hells.

9 *A 'leg-drinker' (pādapaṃ)*: this tree has acquired the name 'leg-drinker' through drinking water through the fibres of its roots which resemble legs. *That was full of shade: chāyāsampannaṃ=sampannaṃ chāyaṃ* (resolution of compound). *Similar in appearance to a black cloud (nīlabbhavaṇṇasadisaṃ)*: similar to a black cloud in appearance. *Resembling the majesty of a thunder cloud (meghavaṇṇasirī nibhaṃ)*: seeming to have taken the shape and colour of a cloud.

13 *A full water-pot (pūraṃ pāniyakarakaṃ)*: a water vessel filled with water. *Some cakes (pūve)*: some hard food. *Delicious (citte)*: he saw some delightful,[31] sweet and pleasing cakes set out on, and filling, the plates that were everywhere.

15 *You are truly not ill-come (atho te adurāgataṃ)*: 'truly' (*atho*) is here a mere particle or is used for the sake of emphasis. We accept that in coming, great king, you are not ill-come and that, moreover, you are quite welcome – this is the meaning. *O tamer of your enemies (arindama)*: you whose nature is the taming of your enemies.

20 *Your advisers and attendants (amaccā pārisajjā)*: let your advisers and attendants hear what I have to say and let your brahmin, that chief priest, hear it too – this is how it should be construed.

21 *I am of Suraṭṭha (Suraṭṭhamhā ahaṃ)*: I am of the Suraṭṭha region. *Your majesty (deva)*: he is addressing the king. *Being of wrong views (micchādiṭṭhī)*: with his outlook perverted by the natthika view. *Badly behaved (dussīlo)*: lacking morality. *Miserly (kadariyo)*: extremely mean. *Abusive (paribhāsako)*: insulting to recluses and brahmins.

22 *I had the habit of obstructing: vārayissaṃ=vāremi* (alternative grammatical form); *I acted as an obstacle (antarāyakaro ahaṃ)*: I acted as an obstacle to those who were giving alms and performing services and whilst others were giving alms for others I had the habit of obstructing many people in performing those meritorious deeds consisting in giving[32] – this is how it should be construed. 'There is no result from giving' and so on is an indication of the form his obstruction took.

23 Herein *there is no result from giving (vipāko n'atthi dānassa)*: [252] he rejects any result saying, 'There is no result for him through giving those alms, no fruit to be gained in the future.' *From where would come the fruit of self-restraint? (saṃyamassa kuto phalaṃ)*: now from where indeed would come the fruit of morality? There is absolutely none whatsoever – this is the meaning. *There is indeed no Teacher (n'atthi ācariyo nāma)*: there is indeed no one who is a Teacher giving precepts as to behaviour and conduct, for beings are either tamed or untamed according

to their nature alone – this is the meaning. For this reason he said, 'So who will tame the untamed?'

24 *All beings are exactly the same (samatulyāni bhūtāni)*: these beings are all equal to one another. Therefore there are none who are superior – why then honour one's superiors? There is indeed no merit from honouring one's superiors – this is the meaning. *There is no power (n' atthi balaṃ)*: he rejects the effort and power of those beings who, relying on their own power, make an effort and bring about anything from worldly[33] prosperity and so on up to attainment of the excellence of arahantship. There is no (power) or effort[34] *so what is the use of man's exertion? (kuto uṭṭhānaporisaṃ)*: it does not result through man's effort, through what a man does – this is said thus in repudiation of the doctrine of (causal) result.[35]

25 *There is indeed no fruit from giving (n' atthi dānaphalaṃ nāma)*: there is indeed no such thing as fruit from giving, meaning giving away merit-offerings is just as fruitless as if one had thrown them into the ashes. *One bearing hostility cannot be cleansed (na visodheti verinaṃ)*: here *one bearing hostility: verinaṃ=veravantaṃ* (alternative grammatical form); the person who has done a wicked deed out of hostility by way of destroying living beings and so on cannot be cleansed, is never made pure, by observances[36] such as giving and morality and so on. 'There is no result from giving' and so on should be regarded as an indication of the manner in which he obstructed others in giving alms and so on, whereas 'There is indeed no fruit from giving' and so forth as an indication of his adherence to wrong (views). *What is his to get: laddheyyaṃ=laddhabbaṃ* (alternative grammatical form). But (how does he get) what is his to get? He said, *through the vicissitudes of fate (niyati pariṇāmajaṃ)*: the creature getting either happiness or misery gets this merely through a change in his fate[37] and not on account of his having done[38] some deed nor on account of a Supreme Deity[39] and so on – this is the meaning.

26 **[253]** *There is neither mother, father nor brother (n' atthi mātā pitā bhātā)*: he speaks with reference to the absence of any fruit from either right or wrong conduct towards one's mother and so on. *There is no world beyond this one (loko n' atthi ito paraṃ)*: there is indeed no such thing as a world beyond this one, beyond this world here. Beings are annihilated right then and there – this is the meaning. *Given (dinnaṃ)*: a great almsgiving. *Sacrificial offering (hutaṃ)*: worshipping with a gift of food;[40] he rejects them both (saying), 'There is no' with reference to the absence of any fruit (from them). *Well laid down: sunihitaṃ=suṭṭhu nihitaṃ* (resolution of compound). *Nothing is known (na vijjati)*: those alms for recluses and brahmins which they call 'that which will follow one as a foundation in

the next world'[41] is not known; it is just a mere figure of speech of theirs – this is the meaning.

27 *It is not a case of someone killing somebody (na koci kiñci hanati)*: if a man should kill another man, should cut off the head of another man, it is not, in the ultimate sense, a case of someone killing somebody – it only looks like killing due to the existence of gaps[42] (between) the seven elementary substances. But what about being struck by a sword? He said, *into the interval between the seven (sattannaṃ vivaraṃ antare)*: the sword enters the gap,[43] that is, the interval, between the seven elementary substances such as earth and so on. For this reason it looks like beings are struck with swords and so on. Like the soul the rest of the elementary substances also cannot be destroyed on account of their permanent nature – this is the meaning.

28 *Indestructible and indivisible is the soul (acchejjabhejjo jīvo)*: the soul of beings is not to be destroyed by swords and so on on account of its permanent nature. *It is octagonal, or spherical like a ball (aṭṭhaṃso guḷaparimaṇḍalo)*: the soul is sometimes octagonal, sometimes spherical like a ball. *And five hundred yojanas (yojanāni satā pañca)*: on attaining its fully accomplished state it is five hundred yojanas in height. *Who then is capable of destroying the soul? (ko jīvaṃ chetuṃ arahati)*: who indeed is capable of destroying with swords and so on a permanent and immutable soul? He is saying that it could not be harmed by anyone.

29 *A ball of thread (suttaguḷe)*:[44] a ball of thread is made when it is wound up. *When cast forth (khitte)*: when cast forth by way of unwinding it. *Runs on unwinding itself (nibbeṭhentaṃ palāyati)*: a ball of thread cast forth, unwinding itself, from a mountain or a tree top [254] just goes on unwinding itself, ceasing to go on when the thread comes to an end.[45] *Even so in that same way (evaṃ evaṃ)*:[46] just as that ball of thread goes on unwinding itself, ceasing to go on when the thread comes to an end, even so in that same way does the soul run on, continue, unwinding its ball of (saṃsāric) existence[47] for just the time stated, for eighty-four hundred thousand great aeons and ceases to continue thereafter.

30 *Even so in that same way does the soul (evaṃ eva ca so jīvo)*: just as some man leaves the village in which he dwells and then enters another village because of something he has to do, even so in that same way does the soul leave a body and enter another subsequent body in accordance with its fate – this is the meaning. *Body: bondiṃ=kāyaṃ* (synonyms).

32 *Eighty-four: cūḷāsīti=caturāsīti* (alternative grammatical form). *Great aeons: mahākappino=mahākappānaṃ* (alternative grammatical form); in this connection if once every hundred years a drop of water were to be removed with the tip of a blade of kusa grass from a great lake

such as Anotatta and so on and that by acting in this manner that lake were to be emptied of its water seven times over then that (period) would be called one great aeon. Having said this he says that the extent of (a soul's running on in) saṃsāra is eighty-four hundred thousand such great aeons. *Both the foolish and the wise (ye bālā ye ca paṇḍitā)*: both those who are blinded by folly and those who possess wisdom – all of these even.[48] *Are cast about in saṃsāra (saṃsāraṃ khepayitvāna)*: are cast about in saṃsāra, arising again and again for the aforesaid length of time. *Before they make an end of misery (dukkhass' antaṃ karissare)*: before they bring to a conclusion, bring to full cycle, the misery of the round[49] (of existences). Even the wise cannot become accomplished during this period and even the fool ceases to continue thereafter – this is his heresy.

33 *Happiness and misery are measured by the doṇa and the basket (mitāni sukhadukkhāni doṇehi piṭakehi ca)*: the vicissitudes of fate are apportioned to this and that being, they are meted out separately, during the aforesaid length of time as though the happiness and misery of beings were indeed measured by the doṇa, the basket and the māna-vessel.[50] The Conqueror knows all this, the one who stands on the plane of the Conqueror knows it in its entirety since he has crossed over saṃsāra, **[255]** whilst other people are bewildered and roam about in saṃsāra.[51]

34 *I was in the past of such a view (evaṃdiṭṭhi pure āsiṃ)*: I was formerly of the aforesaid natthika view. *I was bewildered and enveloped by delusion (samūḷho mohapāruto)*: I was bewildered with the delusion that was caused by the aforesaid view and enveloped by the delusion that arose at the same time; the seed of skilfulness was covered up – this is the meaning. When he had thus indicated the wicked deed done by him, because of the wicked view that had occurred to him in the past he then uttered (the verses) beginning: 'This side of six months' indicating its fruit that he would have to undergo in the future.

38 Herein *after a hundred thousand years: vassasatasahassāni=vassānaṃ satasahassāni* (resolution of compound); 'have passed' are the rest of the words. Or, alternatively this is the accusative case[52] with the force of the locative, meaning when a hundred thousand years have gone by. *A sound is straightway heard (ghoso sūyati tāvade)*: after such a long time has passed a proclamation is straightway, at that time, heard in that hell saying, 'The extent of time that has elapsed whilst you have been being boiled here, good sirs, is one hundred thousand years.' *This is a lakkha, great king, after one hundredth of a koṭi of years (lakkho eso mahārāja satabhāgavassakoṭiyo)*: this is a lakkha, that is, the circumscription of the span of time during which beings have been boiled in hell, great king, after one hundredth, a hundredth part, of a koṭi of years (have passed). This

is what is said: ten times ten is one hundred, ten hundreds are one thousand, ten times ten thousand is one hundred thousand and a hundred times a hundred thousand is one koṭi. By way of these koṭis, one hundred thousand koṭis of years (have passed) after one hundredth of a koṭi of years,[53] but these are to be understood as the means of counting[54] the years of those in hell only, not (those) of men or devas. The life-span of those in hell is countless such hundreds of thousands of koṭis of years. For this reason it was said, 'For a hundred thousand koṭis people are boiled in hell.' To show by means of an illustration the sorts of wicked deeds for which beings are thus boiled in the hells, 'Who are of wrong views, who are badly behaved and who are scoffers at the ariyans' was said.

40 *I will experience (vedissaṃ)*: I will undergo. Having thus indicated the fruit of his wicked deeds that he would have to undergo in the future **[256]** and having explained the matter that the king had enquired about, namely, 'By means of what Brahmafaring comes this majesty of yours?', he then uttered (the verses) beginning: 'Hear this, great king', desiring to establish him in the Refuges and the Precepts.

42 *Who is devoted to the Precepts and Uposatha (sīlesuposathe ratā)*: who delights in those Precepts that are permanently binding and those (additional) precepts observed on the Uposatha.[55]

45 *Gave him: adā=adāsi* (alternative grammatical form).

48 *The Dhamma (taṃ dhammaṃ)*: the eightfold path and the Deathless.

Roused thus by the peta into taking the Refuges and the Precepts the king, with devotion in his heart, praised him on account of the service he had rendered him and, on being established in the Refuges and so on, said the three verses beginning: 'You desire my good', after which he uttered the verse beginning: 'I will shake off', declaring his renunciation of the wicked view that he had previously held.

54 Herein *I will shake off as into a strong wind (odhunāmi mahāvāte)*: I will shake off, will cast off, that wicked view into the wind of your teaching on Dhamma, yakkha, as is chaff when a strong wind is blowing. *Or into a swiftly flowing river (nadiyā vā sīghaṃ gāmiyā)*: or I will cause that wicked view to be swept away as are grass, twigs and fallen[56] leaves in the swift current[57] of a great river – this is the meaning. *I will reject that wicked view (vamāmi pāpakaṃ diṭṭhiṃ)*: I will cast up[58] that wicked view that has been foremost in my mind. He gave his reason for this: *Being devoted to the Teaching of the Buddhas (Buddhānaṃ sāsane rato)*: since I am devoted to the Teaching of the Buddhas, the Lords, that brings one for certain to the Deathless, I will therefore reject this poison known as (wrong) view – this is how it should be construed. Those rehearsing the

texts then inserted[59] the concluding verse (beginning:) 'When (the Soraṭṭha) had said this'.

55 Herein *facing east (pāmokkho)*: heading towards the eastern quarter. *Climbed into his carriage (rathaṃ āruyhi)*: the king mounted his carriage which was ready to leave. He climbed into it and through the majesty of that yakkha reached his city that very same day and entered the royal dwelling. In due course he raised the issue with the monks [257] who in turn raised it with the elders. The elders included it in the rehearsal at the Third Council.

[1] Reading parinibbānato with Se Be for text's parinibbhānato.

[2] Literally the good, or happy, kingdom and identified with modern Kathiawad; cp DPPN ii 1253.

[3] This is the opening phrase of the stock passage summarising wrong view, such a view being attributed at D i 55 to Ajita Kesakambalī where the passage is to be found in full; cp PvA 99 above.

[4] Viñjhāṭavī, the forest, aṭavī, of the Vindhya hills; cp PvA 43, 192. DPPN ii 874, following Mhv xix 6 and Dpv xiv 2, states that through these hills lay the road on which Asoka travelled on his way from Pāṭaliputta (modern Patna) to the port of Tāmalitti (modern Tāmluk on the west bank of the Hooghly near Calcutta) from where the Bodhi tree was to be sent to Laṅkā. However it is usual to understand by the Vindhyas the range of hills in the Indore-Ujjain-Bhopal area of Madhya Pradesh which separated the Āryan north from the Dravidian plateau to the south (and a Dravidian origin is suspected for aṭavī, cp PED sv). There is nothing in the passages of this text in which these hills appear to suggest that they are any other than these latter Vindhyas; indeed it would be expected that Piṅgala would have had to cross these on his return from Pāṭaliputta to Suraṭṭha, identified with Surāṣṭra 'which denoted the modern Kāthiāwār. In its widest denotation the term included the whole of Kāthiāwār, in its narrowest only the southern part of Kāthiāwār, known as Sorath', Hasmukh D. Sankalia, *The Archeology of Gujerat*, Bombay 1941, p. 5; cp A. S. Altekar, 'A History of Important Ancient Towns and Cities in Gujerat and Kathiawad', *Indian Antiquary*, Supplement to Vol. 54, 1925. Moreover since it is probable that the whole of Gujerat came under Mauryan sway, as the presence of many Asokan edicts suggests (Sankalia, p. 7), it would have been quite possible that Piṅgala might have had to visit the Mauryan capital as recorded in this story. This raises the problem as to how the Sinhalese chroniclers came to believe that Asoka, having despatched the Bodhi tree down the Ganges to Tāmalitti, crossed the Vindhyas on his overland journey to that port, surely a somewhat circuitous route. It is possible that the chroniclers have conflated what were originally two separate legends, one of which implying that the Bodhi tree was despatched by the more probable route from a port on the west coast.

[5] The famous Asoka (268–231 BC) of Indian history who in his later life came to be called Dhammāsoka on account of his pious deeds (Mhv v 189; cp DPPN i 216–219).

[6] Reading vissaraṃ with Se Be for text's visaraṃ.

[7] Elephants, cavalry, chariots and infantry – see Vin iv 104f.; cp M ii 69.

[8] Reading paṭippassaddhamaggakilamatho with Se Be for text's paṭipassaddha-.

[9] v 17 below.

[10] Skt Mauryas.

[11] Reading vaṇṇupathaṃ with Be for text's vaṇṇapathaṃ; cp PED sv vaṇṇu and

Stories of the Mansions, p. 148 n. 2. The cty on J i 109 similarly states vaṇṇu vuccati vālukā, vālukāmagge ti attho. Se reads vaṇṇanāpathaṃ.

[12] Text should be amended to read, with Se Be, so that v 3 ends with ito, v 4 beginning with Tena and ending with abravi.

[13] ubbiggarūpo; PED sv ubbigga refers to Th 1, 408, apparently an error for Th 2, 408.

[14] Reading meghavaṇṇasirī nibhaṃ with Se Be for text's meghavaṇṇasirannibhaṃ both here and in the verses that follow.

[15] adurāgataṃ; Gehman has mistakenly analysed this as adura + āgataṃ which is in keeping with neither the context nor the cty; it is to be understood rather as a + dur + āgataṃ.

[16] An epithet of Sakka (Indra), usually taken as 'Breaker of the Fortress' (cp Vedic Puraṃdara applied to Indra). The verse recurs at Vv 62[2] and is rendered in Stories of the Mansions as 'bounteous giver'. At VvA 171 Dhammapāla takes it as being derived from pure dānaṃ dadāti, who gave gifts in the past. See also the interesting discussion at MLS ii 52 n. 5 and cp PvA 118f.

[17] cp Vv 62[3].

[18] Reading niyati with Se Be for text's nīyati.

[19] In detail at D i 56.

[20] Reading dukkhass' antaṃ karissare with v 32; v 33 should then begin with Mitāni, whilst v 34 with Evaṃdiṭṭhi, in accordance with Se Be.

[21] Though Mrs Rhys Davids felt unable to assign the views depicted in these verses (Stories of the Departed, p. 95 n. 1), a comparison with the details given at D i 52–59 may suggest that the views expressed in vv 24, 32 and 29 are those of Makkhali Gosāla (D i 53f.), in vv 26–27 those of Ajita Kesakambalī (D i 55f.) and in v 23 that of Pūraṇa Kassapa (D i 52f.). The rest is more difficult. That some wanderers held views similar to those of v 28 may be seen from the Jaina Sūtrakṛtāṅga II 1 15 (SBE xlv 340). The views found in v 25 remind one of the extreme fatalism attributed to Makkhali Gosāla – see A. L. Basham, *History and Doctrines of the Ajivikas*, London 1951, especially Chapter 2. There is also a note of fatalism about v 33 though reference to an omniscient Conqueror (Jina) suggests the Jainas. It must be the reference to the soul (jīva) that renders the views of vv 30–31 unacceptable since it is precisely these similes (but without any mention of a soul) that are elsewhere used by the Buddha to describe the rebirth process (D i 81, 83).

[22] The lakkha (lac) is usually reckoned at 100,000 and the koṭi (crore) at 10,000,000.

[23] Another name for Kubera, one of the Four Great Kings and sovereign of the yakkhas; cp I 3[3] where this was said to be characteristic of yakkhas.

[24] Cp A ii 17.

[25] amataṃ padaṃ; cp S i 212, ii 280; A ii 51.

[26] The paths and fruits of the four classes of sāvaka: the sotāpanna, sakadāgāmin (once-returner), anāgāmin (non-returner) and arahant; this is an abridged form of the stock paragraph describing the sāvakasaṅgha – see e.g. D iii 227; M i 37; S ii 69f.; A i 222. The sāvakasaṅgha was not identical with the bhikkhusaṅgha, or order of monks, for the former included many laymen and devas and only those monks who belonged to one or other of the four classes. Of saṅghas the Tathāgata's sāvakasaṅgha is reckoned the best, aggaṃ, just as it is this saṅgha that is alone the world's unsurpassed merit-field (It 88).

[27] pāmokkho, mis-spelt pāmokho at Stories of the Departed, p. 97 n. 1. See cty below; it must be assumed he was merely looking in this direction since he was travelling more or less due west.

[28] So verse, Se Be; text mis-spells punam here.

[29] Reading anupaddavo with Se Be for text's anuppaddavo.

[30] Reading bhiṃsanakabhāvena lomānaṃ haṃsāpanaṃ with Se Be for text's bhīsanabhāvena lomānaṃ haṃsanaṃ.

[31] Reading vittijanane with Se Be for text's cittijanane.

[32] Text wrongly punctuates here, beginning a new sentence with dānamayapuññato.

[33] manussa-, literally human but here opposed to the spiritual.

[34] Be reads this as part of the lemma that follows but this does not strictly accord with the verse. Se and text read it as part of the preceding comment. It would seem to make the most sense if it introduces, but is not actually part of, the lemma that follows, as adopted here.

[35] pavattavāda-.

[36] Reading vatato with Se Be for text's vātato.

[37] Reading niyativipariṇāmavasen' eva with Be for text's nīyati pariṇāmavasena (Se niyati parināmajavesena).

[38] Reading katattā with Se Be for text's katāya.

[39] See A i 173ff. where there is a discussion of these three alternatives; at M ii 214ff. the second of these is attributed to the Jainas.

[40] Reading pahenaka- with Se Be for text's pahonaka-; see Childers and BHSD sv prahenaka.

[41] Cp PvA 132.

[42] Reading chiddabhāvato with Se Be for text's chinda-.

[43] Reading chidde with Se Be for text's chinde; cp DA 167 on D i 56.

[44] Text omits ti after suttaguḷe.

[45] sutte khīṇe na gacchati, so Se Be; text omits.

[46] So all texts though this does not accord with the verse. Se reads evaṃ evam pi in vv 29, 30 and 31 whilst Be evam eva ca in all three. Text, however, reads evam eva ca in vv 29–30 but evam eva pi in v 31.

[47] attabhāvaguḷaṃ.

[48] Text is poorly punctuated here and should follow Se Be by beginning a new sentence with Saṃsāraṃ khepayitvāna.

[49] Reading vaṭṭadukkhassa with Se Be for text's vaddha-. In her forward to the 1974 edition of Stories of the Departed (p. iv) Miss Horner remarks that ' "cycle of transmigration" would hardly be accepted now for saṃsāra'. Whilst this may be so in a Buddhist context, it might still be thought to apply here since we are dealing, in both the verse and its cty, with what was clearly regarded as the heretical view of a contemporary rival – indeed it was no doubt partly its viewing saṃsāra as a cycle that rendered it unacceptable.

[50] The doṇa, basket and māna were all measures of rice and other grains whose exact values are uncertain.

[51] Reading saṃsāre . . . pajā with this sentence.

[52] Text wrongly inserts a full stop after vacanaṃ.

[53] It seems Dhammapāla misunderstood vv 38–39 and inferred that the lakkha (100,000 years = one hundredth of the koṭi, 10,000,000), whose passage is marked by a proclamation to this effect, was numerically equivalent to the 100,000 koṭis (or 10,000,000,000,000) of years during which beings are boiled in hell. He therefore felt the need, unnecessarily, to explain how koṭis in hell differ from those on earth. The verses, however, say no more than that after each hundredth part of a koṭi, that is, after one lakkha, a proclamation is made to the effect that one lakkha has passed and that beings in hell are boiled for in all 100,000 koṭis. They would thus hear such a proclamation one hundred times during each of these 100,000 koṭis, that is, 10,000,000 times.

[54] Reading vassagaṇanāvasena with Se Be for text's -gaṇana-.

[55] That is, the usual five, plus not eating after midday, abstaining from dancing, singing and music shows and the use of garlands and scent and so on and the use of luxurious beds; see A iv 248ff.

[56] Reading -paṇṇakasaṭaṃ with Se Be for text's paṇṇakasalaṃ.

[57] Reading sīghasotāya with Se Be for text's sīghaṃ sotāya.

[58] Reading ucchaḍḍayāmi (not listed by PED) with Se Be for text's uḍḍayāmi chaḍḍayāmi.

[59] At PvA 245 above it was stated that all the verses originated with those rehearsing the texts.

IV.4 EXPOSITION OF THE REVATĪ PETA STORY
[Revatipetavatthuvaṇṇanā]

'Rise up, Revatī of very evil character.' This is the Revatī Peta Story.

Since there is no difference between this and the Revatī Mansion Story,[1] what was to be said here with respect to the arisen need and to the verses is therefore to be understood exactly as has already been given in the Exposition of the Mansion Stories (section) of this Elucidation of the Intrinsic Meaning. It is to be regarded as being included in the text of the Mansion Stories on account of the devaputta Nandiya and as being included also in this text as the Revatī Peta Story on account of the verses which are connected with Revatī.

[1] Vv 52; Stories of the Mansions pp. 103–107.

IV.5 EXPOSITION OF THE SUGAR-CANE PETA STORY
[Ucchupetavatthuvaṇṇanā]

'This great grove of sugar-cane of mine.' This is the Sugar-cane Peta Story. How did it originate?

When the Lord was staying in the Bamboo Grove a certain man put a bundle of sugar-cane on his shoulder and went along chewing one sugar-cane. Now a certain layfollower who was virtuous and of a lovely character was going along close behind him with his young child. The child saw the sugar-cane and cried out, 'Give me some!' The layfollower saw the child crying and, catching that man up, tried to make conversation with him. But the man would not converse with him at all, nor would he give the child even a piece of his sugar-cane on account of his ill will.[1] The layfollower pointed to his child and said, 'This child is weeping excessively. Please give him a piece of sugar-cane.' When he heard this the man, unable to bear this, became contemptuous and disrespectfully tossed a stick of sugar-cane behind him. He died in due course and arose amongst the petas on account of his having long been permeated with greed. The fruit [258] of this was indeed in accordance with that deed for there arose for him a great grove of sugar-cane that was thickly covered with jet-black sugar-cane the size of a pestle and that (extended over) an area of as much as eight karīsas.[2] But as soon as he approached it desiring to chew some thinking, 'I will take some sugar-cane', that sugar-cane would strike him on account of which he would fall down fainting. Then one day as the venerable Mahāmoggallāna was going to Rājagaha in search of alms he saw on his way that peta. When he saw the elder he asked[3] him about the deed he had done and there followed an exchange of conversation in verse between the peta and the elder.

1 'This great grove of sugar-cane of mine arose as the fruit of no small amount of meritorious deeds[4] but it is of no use to me now – tell me, sir, of what is this the result?

2 I come to grief and am devoured when I attempt, when I endeavour, to consume any of it. My strength gone[5] and suffering great hardship I wail – of what deed is this the result?

3 In distress I collapse on the ground and writhe in the heat like one that lives in water; my tears trickle down as I cry[6] – tell me, sir, of what is this the result?

4 I am famished, tired and thirsty; I am parched[7] and I do not find either comfort or ease. I ask you of this matter, good sir, how might I get to make use of this sugar-cane?'

5 [259] 'In the past you yourself did a deed – in a former birth whilst in the world of men. Now I will tell you of this matter – if you listen you will understand this matter.

6 You had set out, chewing a sugar-cane, when a man came up behind you. He spoke to you in expectation but you would not converse with him at all.

7 And you who would not speak he begged; "Please give some sugar-cane, good sir", he said to you. You gave him some sugar-cane from behind your back – it is of that deed that this is the result.

8 Look here, you may take some sugar-cane from behind; when you have taken some you can chew it as much as you like – in this way you will become pleased, joyful, elated and satisfied.'

9 He went and took some from behind; when he had taken some he

chewed it as much as he liked – in this way he became pleased, joyful, elated and satisfied.

1 Herein *of what (kissa)*: of what sort of deed – this is the meaning.
2 *I come to grief (vihaññāmi)*:[8] I meet with distress; or, alternatively *I come to grief (vihaññāmi)*: I am oppressed, meaning I am particularly crushed. *Am devoured: khajjāmi=khādiyāmi* (alternative grammatical form), meaning I am cut by the leaves of the sugar-cane as though I were being devoured with sharp sword-leaves.[9] *When I try (vāyamāmi)*: when I make an attempt to eat the sugar-cane. *When I endeavour (parisakkāmi)*: when I make an effort. *To consume (paribhuñjituṃ)*: to consume the juice of the sugar-cane, meaning to chew. *My strength gone (chinnathāmo)*: my endurance gone,[10] my strength curtailed, meaning my strength totally exhausted. **[260]** *And suffering great hardship (kapaṇo)*: in a wretched state. *I wail (lālapāmi)*: I lament extremely afflicted with misery.
3 *In distress (vighāto)*: full of distress[11] or with his strength impaired. *I collapse on the ground (paripatāmi chamāyaṃ)*: being unable to stand I fall to the ground. *Writhe (parivattāmi)*: reel. *Like one that lives in water (vāricaro va)*: like a fish. *In the heat (ghamme)*: on dry ground that is scorched by the heat.
4 *I am parched (santassito)*: very thirsty with the lips, palate and throat gone dry.[12] *Either comfort or ease (sātasukhaṃ)*: a state of comfort or ease. *I do not find (na vinde)*: I do not obtain. *You: taṃ=tuvaṃ* (alternative grammatical form).
5 *You will understand: vijāna=vijānāhi* (alternative grammatical form).
6 *Had set out (payāto)*: had begun to go along. *Came up (anvagacchi)*:[13] followed. *In expectation: paccāsanto=paccāsiṃsamāno* (alternative grammatical form).
7 *It is of that deed (tass' etaṃ kammassa)*: here *etaṃ* (untranslated) is a mere particle; it means it is of that deed.
8 *May take some from behind (piṭṭhito gaṇheyyāsi)*: may take some sugar-cane only from behind your back. *Satisfied: pamodito=pamudito* (alternative grammatical form).
9 *When he had taken some he chewed it as much as he liked (gahetvāna taṃ khādi yāva-d-atthaṃ)*: when he had taken some sugar-cane in the way suggested by the elder and had chewed it as he pleased he took a large bundle of sugar-cane and presented it to the elder. Helping him the elder had him bring it along and went to the Bamboo Grove and (the elder) gave it to the Lord. The Lord together with the order of monks then ate it and showed their appreciation. The peta, with devotion in his heart, saluted (the Lord) and left. From that time henceforward he ate sugar-cane

with ease. He died[14] in due course and arose amongst the Thirty-three.

The incident concerning this peta, however, became well known in the world of men. The people approached the Teacher and asked him about the incident. The Teacher explained the matter in detail and then taught Dhamma. When they heard this those people shrank from the stain of selfishness.

[1] dosena nāma; Se Be omit.

[2] Reading -karīsa- with Se Be and PED for text's -karisa- although PED erroneously includes this reference under karīsa[2], meaning excrement. It is rather an instance of karīsa[1], the square measure of land, the space over which one karīsa of seed could be sown. For further details see PED sv and Childers sv; also Childers sv ammaṇaṃ. Buddhadatta's *English-Pali Dictionary* gives the meaning of karīsamattaṭṭhānaṃ as acre.

[3] Reading pucchi with Be for text's Se pucchanto.

[4] Gehman's 'broad and bearing a plentiful good crop' obscures the point somewhat.

[5] Reading chinnathāmo with Se Be for text's chinnātumo; vll abound here and in the cty below.

[6] Reading rudato with Se Be for text's dūrato.

[7] santassito; not listed by PED.

[8] Se Be read haññāmi, I am thrashed, both here and in the verse but add that this means vihaññāmi here.

[9] Reading asipattasadisehi with Be for text's Se asipattasaṇṭhānasadisehi; this is an allusion to the Sword-leafed Forest – cp PvA 221.

[10] Reading chinnasaho with Se Be for text's chinnasabhāvo.

[11] Reading vighātavā with Se Be for text's vighāṭavā.

[12] Reading sosappattiyā with Se Be for text's so sampattiyā.

[13] So Se Be and verse; text reads anvāgacchi here.

[14] Literally, when he had done his (kammic) time; petas would appear not to die as such but rather fall, perhaps after the manner of devas mentioned at It 76f., and reappear elsewhere.

IV.6 EXPOSITION OF THE BOYS PETA STORY
[Kumārapetavatthuvaṇṇanā]

[261] 'The city named Sāvatthī.' The Teacher who was staying in the Jeta Grove told this concerning two petas.

It is said that in Sāvatthī the two sons of the king of Kosala were handsome and in the prime of life but that drunk with the pride of youth[1] they went with other men's wives. When they died they arose as petas in a moat and at night they would wail with a terrific[2] noise. When the people heard this they were frightened. They gave a great almsgiving to the order of monks with the Buddha at its head thinking, 'Having acted thus, this bad omen may be assuaged', and raised the issue with the Lord. The Lord said, 'Layfollowers, there is no danger[3] whatsoever (that can come) to you from hearing that noise', and then uttered these verses explaining its cause and to teach them Dhamma:

1 'The city named Sāvatthī is flanked by the Himālaya. I have heard that there were there two boys who were sons of the king.

2 Intoxicated with the enticing[4] and finding pleasure in the satisfaction of their sensual desires they hankered after their present happiness and paid no regard to the future.

3 And, fallen from the human state and gone from here to the world beyond, they now unseen bewail[5] the evil they did in the past (saying),

4 "Though many were present and the merit-offerings already prepared we were unable to do even to a limited extent that which would provide us with happiness;[6]

5 What greater evil could there be than this – that we should fall from the royal family and arise on the peta-plane afflicted with hunger and thirst?"

6 After having been rulers here they are no longer rulers there – they roam about in hunger and thirst; of lofty status whilst men they are now of the lowest.

7[7] When the disadvantage stemming from an intoxication with power is realised [262] and this intoxication with power is abandoned, a man is bound for heaven; at the breaking up of the body this wise person arises in heaven.'

1 Herein *I have heard that (iti me sutaṃ)* means not only have I seen this with my own insight for I have also[8] heard[9] that it is so through its being common knowledge in the world.

2 *Finding pleasure in the satisfaction of their sensual desires (kāmassādābhinandino)*: of a nature to find pleasure by way of satisfaction in the pleasures of the senses. *They hankered after their present happiness (paccuppannasukhe giddhā)*: they hankered after, they were greedy for, merely the happiness of the moment.[10] *Paid no regard to the future (na te passiṃsu nāgataṃ)*: they did not think of the happiness to be obtained amongst devas and men in the future, in time to come, by abandoning bad conduct and practising good conduct.

3 *They now unseen bewail (te 'dha ghosentyadissantā)*: those petas who formerly were sons of the king now invisibly bewail, weep, close to Sāvatthī. What were they weeping about? He said, 'The evil they did in

the past'. Then to show by means of an analysis in terms of cause and effect[11] the reason for this weeping of theirs (the verse) beginning: 'Though many were present' was said.

4 Herein *though many were present (bahūsu vata santesu)*: though many worthy of donations were to be found. *And the merit-offerings already prepared (deyyadhamme upaṭṭhite)*: and their own property that was suitable to be given as merit-offerings was to hand, meaning it was available. *Even to a limited extent that which would provide us with happiness (parittaṃ sukhāvahaṃ)*: we were unable to act, alas, towards our own safety, our own security, having done not even the slightest meritorious deed which would provide us with happiness in the future – this is how it should be construed.

5 *What greater evil could there be than this? (kiṃ tato pāpakaṃ assa)*: what else could be, could possibly be, more evil, more despicable, than this? *That we should fall from the royal family (yan no rājakulā cutā)* means that we should fall on account of those wicked deeds from the royal family and now arise on the peta-plane, arise amongst the petas, and wander about afflicted with hunger and thirst.

6 *After having been rulers here (sāmino idha hutvāna)*: they roam about here in this world, in the very same place in which they were formerly rulers, (but) they are no longer rulers[12] there,[13] in that very same place. *Of lofty status whilst men, they are now of the lowest (manussā unnatonatā)*: (though) they were rulers at the time they were men they are now, after death, **[263]** of the lowest and roam about in hunger and thirst on account of their deeds – behold the nature of saṃsāra that is indicated.

7 *When the disadvantage stemming from an intoxication with power is realised (etaṃ ādīnavaṃ ñatvā issaramadasambhavaṃ)*: when the disadvantage, the fault, that stems from an intoxication with authority – namely arising in a state of woe – is realised and this intoxication with power is abandoned, meritorious deeds will be pursued. *A man is bound for heaven (bhave saggagato naro)*: he should be bound solely for heaven, for the devaloka.

When the Teacher had thus explained the issue of those petas and had had the almsgiving that those people had performed dedicated to those petas he taught Dhamma suiting the dispositions[14] of the company assembled there. That teaching was of benefit to those people.

[1] Reading yobbanamadamattā with Se Be for text's yobha-.
[2] bheravena; see PvA 152.

[3] Not 'you will not have any end of hearing that noise' as Gehman suggests, whilst his rendering of the verses that follow is also at fault.

[4] Reading sammattā rajanīyesu with Be for text's pamattā rajaniyesu (Se pamattā rajanīyesu); cp cty on III 7[1].

[5] Reading ghosentyadissantā with Se Be for text's ghosenti na dissanto.

[6] Reading parittaṃ kātuṃ sukhāvahaṃ with Se Be for text's sotthi kātuṃ parittasukhāvahaṃ.

[7] Text erroneously gives this verse the number 9.

[8] Reading na kevalaṃ . . . atha kho with Se Be for text's na kevalaṃ . . . ettha kho.

[9] Reading sutaṃ with Se Be for text's suttaṃ.

[10] Reading vattamānasukhamatte with Se Be for text's vaḍḍha-.

[11] phalato, literally, fruition.

[12] Reading assāmino with Se Be for text's assamikā.

[13] Reading tahiṃ tasmiṃ with Se Be for text's Tahin ti tasmiṃ.

[14] Not 'as was his will' as Gehman suggests.

IV.7 EXPOSITION OF THE KING'S SON PETA STORY [Rājaputtapetavatthuvaṇṇanā]

'Of deeds done in the past.' The Teacher who was staying in the Jeta Grove told this concerning a peta who had been the son of a king. In this connection he who had long ago been the son of a king named Kitava and who had long ago offended a Paccekabuddha arose amongst the petas as a residual effect of that same deed for which he had already been boiled in hell for many thousands of years and it is he who is here meant by 'the peta who had been the son of a king'. His story is exactly as that already given in detail above in the Sānuvāsin Peta Story[1] and should therefore be taken in the same way that it was given there. As the elder was explaining the issue to his peta-relatives the Teacher said, 'This is not only the case with your relations for you too were a peta in your immediately preceding[2] existence and suffered great misery', and at his request related this King's Son Peta Story:

1 'The result of deeds done in the past would disturb the mind as regards sight, sound, taste, smell and touch,[3] (all) pleasing to the mind.

2 When he had enjoyed dancing, singing, pleasure and merriment to no small extent, he amused himself in the park. As he entered Giribbaja,

3 [264] He saw the rishi Sunetta, tamed of self and concentrated, with few needs, possessing modesty and delighting in whatever came into his almsbowl.

4 He got down from the elephant's back and said, "Did you get anything, sir?" That kṣatriya then snatched his bowl and held it above him,

5 And broke the bowl on the hard ground and then went away laughing saying, "I am the son of king Kitava – what can you do to me, you beggar?"[4]

6 The result of that cruel deed which the king's son experienced whilst confined to hell was severe:

7 For six times eighty-four nahutas of years that wrong-doer underwent intense misery in hell;

8 He was boiled[5] lying face upwards and face downwards, on his left and right (sides); feet uppermost and just standing, that fool was boiled[5] for a long time.

9 For many nahutas and for many thousands of years besides that wrong-doer underwent intense misery in hell.

10 Such is the severity for those who harm the faultless ones – those doing wicked deeds (such as) insulting a devout rishi are boiled.

11 He experienced much misery there for many years and when he fell from there he was a peta truly smitten by hunger and thirst.[6]

12 When the disadvantage stemming from an intoxication with power is realised and this intoxication with power is abandoned one should act with humility.

13 He who is full of respect for the Buddhas is in this very life to be praised and at the breaking up of the body this wise person arises in heaven.'

1 Herein *the result of deeds done in the past would disturb the mind (pubbe katānaṃ kammānaṃ vipāko matthaye manam)*: when the fruit of unskilled deeds done in former lives arises and is physically actualised[7] it would disturb, it would overwhelm, the mind of those blinded by folly; they would promote their own good fortune by way of causing misfortune to others – this is the meaning.[**265**] Now it was to illustrate the range of this disturbance of mind that 'as regards sight, sound' and so on was said. Herein *as regards sight (rūpe)*: in the matter of sight, meaning with respect to the acquisition,[8] as desired,[9] of objects of sight that are charming.[10] *As regards sound (sadde)* and so on: the same is also to be applied to these. He then explained in particular (terms) the matter on which he had (so far only) spoken in general (terms) and uttered (the verse) beginning: '(When he had enjoyed) dancing, singing' illustrating this.

2 Herein *pleasure (ratiṃ)*: sensual pleasure. *Merriment (khiddaṃ)*:[11] sporting with one's friends and so on. *Giribbaja (Giribbajaṃ)*: Rājagaha.

3 *Rishi (isiṃ)*: he is a rishi (*isiṃ*) by reason of his striving after (*esanā*) the khandhas of morality and so on of the adepts.[12] *Sunetta (Sunettaṃ)*: the Paccekabuddha of the same name. *Tamed of self (attadantaṃ)*: with the mind tamed with the utmost of taming. *Concentrated (samāhitaṃ)*: concentrated with the concentration of the arahant-fruit. *Delighting in whatever came into his almsbowl (uñche pattagate rataṃ)*: delighting in, content with,[13] whatever food that came into his almsbowl, that was put into his almsbowl, that was received when going about after alms for his sustenance.

4 *And said, 'Did you get anything, sir?' (laddhā bhante ti c' abravi)*: he spoke with the purpose of gaining his confidence saying, 'Haven't you got any alms, sir?' *Held it above him (uccaṃ paggayha)*: lifted it up high, held up the bowl.

5 *And broke the bowl on the hard ground (thaṇḍile pattaṃ bhinditvā)*: and broke the bowl by casting it down on a stony part of the ground. *Went away (apakkami)*: went a short distance away and as he was going the king's son spoke to the Paccekabuddha – who (stood) looking on with compassion thinking how, blinded by folly, he had wrought great misfortune upon himself for no reason – saying, 'I am the son of king Kitava – what can you do to me, you beggar?'

6 *Cruel (pharusassa)*: pitiless. *Severe (kaṭuko)*: disagreeable. *Which (yaṃ)*: the result which. *Confined to (samappito)*: stuck in.

7 *For six times eighty-four nahutas of years (chaḷ eva caturāsīti vassāni nahutāni ca)*: lying face upwards for eighty-four thousand years; (similarly) face downwards, on his left side, on his right side, hanging feet uppermost and just standing – there are thus six[14] (periods each of) eighty-four thousand years. For this reason he said:

> 'He was boiled lying face upwards and face downwards, on his left and right (sides); feet uppermost and just standing, that fool was boiled for a long time.'

9 **[266]** Those years, however, are 'nahutas' since they are many in number – therefore he said 'nahutas'. *Underwent intense misery (bhusaṃ dukkhaṃ nigacchiṭṭho)*: met with extreme misery. *Many (pūgāni)*: a collection of years. (Both this phrase) here and that in the earlier verse[15] are to be regarded as accusative cases in the sense of a continuous period of time.

10 *Such (etādisaṃ)*: of such a form. *The severity (kaṭukaṃ)*: the extreme misery – this description is in the neuter gender just like those of 'he sat down at one side' (*ekamantaṃ nisīdi*) and so on. Of such a form is the severity, the extreme misery, for those persons who harm the

faultless ones; those doing wicked deeds (such as) insulting, offending, a devout rishi are boiled – this is how it should be construed.

11 *He (so)*: the peta who was the king's son. *There (tattha)*: in hell. *Experienced (vedayitvā)*: suffered. *Truly (nāma)*: through being clear and obvious. *When he fell from there (tato cuto)*: when he fell from hell. The rest is just as already given.

Thus by means of this talk concerning a peta who had been the son of a king the Lord agitated the people gathered there and afterwards explained the (Four Noble) Truths at the end of which many arrived at the sotāpatti-fruit and so on.

[1] III 2 above which states, however, that he arose in a fisherman village directly after falling from hell, with no intervening birth.

[2] Gehman's 'in your next existence' is clearly wrong since Sānuvāsin was an arahant and thus one for whom no further rebirth could be expected.

[3] Reading phoṭṭhabbe with Se Be for text's poṭṭhabbe.

[4] bhikkhu presumably here in its more literal sense since given the traditional view that Paccekabuddhas exist at times when there is no Buddhism as such in the world (cp PvA 75) it is unlikely that we were meant to understand this as 'monk' here.

[5] Se Be read paccittha . . . apacchata for text's paccittha . . . apaccittha; I assume these are all 3rd sing aorist forms of paccati since they are not listed by PED, Childers or CPD.

[6] khuppipāsahato nāma peto āsi; Dhammapāla understands nāma as an emphatic particle here but at Miln 294 the khuppipāsa peta seems to be the name of a special class of petas not able to enjoy gifts assigned to them by their relatives. Compare how at PvA 21 Bimbisāra's peta-relatives could receive nothing from him for many aeons. See also A v 269–271, quoted at PvA 27f. above, upon which the Miln passage is based, which similarly distinguishes those petas that subsist on food appropriate to creatures on the peta-plane from those who enjoy gifts offered by their relatives and cp cty on IV 11[1].

[7] This sense of uḷāraṃ is not listed by PED; see however PED sv oḷārika and BHSD sv audāra and audārika.

[8] Reading paṭilābhanimittaṃ with Be (Se ca lābha-) for text's palobhanimittaṃ.

[9] Reading yathicchitassa with Se Be for text's yaticchitassa.

[10] Cp cty on II 9[59] (PvA 136).

[11] Text mis-spells kiddaṃ here.

[12] asekkhānaṃ, that is, of arahants; since Sunetta is a Paccekabuddha it may be assumed that he has already accomplished this. Cp PvA 98, 163.

[13] Reading santuṭṭhaṃ with Se Be for text's santappaṃ.

[14] Reading evaṃ cha with Be for text's evaṃ (Se evaṃ ca).

[15] v 7.

IV.8 EXPOSITION OF THE EXCREMENT EATING PETA STORY [Gūthakhādakapetavatthuvaṇṇanā]

'After getting up out of the latrine.' The Teacher who was staying in the Jeta Grove told this concerning a peta who ate excrement.

It is said that in a certain village not far from Sāvatthī a man of property had a vihāra built for a monk who was dependent upon his family for alms. Monks from various districts would come and stay there. When they saw them the people, with devotion in their hearts, waited upon them with the choicest requisites. Now the monk who was dependent upon that family for alms could not bear this and, overcome by envy, irritated that man of property by telling him of the faults of those monks and the man of property, despising both those monks and the one dependent upon his family for alms, abused them. Then the one dependent upon that family for alms died and arose as a peta in the latrine of that very same vihāra whilst when the man of property died he arose as a peta just above him. When the venerable Mahāmoggallāna saw him he questioned him with this verse:

1 **[267]** 'Who is that standing in that wretched state after getting up out of the latrine? You are without doubt an evil-doer – why do you make that noise?'[1]

When he heard this the peta disclosed his identity with this verse:

2 'I, sir,[2] am a peta gone to a miserable existence in the world of Yama. Having done a wicked deed, I have gone from here to the world of the petas.'

The elder then asked him about the deed he had done with this verse:

3 'Now what evil deed was done by you by body, speech or mind? As a result of which deed do you now undergo this misery?'

The peta then told him about the deed he had done by means of these two verses:

4 'I had one in residence who was envious and selfish about my family; he was attached[3] to my house, miserly and abusive.

5 When I had heard what he had to say I abused the monks – it is as a result of that deed that I have gone from here to the world of the petas.'

4 Herein *I had one in residence (ahu āvāsiko mayhaṃ)*: I had one monk in residence, dwelling continually in the vihāra I built at my residence. *He*

was attached to my house (ajjhosito mayhaṃ ghare): due to his being dependent on my family for alms he clung to my home with a craving adherence.

5 *He (tassa)*: that monk who was dependent upon my family for alms. *The monks: bhikkhavo=bhikkhū* (alternative grammatical form). *I abused (paribhāsissaṃ)*: I insulted. *I went from here to the world of the petas (petalokam ito gato)*: in this way I reached the peta-womb, I became a peta.

When he heard this the elder uttered this verse asking about the destiny of the other:

6 'The one who was dependent upon your family for alms was an enemy in the guise of a friend. To what destiny has that foolish person gone at the breaking up of the body after death?'[4]

6 [268] Herein *in the guise of a friend (mittavaṇṇena)*: with the appearance of a friend, disguised as a friend.

The peta once more uttered two verses explaining the matter to the elder:

7 'I am standing on the head, on the top, of that same one who did that wicked deed. He has reached the other plane and is an attendant to me alone.

8 What others defecate, sir, that becomes my food; whilst what I myself defecate – he has to live on that.'

7 Herein *of that same one (tass' eva)*: of that peta who used formerly to be that monk who was dependent upon my family for alms. *Who did that wicked deed (pāpakammassa)*: who was of wicked conduct. *I am standing on the head, on the top (sīse tiṭṭhāmi matthake)*: I am standing on the head and in so standing I am standing right on the very top, meaning not inside his head.[5] *Has reached the other plane (paravisayaṃ patto)*: has reached the peta-plane which is the other realm compared with the world of men. *To me alone: mam eva=mayhaṃ eva* (alternative grammatical form); the rest of the words are 'he is in attendance'.[6]

8 *What others defecate, sir (yaṃ bhadante hanant' aññe)*: what others discharge in the latrine, the excrement they evacuate, sir, my worthy Mahāmoggallāna. *That becomes my food (etaṃ me hoti bhojanaṃ)*: that excrement becomes my food day in and day out. *What I myself defecate (yaṃ hanāmi)*: that excrement which I also pass after eating that (former) excrement. *He has to live on that (etaṃ so upajīvati)*: the peta who used to be dependent upon my family for alms has to live day in, day out, by way of eating that excrement of mine, meaning he sustains his existence

(in this way). Of these,[7] the man of property insulted the monks who were well behaved saying, 'I hope that you have to eat excrement for enjoying that food', but, as the one dependent upon his family for alms had incited that man of property into speaking in that way,[8] he himself (should also be regarded as having) insulted (the monks) in that way – for this reason his life is more wretched than his.

[269] The venerable Mahāmoggallāna raised the issue with the Lord. The Lord took the matter as an arisen need and, after pointing out the disadvantages of insulting speech, taught Dhamma to the company assembled there. That teaching was of benefit to those people.

[1] Reading saddāyase as recommended by PED sv saddahati and saddāyati; all texts read saddahase as they do also at IV 16[1] below but where the cty, however, repeats as saddāyase (Se Be at least; text mis-spells saddayase).

[2] Reading bhadante with Se Be for text's bhaddan te here and in v 8.

[3] ajjhosito; Se Be read ajjhāsito.

[4] pecca.

[5] na sīsappamāṇe ākāse, literally not in the space that is the size of his head.

[6] Reading paricārako with Se Be for text's paricāriko.

[7] Reading tesu with Se Be for text's tesaṃ.

[8] Reading tathā vacane with Be for text's Se tathā vacanena.

IV.9 EXPOSITION OF THE EXCREMENT EATING PETA STORY [Gūthakhādakapetavatthuvaṇṇanā]

'After getting up out of the latrine.' This was said when the Teacher was staying in the Jeta Grove concerning a petī who ate excrement.

Her story is similar to the preceding story. There, since the vihāra was built by a (male) layfollower, it has been handed down concerning that (male) layfollower. Here, however, it was a female layfollower – this is the only difference. In the rest of the story and verses there is nothing that was not in the foregoing.

IV.10 EXPOSITION OF THE TROOP PETA STORY [Gaṇapetavatthuvaṇṇanā]

'Naked and of hideous appearance are you.' This was said when the Teacher was staying in the Jeta Grove concerning a large number of petas.

It is said that in Sāvatthī there was a large number of people who as a group had neither faith nor devotion, their hearts being possessed of the stain of selfishness and averse to good conduct such as giving and so on.[1] They lived for a long time and at the breaking up of the body (after dying) they arose in the peta-womb close to that city. Now as the venerable Mahāmoggallāna was going to Sāvatthī one day in search of alms he saw those petas on his way and questioned them with this verse:

1 'Naked and of hideous appearance are you, emaciated and with prominent veins. You thin ones, with your ribs standing out, now who are you, good sirs?'

1 Herein *of hideous appearance are you (dubbaṇṇarūpā 'tha)*: you have hideous bodies. *Now who are you? (ke nu tumhe 'tha)*: now who indeed might you be? *Good sirs (mārisā)*: he addresses them as his equals.

When they heard this those petas **[270]** made it known that they were petas with this verse:

2 'We, sir,[2] are petas gone to a miserable existence in the world of Yama. Having done a wicked deed, we have gone from here to the world of the petas.'

Questioned once more about the deed they had done by the elder with this verse:

3 'Now what evil deed was done by you by body, speech or mind? As a result of which deed have you gone from here to the world of the petas?',

they then explained that deed that they had done:

4 'At public bathing places we searched for small coins; though merit-offerings were at hand we made no refuge for ourselves.

5 We approach the river parched but it becomes empty; amidst the heat we approach the shade but it becomes scorched by the sun.

6 And a wind like fire blows on us, burning us, but we deserve this, sir, and other (misery) more terrible than this.

7 Moreover we travel yojanas, famished and desirous of food, but turn back without having obtained anything – indeed our merit is trifling.

8 Famished, fainting and staggering and sinking to the ground, we lie sprawling on our backs or we fall face downwards.
9 As we[3] fall at that very spot, sinking to the ground, we bump our heads and chests – indeed our merit is trifling.
10 But we deserve this, sir, and other (misery) more terrible than this for though merit-offerings were at hand we made no refuge for ourselves.
11 When we[3] have gone, then,[4] from here and gained the human womb we will be affable and endowed with virtue and are determined to do many skilled deeds.'

7 Herein *moreover we travel yojanas (api yojanāni gacchāma)*: we travel many yojanas even. How? *Famished and desirous of food (chātā āhāragiddhino)*: [271] for a long time starved with hunger, we become desirous of food, craving after[5] it, yet though we thus travel we turn back without having obtained any food whatsoever. *(Our) merit is trifling (appapuññatā)*: (we are) lacking in merit, (we have) not done any lovely deeds.[6]
8 *We lie sprawling on our backs (uttānā paṭikirāma)*: we sometimes end up lying on our backs appearing as though all our limbs[7] had been scattered. *We fall face downwards (avakujjā patāmase)*: we sometimes fall ending up face downwards.
9 *We (te ca)*:[8] those of us. *We bump our heads and chests (uraṃ sīsañ ca ghaṭṭema)*: having fallen, ending up face downwards and unable to get up, we just knock against[9] one another's[10] heads and chests as we quiver[11] in pain.

The rest is just as already explained above.

The elder raised the issue with the Lord. The Lord took the matter as an arisen need and taught Dhamma to the company assembled there. When they heard this the people abandoned the stain of selfishness and became given to good conduct, performing meritorious deeds such as giving and so on.[12]

[1] Reading maccheramalapariyuṭṭhitacittā dānādisucaritavimukhā with Se Be for text's maccheramalapariyuṭṭhitā cittādānādīsu caritavimukhā.

[2] Reading bhadante with Se Be for text's bhaddan te.

[3] te, literally they.

[4] nuna; cp PvA 282.

[5] Reading abhigijjhantā with Se Be for text's abhijighacchantā.

[6] Reading apuññatā akatakalyāṇatā with Se Be for text's apuññatāya akatakalyāṇatāya.

[7] Reading -aṅgapaccaṅgā with Se Be for text's -aṅgā.

[8] So Se Be for text's te.

[9] Reading paṭighaṃsāma with Be (Se pati-) for text's paṭihaṃsāma; not listed by PED.

[10] Reading attano attano with Be for text's Se attano.

[11] Reading vedhantā with Se Be for text's vedanantā.

[12] Reading dānādīni puññāni karonto sucaritanirato ahosi with Se (Be dānādisucaritanirato ahosi) for text's dānādīni puññāni karonto ahosi.

IV.11 EXPOSITION OF THE PĀṬALIPUTTA PETA STORY
[Pāṭaliputtapetavatthuvaṇṇanā]

'You have seen the hells and the animal womb.' This was said when the Teacher was staying in the Jeta Grove concerning a certain vimānapeta.

It is said that many traders who were residents of Sāvatthī and Pāṭaliputta[1] were going by ship to Suvaṇṇabhūmi[2] when a layfollower who was attached to a woman fell sick and died. Though he had done skilled deeds he did not arise in the devaloka but instead arose as a vimānapeta in the middle of the ocean on account of his attachment to that woman.[3] The woman to whom he had been attached set out, embarking on a ship that was heading for Suvaṇṇabhūmi. Now that peta, desiring to seize the woman, stopped the ship from moving. Then those traders, wondering what the reason might be for the ship not moving [272] passed round the stick of bad omen[4] which, due to non-human psychic power, came to rest no less than three times with that woman alone to whom he was attached. When they saw this the traders lowered a bundle of bamboo into the ocean and then lowered the woman onto it and as soon as the woman had been lowered the ship quickly proceeded towards Suvaṇṇabhūmi. The non-human led the woman up to his mansion and enjoyed the pleasures of love with her. When she had spent a year (there) she became dissatisfied and begged the peta saying, 'As long as I dwell here I am unable to act towards my welfare in the next world. Please take me to Pāṭaliputta, good sir.' Begged thus by her he uttered this verse:

1 'You have seen the hells and the animal womb, the petas, the asuras as well as men and devas;[5] you have seen for yourself the results of one's deeds. I will take you unharmed to Pāṭaliputta – when you have gone there you must perform skilled deeds.'

1 Herein *you have seen the hells (diṭṭhā tayā nirayā)*: you have even

seen some of the separate hells. *The animal womb (tiracchānayonī)*: you have also seen animals of great majesty such as nāgas and supaṇṇas[6] and so on – this is how it should be construed. *The petas (petā)*: the sort of petas (that are overcome by) hunger and thirst and so on. *The asuras (asurā)*: the Kāḷakañjaka[7] sort of asura. *Devas (devā)*: some of the devas of the Four Great Kings' (devaloka). It is said he would take her with him from time to time by means of his majesty and go around showing her the separate hells and so on. For this reason he said, *you have seen for yourself the results of one's deeds (sayam addasa kammavipākam attano)*: you went to a particular hell and so on and looking around you saw, you did see, for yourself, with your own eyes, the results of deeds done by oneself. *I will take you unharmed to Pāṭaliputta (nessāmi taṃ Pāṭaliputtam akkhataṃ)*: I will now take you unharmed, unhurt by anyone, to Pāṭaliputta in human form[8] but when you have gone there you must perform skilled deeds, meaning since you have seen with your own eyes the results of deeds you should be intent on and delight in (performing) meritorious deeds.

[273] When the woman heard what he had to say she was delighted and uttered this verse:

2 'You desire my good, yakkha, you desire my welfare, devatā; I will do what you say – you are my teacher. I have seen the hells and the animal womb, the petas, the asuras as well as men and devas; I have seen for myself the results of one's deeds. Not trifling are the meritorious deeds I am determined to do.'

The peta then took the woman and travelled through the air and set her in the middle of the city of Pāṭaliputta and then departed. When her friends and relatives and so on saw her they rejoiced thinking that though they had earlier heard that she had been put into the ocean and was dead yet now she was seen and, thankfully, had returned safely. And they assembled and asked her about the incident and she told them of everything that she had seen and experienced, right from the very beginning. Moreover those traders who were residents of Sāvatthī in due course reached Sāvatthī. They approached the Teacher at the proper time, saluted him and, seated at one side, raised the issue with the Lord. The Lord took the matter as an arisen need and taught Dhamma to the four assemblies. The people, filled with agitation, became given to skilled states such as giving and so on.

[1] Modern Patna; in the days of the Buddha it was a mere village and known as Pāṭaligāma and became important only after his death when in time it became the Mauryan capital of Aśoka. Cp DPPN ii 178f. This makes Dhammapāla's suggestion

(PvA 2) that these stories originated with the Buddha himself somewhat suspect.

[2] Cp PvA 47.

[3] Cp PvA 5, 145 where attachment to a woman had similar consequences.

[4] kālakaṇṇisalākaṃ, literally a stick (to determine) the black-eared one, this being considered an inauspicious attribute. It is not known what the process involved. Compare the similar fate of Jonah (Jonah 1 7ff.).

[5] In many places in the Nikāyas only four possible realms of rebirth are mentioned – in the hells, as an animal, as a man and as a deva – e.g. M iii 163ff.; cp D i 83 where a simile describing the rebirth process has men walking along *four* roads. In time a fifth realm, that of the petas, was added and these five, the pañcagati, became the norm for the Theravāda whilst the Mahāyāna further increased the number to six by establishing a separate realm for the asuras. As this verse shows, these six also find mention on occasion in the Pali sources; cp D iii 264 and It 92f.

[6] supaṇṇa, Skt suparṇa, literally beautiful-winged, and an epithet of Garuḍa, the bird of prey that is Viṣṇu's steed and traditional enemy of the nāga, or snake. They often appear paired in this way – see e.g. D ii 259; S iii 240–249; Mahāvastu ii 15, 163f., iii 324.

[7] See the article on the asuras in E. Washburn Hopkins, *Epic Mythology*, Delhi 1974, pp. 46ff. where these are said to be Kāleyas; also R. Spence Hardy, *Manual of Buddhism*, Varanasi 1967, p. 59 where they are said to be a class of peta.

[8] Reading aparikkhataṃ manussarūpen' eva with Se Be for text's aparikkhatamanussarūpen' eva.

IV.12 EXPOSITION OF THE MANGO[1] PETA STORY
[Ambapetavatthuvaṇṇanā]

'This lotus pond of yours is extremely delightful.' This was said when the Teacher was staying at Sāvatthī concerning a 'mango' peta.

It is said that in Sāvatthī there was a certain householder whose wealth had become exhausted. His wife had died and he had an only daughter whom he left at the house of a friend and then, taking goods (he had bought) with a loan of a hundred kahāpaṇas, he set out with a caravan in order to trade and not long afterwards turned back (for home) with the caravan, having gained an interest of five hundred kahāpaṇas on top of his original capital. [274] On the way robbers came upon the caravan and surrounded it and the caravan people ran off in all directions. The householder, however, deposited his kahāpaṇas in a bush and hid nearby but the robbers caught him and took his life. On account of his greed for wealth he arose as a peta in that very spot.

When the traders got back to Sāvatthī they reported the incident to his daughter who was filled with extreme unhappiness and who lamented excessively both at the death of her father and due to her anxiety for her own means of livelihood. A man of property who had been a friend of her father then consoled her saying, 'Just as a potter's vessels all have destruction as their end, even so does the life of living beings have destruction as its end.[2] Death is common to all and has no antidote so you should not grieve and lament too excessively for your father. I will be a father to you and you will be a daughter to me. I will do what has to be done for your father. You can live happily in this house, untroubled just like it were your father's house.' Her grief subsided[3] at these words of his and she became full of respect and esteem for him as though he were her own father and due to her poor circumstances she became his housekeeper. As time went on she desired to perform the rites for the dead on behalf of her father. She cooked some rice-gruel and in a bronze bowl she placed some sweet mango fruits that were fully ripe and the colour of red arsenic. She had her slave-girl carry the rice-gruel and mango fruits and went to the vihāra, saluted the Teacher and then spoke thus, 'May the Lord be kind enough to accept this donation of mine.' The Teacher, his heart stirred with great compassion, fulfilling her wish indicated that he was about to sit down. Overjoyed she spread out a fresh, clean cloth she had brought with her and prepared a seat for the noble Buddha and offered this and the Lord sat down on the seat prepared. Then she presented the rice-gruel to the Lord and the Lord accepted the rice-gruel. She then gave rice-gruel to the monks as well, on behalf of the Saṅgha.[4] After she had given the rice-gruel she once more with clean hands presented the Lord with the mango fruits which the Lord then ate. She saluted the Lord [275] and spoke thus, 'This donation I have made by way of this gift of the spread out cloth, the rice-gruel and the mango fruits, Lord, may that please reach my father.' The Lord said, 'So be it', and showed his appreciation. She saluted the Lord, circumambulated him by the right, and then left. As soon as she dedicated[5] that donation the peta obtained a mango grove, a park, a mansion, a wish-granting tree and a lotus pond as well as great heavenly excellence. Then on a future occasion when those traders were going along in order to trade, they came upon that same road and made their camp for the night at the place they had stayed at before. When he saw them the vimānapeta revealed himself to them together with his park and mansion and so on. On seeing him those traders uttered these two verses enquiring about the excellence he had received:

1 'This lotus pond of yours is extremely delightful. Its beautiful banks[6] are level and it has abundant water. It is in full blossom[7] and is dotted all over with swarms of bees – how did you come by this lovely (pond)?

2 And this mango grove of yours is extremely delightful and bears fruit in all seasons. It is in full blossom[7] and is dotted all over with swarms of bees – how did you come by this mansion?'

1 Herein *extremely delightful: surammā=suṭṭhu ramaṇīyā* (resolution of compound). *Are level (samā)*: have level surfaces. *Beautiful banks (supatitthā)*: beautiful bathing places on account of their stairways made of jewels. *It has abundant water (mahodakā)*: it has plenty of water.
2 *In all seasons (sabbotukaṃ)*: it causes happiness[8] on account of its trees and so on that come into blossom and bear fruit in all seasons. For this reason it was said, 'and bears fruit'. *It is in full blossom (supupphitaṃ)*: it is permanently in blossom.

When he heard this the peta uttered this verse explaining what had been the cause of his obtaining that lotus pond and so on:

3 'A gift of ripe mangoes, water and rice-gruel was given by my daughter – it is because of this that this cool and delightful shade is received by me here.'

3 [276] Herein *it is because of this . . . is received by me here (tena me idha labbhati)*: since that gift of ripe mangoes, water and rice-gruel given by my daughter to the Lord and the monks was given by her on my behalf, it is because of this gift given by my daughter that ripe mangoes (are received by me) here in this heavenly mango grove in all seasons and heavenly water in this lovely heavenly lotus pond; whilst it is because of that gift of the rice-gruel and the spread out (cloth) that this cool and delightful shade (found) in this park, this mansion and this wish-granting tree and so on is received here, that is, is accomplished.

When he had spoken thus the peta took the traders and showed them the five hundred kahāpaṇas saying, 'You may take half of this and give the (other) half to my daughter telling her to clear my debt and to live in comfort.' In due course the traders reached Sāvatthī and told his daughter and gave her (everything including) the portion he had given to them. She gave a hundred kahāpaṇas to his creditors and gave the rest to the man of property who had been a friend of her father and, as for herself, stayed on acting as his housekeeper.[9] But he gave it back to her saying, 'All this is yours alone', and made her mistress of the household of his eldest son. As time went on she had a son and she would utter this verse as she nursed[10] him:

4 'Behold the result, in this life even, of giving, of restraint and self control. I was a slave-girl in my master's family and am now his daughter-in-law and mistress of the house.'

Then one day the Teacher, having perused the maturity of her perception, diffused his radiance and revealed himself as though he were standing face to face with her and then uttered this verse:

5 'He who is not diligent is conquered by the agreeable appearance of the disagreeable, by the lovely appearance of the unlovely and by the pleasant appearance of that which is misery.'[11]

At the end of this verse she was established in the sotāpatti-fruit. On the following day she gave alms to the order of monks with the Buddha at its head [277] and then raised the issue with the Lord. The Lord took the matter as an arisen need and taught Dhamma to the company assembled there. That teaching was of benefit to those people.

[1] Be reads Ambavana-, Mango Grove, here.

[2] Cp Sn 577.

[3] Reading paṭippassaddhasokā with Se Be for text's paṭipassaddhasokā.

[4] Cp PvA 81.

[5] samuddiṭṭha, pp of samuddisati; not listed by PED.

[6] Reading supatitthā with Se for text's Be sutitthā; cp II 1[20], PvA 77.

[7] Reading supupphitā with Se Be for text's sampupphitā in v 1; similarly supupphitaṃ for sampupphitaṁ in v 2.

[8] Reading sukhāvahaṃ with Se Be for text's sukkhāvahaṃ.

[9] Reading attano pitu sahāyassa tassa kuṭumbikassa datvā sayaṃ veyyāvaccaṃ karontī nivasati with Se Be for text's attano pitu sahāyassa datvā sayaṃ veyyāvaccaṃ karontī tassa kuṭumbikassa nīyādesi.

[10] Reading upalālentī with Se Be for text's upālāpentī and not upalāpenti as recommended by PED sv upālāpeti.

[11] This verse recurs at Ud 18 and J i 410, the cty on the latter stating that those who are not diligent and in whom mindfulness is not present are conquered, overcome and smothered by the illusory appearance of these three (tattha asātaṃ sātarūpenā ti amadhuram eva madhurapaṭirūpakena, pamattam ativattatī ti, asātaṃ appiyaṃ dukkhan ti evaṃ tividham pi etena sātarūpādinā ākārena sativippavāsavasena pamattapuggalaṃ ativattati, abhibhavati ajjhottharatī ti attho). Cp the similar sentiments at S iv 127. Gehman's interpretation is quite wrong; moreover the reading of pamattaṃ is common to all texts, including Ud and J, and is clearly preferable to his suggested samattaṃ.

IV.13 EXPOSITION OF THE TREE-AXLE PETA STORY
[Akkharukkhapetavatthuvaṇṇanā]

'When one gives it is not (just) there.' This is the Donor of an Axle Peta Story.[1] How did it originate?

When the Lord was staying at Sāvatthī a certain layfollower who was a resident of Sāvatthī filled some carts with goods and went to Videha[2] in order to trade. He sold his goods there and loaded his carts with goods (he had bought) in return and then took the road leading towards Sāvatthī. As he was going along that road in the forest the axle of one of his carts broke. Now a certain man who had left his village and who was having his hatchet and axe carried along for the purpose of fetching a tree was wandering about in the forest and came upon that place. He saw the layfollower's dejection on account of that broken axle and thought, 'This trader is in distress in the forest on account of that broken axle', and taking pity on him he cut down a tree, made a sturdy axle and presented it (to the trader) and fixed it to the cart. He died in due course and arose as a terrestrial devatā at that same spot in the forest. Having reflected upon his deeds he went by night to the house of that layfollower and uttered this verse as he stood at the door of the house:

1 'When one gives it is not (just) there – you should just give gifts; when one has given one crosses over both, one goes to both by this means. Be alert! Do not be negligent!'

1 Herein *when one gives it is not (just) there (yaṃ dadāti na taṃ hoti)*: when a donor gives a merit-offering it is not just there in the world beyond that the fruit of that gift comes into existence[3] for there is much other agreeable and enjoyable fruit besides. Therefore *you should just give gifts (deth' eva dānaṃ)*: you should just give gifts as are appropriate.[4] Then he stated the reason: *when one has given one crosses over both (datvā ubhayaṃ tarati)*: [278] when one has given gifts one passes beyond misery and misfortune both in this life and in the next world. *One goes to both by this means (ubhayaṃ tena gacchati)*: one reaches, one attains to, both happiness in this life and in the next world by means of these gifts. The meaning is to be construed, moreover,[5] as the well being and happiness both for oneself and for others. *Be alert! Do not be negligent! (jāgaratha mā pamajjatha)* means be alert to procure gifts that yield both (types of) well being and that ward off both (types of) misfortune in this way. Prepare the materials for the gifts[6] and be diligent therein. This is said in a repetitive manner[7] here in order to show respect.

When the trader had accomplished what he had to do he turned back and in due course reached Sāvatthī. He approached the Teacher on the following day, saluted him and, seated at one side, raised the issue with the Lord. The Teacher took the matter as an arisen need and taught Dhamma to the company assembled there. That teaching was of benefit to those people.

[1] Reading Akkhadāyakapetavatthu with Se Be for text's -dāyikapetavatthuṃ; it appears to be an alternative title of the story.

[2] The Videhas and the Licchavis combined to form the Vajjian confederacy. It was located on the north bank of the Ganges to the north of Rājagaha and to the east of Sāvatthī. Its capital was Mithilā, generally identified with Janakapura, just within the Nepalese border to the north of the Mazaffarpur and Darbhaṅga districts. Cp DPPN ii 635, 813ff., 879f.

[3] Reading na tad' eva paraloke tassa dānassa phalabhāvena hoti with Se Be for text's na taṃ devaloke tassa dānassa phalabhāvo hoti.

[4] Reading yathā tathā with Se Be for text's yathā.

[5] Reading hitasukhavasenā 'pi with Se Be for text's -vasenā ti.

[6] Reading dānūpakaraṇāni sajjetvā with Se Be for text's dānupakaraṇā nisajjetvā; cp PvA 105.

[7] āmeṇḍitavasena; not 'sympathy' as suggested by PED – see CPD and SED sv āmreḍita.

IV.14 EXPOSITION OF THE ACCUMULATION OF WEALTH PETA STORY
[Bhogasaṃharaṇapetavatthuvaṇṇanā][1]

'We accumulated wealth.' This is the Accumulation of Wealth Peta Story.[2] How did it originate?

It is said that when the Lord was staying in the Bamboo Grove there were four women in Rājagaha who engaged in trading in ghee, honey, oil and grain and so on, making their living by the improper accumulation of wealth by way of giving false measures and so forth. At the breaking up of the body after dying they arose[3] as petīs in a moat outside that city. At night they[4] were overwhelmed with misery and wandered about making a great and terrific sound howling:

1 'We accumulated wealth properly and improperly. This is now enjoyed by others whilst our share is misery.'

The people were frightened when they heard this and at daybreak they prepared a great almsgiving for the order of monks with the Buddha at its head and having invited the Teacher and the order of monks they served them with the choicest hard and soft foods. When the Lord had finished his meal and had withdrawn his hand from the bowl they sat down nearby and related the incident. The Lord said, 'Layfollowers, [279] there is no danger[5] whatsoever to you in that sound. It is only four petīs who, overwhelmed with misery, lamenting and crying aloud in their distress after talking of the evil deed they had done, uttered this verse:

2 'We accumulated wealth properly and improperly. This is now enjoyed by others whilst our share is misery.'

2 Herein *wealth (bhoge)*: particular possessions and means such as clothes and ornaments and so on that are known as 'wealth' (*bhoga*) because they can be enjoyed (*paribhuñjitabbatthena*). *We accumulated (saṃharimha)*: with our hearts overcome by the stain of selfishness we heaped up, not giving anything to anyone. *Properly and improperly (samena visamena ca)*: rightly and wrongly, or wrongly but with the appearance of being right. That wealth accumulated by us is now enjoyed by others. *Whilst our share is misery (mayaṃ dukkhassa bhāginī)*: through our lack of good conduct towards anyone and our bad conduct we must now share this great misery that belongs to the peta-womb, meaning we are suffering great misery.

When the Lord had thus spoken the verse uttered by the petīs and related the incident he took it as an arisen need and taught Dhamma to the company assembled there, afterwards explaining the (Four Noble) Truths at the end of which many arrived at the sotāpatti-fruit and so on.

[1] So Se Be for text's Bhogasaṃharapetavatthuvaṇṇanā.
[2] Here spelt correctly.
[3] Reading nibbattiṃsu with Se Be for text's nibhattiṃsu.
[4] Reading tā with Se Be for text's ta.
[5] Reading antarāyo with Se Be for text's antārayo.

IV.15 EXPOSITION OF THE WEALTHY MERCHANT'S SONS PETA STORY
[Seṭṭhiputtapetavatthuvaṇṇanā]

'For sixty thousand years.' This is the Wealthy Merchant's Sons Peta Story. How did it originate?

The Lord was staying in the Jeta Grove at Sāvatthī. Now at that time the Kosalan king Pasenadi was going about the city in great royal power, in great royal splendour, dressed and adorned and mounted on the back of the most stately elephant. He saw a woman who was endowed with a beauty resembling that of a deva-nymph[1] who had opened a window on the upper terrace of a certain house and who was looking down at that royal glory.[2] With his heart possessed by the assailing of the defilements that quickly arose upon (sight of) this visual object (the like of which) he had not seen before and although[3] he had [280] a harem whose members were endowed with distinctive qualities such as good family, beauty and good conduct and so on, he nevertheless fell in love with that woman on account of his heart being of a frivolous nature and difficult to tame. He signalled to a man seated nearby as if to say, 'You see that terraced dwelling and that woman', and then entered the royal residence. Everything else[4] is to be understood as already stated earlier in the Ambasakkhara Peta Story[5] but with this difference. Here the man arrived just before sunset when the city gate was closed and hung[6] the red clay and water lilies he had brought on the gate post and then went[7] to the Jeta Grove in order to sleep whilst the king, who had gone to sleep in the royal bed chamber, heard in the middle watch of the night the four syllables *sa, na, du, so* as if uttered in distress from a huge throat. It is said that these are the initial syllables of the verses uttered by the four sons of a wealthy merchant who were long ago residents of Sāvatthī and who in their youth[8] were drunk with the pride of wealth and went with the wives of others thereby producing much demerit. Later on they died and arose close to that very city in the Iron Cauldron.[9] As they were being boiled they would rise up to the rim of the Iron Cauldron, each desiring to utter a verse,[10] but as soon as they had uttered the first syllable they were afflicted with (painful) feelings and sank back into the Iron Cauldron. When the king heard that noise he became frightened and agitated and his hair stood on end. He spent the rest of the night in misery and at dawn had his chief priest sent for and told him of the incident. When the chief priest came to know of the king's fright he, greedy for gain, thought, 'A means of gain for me and the brahmins has indeed arisen',[11] and said, 'Great king, a great calamity has arisen for sure – you must perform the fourfold sacrifice of everything.'[12] On hearing this reply the king commanded his special advisers saying, 'Have prepared whatever is necessary for the fourfold sacrifice of everything!' When she heard this queen Mallikā said to the king, 'Why is it, great king, that you listen to the words of that brahmin and now wish to perform rites in which countless living beings will be harmed and slaughtered? Surely it is the Lord who exercises unobstructed knowledge in all things who should be asked [281] and one should then act in accordance with the Lord's reply.' When the king heard what she had to say he went into the Teacher's presence and raised the issue with the Lord. The Lord said, 'Great king, there is no danger to you whatsoever from that source', and then explained the issue, right from the very beginning, of those creatures who had arisen in the Iron Cauldron hell. He then completed the verses that they had each separately begun to utter saying:

1 'In all we have been boiled in hell for a full sixty thousand years – when will there be an end of this?'

2 'There will be no end – why should there be an end? No end is in sight, for such is the way in which those wicked deeds were done by you and me, good sirs.'[13]

3 'We led a wicked life; though at hand we did not give (therefrom) – though merit-offerings were at hand we made no refuge for ourselves.'

4 'When I[14] have gone, then, from here and gained the human womb I will be affable and endowed with virtue and am determined to do many skilled deeds.'

1 Herein *for sixty thousand years: saṭṭhivassasahassāni=vassānaṃ saṭṭhisahassāni*[15] (resolution of compound). It is said that the creature that arises in the Iron Cauldron hell travels downwards for thirty thousand years until he reaches the lowest level whereupon he travels upwards again for a similar thirty thousand years until he reaches a spot at its rim. In order to make us aware of this he desired to utter the verse (beginning:) 'In all (we have been boiled in hell) for a full sixty thousand years' but after saying *sa*[16] he was afflicted with extremely (painful) feelings and sank back face downwards. The Lord, however, completed it and related it to the king. This is to be applied in the remaining verses too. Herein *when will there be an end of this? (kadā anto bhavissati)*: when will there be an end, a conclusion, of this misery of our being boiled in the Iron Cauldron hell?

2 *For such is the way in which (tathā hi)*: just as there will be no end, no end is in sight, of this misery of yours and mine, such is the way, such is the mode, in which those wicked deeds were done by you and me – it is to be taken thus with this alteration of inflection.[17]

3 *A wicked life (dujjīvitaṃ)*: a life to be reproached by the wise. *Though at hand (ye sante)*: though those merit-offerings were at hand, in existence for us. [282] *We did not give: na dadamhase=na adamha* (alternative grammatical form). To make the meaning of what he had said more clear he then said, 'though merit-offerings were at hand we made no refuge for ourselves'.

4 *I: so 'haṃ=so ahaṃ* (resolution of compound). *Then (nuna)* is a particle of reflection on what is said.[18] *From here (ito)*: from this Iron Cauldron hell. *Have gone (gantvā)*: have departed. *Gained the human womb (yoniṃ laddhāna mānusiṃ)*: gained the human womb, existence in the human state.[19] *Affable (vadaññū)*: of a generous nature, or affable to beggars.[20] *Endowed with virtue (sīlasampanno)*: endowed with virtuous

conduct. *Am determined to do many skilled deeds (kāhāmi kusalaṃ bahuṃ)*: without falling into negligence as I did before I am determined to do many, abundant, skilled deeds, meritorious deeds, meaning I will heap them up.

When the Teacher had spoken these verses he taught Dhamma in detail. At the end of that teaching the man who had fetched the clay and red water lilies was established in the sotāpatti-fruit. The king, full of agitation, abandoned coveting the wives of others and was satisfied with his own wife.

[1] Cp PvA 46.

[2] Reading rājavibhūtiṃ with Se Be for text's rājabhūtiṃ.

[3] Reading sati pi with Se Be for text's sati.

[4] Reading purisassa imaṃ pāsādaṃ imañ ca itthiṃ upadhārehī ti saññaṃ datvā rājagehaṃ paviṭṭho. Aññaṃ sabbaṃ with Se Be (≏ PvA 216) for text's purisassa saññaṃ datvā sabbaṃ.

[5] IV 1.

[6] Reading laggetvā with Se Be for text's laggitvā.

[7] Reading agamāsi with Se Be for text's āgamāsi.

[8] Reading yobbanakāle with Se Be for text's yobhanakāle.

[9] Cp PvA 221.

[10] Reading ekekaṃ gāthaṃ vattukāmehi uccāritānaṃ tāsaṃ with Se Be for text's ekekā gāthā vattukāmā uccāritāni. Tāsaṃ.

[11] Text mispunctuates, the brahmin's opening words being uppanno kho and not just kho.

[12] sabbacatukkaṃ yaññaṃ; this expression occurs at J i 335, where it is rendered 'wherever four roads meet' which cannot be correct given the sequel in which a pit is dug outside the town for the sacrifice, and also in the Iron Cauldron Jātaka (No. 314) which records the same episode as this story and from which it is clear that four of every living creature, including men, were sacrificed and apparently later eaten by the brahmins. The 'dream' also occurs in the cty on S i 142 – see Gehman 109 n. 1 and KS i 102 n. 1.

[13] Reading mārisā with Be for text's Se mārisa.

[14] Reading so 'haṃ with Be for text's Se so hi.

[15] So Se Be for text's vassānaṃ saṭṭhivassāni sahassāni.

[16] Initial syllable of saṭṭhivassasahassāni, first word of the verse; the other three are similarly the initial syllables of the opening words of the other verses: na(tthi), du(jjīvitaṃ) and so('haṃ).

[17] The dative/genitive forms tuyhaṃ mayhaṃ of the verse should be altered to their instrumental forms tayā mayā; they were rendered above with this instrumental sense.

[18] Cp BvA 69 and PvA 123.

[19] Reading manussayoniṃ manussattabhāvaṃ with Be for text's yoniṃ manussattabhāvaṃ; Se reads yoniṃ manussattabhāvaṃ.

[20] Reading pariccāgasīlo yācakānaṃ with Be for text's Se pariccāgasīlo vā yācakānaṃ.

IV.16 EXPOSITION OF THE SIXTY THOUSAND HAMMERS PETA STORY

[Saṭṭhikūṭasahassapetavatthuvaṇṇanā]

'Why do you, like a madman?' This was said when the Teacher was staying in the Bamboo Grove concerning a certain peta.

It is said that long ago in the city of Benares a certain cripple was skilled in the practice of slinging stones. When he had thus reached perfection in the art of throwing gravel he would sit at the foot of a banyan tree at the city gate and by striking banyan leaves with gravel he would cause patterns of elephants, horses, chariots, men, pinnacled houses with flags, full water pots and so on to appear on them.[1] The boys of the city would give him the small change they had been given as pocket-money and had him exercise his arts at their pleasure. Then one day when the king of Benares left the city he came to the foot of that banyan tree. He saw the various forms and patterns such as that of the elephant and so on applied[2] to those banyan leaves and asked the people, 'Who has made these various forms and patterns in this way on these banyan leaves?' The people pointed to the cripple saying, 'They were done by him, your majesty.' [283] The king summoned him and spoke thus, 'Look here, would it be possible for you to fill the belly of a man with pellets of goat dung while he is talking and without his knowing it if I point him out?' 'It should be possible, your majesty' (he replied). The king took him to the royal dwelling and, tired at the constant chatter of his chief priest, had that chief priest sent for. He sat down with him in a secluded space surrounded by a screen wall and, whilst taking counsel (with him) had the cripple sent for. The cripple came bringing a hollow stalk filled with pellets of goat dung and, having noted the king's position, sat down facing the chief priest and when the latter's mouth was open sent the pellets of goat dung through an opening in the screen, one by one, to the bottom of his throat. Being unable, out of shame, to retch (in front of the king) he had to swallow them all. When his stomach was filled with pellets of goat dung the king dismissed him saying, 'Go, brahmin, you have received the fruit of your constant chatter. When you have drunk the drink that is prepared from the crushed fruit and the leaves and so on of the piyaṅgu[3] you will throw up.[4] In this way you will be all right', and, delighted with what the cripple had done, gave him fourteen villages. After obtaining these villages he was himself happy and pleased and he made his attendants happy and pleased too. He lived in comfort but he did not ignore[5] his interests in both this same life and in the next world and would give whatever was appropriate to those in need[6] such as recluses and brahmins and so on, whilst he would give food and remuneration to those who had approached him whilst they trained in his art. Then a man approached him and spoke thus, 'Please be my teacher and train me in this art but I have no use for your food as wages.'[7] He trained that man in the art. As one trained in the art he left desiring to test his art and, by striking him with gravel, he split the head of the Paccekabuddha Sunetta who was sitting on the bank of the Ganges and the Paccekabuddha attained Parinibbāna[8] right there on the bank of the Ganges. [284] When the people heard of this incident they struck him there and then with clods of earth and sticks and so on and took his life. When he died he arose in the great hell of Avīci and was boiled for many thousands of years in that hell. During this Buddha-period he arose, as a residual effect of that same deed, as a peta not far from the city of Rājagaha. As the result must be in accordance with the deed,[9] sixty thousand iron hammers were lifted up morning, noon and night by the impulse of that deed and then fell down upon his head at which, with his head cut and split and afflicted with extremely (painful) feelings, he would fall to the ground – but as soon as the iron hammers had gone away he would stand with his head restored to its original state. Then one day the venerable Mahāmoggallāna, descending from the Vulture Peak, saw him and questioned him with this verse:

1 'Why do you, like a madman, dart about like a startled deer? You are without doubt an evil-doer[10] – why do you make that noise?'[11]

1 Herein *like a madman (ummattarūpo va)*: like one who is by nature mad,[12] like one driven to distraction. *Dart about like a startled deer (migo bhanto va dhāvasi)*: dart about here and there like a startled deer. Not seeing any shelter as the iron hammers are falling he flees this way and that (hoping), 'Maybe it will not[13] strike me here.' But lifted up by the impulse of that deed they fall right on the top of his head wherever he is standing. *Why do you make that noise? (kin nu saddāyase tuvaṃ)*: why do you make that sound, why do you roam about making that cry of utter distress?

When he heard this the peta gave reply with these two verses:

2 'I, sir, am a peta gone to a miserable existence in the world of Yama. Having done a wicked deed I have gone from here to the world of the petas.

3 [285] In all a full sixty thousand hammers fall down on my head and these split my head.'

3 Herein *sixty thousand hammers (saṭṭhikūṭasahassāni)*: as many as sixty thousand iron hammers. *A full (paripuṇṇāni)*: nothing short of. *In all (sabbaso)*: in total. It is said that his head became the size of a mountain

peak, sufficiently large for sixty thousand iron hammers to fall upon.[14] Those falling hammers split his head to the extent that not even a spot through which the tip of a hair could pierce[15] was left. For this reason he makes his agonised cry; for this reason he said, 'in all (a full sixty thousand hammers) fall down on my head and these split my head'.

The elder then spoke two verses enquiring about the deed he had done:

4 'Now what evil deed was done by you by body, speech or mind? As a result of which deed have you gone from here to the world of the petas?

5 (Why do) in all a full sixty thousand hammers fall down on your head and (why do) these split your head?'

The peta spoke three verses explaining the deed that he had done:

6 'I saw[16] the Buddha Sunetta, one in whom the faculties were developed, seated at the foot of a tree, meditating and having nothing to fear from any quarter.

7 By means of a blow through slinging stones I split his head – it is as a result of that deed that I undergo this misery:

8 In all a full sixty thousand hammers fall down on my head and these split my head.'

6 Herein *the Buddha (sambuddhaṃ)*: the Paccekabuddha. *Sunetta (Sunettaṃ)*: the one of that name. *One in whom the faculties were developed (bhāvitindriyaṃ)*: one in whom the faculties of faith and so on[17] were developed by cultivation of the ariyan path.

7 *By means of a blow through slinging stones (sālittakappahārena)*: by striking through slinging stones in the following way: that practice of throwing gravel with the fingers alone or with a small bow called a sling. An alternative reading is 'by striking through slinging stones' (*sālittakappaharaṇena*).[18] *I split: bhindissaṃ=bhindiṃ*[19] (alternative grammatical form).

[286] When he heard this the elder uttered the concluding verse showing that the fruit of that earlier deed that he was now receiving was quite in accordance with the deed he had done:

9 'It serves you right, you wretched man, that in all a full sixty thousand hammers fall down on your head and these split your head.'

9 Herein *it serves you right (dhammena)*: it is with accordant cause.[20] *You: te=tava* (alternative grammatical form). This fruit that has come to you is quite appropriate to that wicked deed that you did in offending that Paccekabuddha. He points out therefore that this cannot be evaded

by anyone whether deva or Māra or Brahmā or, moreover, even a Perfect Buddha.

Now when he had spoken thus he went from there to the city in search of alms and when he had finished his meal he approached the Teacher in the evening and raised the issue with the Lord. The Lord took the matter as an arisen need and, whilst teaching Dhamma to the four assemblies, made known the magnificent qualities of the Paccekabuddhas and how deeds are not barren.[21] The people, filled with agitation, were also filled with faith; they abandoned wicked deeds and became given to meritorious deeds such as giving and so on.

The exposition of the Sixty Thousand Hammers Peta Story is concluded – thus the exposition of the meaning of the fourth, Great, chapter, that is adorned with sixteen stories in these Peta Stories of the Khuddaka Nikāya is concluded.[22]

[1] This part of the story should be compared with the Sālittaka Jātaka (No. 107) in which it is stated that he cut the leaves into these shapes by hurling the gravel at them.

[2] Reading appitā with Be for text's anappakā; Se reads anappaso.

[3] Be reads maddanaphalapiyaṅgutacādīhi for text's madanaphalaṃ piyaṅgupattādīhi with which Se agrees except for making it one compound. I propose reading maddanaphalapiyaṅgupattādīhi on the grounds that the fruit is surely crushed, maddana, rather than intoxicating, madana, and that since such crushing might well include its skin, taca, it is more likely that it was its leaves, patta, that were also added to the concoction. The piyaṅgu is panic seed, Panicum italicum, and was used as an emetic.

[4] ucchaḍḍehi, not listed by Childers or PED, whilst CPD, although noticing the occurrence of this verb in the Be of PvA 256, fails to notice this occurrence upon which all texts are unanimous.

[5] Reading ahāpento with Se Be for text's gāhāpento.

[6] atthikānaṃ; Se Be omit.

[7] mayhaṃ pana alaṃ bhattavetanena; this use of alaṃ with the instrumental is not listed by PED but cp CPD sv.

[8] parinibbāyi.

[9] Cp PvA 206.

[10] Reading pāpakammanto with Be and IV 8[1] for text's Se pāpakammaṃ.

[11] Cp IV 8[1].

[12] Reading ummattakasabhāvo with Be for text's Se ummattasabhāvo; cp PvA 39.

[13] Reading na sīya with Se Be for text's sīya.

[14] The word for 'peak' and 'hammer' is the same here (kūṭa) and some pun is no doubt intended.

[15] Reading vālaggakoṭinittuddanamattaṃ with Se (Be -nitudana-) for text's bālakoṭimattaṃ.

[16] Reading addasāsiṃ with Se Be for text's addusāsiṃ.

[17] That is, the five (spiritual) faculties of faith, energy, mindfulness, concentration and wisdom. See e.g. E. Conze, *The Way of Wisdom*, Kandy 1964, Buddhist Publication Society Wheel Series Nos. 65/66.

[18] Reading -payogo tathā sakkharāya paharaṇena. Sālittakappaharaṇenā ti vā pāṭho

with Se for text's -payogo. Tathā sakkharāya paharaṇena sālittakappahāre ti vā pāṭho. Be differs considerably.

[19] Reading bhindissan ti bhindiṃ with Se Be for text's te bhindissan ti te bhindiṃ.

[20] Cp PvA 125.

[21] Reading avañjhataṃ with Se Be for text's avatthānaṃ (listed by PED as avaṭṭhānaṃ).

[22] So Be.

CONCLUDING REMARKS[1]

Thus:[2]

1 Those who arise amongst the petas have all been doers of evil deeds; on account of those deeds the fruit for them is evil and severe.

2 Demonstrating and explaining[3] this by means of questions and answers [287] is the teaching that by necessity stimulates[4] beings[5] with agitation,

3 That forms a topic of conversation that is skilled[6] and that is well founded on a thorough understanding (of the subject), namely, the Peta Stories that were rehearsed by the Great Masters.

4 Depending thereon, after the manner of their ancient commentary, to clarify their[7] meaning, I have undertaken this exposition of their meaning,

5 Namely, this Elucidation of the Intrinsic Meaning that appropriately clarifies the intrinsic meanings at various places herein,

6 This unconfused resolution (of the subtle meanings) which comprises of as many as fifteen textual recitation sections has now reached conclusion.

7-8 May all creatures plunge into the Teaching of the Saviour of the World[8] by means of the majesty[9] of whatever merit that has been attained by me through its composition in this way and may they partake in the flavour[10] of release through behaviour that is pure and virtuous and so on.

9 May the Teaching of the Perfect Buddha long remain in the world and may all living beings constantly have reverence for it.

10 May the (rain-)deva also rain properly and at the right time and may the Lord of the Earth[11] be devoted to the true Dhamma and rule the world in accordance with that Dhamma[12] alone.

Thus[13] the exposition of the meaning of the Peta Stories performed by the venerable Ācariya Dhammapāla, monk and noble sage and resident of the Badaratittha Vihāra,[14] is concluded.

The Commentary on the Peta Stories is accomplished.

[1] nigamanakathā, Be only.

[2] ettāvatā ca; so Se Be, text omits.

[3] Reading vibhāventī with Se Be for text's vibhāventi.

[4] Reading -vaḍḍhanī with Se Be for text's -vaḍḍhani.

[5] Be reads sataṃ for text's Se satta- in which case the meaning would be 'stimulates a hundredfold with agitation'.

[6] Reading kathāvatthukusalā with Se Be for text's gāthāvatthukusalā; such skilled or profitable topics are enumerated at M iii 113; Miln 344 etc.

[7] Reading tassa with Se Be for text's tattha.

[8] Cp PvA 42.

[9] Reading tassānubhāvena with Be for text's kammassānubhāvena; Se reads assānubhāvena.

[10] See GS i 32 n. 5, iv 139 n. 5.

[11] Reading jagatīpati with Se Be for text's jagati sadā; it is an honorific title for a king.

[12] dhammena; it may mean merely justly.

[13] I follow Be here: Iti Badaratitthavihāravāsinā munivarayatinā Bhadantena Ācariya Dhammapālena katā Petavatthu-atthasaṃvaṇṇanā niṭṭhitā Petavatthu-Aṭṭhakathā samattā.

[14] Dhammapāla was a native of Kāñcipuram and thus in all probability a Tamil and spent most of his time at the Badaratittha Vihāra on the south-east coast of India, a little to the south of Madras. See G. P. Malalasekera, *The Pali Literature of Ceylon*, Colombo 1958, pp. 112ff.; also DPPN i 1145f.

I. INDEX OF WORDS AND SUBJECTS

Numbers refer to page irrespective of whether prose or verse; superscript numbers denote the footnote on the page specified; asterisk (*) denotes a (usually fanciful) etymology.

Abhidhamma 4 139 142
Abhiññās 168
Abuse 14 48 97 149 277 278, -ive 60 61 108 109 256 257 259 277
Adepts 275
Adulterous 158 161 163 164, -tery 158 164, -tress 158
Aeon(s) 24 33[7] 33[8] 175[39] 256 276[6], great – 261 262, simile of the length of a great – 261f.; – long 106[3]
Agitation 3 33 37 43 48 58 61 63 80 82 96 111 112 151 165 172 186 195 205 224 242 243 254 255 276 283 291 293 297 298 299[5]
Ājīvika 82[1]
Alkaline 222 223
Alms vii 20 21 24 25 27 28 29 30 31 32 34[20] 35[60] 39 46 49 58 60 62 63 80 98 99 110 112 114 115 116 117 119 124 125 126 127 128 129 130 131 132 133 134 135 136 146[112] 156 157[9] 189 212 213 254 259 260 275 287, dependent upon a family for – 218 277 278 279, going about for/after – 154 275, in search of – 39 46 51 54 101 138 151 189 190 192 193 217 257 268 280 297
Almsbowl 273 275
Almsfood 16 17 147[126] 151 189 245
Almsgiving 20 22 23 24 25 27 39 56 62 69 85 99 112 112[2] 119 127 129 131 132 134 136 137 138 139 140 142 145[92] 146[111] 156 174[4] 181 195 200 205 211 260 270 272 289
Almshall 136
Almshouse 129
Alms materials 113 135 211, materials for the gifts 288
Almsround 42 193 246, uninterrupted – 257
Almsworthy vii 146[112]
Analysis of the elements 49[1]
Ancestors 21
Anger 59 90 222 229 235, -gry 38 89 90 92 123 150 202 234
Animal 113[22] 172 175[38] 283 284[5], womb of –s 172, -womb 30 282 283
Añjali 54 82[2] 101 149 164 189 190 243
Anoint 53 79 243 247
Antarā-parinibbāyin 147[122]
Antelope, kadalī 161 163
Appreciation 10 20 22 26 28 29 49 51 87 95 149 211 269 285, -ted 81
Arahant(s) ix 3 5 8 9* 10 11 13[23] 13[25] 19[2] 62 63 80 88[22] 104 113[26] 113[30] 148[139] 166[26] 174[3] 187[21] 191 213[2] 239 240 241 252[108] 265[26] 276[2] 276[12], the – ix 3 222 223 224, -fruit 275, -ship 18 57 63 190 242 251[70] 252[108] 260
Ariyan (adj) 220 245 248, (individual) 28 63 143[16] 154 157[9] 257 263, – path(s) 141 148[139] 191 296
Ariyasaṅgha 3 49 64[36] 113[30] 117
Army 254, 255
Arsenic, red 285
Arūpāvacara 147[132]
Āsavas 9 11 51 217 254
Āsava-free 104
Ascetic 18 104 105* 159 160 170 171 172
Assignment of a gift vii 11 35[60] 49 52 53 56 75 86 92 95 98 112 116 117 191 193 212 213 238
Asura(s) 113[22] 282 284[5] 284[7], Kāḷakañjaka- 283
Attendant(s) 42 45[2] 61 65 101 105 154 214 219 247 255 256 259 278 294
Austerity 105
Axle 287 288

Bamboo 185 282
Bandhujīvaka 11[5]
Banyan 8 119 120 125 147[132] 254 255 294
Barber 131 145[81] 180 185
Barren 36 89 203 297
Basket (a measure) 257 262, makers 182 184 185

Bath attendant 131 180 182 185
Bathing places 81 211 212 235 280 286
Bees 285 286
Beggar 84 108 109 119 124 126 127 129 132 133 135 274 275 292
Begging 6 154 202
Blinded 262 274 275
Blind man 243 246, -ness 8 12[15]
Blood 35[60] 38 39 39[8] 41 46 47 48 59 62 66 74 85 86 150 151 215 232 233
Blue-green 163 167[44]
Bodhisatta 23 44 46[16] 66 69[4] 106[3] 168
Bodhi tree 264[4]
Boon(s) 23 132 133 244
Bowl 6 149 172 189 242 246 274 275 285
Brahma-faring 19 34[46] 63 124 125 206 208 209 256 263
Brahmaloka 12[12] 80 147[132] 173 175[47]
Brāhmaṇic 145[98] 146[111] 146[112]
Brahmavihāras 49[1] 173 175[47]
Brahmā-worlds 140
Brahmin(s) 6 24 29 30 31 48 57 58 59 60 65 66 67 68 69 74 84 100 100[6] 104 105 106[16] 109 111 113 114 116 119 120 121 123 126 127 128 146[112] 155 156 187[26] 212 238 241 242 243 256 259 260 291 293[12] 294
Breadfruit trees 159 166[11]
Brick-powder 7
Buddha(s) viii ix 3 4 11[5] 19 22 23 24 25 33[7] 33[8] 43 45[1] 45[2] 45[3] 46[16] 57[24] 63 64[36] 83[41] 101 115 122 140 143[10] 147[128] 147[129] 147[130] 148[142] 148[145] 152[4] 173 175[39] 201[24] 204[12] 205 209[1] 216 216[3] 222 245 247 248 257 258 263 265[21] 274 283[1] 285 296 (Sunetta), Former – (general) 33[7], (Kassapa) 14 16 33[7] 158 197, (Phussa) 23 33[7], (Sujāta) 46[16], Perfect – ix 3 52 102 106 207 224 297 298
Buddha-interval 14 18 24 25 33[8] 51 200
Buddha-period 14 18 189 295
Buffaloes 86
Bull 82[20] 169 170 171, -ock 131
Burmese x 89[25]
Butter 206 208 211

Cakes 254 255 257 259
Cakkavāḷa 140 142 147[126] 147[132] 148[133]
Cakkavatti(n) (see also Wheel-turning (monarch)) 70[21] 83[41] 106[15] 143[26]
Calm 19[3], -ed 173
Caṇḍālas 104 182 185 187[26]
Caravan 47 142[2] 143[13] 284
Carriage 193 195 258 264, -of state 79 83[39]
Cart(s) 108 119 120 288, -load 108 109 136 137
Cattle 85 86 175[38], -rearing 26 31, womb of – 172 175[35]
Cemetery 86 100 169 170 205 206 207 208 218
Cetiya 222
Chandana 144[49]
Chariot 59 60 100[5] 100[6] 131 264[7] 294, -makers 182 185, -eer 169 170 171 221[15], -wheel 68
Charity vii 128 146[112]
Charnel ground 205 206 207 208
Circumambulation 43 78 79 83[36] 96[9] 168 229 285
Class (vaṇṇa) 106[16]
Clay 202 230 291 293
Cloak 47 49 52 98 229
Club(s) 6 7 59
Coins, small 211 212 280
Commentary vii viii ix x 299, ancient – 3 298
Companion(s) 26 30 31 32 91 93 215 217 218 219 229 232 235
Compassion 7 19 55 73 77 80 85 94 167 181 189 229 233 275 285, meditation of the great – 65 205, Saviour of Great – 3, -ate 190, -ate sage for the world x 77 193
Conceit 93
Conqueror, a 265[21], the 257 262
Consign 28 32
Continent(s) 56[10] 79 83[41] 84[58] 147[132]
Cooks 131 136 137
Corpse 18 37 41 223
Couch(es) 161 163 182 198 199 212 213 217
Council, First 149, Second 151, Third 264
Courtesan 7
Cow 86, 119
Co-wife 38 41 90 92
Creeper 11[5], santāna- 127
Cripple 294
Crossroads 7
Crow 206 207 212
Curse 151

Deasil 83[36]
Dedication of alms 24 25 26 27 28 29

39 49 86 87 116 117 192 194 239 240 241 257 272 285
Deer 60 179 214 215 216 217 295, -hunter 214 215 217 218, -stalker 217
Defecate 278
Defilements 9 54(monk*) 154(monk*) 239 240 290
Delusion 6 257 262
Demerit 291, 207 (act of), -torious deed 51
Desert region 128, – wilderness 107 119 125 131
Desire(s) 8 12[12] 19 77 86 153 182 185 199 237 239 240 257 271, hand that grants – 119 120 124 125 127 128
Destiny 66 67 68 82[1] 127 174[3] 182 185 186 278
Destitute 6 68
Deva(s) vii 8 9 10 19 20[10] 21 30 33 103 104 113[30] 116 117 123 124 125 128 132 133 138 139 140 142 143[25] 143[26] 153 156 186 187[31] 192 195 199 206 208 209 216[2] 239 247 255 256 257 258 263 265[26] 270[14] 271 282 283 284[5] 297
Deva, beings 223, -daughters 216[2], -form 100, -nymph 49 290, -sons 216[2], rain- 298, sky- 141
Devas, Deva of 142, terrestrial 7 12[11] 12[15] 47 58 147[132] 229, world of the vii
Devadhītā 214
Devaloka 7 11 12[11] 12[12] 24 69 87 95 111 133 142 143[25] 155 185 187[31] 195 222 238 272 282 283
Devaññatara 20[10]
Devaputta 8 11 20[10] 47 48 49 59 100 119 120 121 124 127 138 141 160 179 214 216[2] 267
Devatā(s) vii 12[15] 20[10] 47 54 55 76 87 88[20] 92 98 117 140 142 198 207 210[29] 216[2] 222 237 238 240 241 243 247 254 256 258 283, guardian- 85, household- 20 21, terrestrial- 119 288, tree- 8 47
Devī 76 87 92 98 198
Dhamma 3 6 13[45] 57[24] 152[4] 245 257 258, became given to the – 200, devotion for – 172, established in the – 235 236, expounded – 149, heard – 58 149 172 235 236 237, hearing – 140, in accordance with the – 28 83[41] 92 95 99 242 252[114] 298, King of the – 181, listen to – 242, proclaim the – 244, respect for – 243, skilled in the – 62, talk on – 32 43 54 69 151 189 240, taught – 15 19 22 39 44 49 56 57 58 63 82 88 96 99 104 112 117 156 165 195 200 204 213 216 224 249 270 279 281 283 287 288 290 293, taught – suiting the dispositions of 186 205 272, teach – 4 217 271, teaching – 8 103 241 297, teaching on – 43 45 49 106 173 181 205 263, took delight in the – 165, Treasurer of the – 4 5[10], true – 298, units of the – 4, Wheel of the (Noble) – 4 24 51 73 83[41] 107 153 165 200
Dhamma-farers 236, -followers 204, -hall 206, -of the worthy man 121 123, -talk 106
Dhammacakkhu 13[45] 19[2] 113[30]
Disposition 92 207
Doe 60
Dog 158 159 161 163 164 206 216
Doṇa 257 262 266[50]
Donation 21 22 26 28 32 49 52 53 56 75 77 86 87 92 95 98 116 117 138 180 181 212 213 243 246 254 272 285
Drum(s) 79 218[5], execution – 7, kettle – 97 198 199
Dust 90 91 92 122, gold- 198, -heap 149 194

Efforts, four right 105
Egg-born 187[19]
Eightfold path 107[21] 257 263, -vow 245 248
Elder(s) 4 7 8 14 15 16 17 39 40 41 42 73 74 75 77 80 84[53] 84 85 86 87 101 138 149 150 188 189 190 191 192 193 194 195 196[18] 200 204 215 216 217 219 240 241 242 243 248 264 268 269 273 277 278 280 281 296
Elementary Substances 256 261
Elephant(s) 54 57 58 59 60* 79 159 179 189 229 254 255 264[7] 274 290 294
Embryo 38 40 41
Enemy(ies) 9 66 161 278, tamer of your – 255 256 257 258 259
Evil 271 272 298, – character 267, – conduct 237, – deed 38 41 74 90 97 108 151 162 211 218 220 222 233 243 277 280 289 296 298, -doer 277 295, – nature 215
Envy 27 36 39 40 90 94 185 277, -ied 94,

-ious 90 92 183 277
Excellence 24 25 29 31 39 55 73 77 79 80 81 104 117 126 136 139 153 154 173 176[49] 185 197 205 206 213 216 260 285, heavenly – x 19 32 78 81 95 99 138 139 151 159 160 197 200 206 208 216 219 224 285
Excrement 35[60] 46 47 48 49 85 91 93 202 203 277 278 279
Excreted 207, -tion 203 204
Executed 230, -tion 7 11[5] 159
Exhausted 114 115 120 128 131 132 133 153 269 284, -tion 6 66 104 115 155 200
Existence(s) 3 31 55 66 94 109 110 158 171 172 173 176[49] 184 191 195 209 223 233 261 262 273 278 292, happy – vii 237 238, miserable – vii 37 41 74 77 91 108 168 190 191 211 212 213 215 216 218 237 238 239 277 280 295
Eye, Buddha 65 205, heavenly 7, – of knowledge 172

Fatalism 265[21]
Fate 256 260 261 262
Fatigue 6 120 121 131 254
Field 3 4 5 9 10 11 13[25] 65 99 139 140 141 142 207, gone to the – 138 200, merit – (see s.v. Merit)
Fire 39[7] 41 44 45 64[10] 65 105 172 182 183 211 212 280, great – 233, hell – 189
First Sermon 63[2]
Fish 189 269
Fisherman(men) 189 276[1]
Fleeces, woollen 161 163 182 217
Flies 36 37 39[8] 40
Former birth(s) 268, knowledge of – 175[39] 250[68]
Former lives 274, remembering – 189
Four assemblies 15 297
Four truths 13[45] 19[2] 45 69 105 106 113[30] 142 173 276 290
Friend(s) vii 26 30 31 32 67 68 93 121 122 185 202 214 219 230 231 232 243 274 278 283 284 285 286, lovely – 197
Friendliness, mind of (mettacittaṃ) (see also Loving kindness) 173 175[47]
Fruit 3 9 10 13[34] 15 20 21 22 26 27 28 29 30 31 49 53 54 55 62 67 68 74 75 76 77 78 87 92 93 98 109 110 111 112 112[2] 114 115 125 126 127 139 140 141 142 153 154 156 159 160 161 162 202 203 204 216 224 248 256 257 259 260 262 263 268 274 286 288 294 296 297[3] 298
Fruit(s) of the life of a recluse 246 249 252[108], (of the paths) 265[26], arahant – 275, lesser – 249, topmost – 239 246
Fruitfulness 156
Fruition 141 258 273[11], – of deeds 3 4 10 28 40 51 52 54 75 109 126 136 146[116] 237 238 241 252[120]
Funeral pile 43 65 86, – pyre 100 167 168 169 170, – rites 78 80 168

Gandhabba 124 125 148[146] 254 256
Garland(s) 11[5] 54 65 91 98 179 180 182 220 223, -ed 219 220
Gate-keeper 230
Generosity 9 10 48 62 114 115 126 127 174[4], -rous 21 32
Gift(s) 10 22 27 28 53 74 78 85 86 88[22] 92 95 99 109 116 117 127 129 130 131 134 135 136 139 140 141 142 144[47] 149 154 205 209 243 247 254 260 265[16] 276[6] 285 286 288, materials for the – 288
Giving 74 75 78 96 108 109 110 112 114 115 118 125 126 130 132 133 134 135 136 137 141 151 165 185 206 236 241 243 256 259 260 280 281 283 286 297
Giving, master in the practice of 60 124 126 128 130 132
Glorious One, the 257
Goat(s) 86, – dung, pellets of 294
Go(ne) forth 8 36 57 58 80 113 114 153 168 172 173 182 184 189 242
Going astray, ways of 168 174[3] 174[4]
Goose, ruddy 161
Grass ix 43 44 65 120 163 232 242 246 263, kusa- 193 195 261
Grassy 161 163
Gravel 193 195 294 295 296 297[1]
Great Lakes 158 165[6] 261
Great Masters 3 298
Great Renunciation 23
Greed 9 21 95 110 112 126 127 159 204[12] 212 268 284
Greedy 271 291
Green 163 167[44]
Grief 8 17 42 43 44 45 46[16] 65 100 101 102 105 106 156 165 167 168 170 172 173 268 269 285
Grieve 45 102 103 105 172 285
Group of Five 24

Hammer(s) 59 60 68 202 203 294 295 296 297[14]
Happy state 91 94 96 183 236 237 238
Hare 101 102 103 106[3]
Harem 88[18] 291
Harlot 50 205 208 210
Harsh speech 59, – spoken 29 30 90 92 97, – words 205 208
Harshly 209
Hawk 207
Heaven 24 45 79 109 111 142 144[49] 148[133] 148[146] 174[3] 182 185 222 271 274, bound for – 165 271 272
Heavenly form 230, – place 9 11* 92 95* 99 200
Hell 7 14 19[5] 24 29 54 55* 73 109 111 113[22] 148[133] 174[3] 175[26] 222 223 233 236 238 242 244 245 257 259 262 263 266[53] 273 274 276 276[1] 282 283 284[5] 291 292 295, – fire 189
Help 7 45 95 120 181 189 191 206 209[6] 243 269, -less state 205 206
Heresy 82 82[1] 84[66] 262
Heretic 73 147[126], -al view 266[49]
Heron 161 162
Hindu 33[11] 82[20]
Honour ix 11 26 29 32 33 111 115 140 148[146] 168 205 208 209 222 223 224 256 260, -ed 9 11 20 53 116 117 121 138 181 205 206, -ing ix 11 132 224 260
Horoscope 207
Horse 54 79 175[38] 179 229 235 241 252[112] 294, -back 120, -sacrifice 146[112]
Human 51 76 92 97 98 103 110 116 117 207 243 266[33], -being(s) 30 66 156 184 203, – body 137 138, – existence 76 94, – form 47 153 230 283, – life 63, – life-span 78, – state 76 127 138 271 292, – womb 223 281 292, beings other than – 230, non- 51 103 153 154 160 164 165 215 216 218 219 243 244 249[9] 255 258 282, -beings 207
Hunger 14 22[9] 36 37 41 47 61 62 73 74 77 85 86 107 108 110 115 130 150 156 159 181 183 184 189 191 271 272 274 281
Hungry 66 131
Hunter 179 185 214 215 219[7], deer- 214 215 217 218

Ill will 267
Impale 229
Impaled 229 230 231 232 235 242 244 245 246 248
Impalement 230
Impermanence 65 67 96[17]
Incest 106[16]
Insect 48 50[14] 73
Insight 18 19[2] 44 67 134 174[21] 175[47] (vipassanā) 215 218 258 271, – into the Dhamma 11 12[14] 13[45] 33 142 186 205 209[6], -meditation 173
Island(s) 79 83[41]
Insult 14 48 49 97 278 279, -ing 61 259 274 276 279(speech)

Jackal 206 207
Jackfruit tree(s) 159 166[11]
Jainas 216[3] 265[21]
Jātaka 69 70[21] 106 157[9]
Javana-moments 252[120]
Jhāna 12[15] 49[1] 80 84[55] 141 168 169 173 175[47] 239

Kahāpaṇa(s) 109 113[17] 160 168 284 286
Kalpa-vṛkṣa 144[49]
Kāmāvacara 12[12] 12[15] 143[25] 147[132]
Kamma 15[2] 67 69[6] 157[13] 221[4] 223 224[10], -ic time 270[14]
Kammaṭṭhāna 49[1] 69[3]
Kaṇavīra 7 11[5]
Kapikacchu 91 93
Karīsa 268 270[2]
Kasina 49[1]
King, tenfold code of a 168 174[4]
Knife 222 223
Kosalan 113[16] 290
Koṭi (crore) 6 11[2] 103 139 142 153 154 206 257 262 263 265[22] 266[53]
Kṣatriya 104 106[16] 119 137 138 185 274

Laity 57[24]
Lakkha 257 262 265[22] 266[53]
Lament 21 42 62 100[5] 284 285 289, -ation 20 21 26 43 44 65 66 67 68
Latrine 91 277 278 279
Layfollower(s) 40 42 43 52 53 55 56 57[24] 58 65 69 82 97 98 99 100 101 106 151 153 158 163 167 173 180 190 204 205 208 209 211 212 213 214 215 217 218 245 248 254 257 267 268 271 279 282 288 289
Layman(men) 88[22] 113[30] 213[2] 265[26]
Learners 9 13[26]
Leg-drinker 255 259

Lent 221[2]
Lie(s) (see also Precepts) 18 19 38 39 40 41 163 164 203 203(lying) 220 220(lying) 245 258
Life-span 11 78 139 146[113] 146[121] 147[122] 147[124] 219 221[4] 224[3] 263(in hell)
Lightning 59 159
Loathsome objects 49[1], -ness of food 49[1]
Lord of Devas 25 128 132
Lotus 25 77 79 81 161 162 193 195 198 222
Lotus ponds viii 25 77 81 108 159 161 162 163 193 197 198 199 230 284 285 286
Lovely friend 197 200[1] 248
Loving kindness (see also Friendliness) 240
Lust 8 98 105 214 240 245

Madman 42 43 101 102 294 295
Mahāyāna 216[3] 284[5]
Maidens 219 220
Man of property 36 39 42 78 89 94 96 205 206 222 277 279 285 286
Māna-vessel 262 266[50]
Mandāra 144[49]
Mango(es) 147[126] 159 160 166[24] 197 284 286, -fruit(s) 159 160 197 285, -grove 160 166[29] 285 286 287[1], -tree(s) 147[126] 159
Mansion vii 47 50 51 54 56 153 154 159 161 197 198 199 200 219 282 285 286
Mantra(s) 103 104 123
Matted-hair ascetics 24 25 239
Matter 38 39 39[8] 41 206 207
Mean 47 48 90 92 97 108 109 113 114 115 183 259
Meanness 129
Means, failure of the 123 139
Meat 179 202 203 204[12]
Medicine(s) 76 82[20] 88[21] 93 103 195 206 207, -nal herbs 91 93 103
Meditating 296
Meditation 104 105, – of the great compassion 65 205, – subject (kammaṭṭhāna) 46 63 69[3] 105
Meditative 239 241
Merit vii 9 10 34[46] 75 78 88[22] 110 126 127 144[47] 168 206 207 212 245 248 260 280 281 298, -field 3 8 12[11] 22 135 142 146[112] 201[30] 224 239 265[26], -offering 8 9 10 11 13[24] 13[34] 24 28 75 78 94 99 109 110 117 129 130 132 133 136 138 139 182 184 211 212 260 271 272 280 281 288 292
Meritorious action 140, – deed(s) ix 7 8 10 11 12[11] 26 32 33 51 52 53 58 61 62 66 69 75 76 78 80 82[16] 87 92 93 98 104 110 111 112 113 118 119 123 124 125 126 127 128 136 137 138 141 153 154 155 156 157 158 159 160 165 182 183 185 186 195 197 200 201[24] 205 206 222 223 224 224[3] 238 241 242 248 252[120] 259 268 272 281 283 293 297
Meritorious ones 216, – service 141, – states 207 248
Meritoriously 214
Middle path 134
Mindfulness 88[8] 174[21] 257 287[11] 297[17], – of death 65 69
Miscarriage 36 38 39 40 41
Miserly 47 48 108 109 113 243 256 257 259 277, -liness 48
Miserable (see also Existence) 52 233 243 246, – state 238
Misery 17 39 41 47 61 62 66 68 73 74 82[1] 90 100 109 111 115 121 126 156 159 167 182 183 184 185 189 195 202 208 211 212 214 215 216 217 218 222 223 229 233 236 237 238 240 242 243 248 256 257 260 262 269 273 274 275 277 280 281 287 288 289 290 291 292 296, state of – 36 37 74 75 77 94 191 215 216 218
Moat 211 270 289
Moisture-born 187[19]
Monkeys 241
Moon 68 82[20] 100 100[5] 102 103 106[3] 140 141 198, full- 198 213[2]
Moriyan (Mauryan) 258 264[4] 283[1]
Mother-of-pearl 229
Mourn 21 44 66 67 68 167 170 171, -ing ix 21 66 68 101 167
Mud 198 229 236, -dy 235 236
Mule 58 59 60
Music 79 165[5], fivefold instrumental – 217 218[5]
Mustard fumigation 206 207, -oil 208

Nāga 60 283 284[6]
Nahuta 274 275
Naked 36 40 47 52 57[27] 73 74 75 77 84 85 89 90 91 94 107 108 113 114 179 181 190 191 192 194 196[23]

210 211 230 235 238 239 280, -ness 114 243 246
Natthika heresy 107 112[2] 229 254 259 262
Needle 114 115 191, -afflicted 190 191, -gone 191, -throated 191, -worker 126, eyes of – 191
Nikāya(s) 4
Nimba wood 231 232
Non-returner (anāgāmin) 8 13[26] 19[2] 113[30] 148[139] 252[108] 265[26]
Novice 57 58 59 61 63 84[53] 189
Nymphs 56

Oath 36 38 40 41 158 159 163 164 202
Oblation vii 104
Ocean 51 56[10] 147[132] 282 283, mighty – 51 56[10] 147[132]
Offering vii 11[5] 87 88[20], sacrificial – 256 260
Oil 51 54 242 289, -cake 51 54, mustard – 208
Omen, bad 271, stick of – 282
Omniscience 207
Once-returner (sakadāgāmin) 8 13[26] 19[2] 113[30] 148[139] 252[108] 265[26]
Opapātika 187[19]
Open-handed 257
Order 58 92 95, – of monks 23 25 87 88[22] 95 101 113[30] 151 181 194 197 205 213 245 248 265[26] 269 289, with the Buddha at its head 22 23 32 56 87 112 181 205 208 270f. 287 289
Ordination 11[5] 57 190
Ox(en) 42 43 44 47 108 131, head of an – 235 236, skull of an – 229

Paccekabuddha 78 80 84[53] 152 153 157 189 273 275 276[4] 276[12] 295 296 297
Paddy 9 202 203 208
Palace 7 80 114 117 161 165 182 185 187[27] 217
Pali viii x
Pali Text Society x xi
Palm tree 59
Palmyra 107 108 112[8]
Parched 107 131 150 211 212 268 269 280
Pāricchattaka 147[130]
Pārijāta 144[49]
Parinibbāna 24 80 149 221 254 295
Path(s) 19[2] 113[30] 258 265[26], ariyan – 141 148[139] 191 296, fruits of the – 3
Pātimokkha 239
Pavāraṇā ceremony 24 33[5] 142(mahā-) 148[144]
Peacock fans 182, – tail feathers 150 185
Perfections, ten 141 148[139]
Perfectly Enlightened One 24
Peta-plane 27 28 30 31 33 35[60] 62 85 86 108 223 271 272 276[6] 278, -state 112 116 117, -womb 11 39 40 58 61 74 75 85 89 97 110 112 150 179 184 278 280 290, former – 20 21, world of the – 37 41 49 56 74 86 90 92 97 98 108 115 190 194 211 212 213 277 278 280 295 296
Pigeon 51
Pilgrimage 147[128] 216[3]
Piṇḍa 146[111]
Pinnacled house 182 185 188[51] 192 194 217 294
Pisāca-demons 207
Piṭakas 4
Pitṛ 35[60] 146[111]
Pitiful 185
Pitiless 275
Pity 17 19 26 27 28 39 45 51 63 66 74 75 105 106 111 117 149 154 170 180 181 190 191 192 193 206 215 218 220 222 231 232 245 288
Piyaṅgu 294 297[3]
Plane, divine vii
Plight 7 8 37 110 120 206 209
Ploughing 9 44 65 69
Potential 42 45[1] 58 101 167
Preceptor 58 59 63
Precepts 54 57[24] 69 105 110 112 213[2] 242 245 248 254 257 259 263, conduct associated with the – 29 38 111 258
Preta 35[60]
Previous birth(s) 3 97 185 205, – existence 110 223 233, – life 48 66 183 214 232 233
Pride 93 189 270 291
Prostitute 211
Psychic power 8 49 56 59 116 123 125 138 143[24] 153 181 199 208 222 230 235 243 247 282
Pukkusas (refuse-clearers) 104 185
Pun ix 50[21] 297[14]
Punish 230, -ment 244 247
Pus 35[60] 46 47 48 59 62 85 86
Puthujjana(s) 17 19[2]
Putrid 16 18 19 36 40 41 191 222 223

Queen-consort 168 171

Rainy season 23 46 148[144], residence of the – 23 33[5] 40 46 47
Rebirth vii 10 39 86 138 140 173 175[47] 265[21] 276[2] 284[5]
Recluse(s) 6 18 48 58 60 74 80 84 109 111 114 119 126 127 150 155 156 172 190 191* 211 212 238 240 241 242 243 246 249 252[108] 259 260 294
Recollecting the Buddha's virtues 222
Recollection 171
Recollections, the 49[1]
Reed(s) 60 61 185
Refuge 32 52 62 63 79 86 91 93 109 182 183 211 212 245 248 257 258 280 281 292
Refuges, the 54 57[24] 112 149 242 254 263
Related 233
Relations 28 29 273, blood – 29 30 232 233
Relative(s) vii 20 21 22 24 25 26 27 28 29 30 31 32 36 38 41 58 66 67 68 74 82[16] 88[20] 91 92 93 99 102 103 106 114 115 149 153 155 156 168 179 186 189 190 192 193 231 232 233 276[6] 283, peta – 24 26 28 29 188 273 276[6]
Relics 80 221 222 223 224[4]
Reptiles 206 207 210[18]
Requisites 9 80 87 151 245 277, four – 17 47 88[21] 195 247
Residual effect 14 273 295, -result 184 188[48]
Retinue 19 139 160 165 185 186 219 224 238
Rice-gruel 16 25 205 208 209 285 286
Right view 30 113[30] 187[21] (mundane) 239
Rishi 80 104 105* 168 169* 170 175[25] 273 274 275* 276
Rites for the dead 285, funeral – 78 80 168
Robber(s) 6 7 57 159 284
Robe(s) 47 78 88[21] 151 153 172 242 245
Royal regalia 79
Rubbish 89 92, -heap 192 194 205
Rūpāvacara 12[12] 147[132]

Sacrifice vii 134 135 136 137 138 293[12], brāhmaṇic – 146[112], fourfold – of everything 291, Great – 137 138, horse – 146[112], human – 146[112]
Sacrificial act 137, – fire vii, – offering 256 260, – ritual 105 145[98]
Sage 63[2] 169 170* 170 239 299, compassionate – x 77 193, great – 170 171 172 223 224, Sakyan – 257
Sāla Grove 222, -trees 221
Saṃsāra 9 66 67 171 172 175[35] 248 256 262 266[49] 272, -mocaka 73 82 84[66], -suddhi 82[1], -ric existence 261
Sandal 219 220, -wood 80 100[5] 220 243 247 249[4]
Saṅgha 21 22 23 26 57[24] 88[22] 95 115 116 117 152[4] 192 193 194 196[51] 197 245 248 258 265[26] 285, – of the four quarters 87 192 193 194
Saṅghika 88[22] 196[36]
Santāna (Saṃtānaka) 127 144[49]
Sāvaka 19[2] 52 57[24] 58 64[36] 80(mahā-) 112 113[30] 143[16] 218 265[26], -saṅgha vii 146[112] 205 265[26]
Saviour of Great Compassion 3, – of the World 45 298
Sayaṃ guttā 93
Scent 53 65 91 98 131 143[32] 149 161 162 168 169 170 181 205 222 229, -sellers 131
Scoffers at the ariyans 257 263
Seed 9 10 13[34] 99 139 140 141 142 147[126] 262
Self, developed 104 105 140 141, tamed of – 273 275
Selfish 60 74 182 185 277, -ness 21 27 48 92 94 95 96 99 112 118 149 151 157 185 190 205 211 212 270 280 281 290
Sense(s), feasting the 61, gratification of the 19 81 238, guarding the doors of the 14 169 239 257, losing one's 106[5], pleasures of the 6 185 186 214 215 271
Sense-sphere 140 147[132] 148[146]
Sensual desires 271, – pleasure(s) 61 164 165 274, what is – 214
Serpent 66
Sesame 211
Sesamum 51 52 54
Shame 51 174[21] 294, -ful 92 94 96[18] 181 183 191
Shaveling 189 205 211
Silence 157[9] 190, consent with/by – 20 23 25 149 181
Sinhalese x 11[5] 264[4]
Sixfold lore 104
Skeleton 159 163 216

Skilled behaviour 125, – deed(s) 8 11 28 52 54 62 73 80 128 152 156 182 183 184 189 200 201[24] 215 216 218 238 245 248 252[120] 281 282 283 292 293, – in proprieties 135, – in right conduct 134, – states 10 126 151 184 190 207 244 245 248 283, – topics 299[6], what is/who are – 9 10 11 19 156 220 298
Skilful means 106, -ness 262
Sky 18 68 77 111 113 114 192 223 224
Slander 16 18 19 220, -rous speech 29 30 219 220, -rousness 219
Snake 65 66 69 152
Some 11 18 27 38 44 61 75 111 137 191 231 236 [alternative readings cited: 31 38 93 150 164 170 171 191 199 200 231 296]
Sorrow ix 20 21 26 32 44 45 69 92 95 99 100 164 172 186, -ful 54 109 257
Sotāpanna 8 12[14] 13[26] 13[45] 19[2] 113[30] 148[139] 158 242 252[108] 265[26]
Sotāpatti- 12[14], -fruit 24 42 43 45 45[1] 46[16] 69 101 106 149 167 173 249 276 287 290 293
Soul 256 261 262 265[21]
Spoon-alms 138 139
Śrāddha 29
Stake 231 232 233 242 244
Star 82[20] 140 141
States of loss 111
Stench 223 255 258
Streamwinner (sotāpanna) 12[14]
Stūpa ix 46[9] 80 222 223 224 224[4]
Successful attainment of the field 10 207, – of those worthy of donations 29 139 142
Suchness 189
Śūdras 104 106[16] 187[26]
Suffered 276
Suffering vii 22[9] 37 222 223 290
Sugar-cane 267 268 269, grove of – 267 268
Sugata 142 148[142] 204 206 207 215 216 218
Sun 61 83[36] 100 100[5] 117 132 139 147[132] 183 211 212 213[2] 219 220 221[15] 230 280
Sunrise 132 160 181 205 218, -set 291, -shade 51 98 131
Supaṇṇas 283 284[6]
Supramundane paths 19[2] 148[139]
Supreme Deity 260
Surveying the world 7 42 101 205
Swan(s) 161 162 166[26] 198 199 201[10], golden – 181, king of the golden – 181
Sweetmeats 7 8
Sympathetic 236 243

Tailor 119 124 126 168, -ing 119 168
Tamāla (blossoms) 222
Tamil 136 146[109] 299[14]
Tathāgata 112 116 117 208
Theft 204[12]
Theravāda 284[5]
Thirst 14 25 36 37 47 61 62 73 85 86 107 108 110 112 150 156 181 183 184 189 191 212 271 272 274 283
Thirsty 131 150 212 268 269
Thoroughbred 229 243
Those making a recension of the Dhamma 190
Those rehearsing the texts 53 56[21] 75 95 98 115 130 136 140 141 150 169 180 200 206 208 213 231 242 254 263f. 267[58]
Those rehearsing the Dhamma 192
Thread 152 153 154 261, ball of – 256 261
Three Jewels 3 52 149 248
Throat 107 112 269 291
Thunderbolt 49
Tongue 107 159 207
Tonsure-hall 57
Trader(s) 51 52 53 106[16] 107 108 111 112 120 128 229 253 282 283 285 286 288, dishonest – 202 203, scoundrel of a – 203
Transience 63
Transfer of merit vii 28(denied)
Turban 83[40], -ed 220
Twin Miracle 139 147[126]

Uddāla flowers 179
Umbrella 79 83[40]
Uncharitable 48
Unselfish 182 185 257
Unskilled deed(s) 17 54 111 184 238 250[57] 274
Uposatha 69 211 213[2] 219 248 257 263
Urine 35[60] 46 47 48 85

Vadamala 11[5]
Vaiśyas 104 106[16]
Vajjhamālā 11[5]
Vajjian(s) 229 230 231 239 289[2] (confederacy)
Vedas 104 146[112]
Vedic deity 152[10]

Venison 66
Vihāra 16 23 25 43 58 59 73 85 88[7] 149 150 158 206 277 279 285 299
Vimāna vii 35[60]
Vimāna-devatā 100 199
Vimānapeta 153 155 214 219 254 282 285
Vimānapetī 51 54 56 158 165 166[29] 197 200 201[25]
Vīṇa 158
Virtue 3 18 40 42[6] 48 55 62 66 74 96 98 105 106[3] 114 115 126 140 151 156 158 168 169 195 222 229 240 241 245 257 258 281 292
Virtuous 73 80 116 122 132 133 135 147[129] 158 184 209 229 267 292 298
Visible, making 25 168 181 192 194
Vision, deva-like 168
Vulture 207

Wail 25 62 165 268 270, -ing 100 168 169 170 255 258
Water lily(ies) 25 77 81 161 162 193 195 198 230 291 293
Water-pot 59 68 190 195 196[16] 197[56] 254 255 257 259 294
Wealthy merchant 3 6 8 20 22 24 107 108 109 119 126 127 130 143[7] 290 291
Weaver 46 47
Weep 21 44 45 66 67 68 105 165 167 169 170 172 271, -ing 8 20 21 22 26 32 44 66 68 100 168 268 271 272
Wheel-turning (monarch) (see also Cakkavatti(n)) 123 143[26]
Wicked character 233, – conduct 278, – deed(s) 7 8 9 15 16 17 37 38 39 41 54 55 59 61 62 74 84[66] 90 91 92 94 97 98 104 108 109 111 112 115 122 125 126 129 151 158 159 164 165 174[3] 181 189 190 197 203 205 211 212 213 214 215 218 221[4] 222 223 233 236 237 238 241 243 248 252[120] 254 257 260 262 263 274 276 277 278 280 292 295 297, – life 292, – mind 256, – states 105 190, – thought 209, – view 258 262 263
Wickedness 111 156 191 215 218
Widow 68 168
Wish 51 107[18] 132 135 150 151 155 157[14] 186 218 285, -granting hand 128, -granting tree (see also Kalpavṛkṣa) 79 127 144[49] 185 285 286
Witness 230 241 242 243 244 247
Wives, of others 291 293, other men's – 270
Woe, a state of 272, states of – 248
Woeful state 62
Womb-born 187[19]
World beyond vii 69[12] 170 256 260 271 288, – of men 37 59 63 69[12] 110 153 154 155 162 166[29] 170 203 209 237 268 270 278, – systems 139 140 148[133]
Worms 18 48 50[14] 202 203 204 222 223
Worthy of donations 28 29 99 115 116 130 132 133 136 139 140 141 142 180 239
Worthy man 121 122 127 135 246, Dhamma of the – 121 123
Wrong-doer 274
Wrong view 29 30 47 58 73 119 187[21] 229 240 247 254 256 257 259 260 263 264[3]

Yakkha 19 35[60] 59 116 117 120 123 125 128 131 140 141 144[34] 152 206 207 234 235 239 240 243 244 246 247 248 253 258 263 264 265[23] 283
Yojana(s) (league) 54 55 78 109 120 139 140 141 148[146] 160 183 230 256 257 261 280 281

Zodiac 207

II. INDEX OF NAMES

Numbers refer to page irrespective of whether prose or verse; superscript numbers denote the footnote on the page specified; asterisk (*) denotes a (usually fanciful) etymology:

Abhidhamma 139 142
Abhidhamma Piṭaka 4
Adam's Peak 147[128]
Adinnapubbaka 100 100[5]
Aggideva 101 119
Agni vii
Agrawala, V. S. 142[2]
Ajātasattu 114 116 117 222 224[2]
Ajita Kesakambalin 112[2] 264[3] 265[21]
Ajjuna 101 119
Altekar, A. S. 264[4]
Ambasakkhara 229 231 242 245 246 249 252[108]
Ambasakkhara Peta Story 291
Ambaṭṭha 104 106[16]
Ambaṭṭha Sutta 106[16]
Amore, R. 146[112]
Ānanda 5[10] 45[2] 101 147[126] 189
Anāthapiṇḍika 20
Andhakavinda 113 114 115 116
Aṅga 34[14] 142[2]
Aṅga-Magadha 24 34[14]
Aṅgati 82[1]
Aṅgīrasa 124 127* 129
Aṅguttara Nikāya 4
Añjanadevī 119
Aṅkura 101 118 119 120 121 123 124 125 128 130 131 132 133 134 136 137 138 139 140 141 145[83]
Aṅkura Peta Story 142
Anotatta 165[6] 262
Anulā 113
Anurādhapura 5[4] 12[16]
Anuruddha 84 87 138
Araṇiya Devas 220
Aruṇa 221[15]
Aruṇavatī Vihāra 73
Āsāḷhī (Āṣāḍha) 139 147[127]
Asayha 124 126 127 128 143[33], -mahāseṭṭhi 119, -seṭṭhi 119 126 127 128 129 145[83]
Asia 142[2]
Asitañjana 118 119
Asoka 83[41] 264[4] 264[5] 283[1]
Avīci 17 55 189 295

Badaratittha Vihāra 229 229[14]
Bāhlīka 142[2]
Baladeva 101 119
Bald-Headed Peta Story 75 111
Bamboo Grove 6 8 13 16 73 84 113 179 188 214 216[3] 217 219 267 269 289 294
Bamyan 142[2]
Basham, A. L. 265[21]
Benares 43 50 57 58 63[2] 65 78 84 113 114 159 160 179 180 181 188 197 294
Bhaddā Kāpilānī 80
Bhaggava 175[39]
Bhairava 165[8]
Bheruva 119 124 125
Bhopal 264[4]
Bhūta 89 91 92 94
Bimbisāra 24 26 27 86 88[22] 179 219 276[6]
Brahmā 104 105 139 147[126] 148[133] 166[26] 175[43] 297, Great – 148[146], Sanaṃkumāra 201[10]
Brahmadatta 167 169 170 171 175[26]
Brahmakund 33[11]
Brahmayoni 33[11]
Budaun 174[1]
Buddhadatta 152[17] 270[2]
Buddhaghosa 145[92] 187[19] 210[29]
Buddhavaṃsa 33[7]
Burma 56[11]

Cakkavatti-Sīhanāda Suttanta 83[41] 143[26]
Calcutta 264[4]
Campā 142[2]
Candadeva 101 119
Cariyāpiṭaka 148[139]
Ceylon 5[4] 11[5] 147[128]
Chaddanta 165[6]
Chambal 174[1]
Chandajōti Thēra, Māpalagama x
Chaudhury, B.N. 142[2] 146[109] 174[1]
Childers, R. 40[10] 50[14] 82[20] 96[18] 166[24] 204[11] 253[122] 266[40] 270[2] 276[5] 297[4]

Citta (Caitra) 138 146[117]
Clarification of the Intrinsic Meaning (Paramatthavibhāvaniyaṃ) 253
Colombo x
Conze, E. 297[17]
Coomaraswamy, A. K. 112[2] 143[21] 165[3]
Coral Tree 139 140 147[130]
Cousins, Lance xi
Cūḷani 170 171, -Brahmadatta 168
Cūḷaseṭṭhi 113
Cūḷataṇhā Saṅkhayasutta 187[27]
Cundaṭṭhila 179 180

Dakkhiṇa-Pañcāla 174[1]
Dakkhiṇāpatha 136
Daṇḍaka 175[25]
Darbhaṅga 289[2]
Dasaṇṇas 107 108 109
Deathless 215 216 218 257 263
Deccan 146[109]
Deer Park 63[2]
Delhi 174[1]
Devadatta 114
Devagabbhā 118
Dhammadinnā 24
Dhammapāla vii viii ix x 5[4] 34[46] 46[16] 50[21] 56[21] 89[26] 100[6] 106[16] 143[10] 148[133] 148[148] 175[35] 186[7] 188[41] 209[10] 252[120] 265[16] 266[53] 276[6] 283[1] 299 299[14]
Dhammapāla (brahmin family) 65
Dhammāsoka 254 258 264[5]
Dhanapāla 107 108 109 112[14], -ka 107
Dhataraṭṭha 20 21 143[32] 181
Dīgha Nikāya 4
Dīgharājī 73 82
Dutt, S. 88[22]
Dvāraka 102 120 124 128 130 131
Dvāravatī 101 102 119 120 128 131

Elucidation of the Intrinsic Meaning 77 100 267 298
Encyclopedia of Buddhism 252[120]
Erakaccha 107 108 109

Farukkhabad 174[1]
Four Great Kings 20 21 123 143[32] 144[34] 147[132] 265[23] 283

Gaṇḍa 147[126], -'amba 139 147[126]
Gandhāra 142[2]
Ganges 50 146[109] 150 151 159 160 179 181 197 264[4] 289[2] 295
Garuḍa 284[6]
Gayā 33[11]
Gayāsīsa 24
Gehman, H. S. 19[3] 39[5] 39[8] 42[6] 45[3] 46[16] 56[4] 56[7] 63[1] 69[10] 89[25] 106[8] 157[2] 166[29] 186[5] 187[27] 187[28] 196[15] 196[16] 196[38] 209[6] 214[4] 221[2] 221[3] 251[90] 251[93] 252[103] 265[15] 270[4] 273[3] 273[14] 276[2] 287[11] 293[12]
Ghaṭa 105, -Jātaka 142[4], -paṇḍita 101 102 103 104 105 106 119
Giribbaja 215 216[3] 218 222 273 274
Godāvarī 146[109]
Gombrich, Richard xi
Gonda, J. 146[112]
Gotama 15[1] 24 29 30 46[16] 83[40] 218
Grand Trunk Road 142[2]
Great Hell (Avīci) 55 189 233
Great Lakes 158f.
Great Sacrifice 137 138
Gujerat 264[4]

Hardy, E. x xi 83[30] 89[26]
Hardy, R. Spence 284[7]
Hare, E. M. 252[120]
Hastinapur 213[1]
Hastināpura 142[2]
Hatthinipura 210 211 213
Healing Star 76 87 92 98
Hewavitarne, Simon x
Himālaya (Himalayas) 63[2] 80 142[2] 150 151* 159 160 168 174[1] 197 271
Hooghly 264[4]
Hopkins, E. Washburn 221[15] 284[7]
Horner, I. B. xi 148[139] 266[49]

Indaka 138 139 140
India 56[10] 84[49] 142[2] 146[109] 147[132] 165[3] 188[51] 299[14]
Indian Antiquary 264[4]
Indore 264[4]
Indra 64[10] 144[57] 265[16]
Iron Cauldron 233 291 292
Iron Cauldron Jātaka 293[12]
Isipatana 57 59
Iṭṭhakāvatī 73 82

Jainas 216[3] 265[21]
Jambudīpa 80 83[41] 119 147[132]
Janakapura 289[2]
Jātaka Stories 11[5] 69[10] 82[1]
Jayasena 23
Jayawickrama, Professor xi
Jeta Grove 20 42 49 56 57 65 89 97 99 100 107 142 200 208 210 229 270 273 277 279 280 282 290 291

Jonah 284[4]

Kakusandha 33[7]
Kāḷakañjaka 283
Kāleyas 284[7]
Kālinga 175[25]
Kamboja 120 142[2]
Kaṃsabhoga 118
Kāñcipuram 299[14]
Kaṇha 100 101 103
Kaṅkhārevata 150
Kaṇṇamuṇḍa 158 160 166[33]
Kaṇṇamuṇḍa Peta Story 197
Kānyakubja 142[2]
Kapila 167 174[1]
Kapinaccanā 240 241 251[82]
Kāpiśī 142[2]
Kappina 84 87
Kappitaka 239 240 244 245 251[82]
Kashmir 142[2]
Kāsi 53 65 75 87 92 98
Kāsipurī 23
Kasmīra-Gandhāra 142[2]
Kassapa (Buddha) 14 16 24 33[7] 158 197
Kassapa (Mahā-) 224
Kathiawad (Kathiāwār) 264[2]
Kaurava 213[1]
Kauśāmbī 142[2]
Kern, H. 209[2]
Kesava 101 102
Khantipālo Bhikkhu 11[5]
Khuddaka Nikāya 3 4 69 173 224 297
Kimbilā 158 163 164
Kitava 188 189 273 274 275
Kolita 87
Koliya 179 180 181 186
Konāgamana 33[7]
Kosala(n) 22 113[16] 174[1] 270 290
Kosambi 149
Kṛṣṇa 142[4]
Kuṇāla 165[6]
Kuṇḍi 188 189 190
Kuru(s) 174[1] 210
Kusinārā 222
Kuvera (Kubera) 20 21 144[34] 265[23]

Lakkhaṇa Suttanta 83[41]
Lancaster xi, University of – 12[14] 113[30]
Laṅkā 264[4]
Licchavi(s) 229 231 233 241 242 243 244 245 246 289[2]
Like a Field Peta Story 4

Madhurā (Mathura) 142[4]
Madhya Pradesh 264[4]
Madras 299[14]
Madurai 142[4]
Magadha 24 32 34[14] 73 145[74]
Mahābhārata 213[1]
Mahādhanaseṭṭhi 6
Mahā-Kaccāyana 149
Mahākaṃsaka 118
Mahākappitaka 249
Mahākassapa 80 222 224
Mahāmandhātu 104
Mahāmoggallāna 7 8 84 86 87 88 89[25] 165 200 202 268 277 278 279 280 295
Mahāsāgara 118
Mahāsudassana 104
Mahā-Ummagga Jātaka 174[2]
Mahāvastu 284[6]
Mahāvihāra (Anurādhapura) 3 5[4] 12[16], (Bamboo Grove) 8
Majjhima Nikāya 4
Makkhali-Gosāla 82[1] 265[21]
Malalasekera, G. P. 33[11] 251[82] 299[14]
Mallas 222
Mallikā 291
Mānavadharmaśāstra 106[16]
Mandākini 165[6]
Mandhātā 106[14]
Mansion Stories vii 100 253 267, *Commentary on the* – 77
Māra 12[15] 175[43] 297
Mātaṅga 175[25]
Mathurā 142[2] 142[4]
Mattā 89 90 92 95 96[3]
Maṭṭakuṇḍalin 99 100 100[5] 100[6]
Maṭṭakuṇḍalin Mansion Story 100
Mauryan 283[1]
Mauryas 264[10]
Mazaffarpur 289[2]
Mejjha 175[25]
Meru 56[10] 147[132]
Metteyya 33[7]
Milinda's Questions 145[78]
Minor Readings and Illustrator viii 5[5] 33[1] 34[33]
Mithilā 289[2]
Moggallāna 7 12[11] 87 187[27]
Moriya(s) 255 258

Nālandā 175[25]
Ñāṇamoli viii 201[9]
Nanda 77 78 79 80 81 192
Nandā 97 98
Nandaka 254
Nandana 144[49] 182 185 186 187[27] 187[31] 197 199 201[13]

Nandasena 97 98 99
Nandiya 267
Ñānissara Thēra, Mahagoda Siri x
Nārada 4 14 15 18 19 214 217 219 220
Nepal 165[8]
Norman, K. R. xi
North Road 142[2]
North-West Frontier 142[2]

Paduma 80
Padumavatī 80
Pajjuna 101 119
Pañcāla 167 169 170 171 174[1]
Paṇḍukambala Rock 139 140
Pāricchattaka 147[130]
Pasenadi 22 290
Pāṭaligāma 283[1]
Pāṭaliputta (Pāṭaliputra) 142[2] 264[4] 282 283
Path of Purification 19[9] 49[1] 69[3] 148[146] 201[9]
Patna 264[4] 283[1]
Perera, L. P. N. xi
Peta Stories 3 4 69 100 173 224 297 298 299
Petavatthu 146[112]
Phussa 23 33[7]
Piṅgala(ka) 254 258 264[4]
Piyaṅkara 113[21]
Poṭṭhapāda 190 191
Puraṃdara 265[16]
Pūraṇa Kassapa 265[21]
Pure Abodes 148[146]
Purindada 124 125 256
Puṣkalāvatī 142[2]

Rāh-i-Azam 142[2]
Rahula, Walpola 5[4]
Rājagaha 4 6 13 14 15 19 23 24 25 33[11] 73 84 86 114 115 214 215 216[3] 217 218 222 268 274 289[2] 289 295
Rajgir 33[11]
Rangoon x
Rathakāra 165[6] 197
Revata 151
Revatī 267
Revatī Mansion Story 267
Rhys Davids, Mrs. 265[21]
Rohiṇeyya 101 102
Rudra 150 152[10] 165[8]

Śākala 142[2]
Sakka 25 65 66 67 69 69[4] 106[3] 119 123 124 125 128 132 133 147[129] 175[43] 187[27] 187[31] 201[13] 206 209 256 265[16]
Sakya 47 58
Sālittaka Jātaka 297[1]
Sāmaññaphala Sutta 252[108]
Saṃkicca 57 58 59 63 63[1]
Saṃyutta Nikāya 4
Sanaṃkumāra, Brahmā 201[10]
Sankalia, Hasmukh D. 264[4]
Saṅkassa 142
Sānu 195[10]
Sānuvāsin 188 190 191 276[2], Mount – 189 190
Sānuvāsin Peta Story 273
Sāriputta 5[11] 35[73] 73 75 81 84 85 86 87 88 88[22] 89[23] 89[26] 107[18]
Sarnath 63[2]
Sasapaṇḍita Jātaka 106[3]
Saturn 195[10]
Sāvatthī 20 36 40 42 46 49 50 51 55 65 89 97 101 107 112 118 139 142 147[126] 152 153 158 165 167 197 200 202 204 249 270 271 277 280 282 283 284 286 288 289[2] 290 291
Scotland 83[36]
Separate Feelings, The 224[7]
Serinī 210
Serissaka 253
Serissaka Mansion Story 253
Sīhapapāta 165[6]
Sikhi 33[8]
Sindh 79
Sindhaka 132 133
Sineru 140 147[128] 147[132]
Sircar, D. C. 142[2]
Sīrimā 23
Siripāda 147[128]
Śiva 152[10] 165[8]
Snake Jātaka 65
Sorath 264[4]
Soraṭṭha, The 255 258 264
Squirrels' Feeding Ground 6 13 16
Ṣonaka 133
Śrughna 142[2]
Stories of the Departed 253[4] 265[21] 265[27] 266[49]
Stories of the Mansions 100[3] 145[79] 253[3] 264[11] 265[16] 267[1]
Sujāta (Buddha) 46[16]
Sujāta (householder's son) 43 44 45 46[16]
Sujāta Jātaka 46[16]
Sulasā 7 8 11 12[15]
Sunetta 189 273 275 276[12] 295 296
Suraṭṭha (Surāṣṭra) 254 255 256 258 259 264[4]
Suriyadeva 101 119

III. SOME PALI WORDS DISCUSSED IN THE NOTES

IV. LIST OF QUOTATIONS AND ALLUSIONS

D iii 58   10 126
D iii 188   134

M i 17   28

S i 108   63
S ii 94   63
S ii 178 = iii 149 = 151 ≏ v 226   172

A v 269–271   29

Dhp 125   122
Dhp 127 = Miln 150   111

Sn 98   27
Sn 577   285

J iii 155   101
Jāt 354   65

V. WORDS AND SENSES NOT LISTED BY PED

accharituṭṭho 253[122]
acchariyatuṭṭho 253[122]
anubalappadāyika 82[20]
apacchatta 276[5]
apaccittha 276[5]
apara 186[1]
aparituṭṭho 253[122]
alaṃ 297[7]
ācerake 251[81]
ucchaḍḍayāmi 267[58]
ucchaḍḍehi 297[4]
uḷāraṃ 276[7]
kirīṭī 221[1]
kopīnaṃ 96[18]
khala 204[11]
tahiṃ 201[29]
namakkāraṃ 225[17]
paccittha 276[5]
pajāpatī 39[1]
paṭighaṃsāma 282[9]
pāṇaka 50[14]
pāṇi 64[14]
bhāra 113[18]
santassito 270[7]
sandassesi 35[73]
samuddiṭṭha 287[5]
sammānetvā 13[38]
sarīrapaṭijagganaṃ 15[5]
surabhi 84[63]
suhajjānaṃ 70[16]
sogandhiyā 166[20]
hīyo 34[18]

VI. AMENDMENTS TO PED SUGGESTED IN THE NOTES

13^{45} 70^{21} 82^{7} 83^{28} 166^{11} 166^{13} 186^{2} 196^{44} 201^{8} 201^{11} 204^{6} 214^{3}
249^{4} 249^{13} 249^{16} 250^{45} 251^{73} 251^{81} 265^{13} 270^{2} 287^{10} 289^{7} 298^{21}